GOD'S
UNFINISHED
BOOK

GOD'S
UNFINISHED
BOOK

JOURNEYING THROUGH
THE BOOK OF ACTS

RAY C. STEDMAN

DISCOVERY HOUSE
PUBLISHERS®

Feeding the Soul with the Word of God

God's Unfinished Book
© 2008 by Elaine Stedman
All rights reserved.

Discovery House Publishers is affiliated with
RBC Ministries, Grand Rapids, Michigan.

Discovery House books are distributed to the trade exclusively by
Barbour Publishing, Inc., Uhrichsville, Ohio.

Requests for permission to quote from this book should be directed to:
Permissions Department, Discovery House Publishers, P.O. Box 3566,
Grand Rapids, MI 49501.

CIP Data Available upon Request

Interior design by Sherri L. Hoffman

PRINTED IN THE UNITED STATES OF AMERICA

08 09 10 11 12 / BP / 10 9 8 7 6 5 4 3 2 1

CONTENTS

PART IV: THE PRISONER OF THE LORD—*Acts 21–28*

PUBLISHER'S PREFACE

Ray Stedman (1917–1992) served as pastor of the Peninsula Bible Church from 1950 to 1990, where he was known and loved as a man of outstanding Bible knowledge, Christian integrity, warmth, and humility. Born in Temvik, North Dakota, Ray grew up on the rugged landscape of Montana. When he was a small child, his mother became ill, and his father, a railroad man, abandoned the family. Ray grew up on his aunt's Montana farm from the time he was six. He came to know the Lord at age ten.

As a young man, Ray lived in Chicago, Denver, Hawaii, and elsewhere. He enlisted in the Navy during World War II and often led Bible studies for civilians and Navy personnel. He sometimes preached on the radio in Hawaii. At the close of the war, Ray was married in Honolulu (he and his wife, Elaine, had first met in Great Falls, Montana). They returned to the mainland in 1946, and Ray graduated from Dallas Theological Seminary in 1950. After two summers interning with Dr. J. Vernon McGee, Ray traveled for several months with Dr. H. A. Ironside, pastor of Moody Church in Chicago.

In 1950, Ray was called by the two-year-old Peninsula Bible Fellowship in Palo Alto, California, to serve as its first pastor. Peninsula Bible Fellowship became Peninsula Bible Church, and Ray served there for forty years, retiring on April 30, 1990. During those years, Ray Stedman authored a number of life-changing Christian books, including the classic work on the meaning and mission of the church, *Body Life*. He went into the presence of his Lord on October 7, 1992.

This important work, *God's Unfinished Book: Adventuring Through the Book of Acts,* was edited from four sermon series that Ray Stedman preached in the early 1970s. Pastor Stedman brings the history, adventure, and profound meaning of Acts to life in readable, everyday language. Acts is truly one of the most exciting and action-filled books of the Bible, and these ancient pages brim with insights and principles that still transform lives in this Internet age. So read on and discover your place in God's unfinished book, the book of Acts.

—Discovery House Publishers

PART I

THE CHURCH IN ACTION

Acts 1:1–8:1a

1

OUT OF THE SHADOWS

Acts 1:1-14

From Tarzan to Indiana Jones, from Buck Rogers to Luke Skywalker, action thrillers have entertained generations of readers and moviegoers. For me, the book of Acts is the action thriller of the New Testament. The very name, Acts, suggests action. Here we find a tale set in the exotic culture of the first-century Roman world. The story is rich in plot twists, peril, narrow escapes, conflict, and intrigue, all set against the backdrop of fast-changing world events.

The book of Acts is truly one of the most exciting books of the Bible. Its full name is The Acts of the Apostles, yet the only apostles prominently featured are James, John, Peter, and Paul. The book should probably be called The Acts of God, for it reveals how God acts through Christians. We see the healing life of Jesus Christ poured out upon a corrupt and dying society through ordinary people like you and me.

We could never understand the New Testament without the book of Acts, for it fills the gap between the four Gospels and Paul's letter to the Romans. At the end of the Gospels, we find a handful of Jews gathered in Jerusalem talking about a coming kingdom. In Romans, we find a letter from an apostle who is not even mentioned in the Gospels and who was not one of the Twelve. The book of Acts tells us how this small band of Jews in Jerusalem became a multiethnic force for global transformation.

THE LORD'S STRATEGY IN THE BOOK OF ACTS

The first fourteen verses of Acts give us the key to the book. They reveal the strategy by which Jesus Christ proposes to change the world. It is His strategy by which His church is to operate. The church ceases to become effective in the world when it departs from this strategy.

I believe most Christians suffer from an inferiority complex when we confront the world around us. Many of us have accepted the notion that the church is irrelevant in the world. Don't be fooled! The church is the most important body in the world today—more important than the United Nations, NATO, and all the governments of the world combined. Whatever happens in the world today is a result of what the church is doing—or failing to do. We shall see this clearly in the book of Acts.

The strategy of the Lord Jesus is given to us: "In my former book, Theophilus, I wrote about all that Jesus began to do and to teach until the day he was taken up to heaven, after giving instructions through the Holy Spirit to the apostles he had chosen" (Acts 1:1-2).

The author of Acts is Luke, the beloved physician, who accompanied Paul on some of his journeys (much of this book is an eyewitness account). When Luke speaks of "my former book," he refers to the Gospel of Luke (Acts could be called The Gospel of Luke: The Sequel). We do not know how Luke became a Christian, though he may have been converted by Paul. There was a close friendship between Paul and Luke, because Luke remained at Paul's side through times of danger, hardship, and trial.

Luke addressed both of his books to a man named Theophilus (Luke 1:3 and Acts 1:1). This name means "friend of God." There is no person named Theophilus mentioned anywhere else in Scripture, so Theophilus may have been the name of a young Greek convert to Christianity, or it may be that Luke addressed his two books to any reader who is a friend of God, much as I might open a general letter to the members of my church by writing, "Dear Friend in Christ."

What is the Lord's great strategy for achieving His work in human history? Luke writes, "In my former book, Theophilus, I wrote about all that Jesus began to do and to teach." Luke says that his previous book, the gospel of Luke, was a record of what Jesus, the incarnate Son of God, "began to do and to teach." This implies that the second book, the book of Acts, is the continuation of what Jesus began to do and teach.

In a real sense, the book of Acts does not recount the acts of the apostles or the acts of the church but the continuing acts of Jesus. In the Gospels, Jesus did His work through His physical body of human flesh. In the book of Acts, He does His work through the bodies of men and women who are indwelt by His life. Thus, whether in the Gospels or in Acts, incarnation—the Son of God taking on human flesh—is the secret strategy by which God changes the world.

Whenever God sends a message to the human race, He clothes His message in flesh and blood. He manifests His own life through the life of a human being, making clear what He has to say. That is the strategy of the book of Acts: Men and women, possessed by Jesus Christ, indwelt by the Holy Spirit, manifest the life and power of God the Father. That's the secret of authentic Christianity. Any so-called Christianity that does not operate by this strategy is false Christianity. Many individuals and institutions have adopted the guise of Christianity but are not indwelt by the life of Jesus Christ—and they do not represent authentic Christianity.

AN UNFINISHED BOOK

The book of Acts begins with Jesus being taken up into heaven, and it ends with Paul in Rome, under house arrest while awaiting trial before Caesar.

As you read the final chapter, it seems you should be able to turn the page and read the rest of Paul's adventure—but no, the book is ended, the story tantalizingly unfinished.

Indeed, Acts is an unfinished book. The story that began in the Gospels and continued in Acts is still being written to this day, to this hour. What we call the book of Acts was volume 1—the record of the Acts of God in the first century A.D. In every century, God, through His church, has written another volume of Acts. As this book goes to press, God is in the midst of writing volume 21, the acts of God in the twenty-first century A.D. It may be the final volume. God alone knows.

The events recorded in the book of Acts continue to shape history to this present day. The first of these historic elements is the resurrection of Jesus:

> After his suffering, he showed himself to these men and gave many convincing proofs that he was alive. He appeared to them over a period of forty days and spoke about the kingdom of God. On one occasion, while he was eating with them, he gave them this command: "Do not leave Jerusalem, but wait for the gift my Father promised, which you have heard me speak about." (Acts 1:3-4)

Notice that Luke stresses the great and central fact of Christian faith: Jesus is alive. The founder of every other religion on earth has died and turned to dust. But the founder of Christianity came out of the tomb and is alive today.

Read your newspaper or watch the news networks, and you'll hear story after story of self-exalted messiahs who claim to be the second coming of Christ on earth. Some attract hundreds or thousands of followers. But when I hear someone claiming to be a new messiah, my first question is: Has he risen from the dead? I have no use for any self-proclaimed messiah who has not risen from the dead!

Luke says that after Jesus was crucified, He gave many convincing proofs that He was alive. Luke lists three categories of proof.

First, Luke says, "He appeared to them over a period of forty days." The Greek word translated "appeared" is *optanomai*, from which we get our word *ophthalmic*, which means "of or relating to or resembling the eyeball." It would be a reasonable translation of Luke's wording to say that Jesus allowed the disciples to eyeball Him over a period of forty days. The disciples saw Him again and again, not once but many times, and it was clear that His appearance before them was not a hallucination.

Second, Luke says, the risen Lord Jesus "spoke about the kingdom of God." The disciples clearly remembered His subject matter when He spoke to them: He talked about the kingdom of God. First the disciples saw Him; then they heard Him. Two objective sensory experiences confirmed that the resurrection was no fantasy or illusion.

Third, Luke says, Jesus "was eating with them." The disciples saw Him eat. They shared meals with Him and saw Him put food in His mouth, chew it, and swallow it. This is the proof, Luke says: He ate with us, so we know He is alive.

The Christian faith rests on the fact of the resurrection of Jesus. Hundreds of eyewitnesses saw Him, heard Him, and ate with Him—and many went to a martyr's death, confident that they would be raised just as they had seen Jesus raised. Over the centuries, skeptics have tried to disprove the resurrection of Jesus, but no one has succeeded. Some who sought to disprove the resurrection were in fact converted by the evidence they found.

Josh McDowell was an atheist college student when he decided to write a paper disproving the Christian faith. While researching the paper, the historical evidence he uncovered persuaded him to become a Christian, and today he is an outspoken Christian speaker and author of *Evidence That Demands a Verdict*.

Lee Strobel was an award-winning journalist for United Press International when his wife became a Christian. An avowed atheist at the time, Strobel decided to investigate the claims of Christianity in order to disprove it. Like Josh McDowell before him, Strobel was persuaded to faith in Christ on the basis of the evidence, including the evidence for the resurrection.

THE PROMISE OF THE FATHER

The next historical fact Luke brings to our attention is the promise of God the Father. He writes:

> On one occasion, while he was eating with them, he gave them this command: "Do not leave Jerusalem, but wait for the gift my Father promised, which you have heard me speak about. For John baptized with water, but in a few days you will be baptized with the Holy Spirit."
>
> So when they met together, they asked him, "Lord, are you at this time going to restore the kingdom to Israel?"
>
> He said to them: "It is not for you to know the times or dates the Father has set by his own authority. But you will receive power when the Holy Spirit comes on you; and you will be my witnesses in Jerusalem, and in all Judea and Samaria, and to the ends of the earth." (Acts 1:4-8)

The disciples were still looking for Jesus to establish a political kingdom in Israel. But Jesus told them that the sovereign God does not reveal His timetable. God would baptize them with the Holy Spirit.

"Do not leave Jerusalem," Jesus said to the Eleven (the Twelve, minus the traitor Judas). Literally, His wording was, "Stick around in Jerusalem." That may sound like American slang, but the Greek word used here, *perimeno*, literally means to stick to a spot as if glued there—don't move!

The disciples were to stick around and wait for the promise of the Father to come upon them. God was commissioning them to be His witnesses "in Jerusalem, and in all Judea and Samaria, and to the ends of the earth." This was a big task, and they would make a hopeless mess of it if they tried to witness in their own human strength. They needed the life and the power of the Holy Spirit.

The same holds true for you and me. We cannot be effective Christians if we do not operate in the power of the Holy Spirit. Our human flesh only gets in the way of God's message. Like those first-century disciples, we need the indwelling presence of the Spirit in our lives.

Notice the contrast Jesus draws between John's baptism and the baptism of the Spirit. John baptized with water; in other words, his baptism was a symbol, a foreshadowing of a coming reality. But the Spirit's coming would not be a ritual; it would be the fulfillment of the Father's promise. So Jesus told the disciples, "Wait for the gift my Father promised."

When did God the Father make that promise? He made that promise to Abraham two thousand years before Jesus came to earth:

> "I will make you into a great nation
>   and I will bless you;
> I will make your name great,
>   and you will be a blessing.
> I will bless those who bless you,
>   and whoever curses you I will curse;
> and all peoples on earth
>   will be blessed through you." (Genesis 12:2-3)

God told Abraham that He would bless Abraham, make his name great, and bless all nations through him. God did not tell Abraham what form that blessing would take, but in Galatians, Paul explains God's promise of blessing through Abraham:

> Christ redeemed us from the curse of the law by becoming a curse for us, for it is written: "Cursed is everyone who is hung on a tree." He redeemed us in order that the blessing given to Abraham might come to the Gentiles through Christ Jesus, so that by faith we might receive the promise of the Spirit. (Galatians 3:13-14)

The promise God made to Abraham was that his spiritual descendents—believing Jews and believing Gentiles—would receive the Holy Spirit. Does this mean that no one received the Holy Spirit until the day of Pentecost, when the Spirit descended on the disciples? The fact is, before the day of Pentecost, no Gentile ever received the Holy Spirit unless he first became a part of Israel.

In the Old Testament, there are several accounts of people who were filled with the Spirit in Israel. We know that Abraham was filled with the Spirit because God promised, "I will bless you," and that blessing, Paul says, is the promise of the Spirit. Moses, Joshua, David, many of the kings of Judah, and all of the prophets received the Spirit because Peter tells us that when the prophets predicted the sufferings of Christ and the glory that would follow, they spoke by "the Spirit of Christ which was in them" (1 Peter 1:11 KJV). They were filled with the Spirit and spoke according to the Spirit.

Yet these Old Testament believers had an incomplete and partial understanding of the Spirit who indwelt them. They experienced the Spirit-filled life by means of shadows and symbols. We find symbolic depictions of the Spirit throughout the Old Testament: Aaron's rod that budded, which was kept in the Ark of the Covenant (Numbers 17), and the seven-branched candlestick in the tabernacle (Exodus 25:31-40) are pictures of the Holy Spirit illuminating the mind and heart. The widow's jar of oil that never ran dry was a picture of the endless flow of the Spirit in our lives (2 Kings 4:1-7).

The two olive trees that dripped oil from their branches into the bowls of the golden lampstand are a picture of the Holy Spirit (Zechariah 4). Ezekiel's river, which flowed from the temple and from the throne of God, is a picture of the overflowing, Spirit-filled life (Ezekiel 47:1-12; see also Revelation 22:1-5).

The last symbolic picture of the promise of God was John's baptism. Jesus said that John the Baptist was the last of the prophets. In his gospel, Luke tells us that John was filled with the Holy Spirit from his mother's womb (Luke 1:15). John experienced the indwelling Spirit, but he could only teach about the Spirit through the ritual of baptism.

In Acts 1, the risen Lord tells His disciples in Jerusalem there will be no more shadows, for the reality is at hand. When the Holy Spirit comes, all believers will live their lives on this new level. Jesus had once told His disciples, "the Spirit of truth . . . lives with you and will be in you" (John 14:17). He was telling them that the Spirit was already with them (alongside them) but did not yet dwell in them. On the day of Pentecost, that would change—and the filling of the Spirit would be available to Jews and Gentiles.

The Holy Spirit is given to us immediately when we believe in Jesus. There may not be any sign or emotional sensation when the Spirit is given to us, but it occurs nonetheless. That is the promise of Jesus.

THE MISTAKE OF THE CHURCH

Next, we see that the Spirit has come to bring us power, not a program.

The disciples said to him, "Lord, are you at this time going to restore the kingdom to Israel?" They wanted to understand His political program for Israel. But Jesus replied, in effect, "Don't concern yourself with God's timetable—that's all under His sovereign authority. Your task is to manifest His power. The Father will take care of the schedule."

Here we see the great mistake of the church. We think it's our job to set up programs to carry out the work of God. But Jesus says we should focus on His power, not on a program. The Lord's promise to us is the same today as it was in Acts 1: "You will receive power when the Holy Spirit comes on you; and you will be my witnesses."

What kind of power do we receive? Resurrection power. But the power of the risen Lord does not draw attention to itself. His power is a quiet power. We tend to think of power as something that dazzles, explodes, and electrifies. But when Jesus came out of the tomb, no one saw, no one heard. The evidence of His resurrection was a quiet, empty tomb.

Resurrection power is quiet but irresistible and unstoppable. Every obstacle thrown in its path only advances the gospel even further. Resurrection power changes lives from within. It doesn't destroy; it heals. It doesn't divide; it harmonizes. It breaks down the "the barrier, the dividing wall of hostility" between humanity and God (Ephesians 2:14). That is the power we receive through the Holy Spirit.

Jesus says, "You will be my witnesses." He doesn't say we will be His propagandists or His salesmen. We will be His witnesses. We are not to go out and recruit people into our religious club or peddle a religious product. When we do that, the church becomes powerless and ineffective. He calls us to be His witnesses, and that means we tell people what Jesus has done in our lives.

The mark of a false church is that it loves to talk about itself. The early Christians never witnessed about the church. They witnessed about the amazing change Jesus made in human hearts. God did not promise us a program. He promised us power—the power of the Spirit who indwells us through faith in the risen Lord.

THE HOPE OF THE LORD'S RETURN

The promise of the Father is not restricted to one point in time and space. It is universal. It begins in Jerusalem and then goes out into Judea and Samaria and to the uttermost parts of the earth. It is all-inclusive, encompassing all places, races, and ages, as attested in the words of the hymn by William Dunkerley:

> In Christ there is no east or west,
> In him no south or north;
> But one great fellowship of love,
> Throughout the whole wide earth.

Throughout the book of Acts and wherever the church becomes what God intended it to be, you see this same inclusive spirit being demonstrated. When the church becomes exclusive, when it ceases to be a place that welcomes all people without partiality or prejudice, it ceases to exhibit the power of God in the world.

Next, Luke stresses the hope of Christ's return. After Jesus promises that the disciples will receive the Spirit and become witnesses, something amazing happens:

> After he said this, he was taken up before their very eyes, and a cloud hid him from their sight.
>
> They were looking intently up into the sky as he was going, when suddenly two men dressed in white stood beside them. "Men of Galilee," they said, "why do you stand here looking into the sky? This same Jesus, who has been taken from you into heaven, will come back in the same way you have seen him go into heaven." (Acts 1:9-11)

As the disciples stood with Jesus on the Mount of Olives, outside of Jerusalem, they saw him ascend into a cloud—and they never saw Him again. Jesus had told them, "It is for your good that I am going away. Unless I go away, the Counselor will not come to you; but if I go, I will send him to you" (John 16:7). Jesus makes His life intimately available to us by means of the Spirit.

Where did Jesus go? Not to some far planet or distant galaxy. It's a mistake to think of heaven as a place beyond the clouds, somewhere in space. I'm convinced that Jesus stepped into a different dimension of existence—into the invisible spiritual kingdom that surrounds us on every side. He is not far away—and He has left us His Spirit, by whom Jesus continues to live through us.

Though Jesus has left, His return is certain. "Men of Galilee," the angels said, "why do you stand here looking into the sky? This same Jesus . . . will come back in the same way you have seen him go into heaven." Just as He stepped into invisibility, He will one day step back into visibility. When He comes, the Scriptures tell us, He will lift the curse from nature (Isaiah 11:9; Habakkuk 2:14; Romans 8:19-22).

People today are frightened of the looming ecological crisis—pollution, global warming, ozone depletion, and an increasingly toxic environment. How shall we solve these problems? The truth is: We shall not. These problems will grow steadily worse, not better. Jesus said that the tribulation of the last days will be so intense that all life will be extinguished unless God intervenes (Matthew 24:21-22).

And God *will* intervene. When Jesus returns, He will remove the curse from nature, and the earth will bloom with life once again. God will draw back the curtain on His masterpiece—a new humanity. As Paul writes, "The creation waits in eager expectation for the sons of God to be revealed" (Romans 8:19). This hope is part of the grand strategy of God.

WAITING AND PRAYING

Next, Luke reveals to us one more essential element in God's plan for the early Christians—and for you and me:

> Then they returned to Jerusalem from the hill called the Mount of Olives, a Sabbath day's walk from the city. When they arrived, they went upstairs to the room where they were staying. Those present were Peter, John, James and Andrew; Philip and Thomas, Bartholomew and Matthew; James son of Alphaeus and Simon the Zealot, and Judas son of James. They all joined together constantly in prayer, along with the women and Mary the mother of Jesus, and with his brothers. (Acts 1:12-14)

The disciples returned to Jerusalem and waited, but they didn't wait passively. They acted because they prayed. Though deprived of the physical presence of Jesus, they were not cut off from God. The Spirit was not yet given, so they didn't possess His indwelling life, but they were still linked to the Father by prayer. They gave themselves to prayer, awaiting the full revelation God intended to give them. Prayer is a crucial ingredient in the Father's strategy for touching and changing the world.

The indwelling power of the Holy Spirit could only be glimpsed through shadows and symbols in the Old Testament. Now it is about to burst forth upon the scene. God's plan for you and me has come out of the shadows and into reality. The indwelling Spirit empowers us to affect our world. That's the secret of authentic Christianity. That's God's strategy for our lives: Possessed by Jesus Christ, indwelt by the Holy Spirit, we go forth to manifest the life and power of God the Father.

The action thriller of the New Testament has begun!

2

THE BIRTH OF THE CHURCH

Acts 1:15–2:4

How does the secular world view the church?

Some see the church as rocked by division and filled with hypocrites who devour each other over minor issues of doctrine and dogma. Others see the church as a greedy, corrupt institution, passing the collection plate while pursuing worldly wealth and power. Others scoff at Christian morality and point to scandal after scandal involving prominent televangelists. I'm reminded of the observation by Friedrich Nietzsche: "If you want me to believe in your Redeemer, you'll have to look a lot more redeemed."

There are people who say the church is irrelevant, impotent, and ineffective—a relic of a bygone era, with nothing to say about life in the twenty-first century. Christians, they say, are a collection of fossils who gather for an hour every Sunday morning with blank stares on their lifeless faces.

In all honesty, these charges are often true, but only when the church forgets what God intended it to be. When we rediscover God's plan for the church and function as He intended, the church becomes the most relevant, dynamic force of all. It becomes attractive and magnetic, drawing people of every class, race, and nation into God's kingdom. It binds the wounds of broken people. It meets the needs of the poor, sick, and hungry. It accepts people in the midst of their sin and shame, offering the healing message of forgiveness. Its righteousness and unity astonish the world. It radically alters the status quo wherever it is planted.

God's true church is the secret government of earth. As the apostle Paul says, "the church of the living God" is "the pillar and foundation of the truth" (1 Timothy 3:15). It is the source and support of all realistic knowledge of life.

THE BODY AND THE BUILDING

In Paul's letter to the Ephesians, he uses two symbols to help us understand the true nature of the church: a body and a building.

First, Paul writes that God appointed Jesus "to be head over everything for the church, which is his body, the fullness of him who fills everything in every way" (Ephesians 1:22b-23). So the church is the living body of Jesus Christ on earth.

Second, Paul writes that Christians are "members of God's household, built on the foundation of the apostles and prophets, with Christ Jesus himself as the chief cornerstone. In him the whole building is joined together and rises to become a holy temple in the Lord" (Ephesians 2:19b-21). So the church is also a building inhabited by the Lord.

These two symbols of the church—a body and a building—help us understand the meaning of this section of Acts. In the last part of chapter 1, the foundation is laid for the building; in the first part of chapter 2, we will see the birth of the body.

Let's put this scene in context. In Luke's introduction, Acts 1:1-14, he describes the ascension of Jesus. This scene in Acts 1:9-11 recaps what Luke had previously recorded in the final chapter of his gospel:

> When he had led them out to the vicinity of Bethany, he lifted up his hands and blessed them. While he was blessing them, he left them and was taken up into heaven. Then they worshiped him and returned to Jerusalem with great joy. And they stayed continually at the temple, praising God. (Luke 24:50-53)

So Jesus ascended to heaven and left the disciples at the Mount of Olives, near the village of Bethany, a short distance from Jerusalem. After His ascension, the disciples returned to Jerusalem. As we piece the accounts together, we see that the next passage, Acts 1:15-16, undoubtedly takes place in the temple courts, since Luke has told us that the disciples were "continually at the temple."

Because Acts 1:13 says that the disciples "went upstairs to the room where they were staying," many people assume that the Holy Spirit later came upon the disciples in the upper room, the place where Jesus served the Passover to the Twelve on the night He was betrayed. That's unlikely. We will later see that 120 people were present at Pentecost—too large a crowd for one small upper room.

So as we link the end of Luke's gospel with Acts 1:15-16, it's clear that the events we are about to examine must have occurred in the courts of the great temple in Jerusalem, probably in Solomon's Porch, the majestic colonnade on the eastern side of the temple. With that setting in mind, we read:

> In those days Peter stood up among the believers (a group numbering about a hundred and twenty) and said, "Brothers, the Scripture had to be fulfilled which the Holy Spirit spoke long ago through the mouth of David concerning Judas, who served as guide for those who arrested Jesus—he was one of our number and shared in this ministry."
>
> (With the reward he got for his wickedness, Judas bought a field; there he fell headlong, his body burst open and all his intestines spilled out. Everyone in Jerusalem heard about this, so they called that field in their language Akeldama, that is, Field of Blood.) (Acts 1:15-19)

Peter speaks of the need to replace Judas, who fell from his place as an apostle by betraying the Lord Jesus. We saw in Paul's letter to the Ephesians that the church is like a building that is "built on the foundation of the apostles and prophets, with Christ Jesus himself as the chief cornerstone" (Ephesians 2:20). So it's not surprising that the broken fellowship of apostles must be mended. They were the Twelve; now there are eleven. The original number must be restored.

The number twelve is significant in Scripture. In Revelation, John sees the magnificent shining city of God coming down out of heaven. There is a wall around the city, with twelve gates. Over each gate is the name of one of the twelve tribes of Israel. The wall also has twelve foundations, and each foundation bears the name of one of the apostles of the Lamb. So there must be twelve apostles.

Some scholars have suggested that Paul should be counted as one of the Twelve, but Paul never makes that claim. Though he was a genuine apostle, he was not one of the Twelve.

Also in this passage, we see that Luke inserts a parenthetical passage about the tragic end of Judas Iscariot. What does Luke mean when he says that Judas bought a field with the reward for his wickedness? He couldn't have purchased real estate with the thirty silver coins he was paid for betraying Jesus. After Jesus was arrested, Judas "was seized with remorse and returned the thirty silver coins to the chief priests and the elders. 'I have sinned,' he said, 'for I have betrayed innocent blood.' . . . Judas threw the money into the temple and left. Then he went away and hanged himself" (Matthew 27:3-5).

How, then, did he buy the field? We know that Jesus appointed Judas as treasurer for the disciples, and John tells us that Judas "was a thief; as keeper of the money bag, he used to help himself to what was put into it" (John 12:6). What did Judas do with the stolen money?

Judas apparently believed that the coming Messiah would overthrow the Roman oppressor and establish a political kingdom. Judas was feathering his nest in anticipation of Jesus becoming king of Israel. A power-hungry embezzler, Judas had chosen a plot of land for his mansion when he became one of the King's right-hand men. He may have been making installment payments from the money he stole.

After betraying Jesus to the soldiers, Judas realized the horrible thing he had done. He returned the blood money to the priests, then went to the property he had purchased and hanged himself there. Perhaps his weight broke the tree limb so that he fell, splitting his body open. In any case, Luke records that Judas "fell headlong, his body burst open and all his intestines spilled out."

When Judas was found dead, the priests used the silver to pay off the property Judas was purchasing. They bought it from a potter, fulfilling Zechariah's prophecy:

I told them, "If you think it best, give me my pay; but if not, keep it." So they paid me thirty pieces of silver.

And the Lord said to me, "Throw it to the potter"—the handsome price at which they priced me! So I took the thirty pieces of silver and threw them into the house of the Lord to the potter. (Zechariah 11:12-13)

Because this potter's field was the site of the suicide of Judas, it was also called the Field of Blood, and you can visit this site in Jerusalem today.

THE SCRIPTURES FULFILLED

Peter quotes from the Psalms to show that the Scriptures had predicted that the traitorous apostle would be replaced. Luke records Peter's words (I have added the Old Testament references Peter cites):

"For," said Peter, "it is written in the book of Psalms,

"'May his place be deserted;
let there be no one to dwell in it,' [from Psalm 69:25]

and,

"'May another take his place of leadership.' [from Psalm 109:8]

Therefore it is necessary to choose one of the men who have been with us the whole time the Lord Jesus went in and out among us, beginning from John's baptism to the time when Jesus was taken up from us. For one of these must become a witness with us of his resurrection."

Peter's words give us a clue as to what the disciples were doing during the ten days after Jesus ascended into heaven, as they waited for the Holy Spirit: They were studying the Scriptures. And there, in the Psalms, they discovered the prophecy that a replacement must be found for the traitor, Judas. So Peter announced that they must replace Judas in the apostolic band. He also stated the qualifications of a genuine apostle:

"Therefore it is necessary to choose one of the men who have been with us the whole time the Lord Jesus went in and out among us, beginning from John's baptism to the time when Jesus was taken up from us. For one of these must become a witness with us of his resurrection." (Acts 1:21-22)

Here we see two qualifications for an apostle.

First, the new twelfth apostle had to have been with Jesus throughout His earthly ministry. There were a number of people who met this qualification. Though Jesus chose the Twelve to be in a special relationship with Him, there were scores of other disciples who also accompanied Him on His journeys. So Peter said that the replacement for Judas would come from that larger circle of disciples who had been with Jesus.

Second, the new apostle had to have witnessed the Lord's appearances after the resurrection. "For one of these," Peter said, "must become a witness with us of his resurrection." The new apostle had to be an eyewitness to the fact that Jesus is alive.

The requirements underscored the truth that our faith is not based on myths or legends but upon historically verified facts. So the new apostle had to be a man who had heard Jesus teach and who could bear witness that these claims were true.

THE THREEFOLD TASK OF THE APOSTLES

The apostles used an interesting means to choose the replacement for Judas:

> So they proposed two men: Joseph called Barsabbas (also known as Justus) and Matthias. Then they prayed, "Lord, you know everyone's heart. Show us which of these two you have chosen to take over this apostolic ministry, which Judas left to go where he belongs." Then they cast lots, and the lot fell to Matthias; so he was added to the eleven apostles. (Acts 1:23-26)

The decision was made in the Old Testament way: They cast lots, which is much like flipping a coin or tossing dice. This is not to say that the disciples made the decision in a casino atmosphere. The casting of lots is a dignified ritual that recognizes that God is present in even the smallest details. The Old Testament tells us, "The lot is cast into the lap, but its every decision is from the Lord" (Proverbs 16:33).

Why did the disciples cast lots? Because the two candidates, Joseph and Matthias, were equally qualified—but there was room for only one apostle in the apostolic band. Since it was humanly impossible to judge between the two, the casting of lots was the chosen means of making the decision. The lot fell to Matthias, and he became the twelfth apostle. The foundation was laid. The apostles were in place and were sent forth by the Lord with a threefold task.

First, the apostles were sent out as pioneers, going where the name of Jesus had never been named in order to plant churches. All twelve apostles fulfilled this task. Church history tells us that Thomas went to India, Peter to Europe, and others to North Africa and elsewhere. These pioneers laid the groundwork for the church.

Second, they were sent out as proclaimers. The apostles uttered the message God had given them. Hours before going to the cross, Jesus told His disciples, "I have much more to say to you, more than you can now bear" (John 16:12). Jesus never revealed what He had to say to them during His earthly ministry—

but these matters were revealed to them when the Holy Spirit came and taught the apostles the thoughts of God. That's why the apostles spoke with authority. As Paul wrote, "When you received the word of God, which you heard from us, you accepted it not as the word of men, but as it actually is, the word of God, which is at work in you who believe" (1 Thessalonians 2:13b).

Third, they were sent out as patterns. The apostles were intended to be examples of how the Spirit of God operates through human beings—how He transforms people and fills them with His newness of life. The apostles did not live on some level far above us. They lived on the same level as we do, and we are to live as they did.

In these three ways—as pioneers, proclaimers, and patterns—the apostles formed the foundation upon which the structure of the Lord's church was built.

THE BIRTH OF THE BODY

As we turn to Acts 2, the metaphor changes. The church is depicted not as a building but as a body, and we witness the birth of the body of Jesus Christ:

> When the day of Pentecost came, they were all together in one place. Suddenly a sound like the blowing of a violent wind came from heaven and filled the whole house where they were sitting. They saw what seemed to be tongues of fire that separated and came to rest on each of them. All of them were filled with the Holy Spirit and began to speak in other tongues as the Spirit enabled them. (Acts 2:1-4)

This passage of Scripture, so often misunderstood, requires careful examination. This event occurred on the day of Pentecost. The Greek word *pentekoste* means "fiftieth day." The day of Pentecost, called Shavuot or Shabuoth in the Hebrew language, occurred fifty days after the Passover feast. It was a Jewish feast day commemorating God's giving of the Ten Commandments to Moses and was called in the Old Testament the Feast of Weeks. It was so called because a week of weeks (seven times seven or forty-nine days) were to be numbered from the Passover. After forty-nine days had passed, the Jews were to celebrate the Feast of Weeks on the fiftieth day.

This feast was also called the Feast of the Wave Loaves. Pentecost came at the end of the wheat harvest in Palestine, and the Jews were to take this new, freshly harvested wheat—the first fruit of the harvest—and bake two loaves. These loaves symbolized the two bodies from which the church would be formed: the Jews and the Gentiles. Jesus said He came first to the lost sheep of the house of Israel (the Jews). But He also said, referring to the Gentiles, "I have other sheep that are not of this sheep pen. I must bring them also. They too will listen to my voice, and there shall be one flock and one shepherd" (John 10:16).

On the day of Pentecost, God brought the Jews and Gentiles together and baptized them into one body. The New Testament has its roots in the Old.

There is another beautiful symbol embedded in this event. The two loaves of the Feast of Weeks were to be baked with leaven (yeast). Leaven is a symbol of sin. The wave loaves were the only sacrifice in all the Old Testament that ever included leaven. Why? Through the symbol of those leavened loaves, God was telling us that the church is not made out of perfect people. It is made up of imperfect people—saints who still battle the old sin nature.

In that beautiful symbolism we glimpse the heart of the church. On the day of Pentecost, the Holy Spirit descended on 120 people who were gathered in one place, and the Spirit made them one. They were baptized by the Spirit into one body. The baptism of the Holy Spirit is not necessarily associated with tongues, or fire, or wind. These were incidentals. The essence of the baptism of the Spirit is that the many become one.

That day was the birthday of the church.

3

SPEAKING OF TONGUES

Acts 2:5-21

In *Symbols of the Holy Spirit,* C. Gordon Brownville tells about the great Norwegian polar explorer Roald Amundsen and his 1903 attempt to lead the first expedition to traverse the Northwest Passage between the Atlantic and Pacific Oceans, north of the Arctic Circle. When Amundsen reached the magnetic North Pole, he opened a cage and released a homing pigeon he had brought with him.

Days later, back home in Norway, Amundsen's wife was delighted when the homing pigeon lighted on her windowsill. Amundsen had promised to send his wife this sign. Even though Mrs. Amundsen could not see her husband, she knew he was alive.

In the same way, Jesus told His disciples that, though he was leaving them, He would send them a sign that He was alive, even though they could not see Him. He promised to the Holy Spirit. Imagine the delight of the disciples when the Holy Spirit descended upon them like a dove at Pentecost! That's the event we now examine.

A PURIFYING FIRE

When Jesus was born in Bethlehem, his birth was attended by shepherds, wise men, angels, and a star. These things happened only once. They never occurred again.

When the church was born in Jerusalem, its birth was attended by wind, fire, and tongues. These things occurred together only once in Scripture. Search the New Testament, and you won't find them occurring together again. Yet many people want to see these same signs occurring whenever the Spirit acts today.

In Scripture, these signs are connected only with the beginning of the body. The only place in Scripture, other than Acts 2, where we find the phrase "baptized with the Spirit" is in 1 Corinthians 12:13: "For we were all baptized by one Spirit into one body—whether Jews or Greeks, slave or free—and we were all given the one Spirit to drink."

The baptism of the Spirit occurred with visible signs at Pentecost. Since then, every person who trusts Jesus as Lord and Savior is instantly baptized into that same Spirit. From the moment of conversion, the new believer partakes in the life of Jesus. No longer living in isolation, the new believer is one with Christ and His body.

Let's examine the symbols associated with Pentecost—the sound of the mighty wind, the appearance of tongues of fire, and the strange phenomenon of people speaking in languages they had never learned before. What do these symbols mean? They are the key to the functioning of the body. This is God's visually impressive way of telling us what this body is going to do and how it is to be characterized.

The wind is the symbol of invisible power. As Jesus said to Nicodemus, "The wind blows wherever it pleases. You hear its sound, but you cannot tell where it comes from or where it is going. So it is with everyone born of the Spirit" (John 3:8). Like the wind, the Spirit is irresistible, invincible, and invisible. When the church operates according to the power of the Spirit, it accomplishes great things. When the Spirit moves through God's people, the church transforms individuals and societies.

Fire is a twofold symbol in the Old Testament. First, it represents that which purifies, because fire consumes impurities. Second, fire represents enthusiasm, passion, and an intense sense of purpose. A church that is on fire has been seized by a purifying, holy passion.

Evangelist Dwight L. Moody was in New York City when someone said to him, "The world has yet to see what God can do with a man who is wholly yielded unto him." Those words stuck in his mind, and for hours afterward, he walked the streets and pondered that statement. Finally, he cried out, "O God, make me that man!"

Instantly, Moody was filled with a sense of the overwhelming love of God. He went to the house of a friend and said, "Please, give me a room where I may pray alone!" The friend showed him to a room. Moody spent an hour or more praising God, his entire being swept up in a purifying love for his Lord.

That was the first of many such experiences in Moody's life. There were numerous times when he felt such an overwhelming love for God that he had to break away and spend time alone with God. His goal was to be totally yielded to God. That intense passion for God is what fire symbolizes in Acts 2.

The ability to speak in foreign tongues is another potent symbol in this passage. Notice that the believers did not speak gibberish or unearthly languages. Luke records:

> Now there were staying in Jerusalem God-fearing Jews from every nation under heaven. When they heard this sound, a crowd came together in bewilderment, because each one heard them speaking in his own language. Utterly amazed, they asked: "Are not all these men who are speaking Galileans? Then how is it that each of us hears them in his own native language? Parthians, Medes and Elamites; residents of Mesopotamia, Judea and Cappadocia, Pontus and Asia, Phrygia and Pamphylia, Egypt

and the parts of Libya near Cyrene; visitors from Rome (both Jews and converts to Judaism); Cretans and Arabs—we hear them declaring the wonders of God in our own tongues!" Amazed and perplexed, they asked one another, "What does this mean?" (Acts 2:5-12)

The disciples spoke in real, known languages that were recognized by people from other nations and cultures. They made powerful, edifying proclamations in these languages. Empowered by the Spirit, they spoke of the wonders of God. These symbols—wind, fire, and tongues—show us that God intended that His church should be filled with power, passion, and proclamation.

WHAT DOES THIS MEAN?

Next, Luke describes the reaction of the onlookers to the miracle of tongues, and he shows that this miracle was given for the benefit of a certain group of people. Of those people, Luke writes: "Now there were staying in Jerusalem God-fearing Jews from every nation under heaven." Thousands of devout Jews had gathered in Jerusalem from around the world to celebrate this holy event, the Feast of Weeks. Many Jews had been dispersed from Palestine into other nations, yet they still made the pilgrimage back to Jerusalem.

Josephus, the Jewish historian of that time, tells us that Jerusalem's normal population of 150,000 would swell to more than a million during the pilgrimages. The city and suburbs would be filled, and thousands would camp out on the hillsides.

In this passage, we see that something called the Jewish pilgrims down off the hillsides and into the temple courts to witness the miracle of God's Spirit coming upon the church. What called the people? The sound of the mighty rushing wind. Luke writes, "Suddenly a sound like the blowing of a violent wind came from heaven. . . . When [the Jewish pilgrims] heard this sound, a crowd came together in bewilderment" (Acts 2:2, 6). It was as if God used a wailing siren to call the people together.

Drawn by that sound, the pilgrims gathered in one place, where they heard an even stranger sound: "Each one heard [the Christians] speaking in his own language." These devout Jews from around the world were amazed. They said to each other, in effect, "Here are a bunch of unlearned Galileans—yet they speak the languages of the world! They're praising God in at least sixteen different tongues! What does this mean?"

In those days, of course, it would have been difficult for a peasant to learn a foreign language. There were no language schools, and a person had to go live in a foreign country in order to learn a foreign tongue. Yet these untrained men and women communicated in a variety of languages.

Luke records the crowd's reaction with two words, translated in Acts 2:12 as "amazed" and "perplexed." The Greek word for "amazed," *existemi*, means literally to be "pushed out of their senses." To translate it into the slang of the 1960s, the experience blew their minds. And the Greek word for "perplexed," *diaporeo*, means that they were stunned and staggered—they doubted their own senses.

As a result of their amazement and perplexity, the people asked themselves, "What does this mean?" They wanted to investigate further before coming to a conclusion about this phenomenon. But there were other people there who were quick to dismiss this phenomenon. Luke records that this group jumped to a hasty conclusion: "Some, however, made fun of them and said, 'They have had too much wine'" (Acts 2:13).

In other words, they said, "These Christians must be drunk!" This explanation explained nothing. After all, how could drunkenness enable anyone to speak a foreign language? The accusation was absurd, but it set the stage for Peter's explanation of this phenomenon.

PETER'S POWERFUL MESSAGE

Luke records Peter's response in these verses:

> Then Peter stood up with the Eleven, raised his voice and addressed the crowd: "Fellow Jews and all of you who live in Jerusalem, let me explain this to you; listen carefully to what I say. These men are not drunk, as you suppose. It's only nine in the morning!" (Acts 2:14-15)

The apostle Peter is alert to an opportunity. He hears the mocking voices but doesn't become defensive or hostile. He seizes the moment as an opportunity for witness. As he speaks, a wonderful thing happens: People listen—and the Holy Spirit moves through the crowd, bringing conviction.

Peter's message consists of three elements: an explanation of the phenomenon of tongues; a declaration concerning Jesus of Nazareth; and an application concerning the crowd. We'll look at Peter's explanation of tongues and then examine the other two elements in the next chapter. Luke records Peter's words:

> "No, this is what was spoken by the prophet Joel:
>
> "'In the last days, God says,
>   I will pour out my Spirit on all people.
> Your sons and daughters will prophesy,
>   your young men will see visions,
>   your old men will dream dreams.
> Even on my servants, both men and women,
>   I will pour out my Spirit in those days,
>   and they will prophesy.
> I will show wonders in the heaven above

and signs on the earth below,
blood and fire and billows of smoke.
The sun will be turned to darkness
and the moon to blood
before the coming of the great and glorious day of the Lord.
And everyone who calls
on the name of the Lord will be saved.'" (Acts 2:16-21)

Peter quotes the prophet Joel, who prophesied that the Spirit of God would come upon His people and they would be controlled by the Spirit. There's an interesting contrast in this passage: Peter says that these Christians are not drunk on wine, as the scoffers suggest, but are under the influence of the Holy Spirit, who has been poured out upon them. The apostle Paul made a similar comparison: "Do not get drunk on wine, which leads to debauchery. Instead, be filled with the Spirit" (Ephesians 5:18).

Peter then quotes from Joel 2: "I will pour out my Spirit on all people." Earlier in the same chapter, Joel depicted the Lord coming among His people, leading Israel's mighty army, defeating Israel's enemies, and blessing the nation with rain and food. Then, as Joel puts it, "And afterward, I will pour out my Spirit on all people." (Joel's term "afterward" is rendered "in the last days" in Peter's version, recorded here in Acts.) That transitional word *afterward* is significant. Joel is saying, in effect, "After this visitation, where God comes to Israel, He will pour out His Spirit on all people."

In other words, after the Lord Jesus has come among the people of Israel, God's Spirit will be poured out on all people, Jews and Gentiles. The good news of Jesus and His kingdom will go out to the Gentile world as well as to Israel. This is a fulfillment (a partial fulfillment, as we shall soon see) of what Jesus promised when He said, "I have other sheep that are not of this sheep pen. I must bring them also. They too will listen to my voice, and there shall be one flock and one shepherd" (John 10:16).

Peter also announces that God will pour out His Spirit on all generations (young and old) and both genders (male and female): "Your sons and daughters will prophesy, your young men will see visions, your old men will dream dreams. Even on my servants, both men and women, I will pour out my Spirit in those days, and they will prophesy." In other words, when God pours out His Spirit, the ability to minister on His behalf will not be limited to the young or the aged but will extend to all generations.

It's important to note that Peter does not use a phrase that we often see whenever someone in the New Testament quotes an Old Testament prophecy. Peter does not say, "Thus is fulfilled what was said by the prophet Joel." From other Scriptures, it's clear that while Joel's prophecy has been partially fulfilled at Pentecost, it remains to be fulfilled in a more complete way. That will take place when God again visits His people at the second coming of Christ and the Spirit is poured out once more.

THE AGE IN WHICH WE LIVE

As we previously noted, Peter's wording, when he quotes the prophet Joel, is significant. Joel originally said, "And afterward, I will pour out my Spirit on all people." But Peter changes "and afterward" to "in the last days." He says, "In the last days, God says, I will pour out my Spirit on all people." Thus Peter, under the guidance of the Holy Spirit, adapts Joel's prophecy to the present age of the Spirit—an age that begins, Peter says, with the outpouring of the Spirit of God.

Notice, too, that Joel makes no mention of tongues. Peter says, "This [Pentecost] is what was spoken by the prophet Joel," but Joel did not mention tongues. Instead, Joel referred to another gift of the Spirit, the gift of prophecy. Prophecy is the ability to declare the Word of God. It will be manifested by young and old, men and women, ordinary people. They shall be equipped by the Spirit to tell forth the Word of God with power. The emphasis is not upon the gift of tongues but upon the Spirit who gives the gifts. The age of the Spirit will begin, Peter says, with the outpouring of the Spirit. It will end, Peter says, when the sun is darkened and the moon turned to blood.

Clearly, these dire events did not take place on the day of Pentecost. According to the prophecy of Jesus, these events will take place in the future:

"For as lightning that comes from the east is visible even in the west, so will be the coming of the Son of Man. . .

'Immediately after the distress of those days

' "the sun will be darkened,
and the moon will not give its light;
the stars will fall from the sky,
and the heavenly bodies will be shaken." ' (Matthew 24:27, 29)

The prophecy of Jesus agrees with that of Joel. A day is coming when God's signs will appear on the earth and in the heavens above—signs of blood and fire and a vapor of smoke. In this Pentecost message, Peter gives us a glimpse of the beginning and end of the present age of the Spirit, the great parentheses that mark the age in which we now live. This age began on Pentecost. It will end after the great tribulation.

But through it all runs one great thematic thread, as Peter declares in Acts 2:21: "Everyone who calls on the name of the Lord will be saved." The age of the Spirit, the age of the church, is an era of faith. When men and women believe what God has said and invite Him to be the Lord of their lives, they will be filled with the Spirit.

WHAT ABOUT TONGUES TODAY?

What about tongues today? Many people say, "We're experiencing a second Pentecost. There is a new outpouring of the Holy Spirit. It's the 'latter rain' that was predicted by Joel to follow the 'early rain' of Pentecost." But Joel prophesied that the latter rain would occur after the second coming of Jesus Christ, not before.

What should we make of the current phenomena where people speak in strange words that no one can understand? Occasionally, these manifestations are accompanied by people who claim to interpret tongues. They say there are messages from God in these manifestations. How can we discern whether this is true?

The test is simple: Does this modern phenomenon behave consistently with the gift of tongues in the Bible? That is the only proper test, yet few people seem willing to ask that question. Most simply assume that the modern manifestation is the same as the manifestation in Acts 2. The apostle John warns, "Dear friends, do not believe every spirit, but test the spirits to see whether they are from God, because many false prophets have gone out into the world" (1 John 4:1). To test the spirits, we must know the biblical standard for the gift of tongues. The Spirit of God always acts consistently with the Word of God, so let's look at the four biblical marks of the gift of tongues.

First, in Scripture, the gift of tongues always involves known languages. The languages may be unknown to the people hearing them, but they are known and spoken somewhere on earth. You might say, "What about 1 Corinthians 14? In that chapter, the phrase 'unknown tongue' occurs six times." Yes, it does—in the King James Version. But the word *unknown* has been inserted by the translators; it does not appear in the original Greek text. While the King James Version incorrectly renders the phrase in 1 Corinthians 14:2 as "he that speaketh in an unknown tongue," the New International Version correctly states, "anyone who speaks in a tongue." When the Scriptures are literally and correctly translated, you find no reference to a so-called unknown tongue.

Second, in the Scriptures, tongues are addressed to God in praise and worship. Tongues are not messages intended for people in the church, nor are they a means of preaching. The Christians in the New Testament did not preach in tongues; they praised God in tongues. Paul confirms this truth: "For anyone who speaks in a tongue does not speak to men but to God" (1 Corinthians 14:2a). So if you ever hear a message being conveyed to other people by means of an unknown tongue, you are witnessing something that is contrary to the view of tongues in the New Testament.

Third, in the Scriptures, the gift of tongues is to be manifested publicly, never privately. Paul writes, "Now to each one the manifestation of the Spirit is given for the common good" (1 Corinthians 12:7). The gifts are not intended for private blessing; they are for the common good. This principle was evident on the day of Pentecost. Though the Christians spoke in praise to God, the miracle occurred for the benefit of the thousands of Jews who had gathered from the four corners of the earth. There is no New Testament record of the private use of tongues.

Fourth, in the Scriptures, the gift of tongues is a sign to unbelievers, not believers. Many who promote the gift of tongues today cite 1 Corinthians 14 yet ignore this verse: "Tongues, then, are a sign, not for believers but for unbelievers" (1 Corinthians 14:22a). This statement appears immediately after Paul quotes the prophet Isaiah:

> "Through men of strange tongues
>   and through the lips of foreigners
> I will speak to this people,
>   but even then they will not listen to me,"
> says the Lord. (1 Corinthians 14:21)

Here Paul quotes Isaiah 28:11-12, in which Isaiah tells the people of Israel that a day will come when God will send men speaking strange tongues. And, says Isaiah, when you hear these strange tongues, you will know that the hour has come when God turns from His limited ministry to Israel and begins to send His message out to people everywhere. That's why tongues were given. They are a sign that the gospel is going out to the Gentile world. Wherever you find tongues in the New Testament, you find unbelievers present, because tongues are a sign to them, not to believers.

How does the biblical gift of tongues compare with the present-day manifestation? After more than thirty years of observation, I must conclude that the present-day manifestation of tongues does not meet the biblical standard. Attempts to square this practice with the Bible's teaching serve only to distort the Scriptures.

The utterance of strange syllables is a common practice in various religions, including Hinduism and several African cults. Plato and other early Greeks wrote of this phenomenon, linking the utterance of strange syllables with experiences of religious ecstasy. So what is practiced in many churches today is nothing new.

How do we explain it? In some instances, this phenomenon is a psychological response to a strong desire to experience spiritual ecstasy or even spiritual superiority. It's a trick the mind plays on us to fulfill a desire to be favored by God. At other times, this false gift appears in connection with a genuine moving of the Holy Spirit, perhaps as an act of subversion by the enemy to undermine a genuine spiritual awakening.

Over the years, I have seen various awakenings and revivals derailed by the practice of tongues. Individual believers who have started strong in the faith have sometimes been detoured into a spiritual dead-end street. Strong, vibrant churches have been divided and destroyed by conflict over tongues.

Where did the present-day practice of tongues come from? For almost nineteen centuries, the gift of tongues seemed lost. The early church father, John Chrysostom, wrote that the gift of tongues had ceased long before his day. It was not practiced in the era of Martin Luther and John Calvin. It was not practiced during the great evangelical awakening when John Wesley and Charles Wesley began the Methodist movement.

The present-day tongues movement dates back to 1900, when Charles Fox Parham, a Methodist minister and Freemason, broke away from the Methodists and founded Bethel Bible School in Topeka, Kansas. Convinced that the American church had become lifeless, he searched for the source of the apostles' power in the book of Acts. He came to the conclusion that the gift of tongues was the key to spiritual vitality.

Beginning on New Year's Eve 1900, Parham and his students prayed around the clock, asking God for "the baptism of the Holy Spirit" and the gift of tongues. Just after midnight on the morning of January 1, 1901, Parham and his students laid hands on one young student, Agnes Ozman, praying that she would be filled with the Spirit. The young woman began speaking in an unknown language (some claimed it was Chinese). Soon, Parham and others began speaking in unknown languages. This practice eventually spread to other churches and cities.

I understand the appeal of speaking in tongues. It offers an ecstatic emotional experience and a seeming shortcut to spirituality. But we should heed Peter's words: "His divine power has given us everything we need for life and godliness through our knowledge of him who called us by his own glory and goodness" (2 Peter 1:3).

We do not need to add anything to what Jesus already gave us the moment we received Him. We need only to claim by faith what is already ours in Him.

4

JESUS THE CHRIST

Acts 2:22-37

John Wesley, the eighteenth-century English preacher who co-founded the Methodist movement, trained many young men to be preachers. He would send them out to preach at churches, parks, and street corners; then they would report back to him the results of their preaching. Wesley would invariably ask them two questions: "When you preached, was anyone converted? And when you preached, did anyone get angry?"

If the answer to both questions was no, Wesley would say, "In that case, I believe you should pursue a different vocation. The Lord has not called you to preach. When the Holy Spirit convicts people of sin, they either get converted—or they get mad!"

In the previous chapter, we heard the first half of Peter's sermon on the day of Pentecost. As we come to the second half of his sermon, Peter will make a confrontational statement and his hearers will either be converted—or get mad!

> "Men of Israel, listen to this: Jesus of Nazareth was a man accredited by God to you by miracles, wonders and signs, which God did among you through him, as you yourselves know. This man was handed over to you by God's set purpose and foreknowledge; and you, with the help of wicked men, put him to death by nailing him to the cross. But God raised him from the dead, freeing him from the agony of death, because it was impossible for death to keep its hold on him." (Acts 2:22-24)

This bold statement hits the crowd with amazing force. It's the opening salvo of a three-part argument that begins with the humanity of Jesus and ends with a bold proclamation of His deity. Peter advances his argument with irrefutable proofs. He begins by recounting the great historical events upon which our Christian faith rests: the life, death, and resurrection of Jesus of Nazareth. If these events had not taken place in recorded history, then Christianity would be a hoax. Our faith rests on historical facts.

No one knows these facts better than Peter's audience. They were present in Jerusalem during the Passover week, when Jesus was arrested, executed, and reported to have risen again. The entire city was in upheaval over these events. If Peter had misreported any of these events, the crowd would have shouted him down. But no one contradicted Peter's message. He set forth the facts that these people had witnessed for themselves—the facts that established the remarkable claims of the Christian faith.

THE LIFE OF JESUS

Each of the events Peter speaks of teaches an important truth.

First, Peter talks about the life and ministry of Jesus. "Jesus of Nazareth," Peter said, "was a man accredited by God to you by miracles, wonders and signs, which God did among you through him, as you yourselves know." Jesus was a real human being, not a legendary figure, and when you see Jesus, you see humanity as God intended it to be.

Jesus was authenticated by God through miracles and signs. He turned water into wine, commanded the wind and waves be still, multiplied the loaves and fishes, healed the sick, cast out demons, raised the dead, and more. He manifested the control over nature that God originally intended for the human race. These signs were not done by Jesus because He was God. Rather, God performed these miracles through a man who was utterly yielded to the indwelling power of God within.

You and I are to function the same way as Jesus did, by continually drawing on His indwelling presence. Jesus was God, and Peter will declare His deity in this message, but the deity of Christ is not the secret of His ministry. Jesus performed amazing works because He was yielded to the Father. He was the pattern of normal humanity.

THE DEATH OF JESUS

Next, Peter focuses on the death of Jesus. His death, Peter says, revealed God's purpose in history: "This man was handed over to you by God's set purpose and foreknowledge; and you, with the help of wicked men, put him to death by nailing him to the cross." Jesus died to fulfill the program of God. The cross was no accident. It was an essential event, for it was the only way God could deal with the problem of human evil.

You may recall Robert Louis Stevenson's novel *Dr. Jekyll and Mr. Hyde*. It's the story of a man who, by day, was the respected Dr. Jekyll, but by night he became the monstrous Mr. Hyde. We are all like Jekyll and Hyde. We are made in God's image, and we want to love and serve Him, but we also have our sin nature, the result of the fall of Adam. We continually turn into Mr. Hyde and commit horrible sins that fill us with shame and self-loathing. It's the Mr. Hyde in us that God seeks to defeat and destroy.

A young man once came to me for prayer and counseling. He was brought up in our Sunday school but had left the church, and I hadn't seen him in years. We sat down, and he told me he had taken some wrong turns and spent time in prison. Now he wanted to get his life straightened out. We talked about God's love and forgiveness, and about how he needed to yield his life to the Lord Jesus. We prayed together. He seemed sincere about wanting to yield his life to Christ.

But that night, just hours after we prayed together, he went to the place where he worked and cleaned out the till. Then he went to his parents' house, stole two hundred dollars from his father, and left town. You might say, "Well, he was never sincere." But we can't know another person's heart. All I know is that I believe I was talking to the repentant Dr. Jekyll side of this young man, but hours later, Mr. Hyde was clearly in control.

God says that the only way to break the power of sin in our lives is through death—the death of Jesus upon the cross. There is no other way. If we try to grapple with our evil by our own efforts, we will lose. Hyde is stronger than Jekyll. We must accept the death of Jesus in order to defeat Mr. Hyde.

THE RESURRECTION OF JESUS

Next, Peter speaks of the resurrection of Jesus and what that means for our lives: "But God raised him from the dead, freeing him from the agony of death, because it was impossible for death to keep its hold on him." Resurrection power is the ability to bring life out of death, to bring hope out of hopelessness, to transform darkness into light.

Ever since death entered the human race, men and women have dreamed of solving the death problem. Some suggested solutions are grotesque. For example, there is the cryogenic approach: When you know you are about to die, you can have yourself deep-frozen in liquid nitrogen, and your body can be put away in a cold-storage vault until a cure is found for your disease—perhaps a century from now. Then (in theory) you will be thawed out, cured, and allowed to go on living.

But that is not the kind of resurrection Jesus offers. That is not the power that raised Jesus from the dead and liberated Him from the tomb. Later, Peter says, "God has raised this Jesus to life, and we are all witnesses of the fact" (Acts 2:32). When Peter makes this amazing statement, not one person in the crowd protests. The people knew that the tomb was empty and that Jesus was risen—no one dared to argue the fact. That is strong evidence for the resurrection: No one in Jerusalem challenged his claim.

Remember, the crucifixion was a recent event. People could go outside the city and inspect the empty tomb with their own eyes. Everyone knew that the Jewish religious authorities and the Romans had not been able to produce the body. The high priest and the Roman governor would have squelched the resurrection rumors if they could—but they couldn't. Jesus was alive. He was appearing again and again to His own followers, and the empty tomb bore mute witness to the fact that the grave couldn't hold Him.

THE PROPHECY OF DAVID

The next section of Peter's Pentecost sermon focuses on the Old Testament predictions of the resurrection:

David said about him:

"'I saw the Lord always before me.
    Because he is at my right hand,
    I will not be shaken.
Therefore my heart is glad and my tongue rejoices;
    my body also will live in hope,
because you will not abandon me to the grave,
    nor will you let your Holy One see decay.
You have made known to me the paths of life;
    you will fill me with joy in your presence.'" (Acts 2:25-28)

Peter is not merely stating that David predicted the resurrection of Jesus Christ. He is pointing out that David declared the resurrection to be absolutely necessary in view of the life Jesus had lived. David prophesied that Jesus would say, "I saw the Lord always before me. Because he is at my right hand, I will not be shaken." David knew that Jesus would live in utter dependence upon the Father. Therefore, David, expressing the attitude of Jesus, said, "My heart is glad and my tongue rejoices; my body also will live in hope, because you will not abandon me to the grave, nor will you let your Holy One see decay." The life Jesus lived guaranteed that death would have no power over him.

Major W. Ian Thomas, founder of Torchbearers International, put it this way: "He had to be what He was in order to do what He did. He had to do what He did in order that we might have what He is. And we must have what He is in order to be what He was." Now, that is Christianity! Ordinary men and women can be what Jesus was, can live the resurrection life He lived, because we have what He is.

Next Peter makes it clear that David was speaking not of himself but of Jesus:

"Brothers, I can tell you confidently that the patriarch David died and was buried, and his tomb is here to this day. But he was a prophet and knew that God had promised him on oath that he would place one of his descendants on his throne. Seeing what was ahead, he spoke of the resurrection of the Christ, that he was not abandoned to the grave, nor did his body see decay. God has raised this Jesus to life, and we are all witnesses of the fact." (Acts 2:29-32)

Skeptics sometimes claim that the messianic psalms, which predict the sufferings and resurrection of Christ (such as Psalm 16 and Psalm 22), are not prophetic but reflect the personal experience of the psalmist. Peter firmly refutes that argument. He says, in effect, "You can't say that Psalm 16 reflects the experience of the psalmist, because it speaks of a man whose body does not rot in the grave. That couldn't refer to the psalmist because David died and was buried in a tomb in Jerusalem. Clearly, this psalm refers to Another. It refers to Jesus the Messiah."

DEATH HAS NO POWER OVER JESUS

Next, Peter speaks about the results of the resurrection—what it means to every person on the planet that Jesus of Nazareth was raised from the dead:

> "Exalted to the right hand of God, he has received from the Father the promised Holy Spirit and has poured out what you now see and hear. For David did not ascend to heaven, and yet he said,
>
>> "'The Lord said to my Lord:
>>   "Sit at my right hand
>> until I make your enemies
>>   a footstool for your feet." '
>
> "Therefore let all Israel be assured of this: God has made this Jesus, whom you crucified, both Lord and Christ."
> When the people heard this, they were cut to the heart and said to Peter and the other apostles, "Brothers, what shall we do?" (Acts 2:33-37)

Again Peter enlists his audience as a crowd of witnesses. He says, in effect, "You see right now the proof of what David predicted." And he quotes from Psalm 110, David's prophecy of what God the Father would say to David's Lord, Jesus the Messiah: "Sit at my right hand until I make your enemies a footstool for your feet."

What is the proof Peter refers to? There is a startling clue in this statement: "Exalted to the right hand of God, he has received from the Father the promised Holy Spirit and has poured out what you now see and hear." Peter says that his audience was at that very moment seeing tongues of fire dancing on the heads of the Christians and hearing the sound of the mighty wind and the strange languages. These manifestations were still going on while Peter spoke.

So, in effect, Peter said, "These manifestations are visible, audible proof that Jesus of Nazareth is Lord and Christ." When Peter says, "God has made this Jesus, whom you crucified, both Lord and Christ," we should examine closely what he means. The word *Lord* refers to Jesus' role as ruler of all things, the One who holds the key to life and death, heaven and hell.

The word *Christ* means "Messiah." Many people, when they hear the name Jesus Christ, think that Jesus is His first name and Christ is His last name. But Christ is His title, meaning the anointed One, the promised Deliverer, the hope of humankind. Peter bluntly tells the people that they are in a precarious position, because this same Jesus, whom Peter had proven to be the Messiah, is the One they had crucified only fifty days earlier. Imagine how these people felt upon hearing Peter's words!

Imagine that you are driving to a job interview and you have a car accident. The other driver comes out of his car, and you beat him, curse him, and kick him. Then you get back in your car, drive on to your job interview, and arrive at the boss's office—and find yourself ushered into the presence of the man you have just cursed, kicked, and beaten! This gives you a faint taste of how these people must have felt as they listened to Peter's sermon. They realize that the Messiah they have been waiting for is the man they crucified. No wonder they cried out, "Brothers, what shall we do?"

Here, Christianity rests its case. Jesus Christ is Lord, whether people know it or not. He is the inevitable Man. There is no way to avoid Him. He is the Lord of all things, and our every heartbeat depends on Him and is a gift from Him. Sooner or later, like it or not, we must deal with Jesus the Christ. Like Peter's audience, we must ask ourselves, "What shall we do?"

Next we shall see Peter's answer to this all-important question.

5

THE YOUNG CHURCH

Acts 2:38-47

On the morning of February 3, 1970, the students of Asbury College in Wilmore, Kentucky, gathered for a 10 o'clock chapel service. The meeting, scheduled to last fifty minutes, continued nonstop, twenty-four hours a day, for the next eight days. Eyewitnesses compared it with the Great Evangelical Awakenings of 1740 and 1800.

The event began when the school's academic dean stood and shared his Christian testimony. Then he invited students to share their experience with Christ. Students stood and spoke, one after another. Soon, some of the students went forward and quietly prayed. Others sang hymns: "How Great Thou Art," "What a Friend We Have in Jesus," "Blessed Assurance." Some wept openly.

As word spread, people streamed into the auditorium and fell under a deep conviction from the Holy Spirit. They recognized that their lives were fragmented and their relationships were damaged by sin and resentment. Hearts melted, and students confessed, repented, and forgave one another. Some embraced while others broke out in spontaneous applause. No one planned this event. It took on a life of its own.

Days passed, and the news media learned of the Asbury revival. A newspaper sent a reporter to find out what was happening. When the reporter asked the college president to explain the event, the president said, "The only way I can account for this is that last Tuesday morning, at about twenty of eleven, the Lord Jesus walked into our auditorium, and He's been there ever since."

The president also remarked on another facet of the event: Everything that happened was amazingly orderly. No one spoke out of turn. No one shouted or fell in a fit of religious frenzy. Everything that happened was quiet and well-behaved, as one might expect of a movement of God's Spirit.

In one report, the wife of the college president came forward and confessed that she had harbored resentment toward the school and the community. She said she had been unhappy there and had blamed the school. But God had replaced her bitterness with love and acceptance. Some said that when she finished her testimony, they felt it was like the day of Pentecost in Acts 2. People were convicted of sin and filled with joy to see hearts changed by the power of God's Spirit.

News of the Asbury revival was reported in newspapers across the country. For months afterward, students continued to meet and pray together. When summer came, the Asbury students went back to their communities—and the revival spread around the country. By the fall of 1970, similar revivals were reported at more than a hundred other colleges and Bible schools across North and South America.

This twentieth-century event is much like the first-century event we see in Acts 2. Here, a revival is about to take place in Jerusalem that will spread throughout Judea, and then to Samaria, and out to the uttermost parts of the world. The fact that the Spirit of God still operates in our day as He did two thousand years ago confirms that we are living in the same age of the Spirit that began on the day of Pentecost.

"REPENT AND BE BAPTIZED"

Previously we saw Peter before the crowd, explaining that the phenomena of rushing wind and tongues of fire were due to the fact that Jesus of Nazareth had ascended and was seated at the right hand of the Father. When the people heard this, they were "cut to the heart." To be cut to the heart is to be deeply convicted by God's Spirit. The people had their eyes opened to their own sinfulness. In a flash of clarity, they understood that Jesus of Nazareth was truly God in human flesh, the long-awaited Messiah—and they had nailed Him to a cross. In despair, they cried out, "Brothers, what shall we do?"

That's how the Spirit works in our lives. He convicts us of sin and makes us aware of the lordship of Jesus Christ. Jesus is the Lord of those who love Him, but He is also the Lord of those who reject Him. Jesus is the inescapable One, and the moment any person recognizes Him and understands who He truly is, there is conviction of sin. That person is cut to the heart.

The people understand that Peter calls them to some sort of action, so they ask, "What shall we do?" So Peter tells them how to be saved:

> Peter replied, "Repent and be baptized, every one of you, in the name of Jesus Christ for the forgiveness of your sins. And you will receive the gift of the Holy Spirit. The promise is for you and your children and for all who are far off—for all whom the Lord our God will call."
>
> With many other words he warned them; and he pleaded with them, "Save yourselves from this corrupt generation." (Acts 2:38-40)

Peter replies, in effect, "There are two things you must do: repent and be baptized. Then there is one thing God will do." We will get to God's response in a moment. First, let's look at our response: repentance and baptism.

"Repentance" is a much-misunderstood word. Many people think repentance means feeling sorry and even weeping over sins. But that's remorse, not repentance. True repentance means that you change your mind. The Greek word *metanoi*, translated "repent" in the Scriptures, means exactly that: change your mind. The English word *repent* comes from the Latin *pentir*, which means "to think." The prefix *re-* means "again." So *re* plus *pentir* means "to think again." If you think everything is all right with your life, well, think again! If you think Jesus was merely a great human teacher but not God in human form, think again! Repent. Change your mind.

The second thing Paul says the people must do is to "be baptized." This is not to say that baptism adds anything to your repentance. Baptism doesn't remove your sins. Why, then, is it important to be baptized? The symbol of baptism is an outward declaration of the inward change. It means, "I am identified with Jesus."

There is no evidence in Scripture that the importance of baptism hinges on the mode of baptism. The three common modes of baptism are immersion (briefly submerging the believer under water), aspersion (sprinkling water over the believer's head), and affusion (pouring water over the believer). All three modes symbolize the beginning of a new life and identification with Christ.

You might ask, "Is Peter telling us that baptism is the means by which we receive forgiveness?" No. The original Greek language of this text could be translated in this way: "Be baptized in the name of Jesus Christ because of the forgiveness of your sins." Later in Acts, Peter will tell the people gathered in the house of Cornelius, "All the prophets testify about [Jesus] that everyone who believes in him receives forgiveness of sins through his name" (Acts 10:43). No mention is made of baptism, only faith.

So baptism doesn't save us. It's the outward symbol of our inward faith relationship with the Lord Jesus Christ. Peter is saying, in effect, "When you repent, you will receive the Holy Spirit, and He will come and live in you. His work in your life will make Jesus real and close to you."

THREE THOUSAND BECOME ONE

The apostle Peter says that this newness of life is available to all: "The promise is for you and your children and for all who are far off—for all whom the Lord our God will call." Take note of that phrase: "for all whom the Lord our God will call." Peter is telling us that we do not find God—He calls us! If you have a hunger in your heart to know God, that hunger was stirred by God. As Jesus once said, "No one can come to me unless the Father who sent me draws him, and I will raise him up at the last day" (John 6:44).

Yet, even though God chooses us, we must also choose Him. Peter says, "Save yourselves from this corrupt generation." We cannot be passive when God calls us. We must actively respond. That's what happened on the day of Pentecost, and we see the results in the next two verses:

> Those who accepted his message were baptized, and about three thousand were added to their number that day.
>
> They devoted themselves to the apostles' teaching and to the fellowship, to the breaking of bread and to prayer. (Acts 2:41-42)

Three thousand human souls were saved and filled with God's Spirit on that day. The moment of conversion is only the beginning of the Christian life. Once we are converted, we start living the adventure of knowing Him in ever deeper and more vital ways. In this brief paragraph, we find four essential ingredients of Christian growth.

Baptism. Luke writes, "Those who accepted his message were baptized." Imagine that scene: In one day, in the city of Jerusalem, three thousand people were baptized into the Christian faith. They all openly identified themselves with the crucified Nazarene. To be baptized in the name of Jesus just fifty days after His execution was a courageous step.

Listening and learning. Luke writes, "They devoted themselves to the apostles' teaching." The apostles taught these three thousand new believers the biblical truth about life. We can never understand ourselves, the world around us, or God's purpose in history apart from the Scriptures.

Fellowship. Luke writes, "They devoted themselves . . . to the fellowship." Fellowship means holding all things in common. These three thousand new Christians began to love one another and share with one another. Aliens became friends. Strangers became brothers. A crowd of three thousand people from different cultures, speaking different languages, became one in Christ. They shared problems and needs. They prayed together. They experienced intense community.

Worship. Luke writes, "They devoted themselves . . . to the breaking of bread and to prayer." The breaking of bread is a reference to the communion service, not merely to eating meals together. The new believers shared together in that symbolic testimony to the life and death of the Lord Jesus.

These are the four fundamentals of Christian growth. Without them you cannot grow. With them you cannot keep from growing.

"THOSE WHO WERE BEING SAVED"

In the last paragraph of Acts 2, we see a beautiful and profound picture of how the newborn church influences individual lives and first-century society:

> Everyone was filled with awe, and many wonders and miraculous signs were done by the apostles. All the believers were together and had everything in common. Selling their possessions and goods, they gave to anyone as he had need. Every day they continued to meet together in the temple courts. They broke bread in their homes and ate together with glad and sincere hearts, praising God and enjoying the favor of all the people. And the Lord added to their number daily those who were being saved. (Acts 2:43-47)

The newborn church affects the surrounding society. "Everyone was filled with awe," Luke writes, "and many wonders and miraculous signs were done by the apostles." The public at large was wonder-struck over the supernatural manifestations that followed the apostles. Clearly, there was more than mere human power at work.

Some Christians today feel that we need to experience again the miracles and signs that were evident in Acts 2. But God never intended for believers to continually seek miraculous signs. In Matthew 12, some Pharisees and teachers of the law approached Jesus and said, "Teacher, we want to see a miraculous sign from you." Jesus replied, "A wicked and adulterous generation asks for a miraculous sign!" (Matthew 12:38-39). Jesus made it clear that miraculous manifestations are not as important as the quiet miracle of spiritual healing. What is done in the spiritual realm is far greater than what is done in the physical realm.

A fascination with physical miracles is the mark of an immature church. As Christians become more mature, they cease to be so fascinated with signs and wonders and grow ever more fascinated with the wonder of knowing Jesus as friend, Lord, and Savior. God still works miracles, but as we grow more mature in Him, we find that His power tends to be manifested in our inner life—in our ability to experience His supernatural peace and forgiveness.

So the first effect we see of this newborn church is the profound affect it has upon the world around it. The people of Jerusalem have become aware of a spiritual force that defies explanation—the power of the Holy Spirit, acting through believers.

The second effect of this newborn church is its effect on individual members: "All the believers were together and had everything in common. Selling their possessions and goods, they gave to anyone as he had need." There were people in the newborn church who had more possessions and goods than they needed, and there were people who were poor and needy. So the rich benefited by serving others, and the poor benefited by having their needs met.

Some commentators on Acts have claimed that these early Christians forsook capitalism and became communists. According to this view, these Christians sold everything they had and pooled all of their resources. But that's not what this passage says.

The early Christians did not start a new form of government or a new economic system based on the theories of Karl Marx. They continued to own private property and work at their jobs, but as Christians, they also practiced a new and deeper level of generosity than the world had ever seen before. They sold a portion of their possessions to establish a common fund that was used to help the needy among them. The world had never before seen such caring and compassion. This deep level of concern for others still defines the Christian community.

During the so-called Jesus People movement of the 1970s, Peninsula Bible Church began an unusual policy concerning the collection plate at the Sunday evening service: Anyone who wants to give to the offering may give—and anyone who has a need may take out enough to meet that need. People told us the policy would never work, yet the first night we tried it, our offering was the largest we had received in years. We continued this policy. and it proved to be an effective means of having everything in common and giving to those who had needs.

The third effect of the newborn church is that it brought glory to God. Luke writes, "Every day they continued to meet together in the temple courts. They broke bread in their homes and ate together with glad and sincere hearts, praising God and enjoying the favor of all the people. And the Lord added to their number daily those who were being saved." God was glorified and praised in the midst of His people.

That is what God wants from our lives. If you have never acknowledged Jesus as your Lord and Savior, you can repent, change your mind—and be saved. You can say, "Lord Jesus, come into my life, take control, and be my Lord and my God!" Then you can express your inward change in an outward way through the symbol of baptism. From this day forward, you can live out your inward change by forgiving those who have hurt you, by asking God to rid you of bitterness and grudges, by confessing your sins and restoring your broken relationships.

So open your heart to Jesus the Lord. Let Him melt the resistance within you. Let Him give you a new heart of compassion and generosity toward others. Let Him fill you with the warmth and peace of His Holy Spirit.

Luke said of that young church, "And the Lord added to their number daily those who were being saved." He has been adding to that number for two thousand years. Make sure that you, too, are part of that number. Make sure you are part of His church.

6

THE POWER TO HEAL

Acts 3:1-10

The church has exploded onto the first-century scene! In one day, the new-born body of believers has grown from 120 members to more than 3,000. As we come to Acts 3, the church takes its first baby steps. We are about to witness the apostles' first effort to spread the good news since the day of Pentecost. Here is Luke's account of that incident:

> One day Peter and John were going up to the temple at the time of prayer—at three in the afternoon. Now a man crippled from birth was being carried to the temple gate called Beautiful, where he was put every day to beg from those going into the temple courts. When he saw Peter and John about to enter, he asked them for money. Peter looked straight at him, as did John. Then Peter said, "Look at us!" So the man gave them his attention, expecting to get something from them.
>
> Then Peter said, "Silver or gold I do not have, but what I have I give you. In the name of Jesus Christ of Nazareth, walk." Taking him by the right hand, he helped him up, and instantly the man's feet and ankles became strong. He jumped to his feet and began to walk. Then he went with them into the temple courts, walking and jumping, and praising God. (Acts 3:1-8)

Near the end of Acts 2, in verse 43, Luke summarized the life of the early church by saying, "Everyone was filled with awe, and many wonders and miraculous signs were done by the apostles." Luke did not record all of those signs and wonders, but he did choose to describe this one—the story of the lame man who was healed at the Beautiful Gate. Because Luke selected this event to record, it must be significant.

It's the story of a man who was lame since birth. He knows he has deep needs, and he thinks the answer to his need is money. So he sits by the gate and begs. When the two apostles find him there, he asks them for money. Peter replies, "Silver or gold I do not have, but what I have I give you. In the name of Jesus Christ of Nazareth, walk."

A story is told of a Renaissance-era pope who was a patron of the arts. The church was rich, and the pope lavished large sums of silver and gold on artists who produced the paintings and sculptures that adorned the cathedrals. As the pope walked through a great hall, admiring the artworks there, he said to a bishop who walked with him, "No longer does the church need to say, 'Silver or gold I do not have!'"

"True," the bishop said, "but then, neither can the church say, 'Rise up and walk.'"

As we look at the story of this healing, we have to ask: Does the church still have the power to heal?

MATERIALLY BANKRUPT, SPIRITUALLY RICH

Every detail of this story is significant. The lame man was seated at the gate of the temple. When Peter and John arrived, it was the ninth hour, or about 3:00 in the afternoon—the usual time of prayer. This hour is significant because it was also the hour when Jesus cried out "It is finished!" before his death on the cross (John 19:30).

We are told that the lame man had come to the temple every day for years. That means that the Lord saw this man many times when He went to the temple, yet He never healed him. I believe this is because God has a perfect time for every event. In His timetable, the Father was saving this man for a later time, so that he would be at the gate, needy and begging, when Peter and James arrived.

When the lame man asks for money, Peter first says, "Look at us!" This is a crucial detail. Peter is acting in the same way Jesus did when He healed people. Before healing someone, Jesus always said something to direct that person's attention to Himself. Why? Because when the needy person focuses his gaze on Jesus, he feels a sense of expectation. His faith is quickened. You can't receive anything from God if you don't expect something from God.

Luke records, "So the man gave them his attention, expecting to get something from them." The moment Peter had the man's attention, he did two things. First, he admitted his material bankruptcy: "As far as silver and gold goes, I'm broke." Second, Peter boldly asserted that, in the spiritual realm, he had limitless resources through Jesus the Lord: "In the name of Jesus Christ of Nazareth, walk."

Then Peter reached out, took the man by the right hand, and pulled him up. That was an electric moment! As the man heard Peter command him in the name of Jesus of Nazareth, he felt strength flow into his feet and ankles. He jumped up and began to walk.

What did it mean that Peter commanded this man "in the name of Jesus Christ of Nazareth"? This was not a magic formula Peter spoke. Rather, Peter was announcing the authority he represented.

When you write a check, you sign your name on that check. Your signature represents you and all of the assets you have on deposit in the bank. The check instructs the bank to release an amount of money to the person named on the face of the check, and your signature states the authority that check represents.

In the same way, Peter was handing that lame man a check that read, "Pay to the order of this man the sum of one complete healing, in the name of Jesus Christ of Nazareth."

OUR BANKRUPTCY AND GOD'S ALL-SUFFICIENCY

This display of God's healing power had a profound effect on those present:

> When all the people saw him walking and praising God, they recognized him as the same man who used to sit begging at the temple gate called Beautiful, and they were filled with wonder and amazement at what had happened to him. (Acts 3:9-10)

Peter has set a powerful example for you and me. He showed us that we are to come and declare our bankruptcy in the material realm and declare the all-sufficiency of Jesus Christ in the spiritual realm. This world may chase after silver and gold, but we have the healing power of God, made available in the name of Jesus.

Do you want to be a witness for Jesus Christ? How do you do that? Too often, we send people out with an evangelistic program, a stack of tracts, or some other gimmick, and say, "Go tell people what God is going to do." That's not witnessing according to the biblical pattern. God doesn't want us to tell people what He's going to do. He wants us to tell people what He's already done in our lives. True witnessing always follows a specific model. First, God works in a human life. Second, that person tells other people what God did. Third, God works in the lives of the hearers—and the process repeats.

After all, what does the word *witness* mean? As a noun, "witness" means a person who has personally experienced or perceived something. As a verb, "to bear witness" means to tell about something that you have experienced or perceived. To be a courtroom witness, you have to have directly seen events or evidence relating to the matter being tried. You can't be a witness to something you haven't seen or experienced, nor can you be a witness to something that hasn't taken place.

So allow God to work in your life. Then go tell others what He has done. As Peter wrote, "Always be ready to give an answer to every man who asks you a reason for the hope that is in you, with gentleness and courtesy" (1 Peter 3:15b KJV). That's authentic witnessing, according to Scripture.

THE MEANING OF HEALING

Some Christians will say, "Healing ought to take place in the church all the time. If anyone is sick, another Christian should say to him, 'In the name of Jesus of Nazareth, be healed!'" Some even say it's a sign of sin and unbelief to be sick or to see a doctor and take medicine. They tell us that Jesus died not only for our sins but for our sicknesses as well. They quote the Old Testament:

"by his stripes we are healed" (Isaiah 53:5 KJV). Many so-called faith healers preach that God expects Christians to be well, and those who are sick have hidden sin or a lack of faith in their lives.

In *Disappointment with God*, Philip Yancey tells of a young friend named Richard, a Christian university student. Richard was going through a crisis of doubt about God's existence. One day, while flipping television channels, he came upon a faith healing service conducted by a woman televangelist. He saw people who claimed to receive healings from cancer, paralysis, heart problems, and more.

Three weeks later, when this woman held a series of meetings in a neighboring state, Richard traveled half a day to attend the meeting. It was an emotionally charged event, with people praying in tongues and occasional shouts of, "I'm healed!"

One man in particular made an impression on Richard. He was carried in on a stretcher—yet he got off the stretcher and walked up onto the stage. The crowd cheered wildly. The man gave his name, said he was a physician, and had incurable lung cancer. The doctors, he said, had given him six months to live. "But now, praise God, I'm healed!" he said.

Richard recalled, "I wrote down the man's name and practically floated out of that meeting. I had never known such certainty of faith before. My search was over. I had seen proof of a living God in those people on the stage."

One week later, Richard decided to contact the doctor, so he dialed directory assistance and got the doctor's number. He called, and a woman answered. Richard asked for the doctor. The woman replied flatly, "My husband is dead," then hung up.

Richard was devastated. His faith was shattered.

I believe God is at work in the world. I believe He heals. But the Scriptures don't teach that healing comes through sensationalized mass meetings staged by so-called faith healers. What does Acts 3 tell us about such beliefs? Does the healing of the lame man at the temple support such practices or contradict them?

THE PURPOSE OF MIRACLES

Two classes of Scripture deal with God's purpose for miraculous healing. First, there are Scripture passages that tell us that God performed healing miracles in order to authenticate the gospel message. Those healings proved that certain people were genuine messengers of God and that God spoke through them. One such passage is in Mark 16, where Jesus meets with His disciples after His resurrection:

> He said to them, "Go into all the world and preach the good news to all creation. Whoever believes and is baptized will be saved, but whoever

does not believe will be condemned. And these signs will accompany those who believe: In my name they will drive out demons; they will speak in new tongues; they will pick up snakes with their hands; and when they drink deadly poison, it will not hurt them at all; they will place their hands on sick people, and they will get well." (Mark 16:15-18)

A number of extreme religious movements have based their theology on this passage, claiming that Jesus wants all believers to perform miracles. Those who advocate this interpretation fail to notice that there is a change in the pronouns our Lord uses. He says, first, "Go into all the world and preach the good news to all creation." Then, switching from plural to singular, He says, "Whoever believes and is baptized will be saved, but whoever does not believe will be condemned." Then He changes back to plural: "And these signs will accompany those who believe . . ."

Why is this change to plural significant? Because it indicates that Jesus is now talking directly to those who are present—that is, His disciples. Just a few verses earlier, Mark wrote that Jesus "rebuked them for their lack of faith and their stubborn refusal to believe those who had seen him after he had risen" (Mark 16:14). Jesus has just scolded them for their unbelief after his resurrection, so now He says, "And these signs will accompany those who believe . . ."

After rebuking unbelief, Jesus promises that those disciples who do believe will be accompanied by miraculous signs. He goes on to list those signs: driving out demons, speaking in new languages, surviving the perils of snakes and poisons, and healing the sick. Then, as if to confirm this interpretation, Mark adds, "Then the disciples went out and preached everywhere, and the Lord worked with them and confirmed his word by the signs that accompanied it" (Mark 16:20).

These miraculous signs are what Paul calls "things that mark an apostle" (2 Corinthians 12:12). So Jesus is promising the apostles—not all believers, just His apostles—that their ministry would be authenticated by these signs, wonders, and miracles. This is not a passage that you and I can claim as pertaining to ourselves.

So, the first class of Scriptures dealing with miraculous healings tell us that miracles authenticated the apostles as genuine representatives of God. The second class of passages tells us that God truly does heal in any age, at any time, according to His sovereign purpose. These verses tell us that we have the right to ask Him for physical healing, and He will often heal us as we ask.

We see an example of this second class of passages in James 5. There we are told that if anyone is sick, he should gather the elders to pray, and God will hear the prayer of faith and raise the sick. James says, "Therefore confess your sins to each other and pray for each other so that you may be healed. The prayer of a righteous man is powerful and effective" (James 5:16).

Now, this is not an absolute promise that God will heal, but God does tell us to pray for the healing of ourselves and our brothers. But when we pray, we must leave the results to God. There are numerous instances in Scripture where righteous people of faith pray for healing, yet God chooses not to heal.

When the apostle Paul wrote to the Philippians, he mentioned his dear friend Epaphroditus. The Christians at Philippi had heard he'd been sick. Paul wrote: "Indeed he was ill, and almost died. But God had mercy on him, and not on him only but also on me, to spare me sorrow upon sorrow" (Philippians 2:27). Paul did not have the ability that faith healers claim—the ability to pray and receive an instantaneous miracle of healing. Epaphroditus survived his near-fatal illness, but there is no mention of a miracle, only a slow period of natural recovery.

So we have to put the miracle of Acts 3 into its proper perspective. It was a great authenticating work. Someone once observed that every miracle is a parable, designed not only to demonstrate the power of God but also to illustrate a deeper truth. When Peter told the man by the temple gate to rise and walk, he was not only demonstrating God's power and his own authority as an apostle. Peter was symbolically illustrating that this man had a deep inner need that the man himself didn't recognize. The beggar asked for silver and gold. God gave him an infinitely greater gift—the gift of healing.

What happens to us spiritually is far more important than what happens to our physical bodies. Though we are dying physically, we can grow spiritually stronger day by day. As Paul said, "Therefore we do not lose heart. Though outwardly we are wasting away, yet inwardly we are being renewed day by day" (2 Corinthians 4:16). These outward miracles of healing are pictures of what happens in the inner being when the power of God invades our lives. We are paralyzed by sin, but in the name of Jesus, we can rise up and walk.

This healing in Acts 3 is a parable of the age in which we live. The miracle occurred at the beginning of the age of the Spirit, the church age, to teach us what this age is like. The lame man is a picture of the world, lying at the gate of the house of God, begging for help. Our world doesn't even know what help to ask for. It seeks material things—silver and gold—and sometimes the church mistakenly offers only material aid.

While it's important to meet physical need, we should not forget that humanity's real need is much deeper. If we, as the church, meet only the physical needs of people, then we might as well be the Red Cross, the Community Chest, or some other secular organization. The church of Jesus Christ has been commissioned to give something of eternal value to the people around us—the same gift Peter and John gave the man at the temple gate: true wholeness. Sometimes God does give outward physical wholeness, but He always gives inner wholeness to those who will receive it.

Are you like the lame man of Acts 3? Have you been lying at the gate of God's house, begging for help? God has made His abundant riches available to you—riches that far exceed mere silver or gold, riches that will enable you to rise up and walk. So I say to you today, "Prepare to live a new life of faith and wholeness. In the name of Jesus Christ of Nazareth, rise up and walk!"

7

BY FAITH IN HIS NAME

Acts 3:11-26

We've just witnessed the miraculous healing of the man who was lame from birth. He now leaps and shouts in the temple courts, praising God, but that's not the end of the story. Luke tells us what happened next:

> While the beggar held on to Peter and John, all the people were aston-ished and came running to them in the place called Solomon's Colon-nade. When Peter saw this, he said to them: "Men of Israel, why does this surprise you? Why do you stare at us as if by our own power or godliness we had made this man walk?" (Acts 3:11-12)

Imagine the scene with me: This healed man, in his unbounded joy, clutches Peter and John with both hands and won't let them go! The original Greek language conveys that he clings to both men with great strength. All around the temple courts, people hear the commotion and rush over to see the formerly lame man leaping for joy.

Peter looks at the gathering crowd and sees two different expressions. First, there is wide-eyed amazement over the healing. Second, there is misplaced awe and reverence for Peter and John. Peter can tell that the people have mis-understood the source of their healing power. They think Peter and John are magicians.

THE GOD OF OUR FATHERS

Peter acts quickly, addressing the crowd. "Men of Israel," he says, "why does this surprise *you*? Why do *you* stare at us as if by our own power or godliness we had made this man walk?" I have twice italicized the word *you* because I want you to catch Peter's emphasis. He's saying, in effect, "Why are *you*, of all people, amazed at this? *You*, as men of Israel, as the chosen people of God, should know that this is the kind of God we serve! *You* should not be so sur-prised!" Then Peter delivers a convicting message:

> "The God of Abraham, Isaac and Jacob, the God of our fathers, has glori-fied his servant Jesus. You handed him over to be killed, and you disowned him before Pilate, though he had decided to let him go. You disowned the Holy and Righteous One and asked that a murderer be released to you.

You killed the author of life, but God raised him from the dead. We are witnesses of this." (Acts 3:13-15)

Peter lays out the facts of the trial and crucifixion of Christ in such a way that it can do nothing but stir the guilt of the people. Psychologists will tell you that the worst thing you can do is to make people feel guilty. Such feelings, they say, shut the door to healing for troubled people. Yet that is where Peter begins.

Peter begins with a series of unchallenged facts regarding events that these people participated in. He draws a stark contrast between the acts of God and the acts of human beings. He says, "The God of Abraham, Isaac and Jacob, the God of our fathers, has glorified his servant Jesus. *You* handed him over to be killed." In other words, God glorified Jesus; humanity killed Him. Peter goes on to say that not only did the people hand Him over to death, but also they disowned him before the Roman governor Pilate, even after Pilate wanted to release Him. They asked a murderer, the worst class of criminal, to be released in His stead.

Peter also hammers home the all-important identity of Jesus, "the Holy and Righteous One," echoing the names for the Messiah in the Old Testament. Peter also calls Jesus "the author of life," and he draws a profound contrast here. The people demanded the crucifixion of "the author of life" while demanding the release of the murderer Barabbas, a destroyer of life.

These facts, Peter says, were attested by witnesses, including himself: "We are witnesses of this." Again, the apostle underscores the fact that the Christian faith rests upon well-attested facts, not feelings or wishful thinking.

THE QUESTION OF GUILT

Before we move on to the next section of his message, we need to say a word about the implications of the guilt that is conveyed in this message. One of the darkest chapters of the history of the institutional church is the anti-Semitism it has shown in various times in history. Though the Jews have been a persecuted people since early Old Testament times, the last two thousand years of history have sometimes been marked by an especially tragic form of anti-Semitism in which people calling themselves Christians have oppressed the Jewish people on the pretext that the Jews are Christ-killers.

Organized massacres (pogroms) against the Jews were often sanctioned by the official church during the Middle Ages, especially during the Spanish Inquisition. These cruel episodes were often rationalized on the basis that the Jewish people were held collectively responsible for the crucifixion of Jesus. Anti-Semitism reached a genocidal level in the Nazi Holocaust of World War II. Genocidal race hatred still threatens Jews in the twenty-first century. Pastor Michael D. Evans writes from his experience:

I am a Christian minister. My father was a Christian, my mother an Orthodox Jew. I was raised as a Christian, but still, I was physically attacked as a child in "Christian America." I was called a "Christ-killer" hundreds of times. I pushed my mother's grocery cart down the street while self-professing Christians threw eggs and tomatoes from their vehicles, and shouted obscenities—including "Christ-killer" and "Jew-witch." I remember waking one morning to the words "Christ-killer" spray-painted on the front door. . . .

When I asked [my mother], "Why am I being beat up for killing Christ?" my mother sat me down and told me the story of her grand-father. He was a rabbi. Russian Orthodox Christians burned him and his entire congregation to death inside the synagogue. She said to me, "They did it while screaming, 'You crucified Christ, you Christ-killers.'"

I can still see the pain in her eyes as she told me of loved ones who were thrown into the ovens of Auschwitz. "The last words many of them heard," she said, "were 'Christ-killers.'" Her last words to me that day were, "Chris-tians hate Jews. They believe that we murdered the Son of God."[1]

Who, truly, are the Christ-killers? Who nailed the Messiah to the cross? I did. You did. Every human being who ever lived nailed Him there. Every sin we committed—every lustful thought, every hateful word—drove the nails deeper into His flesh.

But Jesus wasn't executed against His will. He went to the cross willingly, out of obedience to the Father and love for you and me. He was killed by the human race and for the human race. The Jews do not deserve to be singled out as Christ-killers. They are the people God chose to bring the Messiah into the world, and God is still working out His plan through the people of Israel. As God told Abraham:

"I will make you into a great nation
and I will bless you;
I will make your name great,
and you will be a blessing.
I will bless those who bless you,
and whoever curses you I will curse;
and all peoples on earth
will be blessed through you." (Genesis 12:2-3)

Those who curse and do harm to the Jewish people, Abraham's descen-dents, have made themselves to be God's enemies.

1. Michael D. Evans, "Christ-Killers," World Net Daily Web column, February 20, 2004, retrieved at http://www.worldnetdaily.com/news/article.asp?ARTICLE_ID=37218.

GOD'S RESPONSE TO OUR GUILT

The apostle Peter has stirred up guilt in the hearts of the people. But Peter doesn't leave them there, lost in their guilt. He moves quickly to his next point: God's answer to the problem of guilt is a marvelous thing called grace. Peter declares:

> "By faith in the name of Jesus, this man whom you see and know was made strong. It is Jesus' name and the faith that comes through him that has given this complete healing to him, as you can all see." (Acts 3:16)

What does Peter mean? He is underscoring God's reaction to the guilt of humanity. This miracle is a parable in visual form. While the lame man is an individual, and God loves every individual human being, this man also symbolizes the human race in its lostness, guilt, and sin. His handicap symbolizes humanity's broken and fallen condition—our collective guilt due to sin. The lame man was as guilty before God as anyone else in the crowd that day. Yet now, through a miracle of God's grace, the once-lame man could stand before them, restored to wholeness by God's power.

Only one thing could save this man, as Peter pointed out: "It is Jesus' name and the faith that comes through Him that has given this complete healing to him, as you can all see." Peter wanted the people to know that God responds to human guilt with love and grace, on the basis of the name of Jesus. He doesn't demand rites or rituals or sacrifices—just simple faith.

Peter is saying, in effect, "John and I have no magic powers. We simply spoke the name of Jesus, and this man believed in the authority of that name. The moment he believed, God's healing power flowed into him. Now he stands before you—a living demonstration of God's response to your guilt." Next, Peter goes on to declare to the people what will result in their lives if they respond through faith in Jesus:

> "Now, brothers, I know that you acted in ignorance, as did your leaders. But this is how God fulfilled what he had foretold through all the prophets, saying that his Christ would suffer. Repent, then, and turn to God, so that your sins may be wiped out, that times of refreshing may come from the Lord, and that he may send the Christ, who has been appointed for you—even Jesus. He must remain in heaven until the time comes for God to restore everything, as he promised long ago through his holy prophets." (Acts 3:17-21)

God knows that the people didn't understand that they were crucifying the Holy and Righteous One. It was the blundering action of ignorant minds. In fact, the Father's response to human ignorance echoes the Lord's words from the cross: "Father, forgive them, for they do not know what they are doing" (Luke 23:34).

This is God's view of humanity, and it's an accurate view and a compassionate view: We are ignorant, blind, and stupid. We blunder about in the darkness, causing harm and destruction, not realizing what we are doing. This is how all of us operate when we try to run our own lives. God has compassion on our failings. He makes allowances for our weakness and folly.

TIMES OF REFRESHING

Human ignorance cannot thwart God's eternal plan. It may seem as if we have crucified our only hope, but Peter says that God knew all along that human beings would slay His Son. In fact, God predicted this would happen through the writings of the prophets. "But this is how God fulfilled what he had foretold through all the prophets," Peter says, "saying that his Christ would suffer."

What, then, is God's prescription for human stupidity and deliberate human sin? Peter states it plainly: "Repent, then, and turn to God, so that your sins may be wiped out." And what will happen when we repent? First, "times of refreshing" will come from the Lord. Second, the Father will "send the Christ, who has been appointed for you—even Jesus."

Peter is looking down the corridor of future history and says, "Here are the principles by which God will operate: Whenever people turn to Him in repentance, God will solve the problem of guilt and wipe out their sins." This is hard for us to believe. Even after turning to God in repentance, many of us continue to try to produce some merit or standing before God through our own works or religious legalism. We have a hard time accepting God's promise that our sins are washed away by the blood of Christ. God has forgiven us, but we find it hard to forgive ourselves.

Peter wants us to know that God has stirred up our feelings of guilt for one purpose only: He wants us to turn to Him for forgiveness. He takes no pleasure in our feelings of guilt and remorse. God wants to free us forever from our guilt, so that we can experience what Peter calls "times of refreshing."

Moreover, those who repent and receive forgiveness from the Father have something wonderful to look forward to: the return of Jesus Christ. Peter says that a day will come when the Father will "send the Christ, who has been appointed for you—even Jesus." The world around will be rocked with cataclysm and war, yet there will be a community of God's people who remain steadfast, experiencing times of refreshing from God. In the midst of that, Jesus will return. Peter closes with a call to action:

> "For Moses said, 'The Lord your God will raise up for you a prophet like me from among your own people; you must listen to everything he tells you. Anyone who does not listen to him will be completely cut off from among his people.'

"Indeed, all the prophets from Samuel on, as many as have spoken, have foretold these days. And you are heirs of the prophets and of the covenant God made with your fathers. He said to Abraham, 'Through your offspring all peoples on earth will be blessed.' When God raised up his servant, he sent him first to you to bless you by turning each of you from your wicked ways." (Acts 3:22-26)

In his letter to the Romans, Paul tells us that the gospel was given "first for the Jew, then for the Gentile" (Romans 1:16). That is the program that we will see followed in the book of Acts. For now, the gospel is going out in the temple courts, and the hearers are all Jews. Soon the gospel will go out to the Gentile world.

Peter's argument in this passage is directed to an all-Jewish audience. He says, in effect, "You know the prophets, and you know the Scriptures, and your own Scriptures urge you to put your faith in Jesus." Where did Peter learn about the Old Testament Scriptures and how they pointed to Jesus as the promised Messiah? Peter was a fisherman, not a Bible scholar. It may well be that Jesus taught Peter during those forty days after his resurrection, when "beginning with Moses and all the Prophets, he explained to them what was said in all the Scriptures concerning himself" (Luke 24:27). If so, then Peter had only recently learned these truths from Jesus.

In any case, Peter's message to this crowd is compelling. The issue that each of them must settle, he says, is the question of whether or not they will place their faith in the crucified Lord. That's where Peter leaves the issue, but the story doesn't end there. As we turn to Acts 4, the story of Peter and John is about to take a surprising turn.

8

THE RADICAL RESURRECTION

Acts 4:1-12

Peter has been preaching about the One who made the healing of the lame man possible—Jesus of Nazareth, the promised Messiah, who was crucified and rose again. His message has a profound effect on the crowd. Then Peter is interrupted by a frightening commotion:

> The priests and the captain of the temple guard and the Sadducees came up to Peter and John while they were speaking to the people. They were greatly disturbed because the apostles were teaching the people and proclaiming in Jesus the resurrection of the dead. They seized Peter and John, and because it was evening, they put them in jail until the next day. But many who heard the message believed, and the number of men grew to about five thousand. (Acts 4:1-4)

The religious authorities learned that Peter and John were preaching about the resurrection of Jesus. So they called out the temple guard—the police of the temple—and had Peter and John arrested and tossed into jail. Yet even this bare-knuckled display of authority could not hinder the gospel. Peter's message was heard—and believed. Luke records that five thousand men became Christians that day. Hundreds, if not thousands, of women and children also believed; it was the custom of that time to count only the men.

Peter and John didn't advocate the overthrow of the Roman government. They didn't call for the destruction of the temple. They didn't protest the social evils of the day, which were many, or the widespread practice of slavery, or the cruel and unusual practice of crucifixion. They didn't protest rampant taxation or the warmongering policies of the Roman government. They simply preached Christ.

Yet their message was so disturbing that the authorities had to throw Peter and John into jail to shut them up. Even though their message was cut short, five thousand men and an unknown number of women and children became Christians that day.

UPSETTING THE ESTABLISHMENT

Why was the message of Jesus Christ so troubling to the religious and political establishment? Would the authorities seek to silence such a message today? Yes, they would—and they often do. The message of Jesus is regularly suppressed around the world. By some estimates, more than two hundred million Christians today are persecuted and threatened because of their faith. In Acts 4, we can see three radical elements in the Christian message that drives powerful people to silence those who preach it.

Jesus is risen! Peter and John proclaimed the astonishing fact that Jesus of Nazareth, the crucified One, had risen from the dead. In fact, they were preaching this fact only seven weeks after the resurrection. The two apostles were two out of 120 eyewitnesses to this event.

The disciples had seen Him not once but many times, and the testimony of Peter and John was so convicting that at least five thousand souls were convinced of the truth, just as three thousand had been convinced on the day of Pentecost. These people understood that the death and resurrection of Jesus of Nazareth had solved the greatest of all human problems—the problem of death.

Those who believe in Him will live with Him. Jesus said, "I am the resurrection and the life. He who believes in me will live, even though he dies" (John 11:25), and, "Because I live, you also will live" (John 14:19). On that first Easter, Jesus emerged from the tomb with hope for all humankind.

Joe Bayly is the author of *Psalms of My Life*. I once heard him speak at a Christian writers' conference at Mount Hermon, near Santa Cruz, California. Joe, who passed away in 1983, was a wonderful writer and speaker with a delightful sense of humor. He had also known the unimaginable sorrow of having to bury three beloved sons. One of his boys died at the age of eighteen. Another died when he was less than three weeks old. And one died of leukemia at age five.

In a moving account of the five-year-old boy's final hours, Joe described how, early one morning, his son began to bleed, and the doctors could do nothing to stop it. They took towels and soaked up the blood, then they'd wring out the towels and soak up more blood. Finally, at two in the afternoon, the boy cried out for help—and then he died. Joe and his wife were not spared any horror or sorrow in that experience. They would have gladly taken their son's suffering upon themselves, but they were helpless.

Yet, near the end of this story, an amazing expression of peace and joy came over Joe Bayly's face as he recounted how, by faith, he knew he would see his son again. There would be a resurrection from the dead. Though there is sorrow and separation for a time, there is also a remarkable breakthrough in human experience, symbolized by the empty tomb. Jesus Christ has solved the problem of death.

Physical death and spiritual death are linked. The eventual death of the body is strangely and incomprehensibly linked with spiritual death, eternal death. Jesus came to bring us abundant, eternal life. The glorious proclamation of Peter and John is that Jesus, through the resurrection, has overcome death. We can now have peace instead of turmoil, hope instead of despair, liberty instead of bondage, power instead of weakness, and beauty instead of ashes.

THE STONE THE BUILDERS REJECTED

You'd think that the religious authorities would have been pleased that the people had received such wonderful news. Yet the authorities were angered and threatened by the preaching of Peter and John. Why? We glimpse an answer in the next few verses:

> The next day the rulers, elders and teachers of the law met in Jerusalem. Annas the high priest was there, and so were Caiaphas, John, Alexander and the other men of the high priest's family. They had Peter and John brought before them and began to question them: "By what power or what name did you do this?"
>
> Then Peter, filled with the Holy Spirit, said to them: "Rulers and elders of the people! If we are being called to account today for an act of kindness shown to a cripple and are asked how he was healed, then know this, you and all the people of Israel: It is by the name of Jesus Christ of Nazareth, whom you crucified but whom God raised from the dead, that this man stands before you healed. He is
>
> > "'the stone you builders rejected,
> > which has become the capstone.'
>
> Salvation is found in no one else, for there is no other name under heaven given to men by which we must be saved." (Acts 4:5-12)

You can see how seriously the authorities viewed Peter and John and their message by the list of dignitaries present: Caiaphas, the high priest; Annas, the honorary high priest and the father of Caiaphas; and two brothers of Caiaphas, John and Alexander. This family was the *crème de la crème* of Jerusalem society. They were powerful aristocrats who controlled the vast wealth of the temple, including the profitable monopolies associated with the animal sacrifices. Perhaps they sensed that Jesus, who was sacrificed for our sins upon the cross, spelled the end of the ritual sacrifices in the temple, a system that was crucial to their wealth and power.

So they brought Peter and John before them and demanded an explanation for the healing of the lame man. This gave Peter a wide-open door for testimony. The religious rulers asked, "By what power or what name did you do this?" This was the very question Peter was waiting for. With the healed man standing nearby, Peter answered, "It is by the name of Jesus Christ of Nazareth, whom you crucified but whom God raised from the dead, that this man stands before you healed."

Clearly, this was not the same cringing fishermen who had denied his Lord three times just seven weeks earlier. What made such a dramatic difference in the apostle Peter? Answer: the Holy Spirit! When the Spirit enters a human heart, He imparts the life and power of the risen Lord Jesus. Because Peter was filled with the Holy Spirit, he was as bold as a lion.

Peter goes on to quote Psalm 118:22, saying that Jesus is "'the stone you builders rejected, which has become the capstone.'" The apostle shows these religious rulers from their own Scriptures that the psalmist predicted the resurrection of Jesus.

In Psalm 118 we find another verse we often quote without fully appreciating its meaning: "This is the day the Lord has made; let us rejoice and be glad in it" (Psalm 118:24). What does this verse mean? What day does it refer to as "the day the Lord has made"? It refers to the day of the resurrection of Jesus, the day God took the Stone that the builders had rejected and made him to be the capstone, supreme over all of creation.

Both Peter and the psalmist refer to the construction of Solomon's temple. The Bible tells us that when Solomon built his temple in Jerusalem, there was no sound of hammer or saw. The temple was erected in silence. The stones of the temple were quarried from the rock where the temple now stands. To this day, you can visit Solomon's stables, which were hewn from the solid rock of the Temple Mount (the Muslim mosque, the Dome of the Rock, stands over the site today). The temple of Solomon was built to such precise specifications that every block of stone was fitted perfectly before it left the quarry. Each stone was placed without the sound of hammers.

There is a Jewish tradition that says that one great stone block was quarried out and shaped by the stonemason, but the builders could find no place for it. The block did not fit any of the blueprints, so they set it aside. Eventually, because it seemed to get in the way, someone pushed the block over the edge, and it tumbled into the Kidron Valley and was lost in the dense bushes.

When the time came to place the cornerstone—the great stone block that held everything in position—the quarrymen sent word that it had already been delivered. The builders couldn't find it. Then someone remembered the stone that the builders had rejected. They went down into the valley and found the stone. With great effort, they raised it up and fitted it into place—the capstone of the temple. That's the stone that the psalmist and Peter symbolically spoke of. God planned that Jesus would be the Capstone of His government on earth—but the builders and rulers of the nations had rejected Him.

God has prepared a Capstone, and Peter says of that Capstone, "You rejected Him when He came! You had the chance to build the government of Israel on the Rock that God ordained, but you rejected Him, you crucified Him. But God has raised Him from the dead and has made Him the Capstone."

NO OTHER NAME

Finally, Peter adds these amazing words: "Salvation is found in no one else, for there is no other name under heaven given to men by which we must be saved" (Acts 4:12). This is a startling declaration. Peter says that no one else can fulfill the position that Jesus was intended to fill. There is no other source of salvation. There is no other name that can save us. All of the other religious names in history put together—Buddha, Confucius, Gandhi, Ramakrishna, Joseph Smith, Mary Baker Eddy—cannot equal the power and authority of the name of Jesus.

People often accuse Christians of being intolerant of other faiths. In a sense, this accusation is justified. No, we don't hate or disrespect other religions or the people who believe in them. In fact, we recognize that there is much truth in other faiths. But no other faith is built upon the authority of the resurrected Lord. No other faith has ever solved the problem of death.

Jesus is the Capstone. There is no other name by which we can be saved.

It may not seem at first glance that the gospel has any political implications, but it does. Jesus came to liberate us, and wherever His name is named, tyranny is threatened. Though Jesus did not come to oppose government per se, the freedom He brings is a threat to oppressive governments everywhere. There has never been a more powerful force for human liberation than the power of His resurrection. This is why the message of the risen Lord has been hated by tyrants from the first century to the twenty-first.

Tom Skinner was the head of one of the most violent street gangs in Harlem. His heart was filled with bitterness and rage against American society. One night, he was half-listening to the radio when some words about Jesus caught his attention. The rebellious son of a minister, he had rejected Jesus, but something about those words got through to him. He opened his life to Jesus Christ. No one led him to the Lord. He simply made a decision while listening to the radio—and his life was transformed.

Skinner went to the rest of the members of his gang and told them he had given his life over to the risen Christ. He became an evangelist, founded the Harlem Evangelistic Association, and went around the world, telling audiences about the transforming power of the resurrected Lord Jesus. He had a particularly effective ministry among inner-city youth and eventually became chaplain of the Washington Redskins, as well as the author of such books as *Black and Free* and *How Black Is the Gospel*.

If Tom Skinner had not had the radio on that one evening, if he had not heard those words of resurrection life, he might have ended up dead on the streets of Harlem—and all the thousands of lives he has since touched might never have heard of the transforming power of the risen Lord Jesus. But God had a plan for him and for all the young people who would be changed by Tom's message of hope.

That's what Jesus can do. That's how resurrection power can affect our world. It's the power to set men and women free—and it's a power that makes the rulers and tyrants of this world quake in their boots. You can have that same power in your life when you ask Jesus of Nazareth, the risen Lord, to come and take control of your life.

9

HOW TO OPPOSE AUTHORITY

Acts 4:13-31

A number of years ago, stage magician James Randi began debunking the claims of phony mind readers, fortune tellers, and faith healers. He once investigated a California-based televangelist who claimed to heal the sick and receive personal messages from God. Randi personally attended the healer's meetings and quickly figured out how his miracles were achieved.

The televangelist would call on someone from the audience and say, "You and I have never spoken before, have we? I'm sensing that you're from Pasadena, am I right? And there is pain in your feet and especially your big toes. Is it gout? Well, God is going to heal you tonight!"

How did the televangelist know so much about someone he'd never met before? Simple! The televangelist's wife had interviewed the person and transmitted the information to the televangelist with a miniature radio transmitter. Yet the faith healer claimed the information came straight from God.

But what about the healings? The televangelist would command people to get up out of their wheelchairs—and they would leap out of the wheelchairs and practically dance across the stage. How was that done? Again, it was simple. The people the man healed never needed wheelchairs in the first place. In fact, the wheelchairs were provided by the televangelist's staff, but to television viewers, it seemed that the people he healed had been wheelchair-bound for years.

After completing his investigation, James Randi appeared on *The Tonight Show* with Johnny Carson. He played tapes of intercepted radio transmissions between the wife and the televangelist—and millions of people suddenly knew that the televangelist was a fraud. His television audience shrank, and so did donations to him. Soon, the faith healer was no longer on television.

At the height of his popularity, this healer had often encouraged people to be healed by faith instead of going to the doctor. He even told people to throw away their medicines, including insulin and blood pressure prescriptions. Before he left the air, he may well have injured the health of thousands of viewers.

In the Gospels, Jesus healed many people, but He never taught that miracles of healing should replace doctors, medicine, and proper health care. In fact, Jesus said that people who are sick should see a doctor (Mark 2:17). When we get sick, we should pray for healing and then have faith to accept whatever form of healing God chooses. He may choose to deliver us out of our sickness—or he may choose to take us through our trial of sickness. More than anything else, He wants to unleash a new power called resurrection life.

CONTRARY TO REASON

When we last saw Peter and John, they had been brought before the Sanhedrin, the ruling council in Jerusalem. The rulers, elders, and teachers of the law demanded to know by what power and authority the lame man was healed.

Peter was not cowed by the threats of the religious rulers. In fact, he boldly accused them of plotting the death of Jesus and declared to them that salvation is found in Jesus alone, "for there is no other name under heaven given to men by which we must be saved" (Acts 4:12). Luke continues:

> When they saw the courage of Peter and John and realized that they were unschooled, ordinary men, they were astonished and they took note that these men had been with Jesus. But since they could see the man who had been healed standing there with them, there was nothing they could say. So they ordered them to withdraw from the Sanhedrin and then conferred together. "What are we going to do with these men?" they asked. "Everybody living in Jerusalem knows they have done an outstanding miracle, and we cannot deny it." (Acts 4:13-16)

Here's a remarkable picture of the perversity of human hearts. These men undoubtedly prided themselves on being logical, rational thinkers who acted consistently with known facts. But this account shows that they were utterly self-deceived.

The religious leaders noted an unexpected boldness in Peter and John. The rulers associated this sort of poise with educated people, yet the apostles were untrained, common men. The rulers couldn't understand it, and Luke says they "took note that these men had been with Jesus."

When the religious leaders succeeded in having Jesus crucified, they thought they had heard the last of this troublesome Galilean. Jesus of Nazareth had frustrated them to no end not only with His remarkable message but with his uncanny poise and serene confidence. Again and again, they had tried to trap Him, checkmate Him, and defeat Him, but He had effortlessly turned the tables on them every time.

Now, here were two uneducated Galileans who demonstrated the same poise and confidence. It seemed that anyone who spent time with Jesus absorbed some of His personality. Clearly, Peter and John had been with Jesus—and the religious rulers found them as frustrating and troublesome as Jesus.

RESPECTFUL BUT INFLEXIBLE

Luke also underscores the evidence of the man who was healed. The formerly disabled man stands beside Peter and John—irrefutable evidence of a miracle.

What were the rulers supposed to charge the two apostles with? Is it a crime to heal a sick person? Hardly! The apostles have done a good thing. So the religious leaders are at a loss as to what to do with these men.

The religious rulers are forced to admit that the healing is a sign. They are acquainted with the importance of signs. Throughout the history of Israel, God has manifested His presence through signs and wonders. This healing is such a sign, and it was witnessed by thousands in Jerusalem, so it can't be denied.

The rational response to such evidence would be to acknowledge the sign and give the Sanhedrin's stamp of approval to Peter and John. But that's not what the leaders decide to do. Instead, they say to each other:

> "But to stop this thing from spreading any further among the people, we must warn these men to speak no longer to anyone in this name." Then they called them in again and commanded them not to speak or teach at all in the name of Jesus. (Acts 4:17-18)

The rulers of the people behave in a way that is exactly contrary to the evidence—and contrary to reason and sanity. Luke records the response of the two apostles:

> But Peter and John replied, "Judge for yourselves whether it is right in God's sight to obey you rather than God. For we cannot help speaking about what we have seen and heard."
>
> After further threats they let them go. They could not decide how to punish them, because all the people were praising God for what had happened. For the man who was miraculously healed was over forty years old. (Acts 4:19-22)

As representatives of God to the nation of Israel, the religious rulers were supposed to do the will of God. Despite the fact that God had spoken through the sign of a miraculous healing, these men forbade the apostles from speaking in the name of Jesus. In short, they tried to silence God.

Peter and John responded that they had no choice but to speak the things they had seen and heard from God. Their message could not be silenced. They would remain true to God even if they had to defy human religious authority. The apostles were respectful but inflexible. The rulers and priests could only sputter and threaten, but Peter and John knew that the threats of the Sanhedrin were hollow. The apostles had the support of the people—and the rulers feared the people.

WHEN IT'S RIGHT TO DISOBEY

At this point, we gain some insight into the issue of civil disobedience. As Christians, we are to obey God and respect the government. But what do we do when the orders of government violate the laws of God?

This incident in Acts 4 has often been cited as a model for conscientious objection regarding various issues such as war and peace, labor disputes, and civil rights. This account addresses the question: Is it right for a Christian to disobey the law in order to obey conscience? The answer is yes, sometimes we must disobey men to obey God.

Peter called upon the Sanhedrin rulers to judge what the apostles ought to do. He said, "Judge for yourselves whether it is right in God's sight to obey you rather than God. For we cannot help speaking about what we have seen and heard." Peter says, in effect, "You already know that God's authority is higher than yours. So whom should we obey? You? Or God?" The answer is obvious.

The Scriptures make it clear that governments are instituted by God and governmental authorities are God's servants (Romans 13:1-7). It's instructive to note that the emperor of Rome at that time was Nero, one of the most cruel and irrational of all the Roman rulers. Yet Paul said that all governing authorities, including Nero, were the servants of God—and those who resist the government resist what God has ordained.

Government has the God-given power to tax, to maintain law and order, and to punish evildoers even to the point of death. We may not always approve of what the government does, and governmental officials are often guilty of error, corruption, and wrongdoing. Even so, we are exhorted by Scripture to obey the government. Human conscience, operating alone and without support from the revelation of God's Word, is not sufficient grounds to disobey the law.

The laws of government have authority over the human conscience unless that conscience rests squarely upon a direct word of God. The problem with human conscience is that it can be wrong as well as right. So we need an objective standard against which to measure our conscience. That standard is God's Word.

Henry Clay Trumbull (1830-1903) was a Sunday school missionary and Civil War chaplain. He once observed, "Conscience is not given to a man to instruct him in the right, but to prompt him to choose the right instead of the wrong when he is instructed as to what is right. It tells a man that he ought to do right, but does not tell him what is right. And if a man has made up his mind that a certain wrong course is the right one, the more he follows his conscience the more hopeless he is as a wrongdoer." Conscience is superior to the laws of government only when there is a clear conflict between the Word of God and the orders of government.

THE SOVEREIGN LORD

Next, Luke records the response of Peter and John after their release:

> On their release, Peter and John went back to their own people and reported all that the chief priests and elders had said to them. When they heard this, they raised their voices together in prayer to God. "Sovereign

Lord," they said, "you made the heaven and the earth and the sea, and everything in them. You spoke by the Holy Spirit through the mouth of your servant, our father David:

> "'Why do the nations rage
>> and the peoples plot in vain?
> The kings of the earth take their stand
>> and the rulers gather together
> against the Lord
>> and against his Anointed One.'

Indeed Herod and Pontius Pilate met together with the Gentiles and the people of Israel in this city to conspire against your holy servant Jesus, whom you anointed. They did what your power and will had decided beforehand should happen." (Acts 4:23-28)

The apostles did not organize a revolutionary committee to overthrow the Sanhedrin. They didn't march, demonstrate, or carry signs. They didn't use political or popular pressure against the Sanhedrin. Instead, they called upon the sovereign power of God. They prayed, "Sovereign Lord, you made the heaven and the earth and the sea, and everything in them." They acknowledged that God holds the world in the palm of His hand and that He has authority over every human event.

As we look around the world, we see war, terror, genocide, and unbelievable cruelty. We see governments, which the Bible says are instituted by God, committing horrible acts and making disastrous decisions—and it has always been so. God's purposes are not our purposes, His ways are not our ways, and it is often difficult to understand what He is doing in this troubled world. But God is sovereign nonetheless.

The apostles quoted Psalm 2, which speaks of the opposition they faced from the Sanhedrin: "Why do the nations rage and the peoples plot in vain? The kings of the earth take their stand and the rulers gather together against the Lord and against his Anointed One." Then they said, in effect, "That's what we face. Herod, Pontius Pilate, the Gentiles, and even the people of Israel have set themselves against the Lord Jesus. So it's not surprising that the Sanhedrin opposes our gospel. God told us this would happen."

The disciples knew that nothing could happen to them that God did not permit. The sovereign Lord was on the throne, and they would put their trust in Him.

THE MYSTERY OF HISTORY

Notice again what the disciples said: "Indeed Herod and Pontius Pilate met together with the Gentiles and the people of Israel in this city to conspire against your holy servant Jesus, whom you anointed. They did what your power and will had decided beforehand should happen." In other words, God uses the opposition of human beings to accomplish His purposes. I call this principle the mystery of history. The ultimate example of the mystery of history is the crucifixion, which was supposed to have put an end to Jesus but proved to be the doorway to resurrection. That is God's sovereign power at work.

Resting upon this power, the disciples now make their request to God:

> "Now, Lord, consider their threats and enable your servants to speak your word with great boldness. Stretch out your hand to heal and perform miraculous signs and wonders through the name of your holy servant Jesus." (Acts 4:29-30)

The disciples do not ask for peace and safety. They ask for boldness and power. They are saying, in effect, "Lord, we are in trouble and in danger of our lives—but this is great, Lord! You've made it possible for us to witness before rulers. They've threatened us—and that's what we want! Lord, give us boldness to continue speaking out and defying their threats. Do it again, Lord!" Luke records God's answer to their prayer:

> After they prayed, the place where they were meeting was shaken. And they were all filled with the Holy Spirit and spoke the word of God boldly. (Acts 4:31)

God physically shakes the place where they are praying. This is a symbolic act, similar to the action He took on the day of Pentecost when He sent a mighty wind, tongues of fire, and the ability to speak in other languages. Those symbols expressed the working of the Holy Spirit throughout the age of the Spirit, the age in which we live. The symbolic act of shaking the meeting place symbolizes the fact that God will shake Jerusalem and the world with the message of the gospel.

What does this symbol of shaking say to us in our day? Many people, young and old, are disillusioned by the power structures that govern our world. In those structures they see the power to start wars, oppress the poor, harm the environment, and indoctrinate minds. What can anyone do against such monolithic power?

God's answer: There is a force that can shake nations and societies. That force is the message of Jesus, the crucified and risen Messiah. It is the most revolutionary message the world has ever heard—and God has given us the privilege of speaking that message through the filling of the Holy Spirit. If we would boldly proclaim that message, our world would be shaken to its core.

Governments don't produce peace, prosperity, and blessing. The Declaration of Independence doesn't preserve our liberty and happiness, nor does the Constitution of the United States. In our time, we have seen the meaning of the constitution twisted and distorted by the courts. So what does guarantee these principles for our lives?

We should take note of the motto of Hawaii, adopted during the era of great missionary work in the Hawaiian Islands: *Ua mau ke ea o ka aina i ka pono*. Those words, which mean, "The life of the land is preserved by righteousness," became the Hawaiian motto on July 31, 1843. That's when King Kamehameha III proclaimed the sovereignty of the kingdom of Hawaii after a five-month British occupation.

What preserves justice? What preserves peace and prosperity? One thing: righteousness! And what destroys society? Unrighteousness.

According to historian Arnold Toynbee, twenty-six great civilizations have come and gone during the recorded history of the world. In every case, those civilizations failed because they were not built upon righteousness. As we look around at the civilization of America, this bold experiment that began on July 4, 1776, we have to wonder how long it will last. Righteousness in America is clearly in decline; rebellion against God is on the rise. If America does not turn back, God will shake this land as He has shaken every other society that turned away from righteousness.

There is only one hope for the nations of this world, and it is found in the good news of Jesus Christ. This message is the key to restoring righteousness to society. When we pray for boldness to proclaim this message, something amazing happens: The Spirit of God fills us and empowers us to speak His Word with confidence and power.

Luke tells us that when these disciples prayed for boldness to speak God's message, the place in which they met was shaken and the believers "were all filled with the Holy Spirit and spoke the word of God boldly." That's how God wishes us to oppose corrupt authority in this world. Let's pray for boldness. Then let's go out in the fullness of the Spirit, speaking His Word with confidence, shaking the world to its core.

10

BODY LIFE

Acts 4:32–5:11

Astory is told of a village in the Swiss Alps where a wealthy nobleman wanted to leave a gift to the townspeople. He decided to build a beautiful church, and he hired the best craftsmen and purchased the finest building materials. When the building was finished, everyone in the town was astonished at its beauty.

Then one villager noticed a flaw: There were no lamps in the church. How could the townspeople worship in a darkened building?

The nobleman said, "I deliberately designed the church without lamps. See the brackets on the walls? Each family must bring a lamp to every worship service. If you place your lamp in the bracket by your pew, there will be plenty of light. But if you do not show up with your lamp, your place in the church will be dark."

One villager asked, "Why did you design the church this way?"

The nobleman replied, "To remind you that everyone in the church is important. Whoever does not play his part leaves some corner of God's house in darkness." That is how God views His church and our place in it.

AUTHENTIC CHRISTIANITY

In Acts 4, Luke gives us a glimpse of life in the early church. After the dramatic events of Pentecost and the healing of the lame man, the church experienced an exciting time of rapid growth. At the same time the early church faced the mounting threat of persecution—and faced it all with a joyful confidence in the resurrected Lord Jesus.

Luke continues his account in Acts 4:

> All the believers were one in heart and mind. No one claimed that any of his possessions was his own, but they shared everything they had. (Acts 4:32)

That's authentic Christianity. Later, we'll see a counterfeit Christianity entering the church almost at the beginning. Evidence of this counterfeit Christianity will be seen throughout the book of Acts. Wherever the true church goes throughout the world, the counterfeit appears alongside it.

How do we recognize counterfeit Christianity? Externally, it has the appearance of a religious institution where people come together with a mutual interest in a religious program or cause. How does this differ from genuine Christianity? When Christianity is authentic, it consists of individuals who share the same divine life, who are made up of all ages, backgrounds, and classes, and who regard themselves and one another as brothers and sisters in one family, manifesting the life of Jesus Christ.

In Acts 4:32, we have a snapshot of genuine Christianity. Here we see believers who are united in heart and mind and share all things with their brothers and sisters in Christ. When these early Christians gather together, they share the life of Jesus in the unity of the Holy Spirit.

What does it mean to experience true Christian unity? It means much more than being in the same church building at the same time. The early church had something called body life. It exhibited the intangible and invisible reality of being members together of the body of Christ. Its members visibly demonstrated their body life through the sharing of their tangible possessions with true, heartfelt generosity.

Wherever the invisible reality of body life occurs, there will always be visible results. Human needs will be met. Human hurts will be healed. Human relationships will grow deep and strong. Most important of all, the power of God will be manifested for all to see. That's what Luke describes next:

> With great power the apostles continued to testify to the resurrection of the Lord Jesus, and much grace was upon them all. (Acts 4:33)

Power in witness occurs whenever body life is present.

The body of Christ and our own human bodies function in similar ways. The life within us—the life of the spirit—is invisible but real. If you and I were sitting across from each other, you could see me and I could see you, but neither of us could see the other's spirit. Our innermost reality is hidden from others. It takes the body to make our inner life visible. Our bodies produce the voice, facial expressions, eye contact, and gestures that reveal our innermost thoughts and feelings to the people around us.

The same principle is true for the church. When the church functions as the body of Jesus Christ, the voice of the church, the face of the church, and the hands of the church all work together to express the mind and heart of our invisible God. It takes the body of Christ to make the life of Christ visible to the world. Where the body functions, the heart of Christ is expressed with power and authentic witness takes place.

WITNESSING WITH GREAT POWER

Luke records, "With great power the apostles continued to testify to the resurrection of the Lord Jesus, and much grace was upon them all." The twelve apostles gave witness, but the entire church participated in their ministry and made possible this great unleashing of God's power. This principle still holds true.

I have accompanied evangelistic teams to various college campuses. When we arrive on the campus, we all feel weak and inadequate. We find that most students are indifferent to us, and sometimes the professors and administrators are actively hostile to our presence. We feel intimidated in these halls of learning, and we ask ourselves, "What are we doing here? As soon as we start witnessing, they'll laugh us off the campus!"

But we have learned to always act together. Our first activity is to gather as a team to pray. We prepare our hearts with a sense of oneness in the Holy Spirit before we go out on the campus. Then we make contact with the Christian faculty and students on the campus, and we help them learn not only to pray together but also to love each other, listen to each other, and share with each other. In this way, the life of the body begins to flow, and God's power is released in a dramatic way.

Notice that Luke says that the apostles witnessed with great power, but he adds, "and much grace was upon them all" (Acts 4:33). What does that mean? What is this thing called grace?

The word *grace* is one of those terms we Christians use freely because we find it in the Scriptures. We say it over and over, but do we know what it means? Grace is a word that describes the enrichment of life that results from the love, power, and presence of God. Someone has suggested an acrostic to help us remember the true meaning of grace: God's Riches At Christ's Expense.

That's a beautiful definition of grace, and Luke tells us that "much grace" was upon the early church. The early believers were one in heart and mind, so that great power and grace descended upon them. Luke goes on to describe the results of body life in the newborn church:

> There were no needy persons among them. For from time to time those who owned lands or houses sold them, brought the money from the sales and put it at the apostles' feet, and it was distributed to anyone as he had need. (Acts 4:34-35)

Luke tells us that the grace experienced in the early church took two forms: love and spiritual gifts. We see the love of the early Christians demonstrated in these verses, where we find that the believers shared their resources and carried each other's burdens. These early Christians lived out the command that Paul would later write to one of the churches in Asia Minor: "Carry each other's burdens, and in this way you will fulfill the law of Christ" (Galatians 6:2). The law of Christ is the law of love for one another. It's the most basic and essential expression of authentic Christian living.

Jesus said, "A new command I give you: Love one another. As I have loved you, so you must love one another. By this all men will know that you are my disciples, if you love one another" (John 13:34-35). The mark, therefore, of authentic Christianity is not church involvement or a passion for keeping God's moral law. It is love. If you love others, then you are willing to bear their burdens and so fulfill the law of Christ.

The first form of grace God gave the early church was love for one another.

GRACE DEMONSTRATED THROUGH GIFTS

The second form of grace God gave the church was spiritual gifts. Luke records:

> Joseph, a Levite from Cyprus, whom the apostles called Barnabas (which means Son of Encouragement), sold a field he owned and brought the money and put it at the apostles' feet. (Acts 4:36-37)

At first glance, you may not see what these verses tell us about spiritual gifts. But bear with me. As we shall see, the Holy Spirit distributes gifts within the body of Christ, such as those that are listed in Romans 12, 1 Corinthians 12, and Ephesians 4. These gifts are given by the Spirit in order to fulfill the ministry of the body. The gifts were exercised in the early church, and they are exercised in the church today.

Among the early Christians in Jerusalem there was a man named Joseph, whom the early Christians called Barnabas, meaning "Son of Encouragement." This is the same Barnabas who will later become Paul's missionary traveling companion. The early Christians called him Barnabas because of his accepting, encouraging spirit.

The next time we meet Barnabas is in Acts 9. There, the newly converted Saul (soon to be called Paul) goes to Jerusalem to meet with the apostles, but the disciples fear that it's just a trick to arrest them. So Barnabas the Encourager steps forward, believes in Saul, and brings the new convert to the apostles. The encouragement of Barnabas was the key to establishing Paul in his calling as an evangelist.

In Acts 11, Barnabas brings Paul to Antioch, where a great spiritual awakening has broken out. Barnabas involves Paul in the amazing events in Antioch—and Paul's calling as an evangelist is reaffirmed.

Then, in Acts 13, Barnabas lifts up a discouraged young man named John Mark. The young missionary-in-training has been crushed by failure during Paul's first missionary journey, but Barnabas reinstates him. John Mark goes on to become of great help to Paul—and the writer of the second book of the New Testament, the gospel of Mark. We have Barnabas to thank for putting this young man back into service.

So Barnabas was an encourager. He had the gift of exhortation, comfort, and encouragement. The gift of encouragement is a wonderful gift, and

Barnabas used it so diligently and employed it so widely that most people eventually forgot his given name, Joseph, and simply called him Barnabas, Son of Encouragement. Wouldn't it be wonderful to be so known by the exercise of your spiritual gift that people called you Son of Teaching or Daughter of Mercy?

THE CHURCH IN PERIL

We now come to Acts 5. According to the flow of the narrative, there should be no chapter division here. (While the text of Scripture is inspired by God, the chapter and verse divisions were imposed by men.) The theme of the church in Acts 4 carries on into Acts 5, which begins with the word *now* in the New International Version or "but" in many other versions. The word *now* or *but* serves to signal a particular kind of transition. Luke is saying here that what follows in Acts 5 is in contrast or opposition to what just happened in Acts 4.

We have just seen the church experiencing grace from God in the form of great love and the exercise of spiritual gifts, but now we are going to see something different. Now we are going to see not body life, but that which endangers the life of the body. Luke writes:

> Now a man named Ananias, together with his wife Sapphira, also sold a piece of property. With his wife's full knowledge he kept back part of the money for himself, but brought the rest and put it at the apostles' feet.
>
> Then Peter said, "Ananias, how is it that Satan has so filled your heart that you have lied to the Holy Spirit and have kept for yourself some of the money you received for the land? Didn't it belong to you before it was sold? And after it was sold, wasn't the money at your disposal? What made you think of doing such a thing? You have not lied to men but to God."
>
> When Ananias heard this, he fell down and died. And great fear seized all who heard what had happened. Then the young men came forward, wrapped up his body, and carried him out and buried him. (Acts 5:1-6)

What does this account say to us? Here are two people in the church, a husband and wife, who earnestly want to take part in the life of the church. Like Barnabas, they sold some property, but unlike Barnabas, they brought only part the money they received. They laid this gift at the feet of the apostles.

Was there anything wrong with giving only a portion? No. In fact, Peter said to Ananias, in effect, "While this land was yours, you could do anything you wanted with it. Selling it was your choice, and no one made you do it."

So what was wrong with what Ananias did? Peter, exercising his gift of discernment, said to Ananias, "You lied. To act as if you gave all when you only gave part was a sin. You're a phony, Ananias. You pretended to be more generous than you were." The moment Ananias heard those words, he dropped dead at Peter's feet.

Sapphira, the wife of Ananias, was a knowing party to this deception. Luke records the rest of the story:

> About three hours later his wife came in, not knowing what had happened. Peter asked her, "Tell me, is this the price you and Ananias got for the land?"
>
> "Yes," she said, "that is the price."
>
> Peter said to her, "How could you agree to test the Spirit of the Lord? Look! The feet of the men who buried your husband are at the door, and they will carry you out also."
>
> At that moment she fell down at his feet and died. Then the young men came in and, finding her dead, carried her out and buried her beside her husband. Great fear seized the whole church and all who heard about these events. (Acts 5:7-11)

In Acts 4 and 5, we have seen three "greats" in the early church. There was great power. There was great grace. Now there is great fear. Why did the Holy Spirit act in such a severe way? I once heard someone comment, "Thank God this doesn't happen anymore—or we'd have to put a morgue in every church!" It's true, we don't see such dramatic divine judgment today, but God wants us to heed the lesson of this event. The story of Ananias and Sapphira is a picture of what results from a life of pretense and hypocrisy.

The moment we pretend to be something we're not—especially when we pretend to be more spiritually noble than we are—death enters in. We are cut off from the life of Christ. We become dead and unresponsive cells, and our part of the body becomes weak and paralyzed.

We seldom meet deliberate hypocrites. Most hypocrites are unaware of how phony and pretentious they are. To them, putting on a false show of being religious and outwardly Christian comes naturally. They don't even realize they are spiritually dead and fraudulent.

The mark of authentic Christian living is that we love one another, we share our lives with one another, we carry each other's burdens and so fulfill the law of Christ. Until that occurs, we cannot truly say that our lives are authentically Christian.

That's what the story of Ananias and Sapphira underscores for us. The moment this husband and wife pretended to be something they were not—*death!* When we come to church wearing a mask of adequacy while we are spiritually and emotionally depleted—death! When we are struggling with unmanageable problems at home but we put on a phony smile at church—*death!* When we are too proud to admit that our kids are rebelling, our marriage is failing, or addiction rules our lives—*death!*

The moment we pretend to be something we are not, death sets in. If enough Christians pretend to be what they are not, death soon pervades the church. The flow of life ceases, and the body dies. That's how dishonesty kills the church.

HOW TO BUILD BODY LIFE

How do we build authentic body life in the church? It begins with a few believers who decide to take the law of Christ—the law of love—seriously. So a good way to begin building body life is for a few believers to come together, study the "one another" commands, and start putting those commands into practice in their daily living. From that small nucleus of sincere believers, body life will spread and affect the life of the church.

The English phrase "one another" is a translation of the Greek word *allelon*, a word that appears about a hundred times in the New Testament, most frequently in the form of a command regarding how we should behave toward our fellow believers. Here's a brief list of commands that we should apply in our lives.

The Lord's command to love one another is repeated throughout the New Testament: "This is the message you heard from the beginning: We should love one another" (1 John 3:11; see also Matthew 22:37-40; John 15:12, 17; Romans 13:8-10; 1 Thessalonians 3:12; 4:9-10; 2 Thessalonians 1:3; 1 Peter 1:22; 4:8; 1 John 4:7-21).

In Mark 9:50, Jesus said that our Christian unity makes us salt in the world: "Salt is good, but if it loses its saltiness, how can you make it salty again? Have salt in yourselves, and be at peace with each other" (see also Matthew 5:9; Romans 12:18; 14:19; Ephesians 4:3).

Believers should lighten each other's load by bearing one another's burdens. This is a common theme in Paul's letters: "So that there should be no division in the body, but that its parts should have equal concern for each other. If one part suffers, every part suffers with it; if one part is honored, every part rejoices with it" (1 Corinthians 12:25-26; see also Galatians 6:2).

We are also to be like Barnabas, encouraging one another in every way. Paul wrote, "Therefore encourage one another and build each other up, just as in fact you are doing" (1 Thessalonians 5:11; see also Romans 1:11-12; Hebrews 10:25).

One of the most essential ingredients in body life is harmony, a theme that runs throughout the New Testament: "Live in harmony with one another. . . . May the God who gives endurance and encouragement give you a spirit of unity among yourselves as you follow Christ Jesus" (Romans 12:16a; 15:5).

We are to commit ourselves to the welfare of one another, honoring and deferring to one another in humility and love. Paul writes, "Be devoted to one another in brotherly love. Honor one another above yourselves" (Romans 12:10). And, "Do nothing out of selfish ambition or vain conceit, but in humility consider others better than yourselves" (Philippians 2:3; see also Ephesians 5:21; 1 Peter 5:5).

Mutual acceptance is another key ingredient of body life. Paul wrote, "Accept one another, then, just as Christ accepted you, in order to bring praise to God" (Romans 15:7; see also Romans 14:1-3). Mutual acceptance is often expressed through forgiveness and tolerance: "Be completely humble and gentle; be patient, bearing with one another in love. Make every effort to keep the unity of the Spirit through the bond of peace" (Ephesians 4:2-3; see also Romans 14:13; Ephesians 4:31-32; Colossians 3:12-15).

Body life demands that we confess our faults, needs, and hurts to one another and regularly pray for each other. The apostle James wrote, "Therefore confess your sins to each other and pray for each other so that you may be healed" (James 5:16). As we mutually share our needs and hurts, we should mutually share our comfort as well. Paul wrote, "Therefore encourage each other with these words" (1 Thessalonians 4:18).

Authentic Christianity demands that we also instruct and even admonish one another. Paul wrote, "I myself am convinced, my brothers, that you yourselves are full of goodness, complete in knowledge and competent to instruct one another" (Romans 15:14; see also Hebrews 10:24).

Mutual service is a visible expression of genuine body life. "Serve one another in love," wrote Paul (Galatians 5:13). And Peter said, "Each one should use whatever gift he has received to serve others, faithfully administering God's grace in its various forms" (1 Peter 4:10). One way we can serve one another is through acts of mutual hospitality (Romans 12:13; 1 Peter 4:9).

So there's your starting point. I have laid out a Bible study in these passages that should inspire you and a few Christian friends to form a nucleus of body life in your church. Begin there. Start by meeting in your home, with your spouse and children, your roommate, or a neighbor or a friend. Study the Word together, pray together, and share your hearts together.

As you learn more about what Christian love and unity truly mean, keep moving deeper into the life of the body of Christ. Bring in a few more people. Share your joys and burdens with one another. Listen to each other, and pray together for the problems and concerns that are shared. Get to know and understand each other. Admit your weaknesses. Confess your sins. Celebrate together. Grieve with one another. Forgive and accept one another. Encourage and console one another. Sing songs of faith together.

Don't worry about starting small. Don't worry about feeling inadequate— we are all inadequate, but God is all-sufficient. Don't worry that it seems awkward at first—just drop your mask and plunge right in to the depths of genuine fellowship. Trust God and ask Him to let His love flow through you and throughout the body of Christ. Thank Him for His indwelling Spirit, who makes all believers one.

As we live out the life of Christ in the body of Christ, the world will look at us and say, "See how these Christians love one another!"

That is how His body grows.

11

CONFRONTATION!

Acts 5:12-42

"In the last days perilous times shall come."

The apostle Paul wrote those words to his son in the faith, Timothy (2 Timothy 3:1 KJV). The last days Paul warned of began when our Lord first appeared upon the earth. It's a mistake to think of the last days as some future era. Paul was writing about his day—and our day. He was writing about the period of time between the first coming of Christ and His second coming.

During this present time called the last days, we face danger, violence, and evil. Paul warned Timothy that in this era people would be "lovers of themselves, lovers of money, boastful, proud, abusive, disobedient to their parents, ungrateful, unholy, without love, unforgiving, slanderous, without self-control, brutal, not lovers of the good, treacherous, rash, conceited," and more (2 Timothy 3:2-4). We are clearly surrounded by such people. So, as we continue through Acts 5 and examine the perils and conflict faced by the early church, we find pertinent lessons for our lives.

FACTOR ONE: POWER

In this section of Acts, we shall see four factors that are always present when the church obediently responds to peril and crisis. Luke records the first of these factors:

> The apostles performed many miraculous signs and wonders among the people. And all the believers used to meet together in Solomon's Colonnade. No one else dared join them, even though they were highly regarded by the people. Nevertheless, more and more men and women believed in the Lord and were added to their number. As a result, people brought the sick into the streets and laid them on beds and mats so that at least Peter's shadow might fall on some of them as he passed by. Crowds gathered also from the towns around Jerusalem, bringing their sick and those tormented by evil spirits, and all of them were healed. (Acts 5:12-16)

The first factor is this: When the church faces peril in reliance upon God, power is unleashed. Here, this power is demonstrated through dramatic physical healing at the hands of the apostles. Many people read this account and say, "What's wrong with the church today? Why don't we have healings taking place in churches on a regular basis?"

Some people try to reproduce these miracles in their church. Others travel the country or appear on television, claiming to heal as the apostles did. A few even claim to be modern-day apostles. But on close examination, their so-called miracles are nothing but sleight of hand combined with the placebo effect, in which sick people experience a temporary healing because they believe they've been healed.

As we read Luke's account in Acts 5, it's important to understand what it says—and doesn't say. First, Luke says that these healings were done by the hands of the apostles, not by ordinary believers. The apostles gathered in Solomon's Porch (or Solomon's Colonnade), and no ordinary believer dared attempt to do these miracles. It was clear to all that the apostles were anointed by God with unusual grace. The miraculous signs were intended to confirm the ministry of these mighty apostles who laid the foundations of the church through the giving of the Scriptures.

It's a mistake to put too much emphasis on a physical miracle. People easily miss the point of what God is saying through a miracle. That's why the Lord often told those he healed, "Don't tell anyone about this." He didn't send people out to broadcast the news of His miracles. He knew that an overemphasis on miracles could divert attention from His message and thwart His ministry.

The Lord's concern about an unhealthy fascination with miracles is confirmed here in Acts 5. We read that when the apostles began to heal the sick and cast out demons, the crowds carried the sick into the streets so that Peter's shadow might fall on them. That is sheer superstition, and Luke does not suggest that anyone was ever healed by Peter's shadow. Luke simply recorded the excitement that followed these healings.

Miracles are parables in visible form. They show us a symbolic picture of what God wants to accomplish in every human life. So when God shows us a visual parable, such as a miraculous healing, we need to look beyond the surface of the event and see God's lesson. A spiritual healing is a far greater and more lasting healing than any physical healing.

God wants to heal the whole human being, not just the diseased flesh. Most of all, He wants to heal the wounded human spirit—the invisible dimension of our being that is broken by sin, shame, and despair. That's where our deepest problems lie. Every person who was ever physically healed in the New Testament eventually grew old and died, but everyone who has experienced spiritual healing through faith in Jesus Christ shall never die. There's no miracle greater than the miracle of eternal life.

This is not to say that God no longer heals. He still performs miracles. I knew one woman who was diagnosed with an inoperable brain tumor. The doctors told her to put her affairs in order, because she had only a few months to live. Weeks later, however, tests showed that her tumor was gone. There's no medical explanation for such a phenomenon, but there is a faith explanation: This woman received a miracle of healing. But miracles are a rare gift of God's grace, not an entitlement.

FACTOR TWO: FREEDOM

The second factor we see when the church responds to crises in reliance on God is found in the next few verses:

> Then the high priest and all his associates, who were members of the party of the Sadducees, were filled with jealousy. They arrested the apostles and put them in the public jail. But during the night an angel of the Lord opened the doors of the jail and brought them out. "Go, stand in the temple courts," he said, "and tell the people the full message of this new life."
>
> At daybreak they entered the temple courts, as they had been told, and began to teach the people. (Acts 5:17-21a)

The second factor: Freedom! Evil people can imprison us, but God sets us free. When the jealous religious leaders saw how popular the apostles had become, they arrested the apostles and put them in jail. But that night an angel released the apostles and sent them out with orders from the Lord to go back to the temple and preach the message of new life in Christ. At this point, the story takes an almost comical turn:

> When the high priest and his associates arrived, they called together the Sanhedrin—the full assembly of the elders of Israel—and sent to the jail for the apostles. But on arriving at the jail, the officers did not find them there. So they went back and reported, "We found the jail securely locked, with the guards standing at the doors; but when we opened them, we found no one inside." On hearing this report, the captain of the temple guard and the chief priests were puzzled, wondering what would come of this.
>
> Then someone came and said, "Look! The men you put in jail are standing in the temple courts teaching the people." At that, the captain went with his officers and brought the apostles. They did not use force, because they feared that the people would stone them. (Acts 5:21b-26)

The religious leaders of the Sanhedrin thought they had the twelve apostles safely silenced. But when the jailors reported that the jail was empty, the chief priests were alarmed, thinking the apostles had escaped. But then came the biggest shock of all: Not only had the apostles walked out of jail, they had gone right back to the temple and resumed preaching! They had absolutely no fear of the religious officials; instead, the religious officials feared the apostles.

God wants us to know that there is a liberty in the Spirit which the will of man can never imprison. "Where the Spirit of the Lord is, there is freedom" (2 Corinthians 3:17). Sometimes God chooses to liberate His people literally and physically. There are other times where He allows His people to remain physically in prison while permitting their spirits to soar free.

Near the end of his life, Paul wrote from a Roman prison, "God's word is not chained" (2 Timothy 2:9). The Spirit of the Lord always brings freedom.

FACTOR THREE: OPPOSITION

The first two factors we examined were power and liberty. Next, Luke records the third of these four factors—opposition:

> Having brought the apostles, they made them appear before the Sanhedrin to be questioned by the high priest. "We gave you strict orders not to teach in this name," he said. "Yet you have filled Jerusalem with your teaching and are determined to make us guilty of this man's blood."
>
> Peter and the other apostles replied: "We must obey God rather than men! The God of our fathers raised Jesus from the dead—whom you had killed by hanging him on a tree. God exalted him to his own right hand as Prince and Savior that he might give repentance and forgiveness of sins to Israel. We are witnesses of these things, and so is the Holy Spirit, whom God has given to those who obey him."
>
> When they heard this, they were furious and wanted to put them to death. (Acts 5:27-33)

All Peter and the apostles did was speak the truth: "The God of our fathers raised Jesus from the dead—whom you had killed by hanging him on a tree." That was a simple statement of fact. "God exalted him to his own right hand as Prince and Savior that he might give repentance and forgiveness of sins to Israel." Another statement of fact. "We are witnesses of these things, and so is the Holy Spirit." Another statement of fact.

How did the religious leaders of the Sanhedrin respond? With unreasoning rage! This response shows the fallen and depraved character of humanity, including the humanity of the supposed teachers of God's law.

Whenever God's truth is simply and clearly stated, unregenerate people fly into a rage. They oppose the truth in the only way they can think of—with violence. The truth of the Christian gospel attracts some people but enrages others. It is disturbing because it demands a response. Those who do not respond in repentance must respond in rebellion.

The rage we face from the enemies of the gospel is provoked by malevolent spirits who operate behind the scenes. That's why Paul tells us, "For our struggle is not against flesh and blood, but against the rulers, against the authorities, against the powers of this dark world and against the spiritual forces of evil in the heavenly realms" (Ephesians 6:12).

God does not want us to make the mistake of battling human beings. People are not our enemy. People may attack us and even kill us, but they are not the enemy. Our foe is a spiritual ruler named Satan. If you do not grasp the true nature of our warfare, you will be continually baffled by the struggles of this life.

That's why some people today shake their heads at humanity and say, "What's wrong with human beings? We've tried preaching self-esteem. We've told people again and again to 'give peace a chance.' We've tried to educate people in the techniques of conflict resolution. Yet people keep committing acts of violence, crime, and terrorism! Why can't people just learn to get along?"

The problem is that human beings are continually manipulated by powers they are not aware of. Thoughts and feelings arise in the human mind and heart, planted there by invisible forces that oppose the will of God. That's why physical resistance to evil accomplishes little good. What good does it do to kill a human being when the real enemy is a spiritual being? What good does it do to smash the puppet when our real enemy is the satanic puppetmaster?

It does no good to battle flesh and blood. Only spiritual weapons have power against a spiritual foe. Luke illustrates this truth in the next section:

> But a Pharisee named Gamaliel, a teacher of the law, who was honored by all the people, stood up in the Sanhedrin and ordered that the men be put outside for a little while. Then he addressed them: "Men of Israel, consider carefully what you intend to do to these men. Some time ago Theudas appeared, claiming to be somebody, and about four hundred men rallied to him. He was killed, all his followers were dispersed, and it all came to nothing. After him, Judas the Galilean appeared in the days of the census and led a band of people in revolt. He too was killed, and all his followers were scattered. Therefore, in the present case I advise you: Leave these men alone! Let them go! For if their purpose or activity is of human origin, it will fail. But if it is from God, you will not be able to stop these men; you will only find yourselves fighting against God."
>
> His speech persuaded them. (Acts 5:34-40a)

These religious leaders are the same men who conspired to murder Jesus, and the apostles know it. The men who murdered Jesus would not hesitate to murder His followers. The apostles knew their lives were at stake.

But God had a plan for delivering the apostles that the apostles couldn't even guess. God had arranged to have a man on the council who could reason with the other members of the Sanhedrin—the teacher Gamaliel. I'm not saying that Gamaliel was a Christian; in fact, he gives every indication of being an enemy of Christianity. But though Gamaliel was opposed to the gospel, he was subject to the sovereign influence of God.

The account does not directly tell us that the church in Jerusalem was praying for the twelve apostles. However, it's reasonable to assume that the Christians were on their knees, asking God to protect these leaders of the new-born church. So we can only conclude that God, in answer to that prayer, restrained the evil men of the Sanhedrin. He even used one of them, Gamaliel, to talk the others out of killing the apostles.

God often uses His enemies to achieve His purposes. Don't you love the ironic justice of God's ways? Satan uses these men as puppets to do his bidding, but God uses Satan's puppets to frustrate Satan's plans. What a brilliant tactician is our God.

During the crisis of campus unrest during the Vietnam war, violence broke out on the campus of Stanford University, not far from our church, Peninsula Bible Church. As the crisis worsened, the entire city of Palo Alto was in a state of fear. The campus radicals made a number of extreme and unreasonable demands, and they threatened to burn the university to the ground if their demands were not met.

Christians throughout the community gathered in small groups and prayed for a peaceful solution to the crisis. They asked two things: that God would give the Academic Senate at Stanford the wisdom and courage to yield to the reasonable demands and resist those that were unreasonable and that God would restrain the radicals and thwart their plans to burn down the university.

The Academic Senate wisely decided to yield in some areas but stand firm against any unreasonable demands. In response, the radicals held their own meeting to make plans to carry out their threat. Soon after the radical students gathered, they began squabbling among themselves and accusing each other of betraying the cause. At one point, one radical leader shouted, "What's wrong with us? Why are we fighting each other?" The meeting broke up without reaching a decision. The radicals dispersed—and not a single torch was lit. That night was one of the most peaceful nights the Stanford campus had experienced in months.

What happened to the radicals' plan to destroy the university? It came to nothing because God answered prayer. His restraining hand thwarted the plan of the radicals. The same God who answered the prayers of the early believers in Jerusalem still answers prayers. He may not answer our prayers in exactly the way we expect, but He is still working out His plan through the church.

FACTOR FOUR: SUFFERING

We have seen three of the four factors that are always present when the church responds to crises in reliance upon God: power, liberty, and opposition. Now we come to the fourth and final factor:

> They called the apostles in and had them flogged. Then they ordered them not to speak in the name of Jesus, and let them go.

The apostles left the Sanhedrin, rejoicing because they had been counted worthy of suffering disgrace for the Name. Day after day, in the temple courts and from house to house, they never stopped teaching and proclaiming the good news that Jesus is the Christ. (Acts 5:40b-42)

Even though Gamaliel urged the other members of the Sanhedrin not to kill the apostles, there was still a price to pay for preaching the gospel. The Sanhedrin had the apostles flogged, then ordered them not to speak about Jesus ever again.

And the apostles' response? They were happy and blessed that God found them worthy to suffer for the Lord's sake. If you and I were flogged for the sake of Christ, would we rejoice? Would we feel honored to suffer for His sake?

We tend to think that suffering is foreign to the Christian life. Some Christians even believe that God has promised them a life of ease and prosperity. But I have searched the Scriptures in vain for such a promise. The promise I find from the Lord Jesus reads, "In the world you have tribulation and trials and distress and frustration" (John 16:33b, Amplified Bible). And Paul writes, "For it has been granted to you on behalf of Christ not only to believe on him, but also to suffer for him" (Philippians 1:29). Peter writes, "Dear friends, do not be surprised at the painful trial you are suffering, as though something strange were happening to you" (1 Peter 4:12).

Suffering is an integral part of the Christian experience. The experience of suffering is for all believers in all places and times; it's not an experience reserved for a few select martyrs. When we face opposition, we are not to wring our hands and cry out, "Oh, no! Opposition! Now what do we do?" No, we should rejoice as the apostles did.

The same four factors that characterized the early church should mark the church today. When we face a crisis, we should experience:

Power. The power of God is still available to the church—power to change lives and make broken people whole.

Freedom. The Word of God is not bound. Our physical circumstances and limitations make no difference. God's Word makes all the difference.

Opposition. When the church is living up to its calling in times of crisis, its bold message will stir up resistance. The more effective we are for Christ, the more opposition our enemy will throw at us.

Suffering. We should not be surprised when we are called upon to suffer for Him. Let's rejoice that God gives us the honor of sharing in the sufferings of Jesus.

GOD IS WRITING NEW CHAPTERS

A man once came up to me after I had given a talk at a Christian conference in Colorado. "Sir," he said, "did you mean it when you said that the church today is no different from the church of the first century?"

"Absolutely," I said. "I'm convinced that there is no difference between the church today and the first-century church. God expects us to affect the world today as the church affected the world in Acts."

The man wept for joy! He gripped my hand and said, "Bless you! My heart has been crying out for years to hear someone say that. Most preachers tell me that this is a different age and a different church. You don't know what it means to hear you say that the church of Acts and the church today are the same church!"

When are we going to start believing the Scriptures? When are we going to take up the spiritual weapons God has given us? The book of Acts is still being written. God is writing new chapters of Acts in your life and mine.

12

DEALING WITH DISSENSION

Acts 6:1-8

Great hymns are built on great doctrines of the faith, and great hymns have caused great doctrinal controversies. Evangelist and hymn writer Charles Wesley had a strong belief in the doctrines of free will and sanctification. One of Wesley's former associates, Augustus Toplady, turned against Wesley's doctrinal stance and adopted the Calvinist position of free grace and predestination. Toplady became such a strong opponent of Wesley that he often wrote critical magazine articles about him.

When Wesley published his hymn "Love Divine, All Loves Excelling," Toplady was furious over a line in the second stanza and wrote a scathing refutation of Wesley's hymn in *The Gospel Magazine.* He ended the article with a poem he had written. Today, that poem is known as "Rock of Ages," a hymn many of us have sung hundreds of times.

One of the most beloved hymns of our faith was born out of a dissension between two believers over a doctrinal disagreement. Here is proof that God can use even our foolish discord and controversy to serve His purposes. As we come to Acts 6, we will see Satan sow dissension in the early church—

And we'll see how God turns human discord into heavenly harmony.

DISSENSION AND DIVISION

In Matthew 13, Jesus tells a story that is relevant to the events of Acts 6:

> Jesus told them another parable: "The kingdom of heaven is like a man who sowed good seed in his field. But while everyone was sleeping, his enemy came and sowed weeds among the wheat, and went away. When the wheat sprouted and formed heads, then the weeds also appeared.
>
> "The owner's servants came to him and said, 'Sir, didn't you sow good seed in your field? Where then did the weeds come from?'
>
> "'An enemy did this,' he replied.
>
> "The servants asked him, 'Do you want us to go and pull them up?'
>
> "'No,' he answered, 'because while you are pulling the weeds, you may root up the wheat with them. Let both grow together until the harvest. At that time I will tell the harvesters: First collect the weeds and tie them in bundles to be burned; then gather the wheat and bring it into my barn.'" (Matthew 13:24-30)

The parable of the wheat and the weeds is the Lord's prophecy of conditions in the church during the age between His first and second comings. In this parable, Jesus says He will sow good wheat seeds in the field of the world. The wheat represents His true followers. Soon afterward, the enemy will cause evil things to spring up like weeds among the wheat. In the day of the final harvest, the wheat and weeds will be separated. The wheat will be gathered up; the weeds will be burned.

In the book of Acts, we have seen followers of Jesus springing up like wheat in a field. These believers have a tremendous effect. Though they face threats and opposition, they are courageous and joyful as they bear witness to the truth.

In the first four chapters of Acts, we saw no sign of any weeds springing up in the church. Then, in Acts 5, we see the first indication that Satan had begun sowing evil in the church: the deceit of Ananias and Sapphira, who pretended to be something they were not. Because this form of dishonesty spreads death in the church, the Holy Spirit dropped them dead in their tracks—a vivid parable of what takes place within us when we choose hypocrisy over authenticity.

Now, in Acts 6, we encounter more evidence that Satan is sowing weeds among the wheat of God's church. It's the story of the enemy's attempt to divide the church with dissension and misunderstanding. Luke writes:

> In those days when the number of disciples was increasing, the Grecian Jews among them complained against the Hebraic Jews because their widows were being overlooked in the daily distribution of food. (Acts 6:1)

There were two kinds of Jews in the early church: Hebraic Jews and Grecian (or Hellenized) Jews. Hebraic Jews were mostly from Judea and spoke Aramaic, a form of Hebrew. The Grecian Jews came from the outlying provinces beyond Palestine. They spoke Greek because their native lands had been conquered centuries earlier by Alexander the Great. So the church consisted of Hebrew-Jewish Christians and Greek-Jewish Christians, and there was a language and cultural barrier between the two groups.

Luke previously told us, "All the believers were together and had everything in common. Selling their possessions and goods, they gave to anyone as he had need" (Acts 2:44-45). As part of this compassionate ministry, the church maintained a fund to purchase food for needy widows in the congregation.

Then a problem arose. The Greek-speaking Christians complained that the distribution to the widows was unfair. The Hebraic widows received help, but the Grecian widows were being overlooked. The oversight was probably unintentional, but it became a source of dissension in the early church.

Luke says that "the Grecian Jews among them complained against the Hebraic Jews." In the original text, the word for "complained" means that they grumbled among themselves. They did not go to the leaders for a solution. They gossiped and grumbled.

Satan often divides Christians by prompting them to complain to other people but not to the people who can solve the problem. When you complain to people who are not involved in the problem and can't help solve the problem, you spread bitterness and dissension. That's sin, and it's deadly to the church. In Old Testament times, complaining brought God's judgment upon the Israelites in the wilderness.

The complaining of the Grecian Christians caused dissension throughout the congregation. Over the centuries, many churches have been destroyed by dissension, yet many of these churches could have been saved if the people had simply taken their problems to the rightful authorities for resolution. When Christians allow dissension to spread, Satan gains a foothold in the church and in the lives of Christians.

THE RECOGNITION OF THE GIFTS OF THE SPIRIT

The apostles heard the rumors of murmuring, and they acted:

> So the Twelve gathered all the disciples together and said, "It would not be right for us to neglect the ministry of the word of God in order to wait on tables. Brothers, choose seven men from among you who are known to be full of the Spirit and wisdom. We will turn this responsibility over to them and will give our attention to prayer and the ministry of the word." (Acts 6:2-4)

It would be easy to read the wrong attitude into those words, as if the apostles are saying, "We're too important to wait on tables—let some flunkies do it." But that's not their attitude. The apostles were in the upper room when Jesus took up the basin and towel, then washed their dirty feet. They had heard Him say, "The greatest among you will be your servant" (Matthew 23:11). So they were not belittling servanthood. They were issuing a decision based on differences in spiritual gifts. The apostles needed to devote their time to teaching and preaching God's Word while letting others use their gifts of service to meet the needs of the widows.

The early church was learning to divide responsibilities and duties according to the distribution of spiritual gifts. Not only was it essential that the apostles devote themselves to the ministry of their apostleship, it was equally essential that others in the church discover and use their spiritual gifts. So the apostles gave the congregation the responsibility to elect seven men with gifts of service. They also listed the qualifications for these servants, who would be known as deacons.

First, the deacons were to be men of good reputation. They were to have a good witness in the congregation. "Brothers," the apostles said, "choose seven men from among you who are known to be full of the Spirit and wisdom." Their reputations for godliness and wisdom should be well known to all in the church, so that they would be trusted by all. Controversies can be resolved only when people on all sides trust their leaders to be fair and wise.

Second, the deacons were to be spiritual. To be spiritual does not mean to be a pious Joe, with a big Bible tucked under one arm and a Scripture verse for every occasion. To be spiritual means to be full of the Spirit, in continual contact with the Spirit and obediently sensitive to the Spirit's leading.

Third, the deacons were to have the gift of wisdom—the Spirit-given ability to apply scriptural truth to practical situations. In the Bible, this gift is often linked with the gift of knowledge, the Spirit-given ability to read the Bible and grasp the depths of its many layers of truth.

The deacons would need great wisdom to resolve the dissension. Whether the inequity of distribution was intentional or accidental, the problem needed to be corrected by the application of God's truth, and that would require the gift of wisdom.

So these seven men were chosen on the basis of spiritual qualifications.

THE SEVEN WHO WERE CHOSEN
Next, Luke tells us who the church chose as the first seven deacons:

> This proposal pleased the whole group. They chose Stephen, a man full of faith and of the Holy Spirit; also Philip, Procorus, Nicanor, Timon, Parmenas, and Nicolas from Antioch, a convert to Judaism. They presented these men to the apostles, who prayed and laid their hands on them. (Acts 6:5-6)

All seven names are Greek. This means that the deacons were probably all Grecian Jews. The Grecians were the minority group in the church, yet the church chose Grecian Jews to administer the program of caring for Grecian and Hebraic widows. In a moment of dissension, the infant church chose to replace suspicion with trust. The Hebraic Jews bent over backwards to show the Grecian Jews that they wanted to be fair—and they trusted the Grecian deacons to be fair even to the Hebraic widows.

After being chosen by the congregation, these seven men went before the apostles, who laid hands upon them to commission them. The laying-on of hands signifies that the apostles identified themselves with the ministry of the deacons. The apostles were saying, in effect, "These seven men are part of our ministry as apostles, and we are part of their ministry. Every spiritual gift is important to the life of the body."

My friend Ron Ritchie joined the pastoral staff of Peninsula Bible Church in 1969 and later founded an evangelism ministry called Free at Last. After he joined our staff, he told me of an incident at the Walnut Creek Presbyterian Church, where he had previously served.

The pastors had noticed a great number of new Christians joining the church, all from one part of town. Upon investigating, they discovered that one member of the church worked as a milkman in that area. While going on his route, he got to know his customers and would witness to them. Over time, he led many of his customers to Christ, and they came to church.

When the leaders of the church discovered the effect this milkman was having for Christ, they went to him and said, "We can see that you have the gift of an evangelist. We want to identify with you and stand with you in prayer. When you go out and witness, our prayers will go with you. If there is anything you need, we will help you." So they gathered around this man as he knelt, and they all laid hands on him, prayed for him, and commissioned this milkman-evangelist.

That is body life. When it begins to flow, amazing things happen.

The church is the key to society and to life. If the church is not functioning as it should, society will be dysfunctional. Society has becoming increasingly sick because body life has ceased to flow in the church. That's why we see such a dramatic rise in violence, depravity, pornography, crimes against children, and so forth.

The life of the church, dispersed into the world through its members, is the only hope for healing the social structures and power structures of our world. It's the only hope for healing neighborhoods and promoting brotherhood throughout our world. If we are not practicing body life, if we are not truly loving one another and using our spiritual gifts, then we are not having an effect on our world as God intends us to.

THE RESOLUTION OF DISSENSION: FOUR RESULTS

The dissension in the church has been resolved, and Satan's attempt to divide the church has been thwarted. We now see four results of the healthy resolution of this crisis:

> So the word of God spread. The number of disciples in Jerusalem increased rapidly, and a large number of priests became obedient to the faith.
>
> Now Stephen, a man full of God's grace and power, did great wonders and miraculous signs among the people. (Acts 6:7-8)

The first result is that "the word of God spread." This means that the Word of God was proclaimed more widely and reached many more people. Why did the Word of God spread more widely? One reason is obvious: The apostles had more time to preach and teach because they didn't have to spend time waiting tables. Whenever God's people utilize their gifts, ministry is multiplied.

The second result was a direct consequence of the first: "The number of disciples in Jerusalem increased rapidly." Whenever God's Word goes out, lives are transformed and the church grows. The truth of Jesus Christ affected human lives, and the people responded to the gospel with eager hearts.

The third result is surprising: "A large number of priests became obedient to the faith." Here are men who have devoted their lives to religious ritual, sacrifices, and studying the Old Testament. Many of them had probably wondered why the rituals they practiced seemed empty and meaningless, until they heard the good news of Jesus! Suddenly the sacrifices made sense, for they pointed to the sacrifice of Jesus on the cross. Once the perfect sacrifice had come, the symbolic animal sacrifices became unnecessary.

The fourth and final result was that the deacons performed wonders and miracles. Luke wrote, "Now Stephen, a man full of God's grace and power, did great wonders and miraculous signs among the people." As we shall see in Acts 7, this deacon, Stephen, became the first martyr of the church. In Acts 8, we will see another deacon, Philip, performing wonders and miracles.

Neither Philip nor Stephen did miracles until the apostles laid hands on the seven deacons. This suggests that, in some sense, the ministry of the deacons was an extension of the ministry of the apostles. They did these signs and wonders as a result of having been identified with the apostles by the laying-on of hands.

Signs and miracles always confirmed the introduction of something new in the church. When the apostles first began to proclaim the gospel of the resurrected Lord, their authority was confirmed by signs and wonders. Now, as the deacons are commissioned to serve, their ministry is also confirmed with signs and wonders.

SATAN STRIKES OUT AGAIN

At this point in Acts, the first two attacks of the enemy against God's church have been repulsed. The deceit of Ananias and Sapphira was vanquished by the Spirit of God. The dissension in the church was overcome by the wise intervention of the twelve apostles and the selection of the seven deacons. Satan has struck out twice.

Our ancient enemy still seeks to destroy God's church and still uses the same tactics he used against the early church. He tries to subvert us through pretense and hypocrisy, as he did with Ananias and Sapphira. And he tries to divide us through dissension, as he did with the dispute over caring for the widows.

There is still only one way to defeat Satan: When the enemy attacks, the life of the body must flow in the form of Christian love, righteousness, and the gifts of the Spirit. God is ready to do great things in the midst of His people.

The only question is: Are His people ready?

13

THE MESSAGE OF THE MARTYR

Acts 6:8–8:1a

During my first visit to Jerusalem, I came down from the Mount of Olives and went through St. Stephen's Gate on the eastern side of the ancient city. Though that gate is named for the first Christian martyr, it is not the gate Stephen passed through on his way to his execution. The original gate was destroyed by Roman armies in A.D. 70. The city walls that exist today were built under Sultan Suleiman of the Ottoman Empire, fifty years after Columbus discovered America.

However, St. Stephen's Gate, also called The Lions Gate because of the four lions that decorate the structure, was probably built on the site of the original gate. Not only is that gate significant because of its ancient history. It is significant because, during the Six-Day War of 1967, when Israel captured East Jerusalem, Israeli soldiers entered the city through that gate and raised the Israeli flag over the Temple Mount.

More fascinating than the historical significance of St. Stephen's Gate is the eternal significance of what Stephen said just before his death. Let's pick up the story of the first martyr in Acts 6:

> Now Stephen, a man full of God's grace and power, did great wonders and miraculous signs among the people. Opposition arose, however, from members of the Synagogue of the Freedmen (as it was called)—Jews of Cyrene and Alexandria as well as the provinces of Cilicia and Asia. These men began to argue with Stephen, but they could not stand up against his wisdom or the Spirit by whom he spoke.
>
> Then they secretly persuaded some men to say, "We have heard Stephen speak words of blasphemy against Moses and against God."
>
> So they stirred up the people and the elders and the teachers of the law. They seized Stephen and brought him before the Sanhedrin. They produced false witnesses, who testified, "This fellow never stops speaking against this holy place and against the law. For we have heard him say that this Jesus of Nazareth will destroy this place and change the customs Moses handed down to us."
>
> All who were sitting in the Sanhedrin looked intently at Stephen, and they saw that his face was like the face of an angel. (Acts 6:8-15)

Stephen was one of the Greek-speaking Jews chosen by the church as one of the seven deacons. In Jerusalem, there were a number of synagogues of Greek-speaking Jews. Stephen evidently went to these synagogues and preached in the Greek language.

Luke refers to five of these synagogues, one of which was the Synagogue of the Freedman. It was founded by Jewish freed slaves. The other four synagogues were for Jews from Cyrene, a Roman-ruled Greek colony in north Africa, where Libya is today; Alexandria, in Egypt; the Roman province of Asia, which included the cities of Ephesus and Pergamum; and Cilicia, on the southeast coast of Asia Minor, in modern Turkey.

The capital of Cilicia was Tarsus, the birthplace of Saul, later known as the apostle Paul. Young Saul was undoubtedly one of those who disputed with Stephen at the synagogue of the Cilicians, as Luke records: "These men began to argue with Stephen, but they could not stand up against his wisdom or the Spirit by whom he spoke." Saul was a brilliant Hebrew scholar and was undoubtedly angered by Stephen's message about Jesus of Nazareth. Saul had studied under the great rabbi Gamaliel, a grandson of the legendary teacher Hillel the Elder. It must have been a great blow to Saul's pride to be bested in the debate by Stephen.

When the religious rulers could not answer Stephen's arguments, they became enraged and irrational—the usual reaction of those who cannot win an argument by reason and evidence. So they decided to silence Stephen by lodging false charges against him in court. They lined up false witnesses to testify that Stephen had spoken blasphemy against Moses and God. Then they seized Stephen and hauled him before the Sanhedrin.

GUILTY OR NOT GUILTY?

Stephen stands before the same Sanhedrin that condemned the Lord Jesus to death and that had Peter, John, and the other apostles flogged. Stephen is accused of threatening the temple and speaking against the law of Moses. The evidence against Stephen is a mixture of truth, half-truth, and outright lies. Stephen probably said things similar to what he is accused of saying, but his words have been twisted. So the high priest reads the charges and poses one question.

Then the high priest asked him, "Are these charges true?" (Acts 7:1)

In other words: "How do you plead? Guilty or not guilty?" Because of the mixture of truth and untruth in the charges, Stephen can't simply say guilty or not guilty. He needs to explain himself. Yes, he said that the coming of Jesus meant that the worship in the temple was changed, but he didn't say the things people accused him of saying.

So Stephen proceeds to make his defense by preaching a sermon. It is the longest sermon recorded in the book of Acts, and it contains a concise review of the history of the people of Israel. Stephen selects three great heroes of faith from Israel's past, and he underscores the contrast between those Old Testament heroes and his accusers.

THE FIRST HERO OF FAITH: ABRAHAM
Let's take a closer look at Stephen's powerful message, beginning with his examination of the life and faith of Abraham:

> To this he replied: "Brothers and fathers, listen to me! The God of glory appeared to our father Abraham while he was still in Mesopotamia, before he lived in Haran. 'Leave your country and your people,' God said, 'and go to the land I will show you.'
>
> "So he left the land of the Chaldeans and settled in Haran. After the death of his father, God sent him to this land where you are now living. He gave him no inheritance here, not even a foot of ground. But God promised him that he and his descendants after him would possess the land, even though at that time Abraham had no child. God spoke to him in this way: 'Your descendants will be strangers in a country not their own, and they will be enslaved and mistreated four hundred years. But I will punish the nation they serve as slaves,' God said, 'and afterward they will come out of that country and worship me in this place.' Then he gave Abraham the covenant of circumcision. And Abraham became the father of Isaac and circumcised him eight days after his birth. Later Isaac became the father of Jacob, and Jacob became the father of the twelve patriarchs." (Acts 7:2-8)

Stephen's message is that Abraham was a man of lifelong faith, a man who dared to change his life pattern in obedience to God. He left his father's house and his country, and he moved out into a land he had never seen before. Though Abraham didn't own a square foot of ground and had no children, he trusted that God would do what He promised and give that land to Abraham's descendents. Stephen says, in effect, "Abraham, your father, was a man of faith who dared to welcome enormous change because of his obedience to God."

THE SECOND HERO OF FAITH: JOSEPH
Next, Stephen cites the Old Testament hero of integrity and faith, Joseph:

> "Because the patriarchs were jealous of Joseph, they sold him as a slave into Egypt. But God was with him and rescued him from all his troubles. He gave Joseph wisdom and enabled him to gain the goodwill of Pharaoh king of Egypt; so he made him ruler over Egypt and all his palace.

"Then a famine struck all Egypt and Canaan, bringing great suffering, and our fathers could not find food. When Jacob heard that there was grain in Egypt, he sent our fathers on their first visit. On their second visit, Joseph told his brothers who he was, and Pharaoh learned about Joseph's family. After this, Joseph sent for his father Jacob and his whole family, seventy-five in all. Then Jacob went down to Egypt, where he and our fathers died. Their bodies were brought back to Shechem and placed in the tomb that Abraham had bought from the sons of Hamor at Shechem for a certain sum of money." (Acts 7:9-16)

Joseph trusted God, and God led him through deep waters and dark places, through slavery, betrayal, false accusation, and unjust imprisonment. God eventually exalted him, honored him, and fulfilled His word in everything He had promised. Joseph was a man of faith who obeyed God regardless of his circumstances. Because he did, God fulfilled every letter of His promise to Joseph.

So Stephen highlights the contrast between Joseph and these ungodly accusers. Why do Stephen's accusers refuse to obey God? Because they are stubbornly resistant to change. But Joseph is an example of faith and obedience because he accepted the radical changes that God allowed in his life. Joseph trusted God, and God exalted Joseph.

THE THIRD HERO OF FAITH: MOSES

The third hero is Moses. Stephen spends most of his time discussing Moses because his accusers have charged him with speaking against Moses. Stephen divides the life of Moses into three stages. He describes the first stage in these verses:

"As the time drew near for God to fulfill his promise to Abraham, the number of our people in Egypt greatly increased. Then another king, who knew nothing about Joseph, became ruler of Egypt. He dealt treacherously with our people and oppressed our forefathers by forcing them to throw out their newborn babies so that they would die.

"At that time Moses was born, and he was no ordinary child. For three months he was cared for in his father's house. When he was placed outside, Pharaoh's daughter took him and brought him up as her own son. Moses was educated in all the wisdom of the Egyptians and was powerful in speech and action.

"When Moses was forty years old, he decided to visit his fellow Israelites. He saw one of them being mistreated by an Egyptian, so he went to his defense and avenged him by killing the Egyptian. Moses thought that his own people would realize that God was using him to rescue them, but they did not. The next day Moses came upon two Israelites who were fighting. He tried to reconcile them by saying, 'Men, you are brothers; why do you want to hurt each other?'

"But the man who was mistreating the other pushed Moses aside and said, 'Who made you ruler and judge over us? Do you want to kill me as you killed the Egyptian yesterday?' When Moses heard this, he fled to Midian, where he settled as a foreigner and had two sons." (Acts 7:17-29)

Why does Stephen tell these stories to people who know them by heart? He wants to remind them of something they have missed. He says, in effect, "Have you forgotten that Moses was a failure the first eighty years of his life? In his early life, Moses relied on the wisdom he had learned among the Egyptians. He acted on the basis of human knowledge and wisdom—and he fell flat on his face! The first time Moses tried to deliver his people, he committed murder. He tried to be a deliverer in his own strength, and he became a fugitive instead. Moses failed miserably when he did not act by faith."

Next, Stephen describes the second stage of the life of Moses:

"After forty years had passed, an angel appeared to Moses in the flames of a burning bush in the desert near Mount Sinai. When he saw this, he was amazed at the sight. As he went over to look more closely, he heard the Lord's voice: 'I am the God of your fathers, the God of Abraham, Isaac and Jacob.' Moses trembled with fear and did not dare to look.

"Then the Lord said to him, 'Take off your sandals; the place where you are standing is holy ground. I have indeed seen the oppression of my people in Egypt. I have heard their groaning and have come down to set them free. Now come, I will send you back to Egypt.'

"This is the same Moses whom they had rejected with the words, 'Who made you ruler and judge?' He was sent to be their ruler and deliverer by God himself, through the angel who appeared to him in the bush." (Acts 7:30-35)

Here is Stephen's argument: "You want to follow Moses," he says, in effect. "Well, Moses failed when he walked by the sight of his own eyes and in the wisdom of his own mind. But then God appeared to him, empowered him, and taught him the proper source of strength and authority. God sent Moses back to his people. Though they previously rejected him, he became their deliverer."

Stephen was driving home the point that the only One worth following is God. When people act by faith in God, they have the power of an omnipotent God behind them. When they refuse to obey God, they fall flat on their faces.

Next, Stephen describes the third stage of the life of Moses:

"He led them out of Egypt and did wonders and miraculous signs in Egypt, at the Red Sea and for forty years in the desert.

"This is that Moses who told the Israelites, 'God will send you a prophet like me from your own people.' He was in the assembly in the desert, with the angel who spoke to him on Mount Sinai, and with our fathers; and he received living words to pass on to us.

"But our fathers refused to obey him. Instead, they rejected him and in their hearts turned back to Egypt. They told Aaron, 'Make us gods who will go before us. As for this fellow Moses who led us out of Egypt—we don't know what has happened to him!' That was the time they made an idol in the form of a calf. They brought sacrifices to it and held a celebration in honor of what their hands had made. But God turned away and gave them over to the worship of the heavenly bodies. This agrees with what is written in the book of the prophets:

> "'Did you bring me sacrifices and offerings
>   forty years in the desert, O house of Israel?
> You have lifted up the shrine of Molech
>   and the star of your god Rephan,
>   the idols you made to worship.
> Therefore I will send you into exile' beyond Babylon."
>
> (Acts 7:36-43)

Stephen says that when the people refused to obey Moses, they began a system of idolatrous worship that ultimately moved God to send them into Babylon for seventy years of captivity. Moses had said that it would happen, and when it did, Moses said, "God will send you a prophet like me from your own people." The people would have to listen to that prophet—and that prophet, of course, would be Jesus, the one the people had rejected. They were doing exactly what their ancestors had done.

STEPHEN ACCUSES HIS HEARERS

Stephen's message culminates in these verses:

"Our forefathers had the tabernacle of the Testimony with them in the desert. It had been made as God directed Moses, according to the pattern he had seen. Having received the tabernacle, our fathers under Joshua brought it with them when they took the land from the nations God drove out before them. It remained in the land until the time of David, who enjoyed God's favor and asked that he might provide a dwelling place for the God of Jacob. But it was Solomon who built the house for him.

"However, the Most High does not live in houses made by men. As the prophet says:

> "'Heaven is my throne,
>   and the earth is my footstool.

What kind of house will you build for me? says the Lord.
Or where will my resting place be?
Has not my hand made all these things?'

"You stiff-necked people, with uncircumcised hearts and ears! You are just like your fathers: You always resist the Holy Spirit! Was there ever a prophet your fathers did not persecute? They even killed those who predicted the coming of the Righteous One. And now you have betrayed and murdered him—you who have received the law that was put into effect through angels but have not obeyed it."

Stephen's hearers know exactly what he means. "Stiff-necked" means proud and stubborn, unwilling to bow their heads before God. "With uncircumcised hearts and ears" means that even if though they are circumcised in their flesh, the act of circumcision has not penetrated their inner being. Outwardly circumcised, they are inwardly disobedient and as defiled as any uncircumcised Gentile.

Stephen accuses his hearers of thwarting God's Spirit. Their ancestors persecuted the Old Testament prophets, and they themselves killed Jesus, whom the prophets had announced. Luke records their response to Stephen's charges:

When they heard this, they were furious and gnashed their teeth at him. (Acts 7:54)

In their rage, Stephen's accusers grind the enamel off their molars. That's the power of the truth: You must either submit to it or rebel against it. The truth never allows you to remain neutral. Jesus said of His ministry, "Do not suppose that I have come to bring peace to the earth. I did not come to bring peace, but a sword" (Matthew 10:34). In other words, He came to bring truth to the earth—and the truth always divides people. It separates those who seek God from those who seek their own selfish desires.

Stephen's response to the rage of his accusers is amazing:

But Stephen, full of the Holy Spirit, looked up to heaven and saw the glory of God, and Jesus standing at the right hand of God. "Look," he said, "I see heaven open and the Son of Man standing at the right hand of God." (Acts 7:55-56)

God stands by His faithful martyr. Even before the persecutors drag Stephen out to stone him, Stephen already has one foot on earth and one foot in heaven. He sees that the next event awaiting him is the coming of the Lord Jesus for His own. I believe every believer has such a vision the moment he or she steps out of time and into eternity.

Stephen describes aloud what he sees, and his words are like those Jesus used when He addressed this same Sanhedrin at His trial before the crucifixion. Jesus said, "In the future you will see the Son of Man sitting at the right hand of the Mighty One and coming on the clouds of heaven" (Matthew 26:64). When the Sanhedrin hears Stephen describe a vision of Jesus in those same terms, they know that their real problem is not what they should do with Stephen but what they have already done with Jesus.

Stephen now offers them a second chance. They can respond to the Lord's servant and repent, or they can repeat the sin of murder. They choose to murder the servant, just as they murdered his Lord.

THE DEATH OF STEPHEN

Luke records the response of Stephen's accusers and the Sanhedrin:

> At this they covered their ears and, yelling at the top of their voices, they all rushed at him, dragged him out of the city and began to stone him. Meanwhile, the witnesses laid their clothes at the feet of a young man named Saul.
>
> While they were stoning him, Stephen prayed, "Lord Jesus, receive my spirit." Then he fell on his knees and cried out, "Lord, do not hold this sin against them." When he had said this, he fell asleep.
>
> And Saul was there, giving approval to his death. (Acts 7:57–8:1a)

Unable to bear the truth, Stephen's accusers stop up their ears and try to drown out his words. They seize him and drag him through the streets and out of the gate where St. Stephen's Gate now stands. The take him outside of the eastern walls, and there they stone him. As he dies, Stephen prays for two things, the same two requests Jesus made from the cross: "Lord, receive my spirit," and, "Do not hold this sin against them."

Twice in this account, Luke mentions young Saul of Tarsus. Those who stoned Stephen placed their garments at the feet of Saul, and he approved the murder of this martyr. God wants us to see that the blood of martyrs is the seed from which the church of God grows. As Stephen dies, a man stands by who will one day become the apostle Paul, the great missionary evangelist of the early church.

Paul never forgot this scene. It was etched in his memory. When the Lord Jesus confronted Saul on the road to Damascus, He probably stirred Saul's stinging conscience regarding the death of Stephen when He said, "Saul, Saul, why do you persecute me? It is hard for you to kick against the goads" (Acts 26:14). Jesus was saying, in effect, "Saul, Saul, when you persecute my saints, you persecute me! Do you remember how, as Stephen was being stoned to death, he spoke the same prayer I spoke from the cross? Do you remember how Stephen forgave you as he died? His death has been prodding your conscience, like goads jabbing at your soul. It's time to surrender to me."

With the death of Stephen, we reach the end of the opening phase of the expansion of the church. In Acts 1:8, Jesus set forth His three-phase program for the growth of the early church: "But you will receive power when the Holy Spirit comes on you; and you will be my witnesses in Jerusalem [phase 1], and in all Judea and Samaria [phase 2], and to the ends of the earth [phase 3]." Immediately after the death of Stephen, persecution breaks out against the church in Jerusalem, and the apostles are thrust out into Judea and Samaria. Phase 1 (Jerusalem) has ended; phase 2 (Judea and Samaria) begins.

Later, after Paul is converted and begins his missionary journeys, we will see the beginning of phase 3 (to the ends of the earth). This third and final phase of church growth is still going on at this hour. The book of Acts is an unfinished book. We are still writing this book in the twenty-first century. Perhaps some readers of this book will, like Stephen, be called upon to lay down their lives for Jesus' sake. Around the world, opposition is sharpening, and the enemies of the truth are growing more hostile.

Persecution may come to the United States before this age draws to a close. It may be only a matter of time before it becomes risky and costly to preach the gospel of Jesus Christ. When the day of persecution comes, may God grant that, like Stephen, we will be faithful and courageous unto death.

PART II

THE CHURCH UNDER PRESSURE

Acts 8–12

14

MIRACLES VERSUS MAGIC

Acts 8:1b-24

In the mid-1800s, a sixteen-year-old named J. H. Crowell signed on as a sailor aboard a small sailing vessel. A devout Christian, he promised his mother that he would pray three times a day. The day the sailing boat left the harbor, Crowell learned that he was the only Christian in the twelve-man crew. The other men were vile and cruel, and every other word they spoke was a curse.

Crowell kept his promise to his mother. Three times every day, he went below decks to pray aloud. When the other sailors learned that the teen was a devout Christian, they did everything they could to make his life miserable. Whenever he prayed, they threw planks at him or doused him with buckets of foul water.

The captain thought that a Christian crewman was bad for morale, so he ordered Crowell to stop praying. The young man refused. The captain ordered that Crowell be tied to the mast and flogged. The whip cut his back to bloody ribbons, yet Crowell continued praying three times a day.

Enraged, the captain ordered his men to tie Crowell and toss him overboard. The young man freed his arms and swam back to the sailing vessel, but the crewman beat him back with a pole. The young man knew the captain and crew meant to drown him, so he prayed aloud, "Lord, forgive these men! They don't know what they're doing!" Then he called out, "Send my body to my mother! Tell her I died for Jesus!"

Finally, the crewmen hauled him back into the vessel, more dead than alive. When he came to, he found two sailors bending over him—and they said they wanted the kind of courage he had shown in the face of death. Crowell led both men to the Lord. Within days, all of J. H. Crowell's fellow crewmen, including the captain, had given their lives to Christ.

In Acts 8, we see this same principle at work in the life and death of the first martyr, Stephen. The men of the Sanhedrin may have silenced one voice with the stoning of Stephen, but they have set events in motion that will transform the world. God always turns persecution into greater propagation of the gospel. He uses opposition to advance His cause. This principle is vividly demonstrated throughout Acts 8.

PERSECUTION AND PROCLAMATION

Luke shows us what immediately follows the death of Stephen:

> On that day a great persecution broke out against the church at Jerusalem, and all except the apostles were scattered throughout Judea and Samaria. Godly men buried Stephen and mourned deeply for him. But Saul began to destroy the church. Going from house to house, he dragged off men and women and put them in prison.
>
> Those who had been scattered preached the word wherever they went. Philip went down to a city in Samaria and proclaimed the Christ there. (Acts 8:1b-5)

The murder of Stephen unleashes an onslaught of persecution. After spilling Stephen's blood, the persecutors demand more blood. It's like a feeding frenzy of sharks once they detect blood in the water.

As the persecution of the church begins in Jerusalem, the Christians flee in all directions, dispersing into Judea and Samaria. As they go, they share the gospel, just as God had planned. The persecution of the church is no surprise to Him. When God's opponents put up roadblocks, He uses those roadblocks to create detours and produce even more ministry.

Picture young Saul, enraged over the heresy of this upstart cult called Christianity. He tries to stamp it out with all the energy of his flesh. He enters house after house, dragging off whole families of Christians and tossing them into prison. But the more he persecutes the church, the faster it spreads. As the church is driven out into Judea and Samaria, the Christians are forced to rely not on the apostles but on the gifts of the Spirit.

The apostles were not dispersed. Those who fled the city were plain-vanilla Christians like you and me. Yet even ordinary Christians possess the gifts of the Spirit. These believers might never have discovered their gifts if they hadn't been driven out by persecution. So God used the pressure of persecution to unleash spiritual gifts of evangelism, witnessing, helps, wisdom, knowledge, teaching, and all the other gifts the Spirit has given. When we find ourselves being attacked for our faith, we should allow God to transform our persecution into greater proclamation of His truth.

THREE MARKS OF THE MINISTRY OF THE SPIRIT

Next, Luke takes us to Samaria, where we see one ordinary Christian doing extraordinary things:

> Philip went down to a city in Samaria and proclaimed the Christ there. When the crowds heard Philip and saw the miraculous signs he did, they all paid close attention to what he said. With shrieks, evil spirits came out of many, and many paralytics and cripples were healed. So there was great joy in that city. (Acts 8:5-8)

Here, Luke tells us about the amazing ministry of a Christian layman named Philip. Though Philip is not an apostle, his ministry is accompanied by the power of the Holy Spirit. This brief passage, written under the inspiration of the Holy Spirit, shows us three identifying marks that always accompany the ministry of the Spirit.

The ring of truth. Luke writes, "When the crowds heard Philip . . . they all paid close attention to what he said." Crowds pay attention when they sense the ring of truth. When Jesus spoke at the synagogue in Capernaum, the crowds "were amazed at his teaching, because he taught them as one who had authority, not as the teachers of the law" (Mark 1:22). When the chief priests and Pharisees sent guards out to arrest Jesus, the guards returned empty-handed, saying, "No one ever spoke the way this man does" (John 7:46). God's message has the ring of authority and truth.

The accompaniment of power. Luke writes, "With shrieks, evil spirits came out of many, and many paralytics and cripples were healed." Here is power that sets people free. These miracles of deliverance and healing were evidences of the power of God to liberate and heal human beings on a spiritual level. Wherever the gospel goes, there is liberty.

Joy. Luke writes, "So there was great joy in that city." When people are set free, they always experience joy. In *Walden,* Henry David Thoreau observed, "The mass of men lead lives of quiet desperation." It's true. Walk on any city street, and look around at the people who pass by. You'll see great loneliness, emptiness, and depression everywhere you look.

But when the truth of God breaks through, people are filled with joy! Their circumstances may not change. They don't suddenly go from poverty to riches. But their hearts swell with joy. The gospel is good news of great joy.

I remember one woman who gave her life to Christ, and she was instantly so filled with joy that she began to shout, "Whoopee! Whoopee!" She had not learned any Christian jargon such as "Hallelujah!" or "Praise the Lord!" so she just shouted, "Whoopee! Whoopee!" That's the kind of joy the gospel gives, and it electrified the crowds in Samaria—they were whooping it up!

SIMON MAGUS: SATAN'S THIRD ATTEMPT

Next, Luke introduces a troubling individual named Simon:

> Now for some time a man named Simon had practiced sorcery in the city and amazed all the people of Samaria. He boasted that he was someone great, and all the people, both high and low, gave him their attention and exclaimed, "This man is the divine power known as the Great Power." They followed him because he had amazed them for a long time with his magic. But when they believed Philip as he preached the good news of the kingdom of God and the name of Jesus Christ, they were baptized, both men and women. Simon himself believed and was baptized. And he

followed Philip everywhere, astonished by the great signs and miracles he saw. (Acts 8:9-13)

Here we see a contrast between authentic Christianity and counterfeit Christianity. At first glance, it seems that Simon Magus (Simon the Magician) has sincerely converted to faith in Christ, for Luke writes, "Simon himself believed and was baptized." In reality, however, Simon is another satanic attempt to attack the church from within.

Remember that in Matthew 13:24-30, Jesus said that the enemy would sneak in and sow weeds among the wheat, and the weeds and wheat would grow up together, indistinguishable until the time of harvest. The story of Simon the Magician marks the third time in Acts that we see the devil's weeds sprouting in the wheat field of the church. The first was the story of Ananias and Sapphira (Acts 5), two genuine Christians who yielded to hypocrisy. The second was the dissension that arose in the church over the distribution of food to needy widows (Acts 6).

Now, in Acts 8, we have a man who believes and is baptized, though his conversion is fraudulent. We see the identifying mark of a spiritual counterfeit when Luke writes that Simon "boasted that he was someone great, and all the people, both high and low, gave him their attention." Counterfeit faith exalts personalities and inflates egos. Counterfeit believers may use religious jargon and feign humility, but by their clever words and staged actions, they always draw attention to themselves.

Genuine Christianity exalts Christ, not individual personalities. "For we do not preach ourselves," wrote the apostle Paul, "but Jesus Christ as Lord, and ourselves as your servants for Jesus' sake" (2 Corinthians 4:5).

I once attended a service conducted by a famous faith healer. I wanted to hear his message and see if he preached Christ or himself. As I listened, I was surprised that his message seemed scripturally sound. I thought, "Perhaps I've been wrong about this man." At the end of his sermon, he invited people to accept Christ—

Then he revealed his true nature by saying, "If you want to know God, then have faith in my prayers! My prayers will lead you to God. Come forward, and I will pray for you." Everything in his message had been designed to lull the listener into placing his trust not in Christ but in this man and his prayers. That is counterfeit Christianity, a weed pretending to be wheat.

False Christianity always attempts to insert a human mediator between a believer and his God. As Paul writes, "There is one God and one mediator between God and men, the man Christ Jesus" (1 Timothy 2:5). Counterfeit Christianity will tell you that you need a priest or a faith healer or some other special channel that ordinary people don't have. When you hear such claims, don't believe them.

WIDESPREAD DELUSION AND COUNTERFEIT POWER

Another identifying mark of a spiritual counterfeit is a large following of gullible people. Simon's following is the result of a widespread delusion. Luke writes, "All the people, both high and low, gave him their attention and exclaimed, 'This man is the divine power known as the Great Power.'" What did the people mean?

They thought of God as so remote from them that He would not appear to them but would only send His power, as though the power of God were a separate and distinct personality. They looked at Simon's magic tricks and said, "This man is the power of God." The whole city believed it, from the least to the greatest. One of the identifying characteristics of a counterfeit faith is that it misleads the masses. False leaders always have great followings of gullible people.

Another identifying mark of a spiritual counterfeit is counterfeit power. Luke writes, "They followed him because he had amazed them for a long time with his magic." Note that when the Scriptures refer to magic, they do not mean sleight-of-hand or stage illusions. Simon was a master of the occult, and he had formed a relationship with demonic powers. He performed acts of sorcery by drawing upon satanic forces.

We have seen Simon's ilk before. There was an incident in Exodus 7 where Moses and his brother Aaron appeared in Pharaoh's court. God told Aaron to throw his staff on the ground. Aaron did so, and the staff became a writhing serpent. Then Pharaoh's magicians threw their staffs down, and their staffs also became serpents. It appeared that the Egyptian magicians were as powerful as Moses and Aaron, but then Aaron's serpent swallowed up the magical serpents of the Egyptians. Satan loves to create counterfeits of God's works, but the works of Satan can never equal the works of God.

Simon performed magic that looked like miracles, and the people mistook his magic for the power of God. His occult works led the people into spiritual bondage. It is likely, though it is not specifically stated, that many of the demon-possessed people who were liberated by Philip had been enslaved by the magic of Simon.

We have seen a dramatic rise of occult practices and demonic manifestations in recent decades. In the early twentieth century, witches, warlocks, and occult practices were considered the subject of myth and fantasy. In the early twenty-first century, nearly 150,000 Americans claim to be practitioners of Wicca (witchcraft).

Another identifying mark of a spiritual counterfeit is that counterfeits disguise themselves as followers of Christ. Luke writes, "Simon himself believed and was baptized. And he followed Philip everywhere, astonished by the great signs and miracles he saw" (Acts 8:13). Simon took upon himself the symbol of identification with Jesus Christ—baptism—and openly joined the company of those who belonged to Jesus.

But the rest of the account makes it clear that this man was not an authentic believer. He was a weed among the wheat. Outwardly, Simon said the right words and did the right things. Inwardly, he was unchanged.

One reason the church often seems weak and ineffective is that many fraudulent Christians have entered the church. Down through history, counterfeit Christians have destroyed an untold number of churches and hindered the advance of the gospel. That's the bad news. The good news is that the Spirit of God, working through His people, can expose spiritual fraud and deception in the church.

THE SPIRIT COMES UPON THE SAMARITANS

Next, Luke shows us how God brings spiritual counterfeits to light:

> When the apostles in Jerusalem heard that Samaria had accepted the word of God, they sent Peter and John to them. When they arrived, they prayed for them that they might receive the Holy Spirit, because the Holy Spirit had not yet come upon any of them; they had simply been baptized into the name of the Lord Jesus. Then Peter and John placed their hands on them, and they received the Holy Spirit. (Acts 8:14-17)

Here, in contrast to Simon's counterfeit Christianity, we see a genuine manifestation of authentic Christianity—the coming of the Holy Spirit. This indicates that the believers in Samaria had not yet received the Holy Spirit. The Samaritans had believed and been baptized, but then Peter and John had to pray for them to receive the Holy Spirit, because the Holy Spirit had not yet come upon them. How is that possible? Can a person become a Christian without receiving the Holy Spirit?

This account specifically says is that the Samaritan Christians had not yet experienced the Holy Spirit coming upon them. There are various terms used in Scripture to describe the activities of the Holy Spirit. The Samaritan believers had not yet received a certain manifestation of the Spirit: They had not yet been baptized by the Spirit into the one body. They were individual regenerated Christians, just as the apostles had been before the day of Pentecost.

Prior to Pentecost, the apostles had been born again and regenerated by the Holy Spirit, but the Holy Spirit had not yet fallen on them. When the day of Pentecost came, the Spirit came upon them, and they became members of one body in Jesus Christ and received the gifts of the Spirit. That is what now happens in Samaria.

When Peter and John went to Samaria, they first prayed for the church. Then they laid hands on the Samaritans, and the Samaritans, too, received the baptism of the Spirit, making them one body in Christ. Though Luke does not record any signs or wonders, he does tell us that the Samaritans received the Holy Spirit. This event was probably manifested through spiritual gifts, including the gift of tongues. Perhaps the sight of the Samaritan Christians praising God in foreign languages led Simon to covet that gift and offer money to the apostles.

Some people claim you must have the gift of tongues in order to have the Holy Spirit. The Scriptures show us this is not true. In Acts 13, disciples in Antioch of Pisidia are filled with the Spirit, yet there is no mention of tongues. Some might say, "Well, you must have the apostolic ministry in order to lay hands on people so that they receive the Spirit." But that's not true either. In Acts 9:17, Ananias lays hands on the newly converted Paul, and Paul receives the Holy Spirit, yet Ananias was not an apostle.

Some might say, "It must be the laying on of hands that causes people to receive the Spirit." But in Acts 10, the apostle Peter preaches at the house of Cornelius, and his hearers receive the Spirit before he can lay hands on them. The Spirit of God is sovereign and sometimes does things in different ways, in a different order, because that is His sovereign right.

In those days, the Jews and Samaritans had no dealings with each other. The Holy Spirit came to break down that partition and form a single, unified body of believers. If the Spirit of God had not come upon the Samaritan church, there might have been two separate churches, one Jewish and one Samaritan. But when the Holy Spirit came upon these believers in response to the prayer of Peter and John, it was as if God said, "There is one church body, not two. There is no distinction between Jews and Samaritans. All believers are one in the body of Christ."

HOW TO EXPOSE A COUNTERFEIT

Finally, the Holy Spirit exposes the false ministry of Simon the Magician:

> When Simon saw that the Spirit was given at the laying on of the apostles' hands, he offered them money and said, "Give me also this ability so that everyone on whom I lay my hands may receive the Holy Spirit." (Acts 8:18-19)

Simon's spiritual blindness is astounding! He thinks God's power can be purchased with money. He insults God by suggesting that the apostles sell their power to him. This shows how unregenerate his heart was. To this day, the sin of trying to buy religious power with money is called simony, after Simon Magus.

Next, Peter exposes the counterfeit nature of this man:

> Peter answered: "May your money perish with you, because you thought you could buy the gift of God with money! . . . Repent of this wickedness

and pray to the Lord. Perhaps he will forgive you for having such a thought in your heart. For I see that you are full of bitterness and captive to sin."

Then Simon answered, "Pray to the Lord for me so that nothing you have said may happen to me." (Acts 8:20-24)

In the original Greek, Peter's words are much more forceful than "May your money perish with you!" Peter literally says, "To hell with you and your money!" He goes on to read the man's heart: "For I see that you are full of bitterness and captive to sin." Why is Simon full of bitterness and enslaved by sin? Because he's never been set free. An authentic Christian would not be an embittered slave of sin.

What must Simon do? "Repent of this wickedness and pray to the Lord," Peter says. "Perhaps he will forgive you for having such a thought in your heart."

Simon's heart is so far from repentance that he offers this strange reply: "Pray to the Lord for me so that nothing you have said may happen to me." In other words, Simon refuses to act on his own behalf. He tries to put the responsibility for his soul onto Peter. Simon Magus wants to escape the penalty for his sin, but he doesn't want to take responsibility for his own repentance.

It's no wonder that Simon became one of the earliest and greatest opponents of the gospel. There are accounts of Simon in an apocryphal book, The Acts of Peter, and in the writings of several early church fathers, including Irenaeus, Justin Martyr, and Hippolytus of Rome. The early church fathers called him "the first heretic" and "the father of heresies." He is said to have hindered the gospel wherever he went, and he is reputed to have founded an immoral Gnostic cult called the Simonians.

Counterfeits are ultimately revealed for all to see. May God search our hearts so that we may not have even a trace of Simon Magus lurking within us. May our hearts cry out in transparent honesty to God, "Lord, you alone set me free! I place myself in your hands, Lord. Do with me as you will."

15

THE DIVINE WIND

Acts 8:25-40

If the wind should absolutely cease to blow for a single hour, most of the life on this earth would cease to be." So wrote evangelist R. A. Torrey in *The Person and Work of the Holy Spirit.* Torrey explained that scientific studies had shown that the five healthiest cities in the United States were the five cities located on the Great Lakes. This was true despite the fact that these five cities were urban, industrial centers that were "far from being the cleanest cities or the most sanitary."

How could this be so? Torrey explained, "It is the wind blowing from the lakes that has brought life and health to the cities. Just so, when the Spirit ceases to blow in any heart or any church or any community, death ensues. But when the Spirit blows steadily upon the individual or the church or the community, there is abounding spiritual life and health."[1] The Spirit came upon the church on the day of Pentecost as a mighty rushing wind—the visible and audible symbol of the Spirit in His sovereign authority to control the destiny of the church. Jesus speaks of the Spirit in the same way when he tells Nicodemus, "The wind blows wherever it pleases. You hear its sound, but you cannot tell where it comes from or where it is going. So it is with everyone born of the Spirit" (John 3:8).

The mighty rushing wind is an apt symbol of the sovereign activity of the Holy Spirit. He goes where He wills; you cannot predict what He'll do next.

WITNESSING: THE ORDINARY CHRISTIAN LIFE

We see the Spirit moving again:

> When they had testified and proclaimed the word of the Lord, Peter and John returned to Jerusalem, preaching the gospel in many Samaritan villages. (Acts 8:25)

Three words in this verse speak of what God says should be the normal activity of Christians. These two men, Peter and John, had testified, proclaimed, and evangelized (the NIV text uses the word *preaching*, but

---

1. R. A. Torrey, *The Person and Work of the Holy Spirit* (Grand Rapids: Zondervan, 1985), 39.

"evangelizing" would be a more accurate word). Let's take a closer look at these three words.

Testify (Greek *diamarturomai*). This means that Peter and John shared what they had experienced. It's the word you would use of a person giving testimony in a courtroom. To testify in the Christian sense means to tell other people what God has done in your life through Jesus Christ.

Proclaim (Greek *laleo*). This word means to speak the word of the Lord, to talk about the truth. This is what the Bible calls prophesying. Peter and John spoke the truth of the gospel to the new believers in Samaria.

Evangelize (Greek *euaggelizo*). This word means that Peter and John announced the good news of the gospel. We derive our English word *evangelism* from the Greek word *euaggelizo*. As Peter and John returned to Jerusalem, they evangelized by announcing the good news of Jesus Christ in every village and town.

These three activities—testifying, proclaiming, and evangelizing—describe what our daily lives should look like as we live in obedience to the Holy Spirit.

FROM THE ORDINARY TO THE EXTRAORDINARY

Next, Luke draws a sharp contrast between the ordinary Christian life of witnessing, as depicted in Acts 8:25, and the extraordinary actions the Holy Spirit sometimes takes in our lives. Peter and John were carrying out their ordinary function as Christian witnesses as they made their way back to Jerusalem from Samaria. But in the next verse, we see the unpredictable activity of the Spirit of God:

> Now an angel of the Lord said to Philip, "Go south to the road—the desert road—that goes down from Jerusalem to Gaza." So he started out. (Acts 8:26-27a)

An angel appeared to Philip with a message from God. You may ask, "Does God still work through angels?" and the answer is a resounding yes. The ministry of angels, according to the Bible, goes on all the time. But angels are rarely visible to us.

The book of Hebrews tells us that angels are "ministering spirits sent to serve those who will inherit salvation" (Hebrews 1:14). All of us, at all times, are being touched by the ministry of angels, but we do not see them. There have been well-documented incidences of the appearance of angels in church history beyond the New Testament period. Many missionaries have reported the visible appearance of angels. As we draw nearer to the return of Jesus Christ, we may see a dramatic return of angelic manifestations.

Here, the Holy Spirit sends an angel to Philip. The angel commands Philip to go south along the road from Jerusalem to Gaza. This is an empty stretch of desert road, with no villages en route. Philip never questions God's command. He simply goes in obedience to the word of the angel.

This is a beautiful picture of what we might call the wind of God, the sovereign mobilizing action of the Holy Spirit. Notice how the wind of God blows differently in the lives of different believers. In Acts 8:25, the wind of the Spirit blows Peter and John from Samaria back to Jerusalem, witnessing as they go. In Acts 8:26, the wind of the Spirit blows Philip out into a lonely desert place. Yet in both cases, we see that these believers obediently partake of the Spirit-filled, Spirit-led life. The ministry of God's Spirit is vital and fresh every day. The Holy Spirit moves in ways we can't anticipate, so we need to be sensitive to His influence in our lives.

As Christians, we continually try to control the flow of the river of God. We dig a channel, line it with concrete, and say, "Come, O River of God and flow through this channel we have dug for you." To our dismay, a scant trickle of water comes through our channel. Meanwhile, the great flood of the Spirit's power is moving out through the mud flats. We think, "That's not where God belongs! He belongs here, in this nice channel I've dug!" And we wonder why our lives are spiritually dry.

The Holy Spirit wants us to allow Him to override our plans, to change our course, to make something new. The church is often so rigidly programmed that there is no room for the Spirit to move. I've been amazed to see banners in front of churches that read like this:

REVIVAL HERE!
Beginning June 15th and ending June 24th!

I've always wondered how these churches are able to schedule the Holy Spirit that way. Can you put the wind on a timetable? You can't schedule the Spirit any more than you can schedule a hurricane. The sovereign Spirit is free to move beyond the limits of our plans and schedules. Sometimes He moves through the normal circumstances of our lives, and sometimes He shatters our expectations.

Throughout the book of Acts you see the early Christians being responsive to the Spirit of God, even as He breaks through their expectations and plans. The great need of the church is for us to again break free of our overstructured mindset so that we can respond to God's leading. We need to be open to the unpredictable activity of the Spirit of God.

THE MAN GOD HAS PREPARED

The rest of Acts 8 tells how God prepared everything in advance for Philip's adventure. We now meet the man God has prepared:

So he started out, and on his way he met an Ethiopian eunuch, an impor-tant official in charge of all the treasury of Candace, queen of the Ethiopians. This man had gone to Jerusalem to worship, and on his way home was sitting in his chariot reading the book of Isaiah the prophet. (Acts 8:27-28)

The Ethiopian eunuch was a man of great responsibility, the Secretary of the Treasury of Ethiopia. He had great authority and influence throughout all of Ethiopia and Egypt. He worked with the queen (Candace was the title given to the queens of Ethiopia, in the same way the kings of Egypt were called Pharaoh). Being an Ethiopian, he was probably a black African, and he was spiritually searching. Though not a Jew, he had gone all the way to Jerusalem to worship at the temple of the Jews.

Now he returns home dissatisfied. While in Jerusalem, he evidently purchased a scroll of the prophet Isaiah and is reading the scroll aloud as he rides in his chariot. The Spirit has been preparing these two men, Philip and the Ethiopian eunuch, for this encounter. Luke writes:

> The Spirit told Philip, "Go to that chariot and stay near it."
>
> Then Philip ran up to the chariot and heard the man reading Isaiah the prophet. "Do you understand what you are reading?" Philip asked.
>
> "How can I," he said, "unless someone explains it to me?" So he invited Philip to come up and sit with him.
>
> The eunuch was reading this passage of Scripture:
>
>> "He was led like a sheep to the slaughter,
>>   and as a lamb before the shearer is silent,
>>   so he did not open his mouth.
>> In his humiliation he was deprived of justice.
>>   Who can speak of his descendants?
>>   For his life was taken from the earth."
>
> The eunuch asked Philip, "Tell me, please, who is the prophet talking about, himself or someone else?" (Acts 8:29-34)

Notice the timing of the Holy Spirit. Philip walks along the road. A chariot comes over the hill and passes him by. At the precise moment the chariot passes by, the Ethiopian is reading aloud from Isaiah 53, the passage that predicts the coming Messiah, the suffering Savior. Notice how the Spirit guides the conversation. Philip says, "Do you understand what you are reading?"

The Ethiopian replies, "How can I, unless someone explains it to me?" This man is aware of his need for a teacher to explain God's Word. Many people say, "I'm going to read the Bible for myself. I don't need any teachers!" Many spiritually immature believers have brought great sorrow on themselves by refusing to listen to wise Bible teaching.

As Charles Haddon Spurgeon once said, "I never could understand why some men set such great value on what the Holy Spirit said to them, and so little value on what He said to anyone else." The same Spirit who breathed His truth into the Scriptures has also provided teachers gifted in understanding and explaining that truth. It takes both the Word and teachers of the Word to gain a true understanding of God's truth.

The eunuch invites Philip to come up and sit with him. He was at the passage God wanted him to understand, but he was puzzled by it. Isaiah 53 predicts the sufferings of Jesus the Messiah in amazing detail. Unlike many other Old Testament passages, which depict the Messiah coming in triumph and glory, Isaiah 53 depicts Him as quietly submitting to a humiliating and agonizing death.

The Jewish people have been puzzled by these pictures of a suffering Messiah. They love the prophecies picturing Him in triumph but are baffled by the prophecies of his suffering and death. The Ethiopian eunuch was also puzzled, so he asked Philip, in effect, "Who is the prophet talking about? Why does he say the Messiah must die? Or is he even speaking of the Messiah? Is he, perhaps, speaking of himself?"

At this point, Philip knew exactly what to say. He knew the Scriptures, and he knew the Messiah. Luke tells us what Philip did next:

> Then Philip began with that very passage of Scripture and told him the good news about Jesus.
>
> As they traveled along the road, they came to some water and the eunuch said, "Look, here is water. Why shouldn't I be baptized?" And he gave orders to stop the chariot. Then both Philip and the eunuch went down into the water and Philip baptized him. (Acts 8:35-38)

Philip told the Ethiopian eunuch that the passage he was reading, Isaiah 53, predicted the suffering and death of Jesus the Messiah. He told this man the good news of Jesus Christ—that the life, death, and resurrection of Jesus had solved the problem of human guilt, because all of our sin had been laid on Him. How this African man must have rejoiced to hear the story of Jesus!

Philip was keenly aware of the Great Commission: "Therefore go and make disciples of all nations, baptizing them in the name of the Father and of the Son and of the Holy Spirit, and teaching them to obey everything I have commanded you" (Matthew 28:19-20). He undoubtedly explained the symbol of baptism to this Ethiopian man, and in the timing of the Spirit, they came to a place where there was water by the side of the road. So Philip took the man into the water and baptized him.

THE SPIRIT TAKES PHILIP AWAY

There are some profound insights to observe in the closing verses:

> When they came up out of the water, the Spirit of the Lord suddenly took Philip away, and the eunuch did not see him again, but went on his way

rejoicing. Philip, however, appeared at Azotus and traveled about, preaching the gospel in all the towns until he reached Caesarea. (Acts 8:39-40)

At first glance, it appears that a miracle occurred, and you can certainly read the passage that way. While I do believe in miracles, I don't believe that this passage describes a miraculous event. I may be mistaken, but here's what I think happened.

I believe that Philip and the African man were so caught up with excitement and joy over what God had done in bringing them together that they didn't even realize that they had gone their separate ways. The Ethiopian eunuch came up out of the water overwhelmed with joy because he was now a new creation in Christ. All the answers his tortured soul had longed for were suddenly his, and he didn't notice that Philip didn't get back into the chariot with him.

Philip, meanwhile, was so caught up with what God had done and how the Spirit had prepared this African man to receive the gospel that he didn't realize that the man had driven off and left him there. He didn't realize where he was until he reached Azotus on the coast road. There he began to preach in the coastal towns as he went toward Caesarea.

I've had similar experiences myself. There have been times when I have seen God work so dramatically that I have gotten in my car to drive to the next city and didn't realize where I was until I had driven an hour beyond my destination. That's what the adventure of the Spirit-led life is often like.

When Philip got to Azotus, he began preaching while moving up the coast until he reached Caesarea. That's the adventure of the Spirit-filled life. It is an ordinary life, filled with plenty of routine, but even that routine is touched with the flame of heaven! The ordinary Christian life is an adventure in which extraordinary things may happen at any moment. The Spirit-led believer should expect the unexpected. In any ordinary day, we may see the Holy Spirit connect seemingly disconnected events to form a chain of circumstances that can only be described as miraculous.

That's the normal Christian life.

16

THE BELOVED ENEMY

Acts 9:1-19a

In 1885, young Francis Thompson moved to London to pursue his dream of becoming a writer. He wrote hundreds of poems and essays, but his work was rejected by publisher after publisher. Forced to work at menial jobs, often living on the streets without a friend in the world, Thompson became addicted to opium and once attempted suicide—but he even failed at that.

After Thompson had spent three hardscrabble years in London, Wilfrid and Alice Meynell, the editors of the magazine *Merrie England,* discovered some poems he had submitted. They thought his poems were brilliant, though they were written on scrap paper and old grocery wrappers. When they sought Thompson out, they found him homeless and on the brink of death from addiction and depression. The Meynells published his first volume of poems in 1893 and helped him find a place to live in a Franciscan Christian community. There, Thompson found faith in Christ, which enabled him to escape his addiction, though his health was permanently impaired.

As a Christian, Thompson continued to write until his death from tuberculosis in 1907. Though he died at age forty-eight, his most famous poem, "The Hound of Heaven," lives on, touching hearts to this day. It opens with these lines:

> I fled Him, down the nights and down the days;
> I fled Him, down the arches of the years;
> I fled Him, down the labyrinthine ways
> Of my own mind; and in the mist of tears
> I hid from Him . . .

The title "The Hound of Heaven" is startling. The imagery is of a hound hunting a rabbit, chasing the frightened animal until it is cornered and resigned to death. At the moment of despair, the poet realizes that the Hound of Heaven has not pursued him to destroy him but has chased his fleeing soul with love and grace. To the poet's everlasting amazement, the pursuit has ended in salvation. "The Hound of Heaven" is the story of how God pursued Thompson until he surrendered his life to Christ.

It is also the story of the man known as the apostle Paul.

THE BEGINNING OF PHASE 3

In Acts 1:8, Jesus gave His disciples a great three-phase outline of the progress of the gospel through the course of this age: "But you will receive power when the Holy Spirit comes on you; and you will be my witnesses in Jerusalem, and in all Judea and Samaria, and to the ends of the earth." Phase 1: Jerusalem. Phase 2: Judea and Samaria. Phase 3: The ends of the earth.

As we come to Acts 9, we see the second stage. The gospel now goes out to Judea and Samaria as it is systematically preached throughout every village of Samaria and Judea by Philip, Peter, John, and others. At the same time, the Lord is preparing the instrument by which the gospel will move into the third stage—the stage in which we are still involved: to the ends of the earth. God's instrument for implementing phase 3 is a man named Saul of Tarsus, later known as the apostle Paul.

As Acts 9 opens, we find young Saul, the enemy and persecutor of the early Christian movement, doing everything in his power to destroy the infant church:

> Meanwhile, Saul was still breathing out murderous threats against the Lord's disciples. He went to the high priest and asked him for letters to the synagogues in Damascus, so that if he found any there who belonged to the Way, whether men or women, he might take them as prisoners to Jerusalem. (Acts 9:1-2)

There are three noteworthy facets to this story.

First, Saul seeks to destroy the church. In the King James Version, he is "breathing out threats and slaughter"; however, the literal Greek text says he is "breathing in threats and slaughter." In other words, violence and murder are the atmosphere he breathes. He lives on death. Hatred sustains him.

Later, when Paul gave his testimony before King Agrippa, he said, "I too was convinced that I ought to do all that was possible to oppose the name of Jesus of Nazareth. And that is just what I did in Jerusalem. On the authority of the chief priests I put many of the saints in prison, and when they were put to death, I cast my vote against them. Many a time I went from one synagogue to another to have them punished, and I tried to force them to blaspheme. In my obsession against them, I even went to foreign cities to persecute them" (Acts 26:9-11).

Saul of Tarsus is driven by religious zeal. He has not forgotten the death of Stephen—and that memory probably disturbed his conscience. To silence the nagging of his conscience, Saul relentlessly persecuted the church.

Second, Luke records that the Christians are known by a certain name. Later, in the city of Antioch, they will be called Christians for the first time. But here they are referred to as those "who belonged to the Way." Names like this are invariably coined by opponents. This reference to the believers as people of the Way indicates how their opponents view them. They see the Christians as odd and different, as belonging to a different way of life.

Genuine Christians are characterized by love, acceptance, and forgiveness—not by the selfishness and hatred that marks the world. There is something about these early Christians that reminds people of Jesus, who called Himself "the way, the truth, and the life." So the earliest Christians are said to belong to the Way.

Third, Saul of Tarsus is going to Damascus to arrest the Christians there, but the Lord has other plans. Once Saul is outside the borders of Israel, Jesus will meet Paul on the road and take him prisoner.

This is significant. In His program to reach the world with the gospel, God intends to transform Saul into Paul, the mighty apostle to the Gentiles. Until now, the gospel has gone only as far as the traditional boundaries of Israel—to Jerusalem, Judea, and Samaria. Judea is the mountainous southern portion of Israel; Samaria is the middle portion between Galilee on the north and Judea on the south (today, this region is called the West Bank of the Jordan).

God wants a special apostle for a special task. He wants Saul, as the apostle Paul, to take the gospel beyond the boundaries of Israel. He underscores His intent with a symbolic event. He leads Saul outside the boundaries of Israel and there, on the road to Damascus, He arrests Saul and takes him captive.

THE CONVERSION OF SAUL

Next Luke tells us of Saul's life-altering encounter on the Damascus road:

> As he neared Damascus on his journey, suddenly a light from heaven flashed around him. He fell to the ground and heard a voice say to him, "Saul, Saul, why do you persecute me?"
>
> "Who are you, Lord?" Saul asked.
>
> "I am Jesus, whom you are persecuting," he replied. "Now get up and go into the city, and you will be told what you must do.'
>
> The men traveling with Saul stood there speechless; they heard the sound but did not see anyone. Saul got up from the ground, but when he opened his eyes he could see nothing. So they led him by the hand into Damascus. For three days he was blind, and did not eat or drink anything. (Acts 9:3-9)

Many skeptics try to explain this story on a natural basis. Some suggest that Saul's encounter was an epileptic seizure in which he imagined he heard voices. To this theory, Charles Haddon Spurgeon replied, "O blessed epilepsy! Would that every man in London could have epilepsy like that!" Others suggest that Saul was hit by lightning. As he fell dazed to the ground, they say, he thought he heard a voice.

Throughout his life, Paul refers to this event many times, and the various descriptions of his conversion are always consistent. He saw the Lord Jesus, and this was the first of many occasions in which he saw the Lord. Paul based his claim to be an apostle on the fact that he had personally seen Jesus. He heard the Lord's voice, responded to the Lord's call, and was transformed into a mighty apostle to the Gentiles.

JESUS QUESTIONS SAUL

The Lord's first words to Saul are significant: "Saul, Saul, why do you persecute me?" This question forces Saul to think about the course of his life. I'm reminded of the question God asked Adam in the Garden of Eden on the fateful day when Adam fell. God came into the garden and called out, "Where are you?" (Genesis 3:9). If Adam would think through that question, he would find himself on the road back to God. You cannot know the way back until you know where you are.

This is still the first question God asks every lost soul: "Where are you in your life? Are you going in the wrong direction?" Once you answer that question, you can begin to find your way back home.

The Lord's question probes Saul's motivations: "Saul, why are you persecuting me? What is your motive for all the suffering you are causing? What do you hope to accomplish with all of this violence and terror? What drives you, Saul?" In the dark hours that followed his blinding encounter with the Lord, Saul of Tarsus probably asked himself many times, "Why did I do it? What drove me to such hatred and violence toward these 'people of the Way'?"

Next, Jesus says, "I am Jesus, whom you are persecuting. Now get up and go into the city, and you will be told what you must do." Here Jesus shows Saul that his approach to life is going to be turned upside down. Instead of capturing others, Saul is now captured. He is not his own man anymore. He has been bought with a price, and he will be told what to do.

Conversion is a radical transformation in your thinking and your will. Instead of running your own life, you acknowledge that God has the sovereign right to tell you what to do. This was the first change Saul experienced at the moment of his conversion. It was a change of government; the self had been dethroned and the Lord Jesus had ascended the throne. Saul now recognized the right of King Jesus to tell him what to do.

I once heard Major W. Ian Thomas, founder of Torchbearers International, describe Saul's mindset before and after his conversion on the Damascus road. Putting himself in Saul's place, Major Thomas said:

"When I, Saul of Tarsus, investigated the life of this man, Jesus of Nazareth, to see what this cult of Christians was all about, I looked first into his ancestry and discovered a cloud of illegitimacy over his birth. It was clear to me that this Jesus was the son of a faithless woman, born in a cave and laid in a borrowed manger. No one knew who his real father was, but he was raised as the son of a carpenter named Joseph. The family was of Galilean peasant stock, and the boy attended no schools. He had no rabbinical training; in fact, the rabbis and scribes all said he was nothing but a street preacher and a troublemaker.

"Furthermore, he owned no property or possessions and had no bank account. He lived in borrowed housing, ate food provided by friends, rode on a borrowed donkey, and when he died, was buried in a borrowed tomb. His net worth was zero. In the estimation of this world, the man was worth exactly nothing.

"But on the road to Damascus, I encountered this man. In a blinding flash, I looked into his face—and I saw the face of God. In that instant of time, I realized that the man I thought to be worth nothing was in fact the Lord of everything. And I saw myself in a whole new light. Before, I thought I was really something; suddenly I realized I was nothing. Everything I thought I knew was turned upside down. Later, I came to understand that though I was nothing, I could be filled with the One who is everything, and He would make something of my life."

I believe those words capture a sense of what Paul's thoughts must have been soon after his soul-shattering conversion on the road to Damascus.

SAUL THE DISCIPLE

Next, we see how the Lord Jesus prepares Saul for ministry, how He reclaims this man from the bitterness of his empty life and sets him on a path of service to God:

> In Damascus there was a disciple named Ananias. The Lord called to him in a vision, "Ananias!"
>
> "Yes, Lord," he answered.
>
> The Lord told him, "Go to the house of Judas on Straight Street and ask for a man from Tarsus named Saul, for he is praying. In a vision he has seen a man named Ananias come and place his hands on him to restore his sight."
>
> "Lord," Ananias answered, "I have heard many reports about this man and all the harm he has done to your saints in Jerusalem. And he has come here with authority from the chief priests to arrest all who call on your name."
>
> But the Lord said to Ananias, "Go! This man is my chosen instrument . . ." (Acts 9:10-15a)

Saul is now a Christian, and the first thing he experiences as a Christian is the life of the body of Christ. This is a wonderful insight. We see here that Jesus sends two previously unknown Christians to Saul: Judas and Ananias. We know nothing about Judas except that he owns a house on Straight Street and has opened his home to Saul. And we know little about Ananias except that God chose him to be a mentor and friend to Saul. God sent these two men into Saul's life, and Saul was discipled by them.

I don't believe it's an accident that the Holy Spirit chose these two men, with these particular names, to reach out to Saul. You may recall that, earlier in Acts, we have seen that both of these names, Judas and Ananias, have become tainted. In Acts 1, Judas was the betrayer of our Lord. And in Acts 5, a man named Ananias became the first Christian to manifest hypocrisy in the church. Here, in Acts 9, two people with the same names are honored and used by God to bring Saul, the future apostle Paul, into the fellowship of the church. Here the Holy Spirit redeems even the names of sinful men.

Ananias is understandably reluctant to go to Saul, because this man is infamous for dragging Christians off to their deaths. But the Lord reassures Ananias, telling him to go to Saul, "for he is praying." Prayer is a mark of a genuine believer. The Lord wants Ananias to be unafraid, so He tells Ananias that Saul, the former enemy of Christians, can now be trusted because he prays.

CALLED TO SUFFER

Next, God tells Ananias that Saul has been called to a specific ministry:

> But the Lord said to Ananias, "Go! This man is my chosen instrument to carry my name before the Gentiles and their kings and before the people of Israel. I will show him how much he must suffer for my name." (Acts 9:15-16)

Here God states two facts about the ministry of the apostle Paul. First, Paul's ministry will be manifested to three groups of people: the Gentiles, the pagan people of the non-Jewish nations; kings, the power structure of the first-century world; and the people of Israel. As we read Acts and the epistles of Paul, we will see that Paul had a great longing to minister to the Jews and felt equipped to do so, but he was not running the program anymore; God was. Though Paul had a great effect on the people of Israel, he was primarily the apostle to the Gentiles.

The second fact the Lord revealed was that Paul was called to suffer. The Lord said, "I will show him how much he must suffer for my name." The Christian life invariably involves suffering. Paul will later write to the Philippians and tell them that they were called not only to believe in Jesus but also to suffer for his name. Why is suffering a part of Christian life? Because suffering is the activity of love.

Love suffers. It bears the hurt and endures the shame. Anyone who is called to be a Christian is called to love. In this fallen world, there is no love without hurt. Paul cannot be the Lord's chosen instrument unless he accepts the call to suffering.

RENEWED VISION

Next, we see the obedience of Ananias and the effect that this man has on the life of the newly converted Saul:

> Then Ananias went to the house and entered it. Placing his hands on Saul, he said, "Brother Saul, the Lord—Jesus, who appeared to you on the road as you were coming here—has sent me so that you may see again and be filled with the Holy Spirit." Immediately, something like scales fell from Saul's eyes, and he could see again. He got up and was baptized, and after taking some food, he regained his strength. (Acts 9:17-19a)

Ananias laid his hands on Saul, and Saul was filled with the Holy Spirit. There were no tongues or other miraculous manifestations. There was simply a quiet infilling of the Holy Spirit, just as occurs today when a person believes in Jesus Christ. The Holy Spirit came to dwell in Saul and equip him to manifest the suffering love of Jesus Christ.

The only manifestation at that moment was that Saul's vision was changed. The scales fell from his eyes. I think this change in Saul's vision was both literal and symbolic. His eyes could see again, but even more important, the eyes of his soul could see as well. All of his deep-rooted prejudice against the Gentiles disappeared in a moment. He could suddenly see all of humanity, Jews and Gentiles, as a single human race, made in God's image and desperate for redemption.

After the scales fell from his eyes, Saul "got up and was baptized, and after taking some food, he regained his strength." By being baptized, Saul identified himself with Christ and with all who bear the name of Christ. God has now prepared His instrument to carry the gospel to the nations of the world. You and I have been blessed by the conversion of this man. His life has affected the world as few other lives ever have. Saul, this beloved enemy of the faith, was pursued by the Hound of Heaven down the nights and the days, down the arches of the years, down the labyrinthine ways of his own proud Pharisaic mind, until he was captured by love.

Saul, the apostle Paul, has shown us what God can do when we who are nothing are filled by Him who is everything. He calls us to love and to suffer and to influence our world with the story of His love and grace.

17

THE YOKE OF CHRIST

Acts 9:19b-31

Many people mistakenly think that Saul of Tarsus became the mighty apostle Paul during a single lightning-like encounter with Christ. Though Saul became a believer on the road to Damascus, he did not begin to live the fullness of the Christian life until years later. Saul of Tarsus had much to learn before he could become the apostle Paul.

Jesus told His disciples, "Come to me, all you who are weary and burdened, and I will give you rest" (Matthew 11:28). Then he added, "Take my yoke upon you and learn from me, for I am gentle and humble in heart, and you will find rest for your souls" (Matthew 11:29). Those verses describe two separate stages in Christian development. Verse 28 speaks of conversion, and it contains the simplest possible statement of the gospel: "Come to me." Come to Jesus, bring Him your guilt and problems, and He will give you rest. That is His invitation.

Then, in verse 29, He adds, "Take my yoke upon you and learn from me." Coming to Jesus takes away your sin and care, but He's not finished with you. You still need to learn to live like Christ. How? By taking His yoke upon you.

A yoke is a massive wooden tie-bar that fits over the necks of two oxen. By yoking the animals together, you make them work together to pull a load. To take on the yoke of Christ means to be tied together with Him in His work. As you work beside Jesus, with His yoke upon your neck, you discover what it means to live like Him.

Paul had to learn the Christian life. He had to wear the yoke of Christ and learn the Christian life, day by day, lesson by lesson. In the rest of Acts 9, we will watch Saul take the yoke of Christ upon himself so that he can become the dynamic apostle Paul.

THE EAGER YOUNG WITNESS

Luke continues his narrative of the post-conversion life of Saul:

> Saul spent several days with the disciples in Damascus. At once he began to preach in the synagogues that Jesus is the Son of God. All those who heard him were astonished and asked, "Isn't he the man who raised havoc in Jerusalem among those who call on this name? And hasn't he

come here to take them as prisoners to the chief priests?" (Acts 9:19b-21)

Following his blinding conversion on the road, Saul went to Damascus and stayed there for three days and nights. After Ananias came and prayed for him, Saul received his sight, was filled with the Holy Spirit, and was baptized. Then Saul immediately went out and enthusiastically proclaimed Jesus, saying, "He is the Son of God!" In other words, Saul announced that Jesus is Lord and He is God. He is the purpose behind all of life. Saul understood these truths in a flash of insight on the road to Damascus.

The lordship of Christ would remain the theme of Paul's life throughout his days. In his letter to the Philippians, written late in his life, Paul foresees a coming day when "at the name of Jesus every knee should bow, in heaven and on earth and under the earth, and every tongue confess that Jesus Christ is Lord, to the glory of God the Father" (Philippians 2:10-11). This is Paul's fundamental declaration: Jesus of Nazareth is the Lord of heaven and earth.

That's the gospel Paul preached from the time of his conversion to the day of his death. He wrote to the Romans, "If you confess with your mouth, 'Jesus is Lord,' and believe in your heart that God raised him from the dead, you will be saved" (Romans 10:9). Paul never preached that we should receive Jesus as Savior. He preached that we should accept Him as Lord. Only when He becomes Lord does He become Savior.

Next, Luke records Saul's spiritual growth as he takes the yoke of Jesus upon himself and learns what it means to be a follower of Christ:

Yet Saul grew more and more powerful and baffled the Jews living in Damascus by proving that Jesus is the Christ. (Acts 9:22)

"Christ" is the Greek word for "Messiah." Paul confounded the Jewish religious leaders in Damascus by proving from the Scriptures that Jesus of Nazareth was the Messiah. But Paul did not contend with the religious leaders at first. He did so only after another experience that Luke does not recount in Acts but that Paul recalled in one of his letters. There is a three-year gap between Acts 9:21 and Acts 9:22. What happened during those three years? Paul tells us in his letter to the Galatians:

For you have heard of my previous way of life in Judaism, how intensely I persecuted the church of God and tried to destroy it. I was advancing in Judaism beyond many Jews of my own age and was extremely zealous for the traditions of my fathers. But when God, who set me apart from birth and called me by his grace, was pleased to reveal his Son in me so that I might preach him among the Gentiles, I did not consult any man, nor did I go up to Jerusalem to see those who were apostles before I was, but I went immediately into Arabia and later returned to Damascus.

Then after three years, I went up to Jerusalem to get acquainted with Peter and stayed with him fifteen days. I saw none of the other apostles— only James, the Lord's brother. (Galatians 1:13-19)

Immediately after his conversion, Saul began to proclaim Jesus as Lord. But after a few days, Saul found it necessary to see how this good news squared with the truth of the Old Testament Scriptures. Taking the Scriptures under his arm, Saul went away into the Arabian desert. We don't know how long he was there; he doesn't tell us. But he was there long enough to search the Scriptures in light of his encounter on the Damascus road.

As Saul read the Old Testament, he saw Jesus Christ on every page. He discovered what so many others have discovered since: the Old Testament is as much about Christ as the New. The sacrifices and offerings are all pictures of the sacrifice of Jesus. The very configuration of the tabernacle is a picture of the life of Jesus. The Lord appears in symbols and pictures throughout the Old Testament in the books of Moses, in the Prophets, and in the Psalms.

As Saul studied, he probably wondered why Christ had arrested him in such dramatic fashion on the Damascus road. He came to a conclusion (the Bible doesn't say this explicitly, but it's implied in his letters) that God had selected him to go to the nation of Israel and show the Hebrew people from their own Scriptures that Jesus was the long-awaited Messiah.

Saul probably reasoned, "I am a Hebrew of the Hebrews, trained as a strict Pharisee, a scholar of the Scriptures from Genesis to Malachi! I have an intense desire to reach my people—so intense that I would wish myself cut off from Christ if it would help me reach my Jewish brothers! Who is better equipped than I to reach my people?"

Emerging from the Arabian desert, Saul returned to Damascus, confident that he could win his Jewish brethren by proving to them from the Scriptures that Jesus is the Messiah. He went to the synagogues and debated his Jewish brothers, His proof was irrefutable. He won every battle—

But he lost the war. He didn't win a single soul. He thought he could debate his fellow Jews into the kingdom, but he couldn't. The people listened to his arguments and had no answer for them, but still they remained locked in unbelief. In fact, Saul succeeded only in angering the people he sought to win.

THE MAN IN THE BASKET

Luke next records what resulted from Saul's disputes with the religious people in Damascus: They wanted to kill him.

After many days had gone by, the Jews conspired to kill him, but Saul learned of their plan. Day and night they kept close watch on the city gates in order to kill him. But his followers took him by night and lowered him in a basket through an opening in the wall. (Acts 9:23-25)

How humiliating. Here was Saul, eager to win the Jewish people to the Lord—and instead, he was rejected, forced to flee by being lowered in a basket through an opening in the city wall. He left Damascus in the dead of night, an utter failure.

Years later, Paul learned to view that humiliating night in a different way. He wrote, "If I must boast, I will boast of the things that show my weakness. . . . In Damascus the governor under King Aretas had the city of the Damascenes guarded in order to arrest me. But I was lowered in a basket from a window in the wall and slipped through his hands" (2 Corinthians 11:30-33). Isn't that amazing?

Paul says, in effect, "If you ask me what I will boast of, it's the time I was at my weakest, when I was lowered in a basket from a window in the city wall. That's when I learned a lesson in humility. That's when I discovered that God didn't want my ability, just my availability. He didn't need my knowledge. He wanted my obedience." During that basket ride, Saul's Pharisaic pride was choked to death, but it died hard, and not without a struggle. Luke records what happened next:

> When he came to Jerusalem, he tried to join the disciples, but they were all afraid of him, not believing that he really was a disciple. But Barnabas took him and brought him to the apostles. He told them how Saul on his journey had seen the Lord and that the Lord had spoken to him, and how in Damascus he had preached fearlessly in the name of Jesus. So Saul stayed with them and moved about freely in Jerusalem, speaking boldly in the name of the Lord. He talked and debated with the Grecian Jews, but they tried to kill him. (Acts 9:26-29)

After escaping from Damascus, Saul arrives in Jerusalem—and he's still determined to debate his opponents into the kingdom. He still thinks he can win people over by the power of his intellect. So God humbles him again. Not only do the Grecian Jews hate him and want to kill him, but even the Christians keep their distance from him.

Finally, Barnabas (the Son of Encouragement we met in Acts 4:36-37) takes Saul by the hand and leads him to where the apostles are gathered. Barnabas tells them about Saul's conversion and his bold preaching in Damascus.

During the next fifteen days, Saul stays in Jerusalem and goes from synagogue to synagogue, engaging in one argument after another, trying to prove to the Jews that Jesus is the Messiah. As in Damascus, Saul succeeds only in stirring up murderous hostility.

SAUL SEES JESUS AGAIN

During the fifteen days that Saul is in Jerusalem, he has another fascinating experience. This story is not recorded in Acts 9. Instead, we find it in Acts

22, where the apostle Paul has been arrested in Jerusalem and is addressing an angry mob:

> "When I returned to Jerusalem and was praying at the temple, I fell into a trance and saw the Lord speaking. 'Quick!' he said to me. 'Leave Jerusalem immediately, because they will not accept your testimony about me.'
>
> "'Lord,' I replied, 'these men know that I went from one synagogue to another to imprison and beat those who believe in you. And when the blood of your martyr Stephen was shed, I stood there giving my approval and guarding the clothes of those who were killing him.'
>
> "Then the Lord said to me, 'Go; I will send you far away to the Gentiles.'" (Acts 22:17-21)

Here, the Lord tells Saul to leave the city because the people have rejected his testimony. How does Saul respond? He argues. He says, in effect, "Lord, you don't understand! These people know that I used to persecute the church. They know I was there when Stephen was martyred. You're wrong, Lord. The people won't harm me. When they remember how I used to persecute the church, and they see how I've changed since I became a Christian, they'll listen to me. You'll see."

What nerve. Saul thinks he can even win over the Lord Jesus with his debating skills. But the Lord's reply is blunt: "Go!" In the original Greek, this expression is curt and forceful, as if Jesus is saying, "Move it! On the double! Get out of town!" And Jesus adds, "For I will send you far away to the Gentiles."

Jesus is saying, "I have a different program for you, Saul. You're not running your life any longer. I am—and I have something entirely different planned for you. Don't argue with me. Obey me. That's the only way I can work through you. Until you learn that, you will never be of any use to me."

So Saul stopped arguing and started obeying. Returning to Acts 9, we read:

> When the brothers learned of this, they took him down to Caesarea and sent him off to Tarsus (Acts 9:30).

Saul's fellow believers in Jerusalem helped him get out of town. They took him to Caesarea, where he could catch a boat to take him back to Tarsus. Then we read:

> Then the church throughout Judea, Galilee and Samaria enjoyed a time of peace. It was strengthened; and encouraged by the Holy Spirit, it grew in numbers, living in the fear of the Lord. (Acts 9:31)

If you read only the account in Acts 9, you would never understand these verses, would you? As you read through this chapter, it sounds as though Saul is being mightily used by God in Damascus and Jerusalem. It seems to come as a strange twist that Luke should add here that the church would have peace as soon as Saul got out of town. But when we add in these other Scripture passages, Acts 9 makes perfect sense.

We have here a young Christian, a new convert, full of all the zeal of the flesh. He is trying to do God's work in his own argumentative way, and all he does is stir up trouble. Many immature Christians are like that. They need to take the yoke of Christ upon them and learn from Him. What do they need to learn? Jesus said, "Learn from me, for I am gentle and humble in heart" (Matthew 11:29). Immature Christians need to temper their zeal with gentleness and humility. If we have zeal like Saul but lack the humility of Christ, we only get in the way of the gospel.

Saul had to learn this lesson. So, at the insistence of the Lord, Saul reluctantly left Jerusalem and headed home to Tarsus. He stayed there at least seven years and possibly as long as ten. During those years, he learned gentleness and humility.

At this point, Saul drops out of the narrative for a while. Near the end of Acts 11, a spiritual awakening takes place in Antioch. At that point, the Spirit of God leads Barnabas the Encourager to go to Tarsus, find Saul, and bring him to Antioch to take part in that revival. When Saul makes his next appearance, we will see that he is a changed man—humbled, chastened, and obedient to God.

How will we recognize this new Saul, this man who will soon become the mighty apostle Paul? We will recognize him by the yoke of Christ upon his neck.

18

THE CURE FOR DEATH

Acts 9:32–10:23a

We tend to think of death as something that lies far in our future—an event we can avoid facing for years and years. But we begin to die long before we take our last breath. Death is all one thing. Spiritual death, the inner death, can take the form of loneliness, boredom, bitterness, hate, malice, emptiness, depression, and despair. When sin entered the human race, death also entered in all of its forms.

God never intended for us to suffer physical death or spiritual death. The good news is that Jesus has abolished death in all its forms. He has come so that we might have abundant life, even in the valley of the shadow of death.

Near the end of his life, Paul wrote to Timothy from a prison in Rome. Looking back across the years of his ministry, he spoke of the coming of "our Savior, Christ Jesus, who has destroyed death and has brought life and immortality to light through the gospel" (2 Timothy 1:10). That is the central and unique fact of the gospel. Jesus has done what no one else could ever do: He has abolished death.

"JESUS CHRIST HEALS YOU!"

At this point in Acts 9, Saul has returned to Tarsus. There he will live in obscurity for a number of years.

Meanwhile, we return to the story of the apostle Peter. We find him where we left him, traveling among the churches in Judea and Samaria, preaching and ministering. Like all true Christians, Peter is a channel of the power of Jesus Christ to abolish death. There are three forms of death involved in the incidents we examine in Acts 9 and Acts 10. In each case, we'll see a different way that Jesus abolishes death.

First, we see that death has the power to paralyze. Luke writes:

As Peter traveled about the country, he went to visit the saints in Lydda. There he found a man named Aeneas, a paralytic who had been bedridden for eight years. "Aeneas," Peter said to him, "Jesus Christ heals you. Get up and take care of your mat." Immediately Aeneas got up. All those who lived in Lydda and Sharon saw him and turned to the Lord. (Acts 9:32-35)

THE CURE FOR DEATH

If you've ever visited Israel, you have probably been to Lydda. Ben Gurion International Airport, which serves Tel Aviv, is at the ancient town of Lydda, now called Lod. Peter came through Lydda on his way through Judea and Samaria, where Christian communities had sprung up. There Peter encountered Aeneas, a man who had been paralyzed for eight years. "Aeneas," Peter said, "Jesus Christ heals you. Get up and take care of your mat."

Peter does not claim to be a faith healer. He simply says, "Jesus Christ heals you." When Peter says those words as a servant of the Lord, the man is instantly well.

As we have seen before, physical miracles are visual parables that show us the kind of spiritual miracle God wants to perform in every human being. God still performs miraculous physical healings, but today as in New Testament days, miraculous healings are selective and rare. God does not heal everyone who is sick. He heals selectively, and His healings usually illustrate a spiritual truth.

Any physical healing is, at best, temporary. Everyone who was ever healed in the New Testament eventually died. Even Lazarus, who was raised from the dead, eventually died and was laid to rest in a tomb. Here, in Acts 9, we have a man named Aeneas who is paralyzed. For eight years, he has been unable to move. He suffers a paralysis of the body; we sometimes suffer a paralysis of the spirit when we rely on our own inadequate resources. That's the condition this story speaks to.

God wants to show us that Jesus Christ can heal us from the death-like paralysis of trying to live our lives our own way. He says to you and me, just as Peter said to Aeneas, "Jesus Christ heals you!" Now it's up to us to stand and be strong in His name.

DEATH AND RESTORATION

The next incident is even more dramatic. Here, Peter confronts not just paralysis but death itself:

> In Joppa there was a disciple named Tabitha (which, when translated, is Dorcas), who was always doing good and helping the poor. About that time she became sick and died, and her body was washed and placed in an upstairs room. Lydda was near Joppa; so when the disciples heard that Peter was in Lydda, they sent two men to him and urged him, "Please come at once!" (Acts 9:36-38)

Dorcas, a woman of selfless love, became sick and died. Her name, in Hebrew and Greek, means "gazelle." A gazelle is a beautiful, graceful, deer-like creature with captivating eyes. The fact that Luke makes a point of her name in Hebrew (Tabitha) and in Greek (Dorcas) suggests that her name underscored her gracious spirit. Death has snatched this woman's life from her, tragically cutting short her service to God and others. But death does not have the last word. Luke writes:

> Peter went with them, and when he arrived he was taken upstairs to the room. All the widows stood around him, crying and showing him the robes and other clothing that Dorcas had made while she was still with them.
>
> Peter sent them all out of the room; then he got down on his knees and prayed. Turning toward the dead woman, he said, "Tabitha, get up." She opened her eyes, and seeing Peter she sat up. He took her by the hand and helped her to her feet. Then he called the believers and the widows and presented her to them alive. This became known all over Joppa, and many people believed in the Lord. Peter stayed in Joppa for some time with a tanner named Simon. (Acts 9:39-43)

Like Lazarus, whom Jesus called forth from the grave, this woman has been restored from death and restored to a ministry of good works. But though she has been restored, she has not been resurrected. There's an important distinction. Dorcas has been made alive, but only temporarily. She will die again. Her restoration is a visual parable, intended to teach us a spiritual lesson: Death can interrupt a life that is beginning to flourish for God. People can lose their love for God and their desire to serve Him. When that happens, the spirit dies.

There are people around us who have been dead for years, though their body doesn't know it. They have a pulse and respiration, but they are spiritually lifeless, the very picture of death. Jesus, the Lord of Life, can heal a dead spirit and restore it to life.

THE HEALING OF PETER

The third incident in this section of Acts concerns a healing in the spirit of the apostle Peter. It begins with another man who is living twenty-seven miles up the coast from Joppa, in the Roman garrison headquarters at Caesarea. Luke writes:

> At Caesarea there was a man named Cornelius, a centurion in what was known as the Italian Regiment. He and all his family were devout and God-fearing; he gave generously to those in need and prayed to God regularly. One day at about three in the afternoon he had a vision. He distinctly saw an angel of God, who came to him and said, "Cornelius!" Cornelius stared at him in fear. "What is it, Lord?" he asked.
>
> The angel answered, "Your prayers and gifts to the poor have come up as a memorial offering before God. Now send men to Joppa to bring back a man named Simon who is called Peter. He is staying with Simon the tanner, whose house is by the sea."

When the angel who spoke to him had gone, Cornelius called two of his servants and a devout soldier who was one of his attendants. He told them everything that had happened and sent them to Joppa. (Acts 10:1-8)

This is one of the most significant events in the book of Acts. Here, for the first time, we have an account of the gospel going out to a Gentile household. This Gentile, Cornelius, was a centurion in the Roman army. As a centurion (a captain over a hundred men), he was a logical, military-minded man. His fellow centurions were cruel and profane, but Cornelius was a devout and generous man who prayed to the one true God.

Cornelius was not yet saved. He did not know Jesus as his Lord. Many people think that sincerity is all we need to be saved. Cornelius was sincere, but he was not born again. His heart was ready, but he had not yet received Christ.

This story answers the question I'm asked more often than any other, especially by non-Christians: "What about those who have never heard of Jesus?" We see that Cornelius had received some light and was faithful to the light he had received. So God gave Cornelius more light and led him to a man who could introduce him to Jesus.

The Book of Hebrews tells us, "And without faith it is impossible to please God, because anyone who comes to him must believe that he exists and that he rewards those who earnestly seek him" (Hebrews 11:6). Note those two qualifications: Those who come to God must believe that He exists and that He rewards those who seek Him. You see this principle in the life of Cornelius. This Roman soldier believed that God existed. He had forsaken the pagan gods of the Romans and was seeking to live a godly life. So God sent help to Cornelius.

Notice that while God sent an angel, He didn't have the angel preach the gospel to Cornelius. Angels are not commissioned to evangelize the human race. Only human beings may do that. God sent the angel to tell Cornelius where he could find a man to share the gospel with him.

The arrival of the angel frightened Cornelius, and that's understandable. The angel told him to send to Joppa for a man named Peter. So Cornelius sent two servants and a soldier to Joppa. Luke recounts what happened next:

About noon the following day as they were on their journey and approaching the city, Peter went up on the roof to pray. He became hungry and wanted something to eat, and while the meal was being prepared, he fell into a trance. He saw heaven opened and something like a large sheet being let down to earth by its four corners. It contained all kinds of four-footed animals, as well as reptiles of the earth and birds of the air. Then a voice told him, "Get up, Peter. Kill and eat."

"Surely not, Lord!" Peter replied. "I have never eaten anything impure or unclean."

The voice spoke to him a second time, "Do not call anything impure that God has made clean."

This happened three times, and immediately the sheet was taken back to heaven. (Acts 10:9-16)

Why did God give Peter this vision? Because Peter needed healing. God wanted to heal the death in Peter's spirit—the death of prejudice and bigotry. Here was Peter—an apostle, filled with the Holy Spirit—yet he had a huge blind spot of bigotry in his soul.

Peter understood that God had chosen the Jews to be a special people. However, Peter had mistakenly concluded that God had chosen the Jews because they were somehow superior to the Gentiles. He thought that God had rejected the Gentiles, and so should he.

To cure Peter of bigotry, God sent him a vision of sheets filled with animals that Peter was taught were unclean. In the vision, God commanded Peter to rise, kill, and eat. Peter protested, saying (in the King James Version), "Not so, Lord; for I have never eaten anything that is common or unclean." Notice Peter's legalistic mindset. He says, "I have never eaten anything impure or unclean." The words "I have never" are the words of a legalist. Peter is proud of his negative morality.

Though moral purity is important to our Christian walk, we shouldn't define ourselves primarily by our negatives, by what we refuse to do. The grace of God is made manifest in us by our positive way of life, our love for God and others, our joy, our inner peace. The world is neither impressed nor attracted by the negative rules we keep.

Peter is proud of his legalism—and God rebukes him for his pride. When Peter says, "I have never eaten anything impure or unclean," the Lord says, "Do not call anything impure that God has made clean." That's the lesson Peter needed to learn.

I have sometimes counseled people who can't forgive themselves. They say, "What I did was so horrible God can never forgive me." I have counseled people who can't forgive others. They say, "I will never forgive what she said." My answer in either case is, "Do not call anything impure that God has made clean." It grieves the heart of God when we brand any of His children, including ourselves, as unclean, unacceptable, or unforgivable.

THE STUBBORNNESS OF PETER

It's significant that the vision had to be shown to Peter three times. Perhaps it was shown to him three times as a stamp of the full authority of the Trinity upon this revelation. Father, Son, and Holy Spirit all said, "We agree on this.

Put an end to your bigotry, Peter. Don't call impure what the Father, Son, and Holy Spirit have made clean!" Or it may have been a subtle reminder that God accepted and forgave Peter after his three denials of the Lord Jesus before the crucifixion. In any case, God underscored his lesson to Peter through three experiences of this vision.

In the early 1970s, when Dr. Hudson Armerding was president of Wheaton College, he stood up in chapel and addressed the student body regarding a dilemma he faced. He said that many of the financial supporters of the school were upset because they had visited the campus and had seen a number of young men with long hair and beards—so-called hippies. Many donors felt that the school, in allowing so many hippies to enroll, had compromised its values. Donations were down, and the school was in a financial bind.

Dr. Armerding called a young man out of the audience. The young man had the longest hair and beard of anyone in the student body. He walked up to the platform, and Dr. Armerding said, "Young man, everyone can see that you represent the very thing these donors oppose. But I want you to know that the administration of this college does not agree with their view. We believe you're here to seek a deeper understanding of Jesus Christ and His truth. We love you, and we accept you."

The college president embraced the young man—and the students stood and cheered for their president's bold expression of love and acceptance.

Jesus came to break down the walls of partition between God and humanity and between people of different races, cultures, and generations. Our Lord said, "He who is not with me is against me, and he who does not gather with me, scatters" (Luke 11:23). We can judge our lives by that statement. What is our effect on others? Are we gathering? Or are we scattering? Are we reconciling? Or are we dividing?

The great lesson God taught the apostle Peter was that He accepted the Gentiles—and Peter should accept them, too. Luke records Peter's response to the vision:

> While Peter was wondering about the meaning of the vision, the men sent by Cornelius found out where Simon's house was and stopped at the gate. They called out, asking if Simon who was known as Peter was staying there.
>
> While Peter was still thinking about the vision, the Spirit said to him, "Simon, three men are looking for you. So get up and go downstairs. Do not hesitate to go with them, for I have sent them."
>
> Peter went down and said to the men, "I'm the one you're looking for. Why have you come?"
>
> The men replied, "We have come from Cornelius the centurion. He is a righteous and God-fearing man, who is respected by all the Jewish

people. A holy angel told him to have you come to his house so that he could hear what you have to say." Then Peter invited the men into the house to be his guests. (Acts 10:17-23a)

The barriers are crumbling. Peter now invites these Gentiles to be his guests. That's the first step. He had never done anything like that before. Peter is learning to speak the language of liberty. Legalism says, "I have never . . ." But true liberty in Christ says, "I can do what I've never done before!" Peter has been healed of his bigotry.

God seeks to remove every trace of prejudice from our lives. Whether we are Gentiles or Jews, whites, blacks, browns, or any other color under the sun, we are all members of one human race. We all need the redeeming grace of our Lord Jesus Christ.

19

LIFE FOR ALL

Acts 10:23b–11:18

The young man was a stranger to the church. He felt empty and despondent, and he knew something was missing from his life. So his footsteps led him to our church one Sunday morning.

I was speaking from 1 Corinthians that day. As I reading the Scripture text, I came to these words: "Do you not know that the wicked will not inherit the kingdom of God? Do not be deceived: Neither the sexually immoral nor idolaters nor adulterers nor male prostitutes nor homosexual offenders nor thieves nor the greedy nor drunkards nor slanderers nor swindlers will inherit the kingdom of God. And that is what some of you were" (1 Corinthians 6:9-11a).

I felt moved to interrupt. I looked out over the congregation and said, "How many of you identify with these words? How many have ever been guilty of sins listed here? Sexual immorality? Idolatry? Adultery? Homosexuality? Theft? Greed? Drunkenness? Slander? Swindling?" All over the congregation, hundreds of hands went up.

The young man came up to me later and said, "When I saw all those hands go up, I thought to myself, 'These are my kind of people!'"

"And that is what some of you were," Paul said—but Jesus Christ has cleansed us and made us acceptable to God. Let no one call impure whom God has made clean.

ONLY A MAN

We've seen God respond to the prayer of Cornelius, sending an angel to him with a message to send for a man named Peter. Meanwhile, God is working on the heart of Peter, removing his prejudice and preparing him to take the good news of Jesus to a man he would have once called unclean. Luke continues the narrative:

> The next day Peter started out with them, and some of the brothers from Joppa went along. The following day he arrived in Caesarea. Cornelius was expecting them and had called together his relatives and close friends. As Peter entered the house, Cornelius met him and fell at his feet in reverence. But Peter made him get up. "Stand up," he said, "I am only a man myself."
>
> Talking with him, Peter went inside and found a large gathering of people. He said to them: "You are well aware that it is against our law

for a Jew to associate with a Gentile or visit him. But God has shown me that I should not call any man impure or unclean. So when I was sent for, I came without raising any objection. May I ask why you sent for me?" (Acts 10:23b-29)

This passage contains details that mark it as an authentic account of an actual event. When Peter entered Cornelius's house, the proud Roman centurion fell at Peter's feet and worshiped him. It's remarkable that a member of the imperial military force would fall at the feet of one of the conquered people. But Cornelius was so hungry for the truth and so deeply moved by the angel's visit that he believes this Jew must be worthy of worship.

Embarrassed, Peter helps Cornelius to his feet. "Stand up," he says. "I am only a man myself." Peter refused the man's homage, because worship is for God alone.

Peter is uneasy entering the house of a Gentile. He feels he must explain his action, saying, "You are well aware that it is against our law for a Jew to associate with a Gentile or visit him." Peter was citing human law, not God's law. God never prohibited Jews from associating with Gentiles. The Jews had adopted those rules on their own.

Peter then tells Cornelius of the lesson God taught him about the sin of prejudice: "But God has shown me that I should not call any man impure or unclean. So when I was sent for, I came without raising any objection."

THE FIRST HOME BIBLE STUDY

Cornelius replies, telling his side of the story:

Cornelius answered: "Four days ago I was in my house praying at this hour, at three in the afternoon. Suddenly a man in shining clothes stood before me and said, 'Cornelius, God has heard your prayer and remembered your gifts to the poor. Send to Joppa for Simon who is called Peter. He is a guest in the home of Simon the tanner, who lives by the sea.' So I sent for you immediately, and it was good of you to come. Now we are all here in the presence of God to listen to everything the Lord has commanded you to tell us." (Acts 10:30-33)

It's interesting to note what has happened in these verses: Cornelius has invented the home Bible study! He has gathered friends and relatives to his house, and in that culture, a gathering of people always means food and hospitality. When Peter arrived, he found a house filled with people, all eager to hear the Word of the Lord.

In our church, we have encouraged home Bible studies for years, and they have followed this very format: People open their homes, gather friends and neighbors, serve refreshments, and have someone lead a study in God's Word.

These home Bible studies have been a powerful means of witness and outreach, and in two thousand years, the format has remained essentially unchanged.

This gathering is an answer to the prayers of Cornelius. When we first met him, we're told that he and his family "were devout and God-fearing; he gave generously to those in need and prayed to God regularly" (Acts 10:2). What did he pray for? No doubt, he prayed for a deeper understanding of God's truth. With the arrival of Peter, his prayer is being answered.

Some people say that God doesn't hear the prayers of non-Christians. This account shows that He does. Cornelius was religious but not a Christian. God hears every honest and sincere prayer, even the prayers of those who are not yet in a relationship with Him.

Now we come to Peter's message, which is the reason the Holy Spirit has brought Peter and Cornelius together. Luke records:

> Then Peter began to speak: "I now realize how true it is that God does not show favoritism but accepts men from every nation who fear him and do what is right." (Acts 10:34-35)

Peter begins by stating that God shows no favoritism. The Lord receives all who come to Him, regardless of background, social class, or station in life. God does not favor one race over another or one individual over another. He is impartial.

Note what Peter says: God "accepts men from every nation who fear him and do what is right." Don't misread that. Peter is not saying that this is all that God asks of people. Peter is noting that God recognizes an honest heart and a receptive attitude, and Cornelius has that. But Cornelius was not yet saved. Peter continues:

> "You know the message God sent to the people of Israel, telling the good news of peace through Jesus Christ, who is Lord of all. You know what has happened throughout Judea, beginning in Galilee after the baptism that John preached—how God anointed Jesus of Nazareth with the Holy Spirit and power, and how he went around doing good and healing all who were under the power of the devil, because God was with him." (Acts 10:36-38)

Peter explains the story of the incarnation: Jesus came as a man through whom God worked in love and power. He came to show us how a human being can live in utter dependence upon God. We cannot be fully human, as God intended us to be, until God dwells in us and lives His life through us. That's what Jesus came to show us.

Notice too that Peter does not preach Jesus as Savior. He preaches Jesus as Lord. Only when Jesus becomes Lord does He become our Savior.

"WHAT DID YOU DO WITH JESUS?"

Next, Peter says:

> "He went around doing good and healing all who were under the power
> of the devil, because God was with him.
>   "We are witnesses of everything he did in the country of the Jews and
> in Jerusalem." (Acts 10:38b-39a)

When Jesus Christ arrived, He destroyed the effects of evil and sin every-where He went. He did these works openly, before witnesses, where everyone could see. He came to a world that was lost, and He liberated people from Satan's power. Though our world seems darker than ever before, Jesus still sets people free and gives hope to hopeless men and women. Next, Peter tells the story of Good Friday:

> "They killed him by hanging him on a tree." (Acts 10:39b)

Peter does not want to dwell on that day—and who can blame him? The death of the Lord came after Peter had denied Him three times. It was the worst day of the apostle's life. So he simply says, "They killed Him by hanging Him on a tree."

Jesus was killed by the most shameful means possible. Even the Romans recognized this fact. Cicero, the Roman orator, said, "The cross is so terrible that it should not be mentioned in polite company." Jesus, who did nothing but good, was killed in the cruelest way imaginable. Next, Peter says:

> "But God raised him from the dead on the third day and caused him to
> be seen. He was not seen by all the people, but by witnesses whom God
> had already chosen—by us who ate and drank with him after he rose from
> the dead." (Acts 10:40-41)

Peter says, "God raised Jesus from the dead—and I'm an eyewitness, one of many eyewitnesses. Not only did I see Him, but also I ate and drank with Him." That is impressive testimony. The resurrected Lord Jesus was not a ghost but a physical man in a new kind of body—a resurrection body. Peter under-scored the fact that the resurrected Jesus is the Lord of life and the answer to death in all its forms. He then went on to say:

> "He commanded us to preach to the people and to testify that he is the
> one whom God appointed as judge of the living and the dead." (Acts
> 10:42)

This, says Peter, is good news that goes out to all people: Jesus is not dead. He is alive, and He shall judge every human being, living and dead, saved and unsaved, condemned and redeemed. He is the inescapable One. He stands in the path of every human being who has ever been born or will be born. We must all answer the question, "What did you do with Jesus?"

THE SPIRIT INTERRUPTS PETER
Finally, Peter says:

> "All the prophets testify about him that everyone who believes in him receives forgiveness of sins through his name." (Acts 10:43)

Speaking to a Gentile audience, Peter says, in other words, "You Romans may not appreciate this fully, but everything Jesus did was predicted by the prophets. Long before He came to us in human form, the prophets bore witness to one fact: The only way to be forgiven of sin is through faith in Him."

That's the good news that all human beings, whether Jew or Gentile, long to hear. We are guilty people, and that's why we can't stand to be alone with ourselves. Guilt oppresses us. The basic need of our lives is forgiveness—and Jesus alone makes forgiveness possible. No one should take forgiveness for granted and make it a license to sin. But if you are born again, you have received the greatest blessing of your life. You can wake up every morning and know you are accepted as a beloved child of the King.

Peter had intended to continue, but at this point an interruption occurs:

> While Peter was still speaking these words, the Holy Spirit came on all who heard the message. The circumcised believers who had come with Peter were astonished that the gift of the Holy Spirit had been poured out even on the Gentiles. For they heard them speaking in tongues and praising God.
>
> Then Peter said, "Can anyone keep these people from being baptized with water? They have received the Holy Spirit just as we have." So he ordered that they be baptized in the name of Jesus Christ. Then they asked Peter to stay with them for a few days. (Acts 10:44-48)

The Holy Spirit interrupted Peter, just as He interrupted Peter's sermon on the day of Pentecost. Why did the Spirit interrupt the apostle? Notice Peter's words: "Everyone who believes in him receives forgiveness of sins through his name." Luke then records, "While Peter was still speaking these words, the Holy Spirit came on all who heard the message." Peter said that those who believe in Jesus receive forgiveness of sins—and the moment the people heard that, they believed! The instant they believed, they received the Holy Spirit, just as Jesus had promised they would:

> On the last and greatest day of the Feast, Jesus stood and said in a loud voice, "If anyone is thirsty, let him come to me and drink. Whoever believes in me, as the Scripture has said, streams of living water will flow

from within him." By this he meant the Spirit, whom those who believed in him were later to receive. Up to that time the Spirit had not been given, since Jesus had not yet been glorified. (John 7:37-39)

The moment the friends and family of Cornelius heard, they believed. And the moment they believed, they received. The Spirit didn't wait. He descended upon all who were gathered there. As on the day of Pentecost, the sign of the coming of the Holy Spirit was the gift of tongues. This was proof that the Gentiles had been received into the body of Christ on the same basis as the Jews.

Peter said, "Can anyone keep these people from being baptized with water? They have received the Holy Spirit just as we have." The first Gentile believers spoke in tongues not because tongues are always essential to receiving the Spirit but to demonstrate to the Jews that these Gentiles were equally accepted into the body.

The gift of tongues that we see here is the same gift given on the day of Pentecost. The believers spoke languages that were spoken on earth and were not addressed to people. They were tongues of praise to God. The tongues were demonstrated publicly, for the common good, not in private. They were a sign to unbelievers, not believers.

Who were the unbelievers on this occasion? The Jewish Christians who accompanied Peter. You may say, "What? How can they be Christians and still be unbelievers?" Well, they were what I would call unbelieving believers. They had a saving faith in Jesus Christ, but they didn't believe that the gospel was for the Gentiles. In order to convince these unbelieving believers, God gave the gift of tongues to the newly converted Gentiles as a sign that God had accepted them on the same basis as the Jewish Christians.

Peter ordered that the new believers be baptized in the name of Jesus Christ. Notice that the baptism of the Holy Spirit does not do away with the baptism of water. The water baptism is a symbol of the baptism by the Spirit.

THE SPIRIT INTERRUPTS PETER—AGAIN!

The next section shows what happens when truth collides with prejudice:

The apostles and the brothers throughout Judea heard that the Gentiles also had received the word of God. So when Peter went up to Jerusalem, the circumcised believers criticized him and said, "You went into the house of uncircumcised men and ate with them."

Peter began and explained everything to them precisely as it had happened: "I was in the city of Joppa praying, and in a trance I saw a vision. I saw something like a large sheet being let down from heaven by its four corners, and it came down to where I was. I looked into it and saw four-footed animals of the earth, wild beasts, reptiles, and birds of the air. Then I heard a voice telling me, 'Get up, Peter. Kill and eat.'

"I replied, 'Surely not, Lord! Nothing impure or unclean has ever entered my mouth.'" (Acts 11:1-8)

Peter had to face the same prejudiced attitudes that he once held. He found himself in conflict with Christians who could not believe that the gospel was meant for the Gentiles as well as the Jews. So Peter told these prejudiced Christians how God had overcome his own prejudice.

That's the way to answer arguments: Tell people what God has done in your life. When Peter's opponents heard what God had done in Peter's life, there was nothing more that they could say. Faith always rests on what God has done.

Peter had learned a lesson that would soon transform the world: Jesus, the Lord of Life, died and rose again to bring new life to the Jews, new life to the Gentiles—

New life for all!

20

EXPANDING HORIZONS

Acts 11:19-30

Question: When did the gospel first go out to the Gentiles?

If you think it was when Philip shared the gospel with the Ethiopian eunuch, you'd be wrong. If you think it was when Peter shared the gospel with the Roman centurion, Cornelius, and his family, you'd be wrong again.

So when did God first break through this rigid cultural barrier toward the Gentiles? When did the Jewish Christians first take the gospel to the Gentiles? We find the answer here, in Acts 11. Luke writes:

> Now those who had been scattered by the persecution in connection with Stephen traveled as far as Phoenicia, Cyprus and Antioch, telling the message only to Jews. Some of them, however, men from Cyprus and Cyrene, went to Antioch and began to speak to Greeks also, telling them the good news about the Lord Jesus. (Acts 11:19-20)

It's not easy for a writer to relate a number of events that occur at different places at about the same time. It's hard to place these events in chronological order. If you read carefully what Luke is saying, you see that he is backtracking to the days immediately following the death of Stephen, when a great persecution broke out against the Christians.

Some of the Christians—Grecian Jewish Christians who had originally come from Cyprus and Cyrene—went to Antioch. There, these Greek-speaking Jewish Christians told the Greeks the good news of Jesus Christ. This took place shortly after Pentecost, before Philip's encounter with the Ethiopian or Peter's encounter with Cornelius. So the gospel began to penetrate the Gentile world almost from the beginning, and it was carried into the Gentile world by men and women whose names are not recorded.

BARNABAS GOES TO ANTIOCH

Next, Luke records what took place as the gospel was preached far and wide, and the church grew in numbers and geographical extent:

> The Lord's hand was with them, and a great number of people believed and turned to the Lord.
> News of this reached the ears of the church at Jerusalem, and they sent Barnabas to Antioch. When he arrived and saw the evidence of the

grace of God, he was glad and encouraged them all to remain true to the Lord with all their hearts. He was a good man, full of the Holy Spirit and faith, and a great number of people were brought to the Lord. (Acts 11:21-24)

Many people, including Gentiles, came to Christ. The disciples at Jerusalem didn't know what to do about this movement of the Holy Spirit. Since they were Jews, raised as God's chosen people, they were skeptical of any outreach to the Gentiles. News of so many Gentile converts was troubling. Was it possible that Gentiles could come to Christ just as a Jew could? It hardly seemed possible.

To settle the issue, the disciples at Jerusalem sent Barnabas to Antioch. They couldn't have made a better choice than big-hearted Barnabas. He didn't go to Antioch to control what the Spirit was doing. He went to understand this new movement of the Spirit. Barnabas was a Greek-speaking Jew from Cyprus, so he could identify with the Christians from Cyprus and Cyrene who were preaching to the Greeks.

Antioch was a strategic city, the third largest in the Roman Empire. It was a hub of sports competition (the chariot race in the novel *Ben Hur* by Lew Wallace was set in Antioch). The city was also a hub of pagan religion. About five miles outside the city was the temple of Daphne, where sex was worshiped through temple prostitutes. The new church in Antioch arose in the midst of this culture of corruption. Luke tells us that Barnabas was chosen to go to Antioch for three reasons: he was a good man, full of the Spirit and full of faith.

The fact that Barnabas was a good man means that he had a cheerful disposition, an encourager's heart. Being "full of the Holy Spirit" was the supreme qualification. The fruit of the Spirit was evident in his life; he demonstrated qualities of love, joy, patience, and gentleness. Being "full of faith" means that Barnabas acted in trust upon what God said to be true.

What did Barnabas find when he came to Antioch? He found men and women who were undoubtedly Christians. "When he arrived and saw the evidence of the grace of God, he was glad and encouraged them all to remain true to the Lord with all their heart." What convinced Barnabas that they were genuine Christians? He saw the grace of God.

How do you see grace? Isn't grace an invisible quality? Not necessarily. Grace is the goodness of God poured out upon a human life—and the grace of God is always visibly manifested in the life of a genuine believer in specific ways.

In the original Greek, the word for "grace" is *charis*, from which we get the English word *charisma*. It's the same word Paul employs when he speaks of the gifts of the Spirit: "But to each one of us grace has been given as Christ apportioned it" (Ephesians 4:7). The grace Paul refers to is one of the gifts mentioned in Romans 12 and 1 Corinthians 12.

When Barnabas saw the gifts of the Spirit being used in Antioch, he knew that these were genuine Christians. The Book of Hebrews tells us that the reality of salvation is confirmed in several ways, including by "gifts of the Holy Spirit distributed according to his will" (Hebrews 2:4). So the possession of the gifts is a sign of authentic Christianity. Barnabas saw the gifts in use, and he was glad.

BARNABAS ENCOURAGES THE BELIEVERS

Luke tells us that Barnabas spoke to the believers in Antioch, encouraging them to remain true to the Lord with all their hearts. In the original Greek, the sense of Barnabas's words was, "Remain faithful to the Lord with a steadfast purpose, with a set plan."

The Christians in Antioch were not simply to come to church and enjoy the fellowship. They were to seek a deeper knowledge of Jesus Christ and His Word. They were to study the Scriptures, because the Scriptures reveal Christ. Whenever a new challenge or crisis came their way, they were to turn to Him in prayer, not as a last resort but as a first response. New Christians need to learn these principles, and Barnabas wisely instructed them in these principles.

Many new Christians come to Christ and enjoy the fellowship and excitement of being a Christian. But gradually their mindset shifts. They start focusing on feelings and circumstances instead of Jesus. If the excitement they felt in their early Christian experience wears off, they begin to doubt that their relationship with Christ was real. If they encounter difficult circumstances, they doubt God's guidance. It's dangerous to take our eyes off of Jesus and focus on feelings and circumstances.

We see this principle in the life of Peter. In Matthew 14, Peter and the other disciples were in their boat in the middle of a stormy night. They saw Jesus coming toward them, walking on the water. Peter said, "Lord, if it's you, tell me to come to you on the water." Jesus invited Peter to come. So Peter got out of the boat and began walking. As long as he kept his eyes on Jesus, he could walk on water.

But then Peter took his eyes off of Jesus. He looked at the wind and the waves (his circumstances), and he became aware of his fear (his feelings), and he began to sink. "Lord, save me!" he called—and Jesus reached him and pulled him out of the water. "You of little faith," Jesus said, "why did you doubt?"

That's exactly what happens to us whenever we stop focusing on Jesus and start focusing on our circumstances and our feelings. We sink! Some new Christians become discouraged and fall away from the faith. Barnabas wants to guard them against this risk, so he urges the believers in Antioch to remain faithful to the Lord.

Luke tells us that after Barnabas encouraged the church in Antioch, "a great number of people were brought to the Lord." When people look to the Lord and not to themselves or their circumstances, wonderful things happen: People are brought to the Lord. That's God's plan for increasing the church.

Many churches make the mistake of trying to increase the church through programs and campaigns. The harder we try to increase the church through human effort, the more the church seems to decline. The way to grow the church is to become the kind of people He wants us to be. If we demonstrate Christlike love and acceptance for one another, if we exercise the gifts of the Spirit, if we focus on Christ and not on our feelings and circumstances, then the world will beat a path to our door. People will demand to know why we love one another so. That's how the church increases.

THE RE-EMERGENCE OF SAUL OF TARSUS

Next, Barnabas brings Saul of Tarsus back to the forefront of Acts:

> Then Barnabas went to Tarsus to look for Saul. (Acts 11:25)

Luke has just told us, "A great number of people were brought to the Lord," and then he said, "Then Barnabas went to Tarsus to look for Saul." The church in Antioch had grown dramatically, and the new believers needed to be discipled and taught. So Barnabas went to Tarsus to get Saul. Luke records what happened next:

> And when he found him, he brought him to Antioch. So for a whole year Barnabas and Saul met with the church and taught great numbers of people. The disciples were called Christians first at Antioch. (Acts 11:26)

Saul has been gone for seven to ten years. As a new convert, he was constantly getting into heated debates with the religious leaders, trying to convince them from the Scriptures that Jesus was the long-awaited Messiah. He stirred up so much hostility in Damascus and Jerusalem that his opponents sought to kill him.

But during his exile in Tarsus, Saul learned a great deal. In his letter to the Galatians, he tells us that he was not idle during that time. He preached God's Word throughout the regions of Syria and Cilicia, near Tarsus. This way, he sharpened his preaching skills while God knocked some of the rough edges off his character. During that time he also experienced visions and revelations from the Lord, which he mentions in several of his letters.

After Saul had spent time learning and growing more spiritually mature, the Lord sent Barnabas to Tarsus to find him. When Barnabas found Saul, he brought him to Antioch to begin a ministry that would ultimately change the course of human history.

A TERM OF DERISION

Luke notes that the disciples were first called Christians at Antioch (Acts 11:26). It's clear that the term *Christian* was not coined by the Christians but by the people of the surrounding culture. Before the term came into use, the believers called themselves disciples, saints, or brothers and sisters.

The Greek term *Christianos* (Christian) meant "those belonging to Christ," or "the Messiah's men." The people who mockingly used this term didn't believe that Jesus was the Messiah, the Christ, so "Christian" was originally a term of contempt. The people of Antioch said, in effect, "Look at these crazy people! They reject our gods and worship a crucified god instead. They don't enjoy the temple prostitutes as we do but live by a strange moral code. Yet they seem more joyful than we are, even with our hedonistic pleasures. These 'Messiah's men,' these 'Christians,' are out of touch with reality."

But the disciples thought it was wonderful to be called "the Messiah's men." So they adopted the name and called themselves Christians—and the Lord's followers have been called Christians ever since.

During the Jesus People years of the late 1960s and early 1970s, I spoke at a student meeting in a large house just off the UCLA campus. When I arrived, I noticed a number of students on the porch of the house, busily at work. Those students, members of the Christian World Liberation Front, had set up an assembly line. At one end of the line, they had stacks of blue denim work shirts. The shirts were passed to someone who placed them in an aluminum silk-screening frame. The shirts were printed with words, then handed to other people who hung them on clotheslines to dry. The printed shirts read:

I AM ANOTHER JESUS FREAK

The term *freak* came from the hippie drug culture. LSD users were called acid freaks, amphetamine users were called speed freaks, and so forth. As the Jesus People witnessed on campuses and held Jesus Music concerts, people in the hippie culture called them Jesus Freaks—people who were high on Jesus. It was a term of ridicule. (Remember Elton John's song about Jesus Freaks in the streets "handing tickets out for God"?)

The Jesus Freaks didn't mind being mocked. In fact, they adopted the label proudly! They wore the slogan "I am another Jesus Freak" on their backs. Years later, the Christian rock band DC Talk released an album boldly titled *Jesus Freak*. As the Christians at Antioch gladly claimed the title Christian, many Christians today call themselves Jesus Freaks to show they are not ashamed of Christ.

The example of the Christians in Antioch speaks across the centuries: We count it a privilege to endure reproach for the sake of the Lord Jesus Christ.

A PROPHETIC WORD

The chapter closes with this touching scene:

> During this time some prophets came down from Jerusalem to Antioch. One of them, named Agabus, stood up and through the Spirit predicted that a severe famine would spread over the entire Roman world. (This happened during the reign of Claudius.) The disciples, each according to his ability, decided to provide help for the brothers living in Judea. This they did, sending their gift to the elders by Barnabas and Saul. (Acts 11:27-30)

Here we see one of the gifts of the Spirit in action—the gift of prophecy. Many people associate prophecy with the ability to predict the future. But that's not the primary meaning of the word in the original language. "Prophecy" means "to cause to shine." It's the ability to illuminate the Word of God.

These prophets who came down from Jerusalem could take the Word of God and make it shine. They illuminated the darkness in people's lives with the truth of God. Occasionally they could illuminate the future, as we see here, but foretelling the future is not what prophecy is primarily about.

On this occasion, a prophet named Agabus stood up and, by the Spirit, predicted a great famine. This prophecy was fulfilled a few months later. Not only does Josephus, the Jewish historian, record this famine, but two Roman historians speak of it as well. According to Suetonius and Tacitus, this great famine took place during the days of Claudius. We can positively date this famine as taking place in A.D. 44-45.

When the Holy Spirit told Agabus and the other prophets from Jerusalem about the coming famine, the Christians believed the Spirit and began to prepare for the famine. They realized that the famine would be especially severe in Judea, so they prepared to send a gift to Judea. They had to begin before the famine came because they couldn't write a check. They needed time to make and sell a product—some wheat or vegetables they had raised or a tent or pottery they had made—and send the proceeds to Judea.

This account gives us a beautiful picture of the concern these Christians had for the entire body. The believers in Antioch wanted to meet the needs of the Christians in Judea, so they raised the money and sent it with their two favorite teachers, Barnabas and Saul, who had ministered among them for a year. They understood the essential principle of the church: the life of the body must be commonly shared.

Luke does not record a hint of hierarchy in the early church. There's no priesthood, no class of super-saints called the clergy. There's just the body of Christians. Though spread out in Jerusalem, Damascus, and Antioch, and across the countryside of Judea and Samaria and beyond, they are all one body.

They exhibit the gifts of one Spirit. They proclaim one gospel and teach one Word. This is what the church was meant to be.

Over time, it seems, we add layers of religiosity and ritual, hierarchy and tradition, until the simple pattern of the church becomes unrecognizable in all its complexity. Then, after the church has drifted away from that simple New Testament pattern, the Holy Spirit breaks through and shows us the original pattern all over again.

There's nothing more exciting than the sense of renewal that comes when we rediscover the original New Testament model for the church. The mighty wind of the Spirit is blowing through our midst right now. Let's abandon churchianity and rediscover authentic Christianity. Let's believe that make way for a fresh new movement of the Spirit. May God open our eyes to see the church as it was in New Testament times—and as it can yet be again.

21

WHEN PRISON DOORS SWING OPEN

Acts 12

It was a case of cold-blooded, premeditated murder, and the crime was fore-told by Jesus. The victim was the apostle James, a leader in the early church.

Before he became an apostle, James was a rough Galilean fisherman with a loud, boisterous personality. He was the brother of John, who later wrote the gospel of John, and a business partner with Peter and Andrew. While these four men were fishing in the Sea of Galilee, Jesus called them to follow Him. They left their nets and followed Jesus (Matthew 4:18-22; Luke 5:1-11). Because of their bold personalities, Jesus nicknamed James and John "the Sons of Thunder" (Mark 3:17). They were probably in their late teens at the time.

Their ambitious mother, Salome, once tried to manipulate Jesus into giving James and John prominent political appointments (Matthew 20:21). Jesus asked the two young men if they were able to drink the cup He was about to drink, referring to His death on the cross. In their teenage enthusiasm, they said, "We can." Jesus said, "You will drink the cup I drink and be baptized with the baptism I am baptized with, but to sit at my right or left is not for me to grant" (Mark 10:39-40). So Jesus prophesied that the two brothers would share His suffering and die a martyr's death.

As we come to Acts 12, we witness the fulfillment of that prophecy in the life of James. Here we meet Herod Agrippa I, grandson of Herod the Great. He is a cruel man who commits senseless acts of violence against the church. Because James is so outspoken in his zeal for the Lord, Herod Agrippa decides to silence him—with a sword.

THE EXECUTION OF JAMES

Luke records the death of James:

> It was about this time that King Herod arrested some who belonged to the church, intending to persecute them. He had James, the brother of John, put to death with the sword. When he saw that this pleased the Jews, he proceeded to seize Peter also. This happened during the Feast of Unleavened Bread. (Acts 12:1-3)

The Feast of Unleavened Bread means that this execution took place during the Passover season, the same time of year when Jesus was crucified. The execution of James occurred in A.D. 44. We can date this event precisely because the date of Herod's death, recorded in Acts 12:23, is well known in history. These events occurred about twelve years after the crucifixion and resurrection of Jesus.

The church has been growing dramatically during those twelve years, spreading to Judea and Samaria and beyond while reaching out to the Gentiles. Now Satan strikes hard and moves Herod Agrippa to behead James, the brother of John. (Herod Agrippa is the brother of the Herod before whom Jesus appeared prior to the crucifixion.)

James was an important leader in the early church, and Herod may well have thought that the execution of James would intimidate the church. James was the first of the apostles to die; his brother John was the last. So the deaths of these two brothers form a parenthesis within which all the apostles lived and labored and eventually died. James was beheaded with a sword. We are not told how John died, though tradition says he was thrown into a cauldron of boiling oil. Both men died violently as Jesus predicted.

The church may have expected that God would release James from prison, just as He had released Peter and John and all of the apostles on previous occasions. So the believers were undoubtedly stunned and shattered when they learned that James had been beheaded—the first apostle to die.

THE ARREST OF PETER

And there was more bad news: When Herod Agrippa saw that the execution of James pleased the religious leaders, he arrested Peter. Luke writes:

> After arresting him, he put him in prison, handing him over to be guarded by four squads of four soldiers each. Herod intended to bring him out for public trial after the Passover.
>
> So Peter was kept in prison, but the church was earnestly praying to God for him. (Acts 12:4-5)

Though the church had lost members due to persecution and martyrdom over the years, they may have viewed the apostles as beyond the reach of the persecutor's sword. No longer. Now they knew that God would not automatically deliver His saints from suffering and death. So the believers gathered and offered earnest prayers for Peter.

Note the care that Herod took in placing Peter under guard. He detailed four squads, sixteen soldiers total, to watch one man. These extraordinary measures speak of Herod's fear of Peter and the church. The king took no chances that Peter's supporters might attempt a rescue.

The church feared for Peter. The king was afraid of Peter. It seems that only Peter was unafraid. He slept peacefully in the dungeon, despite the chains and guards:

The night before Herod was to bring him to trial, Peter was sleeping between two soldiers, bound with two chains, and sentries stood guard at the entrance. Suddenly an angel of the Lord appeared and a light shone in the cell. He struck Peter on the side and woke him up. "Quick, get up!" he said, and the chains fell off Peter's wrists.

Then the angel said to him, "Put on your clothes and sandals." And Peter did so. "Wrap your cloak around you and follow me," the angel told him. Peter followed him out of the prison, but he had no idea that what the angel was doing was really happening; he thought he was seeing a vision. They passed the first and second guards and came to the iron gate leading to the city. It opened for them by itself, and they went through it. When they had walked the length of one street, suddenly the angel left him.

Then Peter came to himself and said, "Now I know without a doubt that the Lord sent his angel and rescued me from Herod's clutches and from everything the Jewish people were anticipating." (Acts 12:6-11)

Peter had two soldiers chained to his wrists and two guards at the door of his cell. He probably expected to be executed as James has been. Remarkably, he slept! He trusted that whether he died or was delivered, God would be glorified—and he was willing to accept either outcome.

But Peter was not ready for what happened next: An angel of the Lord appeared in his prison cell. The angel had no concern about the guards; they were probably deep in a divinely induced sleep. The angel struck the chains from Peter's arms and told him what to do. Peter was so bewildered that the angel had to tell Peter, step by step, "Now get up. Get dressed. Put on your shoes. Wrap your cloak around you." The angel led Peter by the hand into the streets, and Peter hardly knew what was happening. When he saw the iron gate of the prison swing open of its own accord, he knew God was at work.

THE FUNNIEST SCENE IN SCRIPTURE

Next, Luke gives us a profoundly human account of the church's response to Peter's release from prison:

When this had dawned on him, he went to the house of Mary the mother of John, also called Mark, where many people had gathered and were praying. Peter knocked at the outer entrance, and a servant girl named Rhoda came to answer the door. When she recognized Peter's voice, she was so overjoyed she ran back without opening it and exclaimed, "Peter is at the door!"

"You're out of your mind," they told her. When she kept insisting that it was so, they said, "It must be his angel."

But Peter kept on knocking, and when they opened the door and saw him, they were astonished. Peter motioned with his hand for them to be quiet and described how the Lord had brought him out of prison. "Tell James and the brothers about this," he said, and then he left for another place. (Acts 12:12-17)

This passage reminds me of so many prayer meetings today. We ask God in prayer to act on our behalf—and when He answers, we can't believe it! Nothing in Scripture is funnier than this scene. Peter is left pounding on the door while the servant girl forgets to let him in. She tries to convince the others in the house that it really is Peter standing at the door, and they refuse to believe her.

The Christians in the house say that the girl must be crazy. Perhaps it's not Peter at the door, but his guardian angel. For some reason, it takes a while for someone to think of going and seeing who is knocking on the door. When the door is finally opened, there is Peter. God has answered the believers' prayers, though it may not be accurate at this moment to call them believers. If they had truly believed, they wouldn't have been so amazed that God answered their prayers.

It's strange how weak our faith is. I'm sure these Christians believed that God could deliver Peter, but they didn't expect Him to answer in such a dramatic way.

THE END OF HEROD

Next, Luke relates the cruel rage of Herod the king:

In the morning, there was no small commotion among the soldiers as to what had become of Peter. After Herod had a thorough search made for him and did not find him, he cross-examined the guards and ordered that they be executed.

Then Herod went from Judea to Caesarea and stayed there a while. (Acts 12:18-19)

Sixteen good soldiers died because of Herod's stubborn unbelief. The king refused to believe that God had overruled his decree. As the soldiers told their tale, the only explanation he could accept was that these men were derelict in their duty. So he ordered their execution. Herod then went down to his headquarters in Caesarea. Luke relates what then happened to the king:

He had been quarreling with the people of Tyre and Sidon; they now joined together and sought an audience with him. Having secured the support of Blastus, a trusted personal servant of the king, they asked for peace, because they depended on the king's country for their food supply.

On the appointed day Herod, wearing his royal robes, sat on his throne and delivered a public address to the people. They shouted, "This is the voice of a god, not of a man." Immediately, because Herod did not give praise to God, an angel of the Lord struck him down, and he was eaten by worms and died.

But the word of God continued to increase and spread.

When Barnabas and Saul had finished their mission, they returned from Jerusalem, taking with them John, also called Mark. (Acts 12:20-25)

The Jewish historian Josephus also records the death of Herod. Josephus describes the event when Herod met with the people of Tyre and Sidon in the region we now call Lebanon. When he came out, dressed in his robes, they flattered him. When he spoke, they worshiped him as a god. This pompous, egomaniacal king accepted their praise and worship and seemed to believe himself to be a god. We still see this kind of narcissistic self-importance in some people. Those who let their egos run away with them are on thin ice.

Luke tells us that Herod was stricken by an angel of the Lord, then worms consumed him, and he died. Luke writes as a physician. I don't know exactly what his diagnosis is in Herod's case, but Herod's death was horrific. The historian Josephus tells us that Herod Agrippa died within two or three days of being stricken by this illness.

What does Herod's death mean? This is God's way of demonstrating the folly of the thinking we can live apart from God. Herod had bought into the oldest lie of all, the same lie the serpent used to trick Eve in Genesis 3:5: "You will be like God." Herod's heart was darkened, and the result was physical and spiritual death.

THE LESSON OF JAMES AND PETER

As we step back from these events in Acts 12, we have to ask ourselves: Why was James killed while Peter was delivered? God could have saved James as well, but He didn't. Why? The only answer we find is in Acts 12:5. I believe this verse is the key to understanding the entire chapter:

So Peter was kept in prison, but the church was earnestly praying to God for him (Acts 12:5).

James was executed. Peter was released. What made the difference? Prayer! Note that little word *but*. It indicates a change in direction. Peter was kept in prison, *but* the church was earnestly praying for him. That word *but* tells us that the prayer of believers affected the outcome of the crisis.

As you read about the arrest and execution of James, you find no word that the Christians gathered to pray for him. Perhaps they had grown complacent and assumed that God would never let any harm come to James. In any case, no prayer is mentioned regarding the arrest of James, yet Peter's release is clearly an answer to prayer.

That's the great lesson of Acts 12. We are not to take events for granted, as though we can do nothing to affect them. The old adage, "Prayer changes things," is true. Prayer is a mighty, powerful force by which God's people connect with God's power to change events. That's the message Acts 12 shouts to us.

God still works today as He did in New Testament times. He responds when we pray. This doesn't mean that everything we ask for in prayer will be granted, because we don't always pray according to His will. But God wants us to live in dependence on Him and to work in partnership with Him. The means He has given us is prayer.

Peter slept peacefully while in prison, though he knew he could be executed at any moment. Here we see an important principle of prayer: Our prayers sustain others who are going through trials. The reason Peter slept peacefully is found in verse 5: "So Peter was kept in prison, but the church was earnestly praying to God for him." The church prayed for Peter, and that's where his strength came from.

That's why the apostle Paul repeatedly asked his friends to pray for him: "Pray also for me, that whenever I open my mouth, words may be given me so that I will fearlessly make known the mystery of the gospel, for which I am an ambassador in chains. Pray that I may declare it fearlessly, as I should" (Ephesians 6:19-20). Prayer emboldens the faith and calms the fears of those who are going through trials.

The prayers of God's people can produce important changes in the world, such as the death of Herod. I don't think the church prayed for the king to die. We are not told in Scripture to pray that way. But the church was praying that God would intervene and accomplish His will. As a result of their intercession, God could act in a remarkable way.

God's will was that the vicious tyrant Herod should be removed from the throne. But since the creation of the human race, God has limited Himself and does not interfere with human free will. When God's people, of their own free will, went to their knees and prayed as Jesus had taught them, "Your will be done on earth as it is in heaven," God could do His will and remove Herod from the scene.

This is what Paul means when he writes, "We do not know what we ought to pray for, but the Spirit himself intercedes for us with groans that words cannot express" (Romans 8:26). The world is too complicated and intricate for us to understand. But the Spirit of God helps us in our weakness and responds to the deep longings in our hearts. He intercedes for us, and the Father sends the answer we need for that situation.

My friend, Pastor Dave Roper, told me of an incident at Woodleaf Young Life Camp. One night at about eleven o'clock, the camp trumpeter was practicing alone by the creek (a good place for trumpeters to practice!). When he was finished, he walked back into camp. As he walked through the middle of the camp, he felt an urge to play his trumpet. He was convinced the urging came from God.

The young man quietly asked, "God, what should I play?" The thought came: "Play 'Taps.'" So, at eleven-thirty at night, in the middle of the camp, the young man played 'Taps." Then he put his instrument away, went to his cabin, and went to bed.

The next day, during a meeting, the speaker asked if anyone wanted to give a testimony. Everyone was astonished when a certain young camper stood to speak. This boy was well known for his belligerent attitude. He had come only to get away from his parents and was dismayed to find out that it was a Christian camp where he had to hear about the Bible! He made it clear that he wanted nothing to do with Jesus.

"But late last night," he said, "around eleven-thirty, I was walking out of the camp. I was heading for the highway so I could hitchhike home. I'd had enough of this place and all the Jesus talk.

"But then I heard somebody in the camp playing 'Taps' on the trumpet. It's that song they play when somebody dies. So I said to myself, 'Who died?' Then it hit me, 'Hey, Jesus died—and He died for me.' So I sat down beside the road and I asked Jesus to take over my life. So, here I am—and I'm a Christian now."

Who can doubt that God was at work in the heart of that trumpeter, leading him to play that tune at such an odd hour? The trumpeter had no idea that a rebellious boy was sneaking away and planning to hitchhike home, but God knew. That's why we need to be sensitive to God's indwelling Spirit, and that's why prayer is important.

BARNABAS AND SAUL

Finally, notice how Luke concludes this chapter:

> But the word of God continued to increase and spread.
>
> When Barnabas and Saul had finished their mission, they returned from Jerusalem, taking with them John, also called Mark. (Acts 12:24-25)

The gospel of Jesus Christ continued to spread in spite of opposition and persecution. Luke now focuses on two men God has been preparing: Barnabas and Saul. They have been witnesses to the dramatic acts of the Holy Spirit in Jerusalem, Antioch, and elsewhere. They have learned the lessons of the arrest and deliverance of Peter.

Saul, the future apostle Paul, would later recall how God set captives free, opened prison doors, and deposed a tyrannical ruler, all in response to the prayers of His people. Throughout the book of Acts, we see that prayer is the key to effective ministry, deliverance from danger, and peace in turbulent times. Prayer is our most potent weapon in the struggle against the enemy of our souls.

That's the central theme of Acts 12: Prayer changes things.

PART III

THE PATTERN SETTERS

Acts 13–20

22

THE STRATEGY OF THE SPIRIT

Acts 13:1-13

In September 1939, Nazi Germany invaded Poland, the first step in an all-out bid to conquer the world. After crushing Poland, Adolf Hitler sent storm troopers into Denmark, Norway, Belgium, the Netherlands, France, Eastern Europe, Russia, and North Africa. Nation after nation fell before the onslaught. "We have only to kick in the door," Hitler boasted, "and the whole rotten structure will come crashing down!"

By the summer of 1940, Hitler hurled his forces against the British Isles. German bombers attacked the island nation with unbelievable ferocity, attacking not only military targets but also civilian population centers. As raid after raid pounded London into rubble, it seemed like just a matter of time before Britain, too, would fall.

Then, on May 9, 1941, the British destroyer HMS *Bulldog* forced a German submarine, the U-110, to the surface. As the destroyer's guns pummeled the sub, the Nazi crew poured out of the hatches and leaped into the sea. The *Bulldog's* captain ordered a twenty-year-old lieutenant, David Balme, to capture the abandoned sub. Lt. Balme boarded the crippled sub and descended into its innards. Searching the boat, Lt. Balme found an amazing prize: A working Enigma code machine. From then on, the Allies were able to read even the most carefully encrypted Nazi communications.

A few months later, in December 1941, after the Japanese attack on Pearl Harbor, the United States entered the war. These two events—the cracking of the Enigma code and the added might of the American military—turned the tide against the Nazi war machine. By late 1942, the Allies began to push back Hitler's armies, and the British prime minister, Winston Churchill, was able to declare, "the hinges of history have turned."

As we come to Acts 13, we reach another moment which could be called one of the hinges of history. This chapter marks the beginning of the third phase of the Great Commission of the Lord Jesus Christ. It also marks the beginning of a section of Acts that I call The Pattern Setters. Here, in Acts 13 through 20, we find the pattern for all Christian witness in any culture, in any era of history.

THE BEGINNING OF PHASE 3

You'll recall that in Acts 1:8, Jesus laid out His three-phase program for church expansion: "But you will receive power when the Holy Spirit comes on you; and you will be my witnesses in Jerusalem [phase 1], and in all Judea and Samaria [phase 2], and to the ends of the earth [phase 3]." We saw the beginning of phase 2 in Acts 8:1, following the death of Stephen, when a persecution broke out against the church in Jerusalem and the church moved out to Judea and Samaria.

Now, in Acts 13, we see the beginning of the third and final phase—"to the ends of the earth." This chapter also marks the beginning of a new phase in the life of Saul of Tarsus. Roughly a dozen years after his conversion, Saul, or Paul, as he is about to be known, begins to take on his ministry as an apostle of Jesus Christ.

The key theme of Acts 13 is what I call the strategy of the Spirit. This chapter reveals how the Holy Spirit leads and guides individual believers in order to fulfill His overall strategy for the church. In the first three verses, Luke gives us the setting for the Spirit's calling of Barnabas and Saul:

> In the church at Antioch there were prophets and teachers: Barnabas, Simeon called Niger, Lucius of Cyrene, Manaen (who had been brought up with Herod the tetrarch) and Saul. While they were worshiping the Lord and fasting, the Holy Spirit said, "Set apart for me Barnabas and Saul for the work to which I have called them." So after they had fasted and prayed, they placed their hands on them and sent them off. (Acts 13:1-3)

This scene opens with a group of Christians in Antioch exercising their spiritual gifts. They are believers who have received the spiritual gifts of prophecy and teaching. Although it is not apparent in the English text, the Greek text makes it clear that three of the men (Barnabas, Simeon, and Lucius of Cyrene) were prophets and two (Manaen and Saul) were teachers.

We meet several of these men for the first time. Simeon, a prophet, was also called Niger because he came from the region of western Africa where the Republic of Niger is today. Many Bible scholars believe Simeon was a black African. Another prophet, Lucius, was from Cyrene, a Roman-ruled Greek colony where Libya is today.

Manaen had been a member of the court of Herod the tetrarch (the Herod who interviewed Jesus prior to the crucifixion, not Herod Agrippa from Acts 12). The Greek text makes clear something the English translation does not convey: Manaen was a foster brother of Herod.

So here we have a diverse collection of people from various walks of life, a demonstration of the diversity that characterized the early church: Simeon, a black African; Lucius, a Grecian Jew from North Africa; Manaen, a Jewish aristocrat; Barnabas, a Grecian Jew from Cyprus; Saul, a trained Pharisee, a Jew among Jews.

THE CALLING OF BARNABAS AND SAUL

These five men were all fasting. In the Bible, fasting is the mark of deep spiritual concern. When a believer fasts, it means that he or she is willing to forego the normal comforts and necessities of life in order to concentrate on prayer. Fasting is a symbolic expression of a person's inner hunger for God.

At this point in Acts, Saul was not affirmed as an apostle, but he was a teacher at the Antioch church. The only spiritual gift manifested in his life was a profound ability to teach the Word of God. While these five men were fasting, praying, worshiping, and exercising their spiritual gifts, they sensed the Spirit speaking to them in a clear way: "Set apart for me Barnabas and Saul for the work to which I have called them."

This is a significant insight. Many people sit and wait for God to lead them in a dramatic way, and they wonder why they don't hear God speaking. It's probably because God rarely calls people who are sitting and waiting. He usually calls people who are busy exercising their spiritual gifts right where they are. That's how He called Barnabas and Saul. These men were not off on some retreat when they heard the Spirit speak. They had their sleeves rolled up and were actively serving God and others.

I don't know how the Spirit spoke to these men. The voice of the Spirit may have come to them through a prophetic utterance of one of the prophets. Or the Spirit may have spoken through a deep sense of conviction shared by all five men. In any case, the Spirit spoke to them as they were engaged in the ministry God had given them.

You can't steer a car that's standing still. You can only steer a car that's moving. When God's people are on the move, He will steer them to greater heights of ministry.

Notice two elements of the Spirit's sovereign choice of Barnabas and Saul. First, He chose the men. Second, He chose the work they would do. He said, "Set apart for me Barnabas and Saul for the work to which I have called them." In this way, the Spirit of God called two men to take the gospel to the uttermost parts of the earth.

THE COMMISSIONING OF BARNABAS AND SAUL

The church at Antioch held a commissioning ceremony for Barnabas and Saul: "So after they had fasted and prayed, they placed their hands on them and sent them off." This means that the entire church was involved in sending these two men. When Luke says that the church sent them off, it doesn't mean that the believers patted these two men on the back and said, "Off you go!" It means that the entire body of believers in Antioch provided prayer support and financial resources for their mission.

We next see a beautiful blending of the sovereignty of the Spirit with human activity in the sending of these two men:

> The two of them, sent on their way by the Holy Spirit, went down to Seleucia and sailed from there to Cyprus. When they arrived at Salamis, they proclaimed the word of God in the Jewish synagogues. John was with them as their helper. (Acts 13:4-5)

Notice the blend of two factors: God's sovereign choice and people's real but limited power of choice. The Holy Spirit sent these men on their way. This means that the Spirit gave them the urge to venture forth. But the passage also says that Barnabas and Saul "went down to Seleucia and sailed from there to Cyprus." The Spirit urged Barnabas and Saul to move out, but the two men chose their own route. The Spirit didn't say, "Go to Cyprus." The Spirit simply said, "Go." The route was theirs to choose.

That's what it means to be led by the Spirit. God's Spirit may lay a need on your heart, and He will impress upon you the desire to meet it. But the Spirit does not tell you how to go about it. God wants you to grow in the confidence that He is leading you while allowing you to make your own choices.

When I was at Dallas Seminary, one of my fellow students used to pray about every little decision: Should he put his hat on in the morning or not? Should he order the apple pie or the pumpkin pie? If God dictated every little choice in our lives, we'd be robots, without any free will. God could have created robots, but He created us to be partners with Him, living in obedience yet able to think and act of our own volition.

God does actively direct us at times, and when we hear His urging, we should not ignore it. But in the absence of a specific directive from God, either through His Word or the prompting of His Spirit, we can move confidently, knowing that He will open doors of opportunity for us.

THE HELPER, JOHN MARK

Barnabas and Saul began their ministry in the synagogues. Paul explains his reason for this pattern in his letter to the Romans. There he writes that it was God's intention that the gospel go to the Jews first, then to the Gentiles. As you look over the span of Paul's ministry, you see that he always obeyed this pattern. He went to the Jews in the synagogues, and, if they rejected his message, he went to the Gentiles.

These two missionaries took a young man with them as a helper and ministry trainee. His name was John Mark, referred to in Acts 13 only as John.

God did not command them to take a helper with them, but Saul and Barnabas chose him. Here again, the human element combines with God's sovereignty in this passage. It was probably Barnabas's idea, more than Saul's, to bring John Mark along.

John Mark was a cousin of Barnabas (Colossians 4:10). His mother was a wealthy widow in Jerusalem. When Peter was released from prison by an angel of the Lord, we are told that he went to "the house of Mary the mother of John, also called Mark, where many people had gathered and were praying" (Acts 12:12).

Because he grew up around wealth, John Mark may have been somewhat spoiled and immature. Barnabas probably saw great potential in John Mark but also knew he needed to experience some hardships on the missionary road in order for God to truly use him. John Mark's immaturity will later become a source of intense conflict between Barnabas and Paul (Acts 15:36-40).

John Mark is also known as Mark the Evangelist because he is the author of the gospel of Mark. In that gospel account, he tells the story of the rich young ruler who asked Jesus, "Good teacher, what must I do to inherit eternal life?" In the course of their conversation, Jesus told the young ruler, "One thing you lack. Go, sell everything you have and give to the poor, and you will have treasure in heaven. Then come, follow me." But the young man turned away from Jesus because he had great wealth and was unwilling to part with it (Mark 10:17-23).

Who was that rich young ruler? I'm convinced that it was John Mark. Mark's description of the young nobleman's thoughts and feelings in that account is the most personal and detailed narrative in the gospel of Mark. The description of the young ruler fits John Mark to a T.

Barnabas and Saul, accompanied by John Mark, went to Cyprus, landed at Salamis, and began to preach. They were confident that God was opening doors of opportunity for them, but they didn't wait for specific orders for every action they took. The strategy belongs to the Holy Spirit, but He allows us to make choices and decisions as to how we will implement His strategy.

THE RADICALISM OF THE HOLY SPIRIT

Some years ago, a San Francisco-based Christian group wanted to do something about the sex-oriented nightspots in the city's infamous North Beach area. Several dozen Christians would gather in front of The Condor Club and other striptease clubs and would carry protest signs. Protesting is one of the most highly protected activities in San Francisco, so there was nothing the clubs could do to stop these protesters.

As a result of the Christian protests, attendance at the clubs declined sharply. The manager of one of the clubs finally had enough, and he sent a bouncer out to intimidate the Christians and order them to leave. The Christians, knowing they had a legal right to be there, stayed put. The bouncer confronted them several nights in a row and finally got so angry that he punched one of the Christians in the mouth.

Clearly, these protests were risky, but the Christians refused to back down. When they arrived the next night, the bouncer again ordered them to leave. "We'll go under one condition," the leader of the Christian group said. "Just let us go inside and pray for all the people there."

The club manager agreed—anything to get rid of those Christians! So the Christians filed into the club and went up on the stage where a number of ill-clad dancers stood. The band went silent. The patrons sat slack-jawed at their tables. The Christians took the microphone and prayed for the manager, the bouncer, the young women on the stage, and the customers at the tables. They asked God to reveal His truth to these people and show them their need of a Savior.

As the Christians prayed, the bouncer closed the doors so the street noise wouldn't disturb the prayer meeting. The patrons and performers bowed their heads as they were being prayed for. The place was as quiet as a church. When it was over, there was no mocking or sneering, just a respectful silence as the Christians filed out.

That is the radicalism of the Holy Spirit. Radicalism is defined as an inclination to use revolutionary methods to change society—and without question, the Spirit's methods are revolutionary. No church evangelism committee could ever dream up an idea as radical as a prayer meeting in a striptease club. Unplanned, impromptu events like that prayer meeting happen only when the creative Holy Spirit moves unhindered through the events of our lives. When the Spirit moves, we must follow.

This is an example of God's sovereignty working hand in hand with human activity, as God's people make themselves available as co-laborers with God. We see God and Christians working together this way throughout the book of Acts. The result is that God's message goes out in surprising ways as God opens doors for fruitful ministry.

OPPOSED BY A CULTIST

Luke does not tell us everything Barnabas and Saul did on Cyprus, but we know they had an effective ministry because Christian churches were established there from the beginning. Luke tells us that Saul and Barnabas passed through the island from east to west, probably visiting each city along the way. Their travels may have taken two or three months. Finally, they arrived in Paphos, the capital of Cyprus, on the western coast of the island. There a startling incident took place.

They traveled through the whole island until they came to Paphos. There they met a Jewish sorcerer and false prophet named Bar-Jesus, who was an attendant of the proconsul, Sergius Paulus. The proconsul, an intelligent man, sent for Barnabas and Saul because he wanted to hear the word of God. But Elymas the sorcerer (for that is what his name means) opposed them and tried to turn the proconsul from the faith. (Acts 13:6-8)

Notice the activity of the Holy Spirit behind the scenes of this incident. Barnabas and Saul had no idea that they would have a hearing before the proconsul of the island. Sergius Paulus was appointed to govern the isle of Cyprus by the Roman Senate. Though a pagan, he was prompted by the Holy Spirit to send for Barnabas and Saul because he wanted to hear the word of God.

When Barnabas and Saul came and began to teach Sergius Paulus, they were opposed by a Jewish magician who had adopted the name Elymas. The origin of this name is obscure but may be derived from the Arabic word *alim*, meaning "wise" (the Greek word for sorcerer in verse 8 is *magos*, which literally means "wise man").

The sorcerer's Hebrew name was Bar-Jesus, which means "the son of Jesus." In the Hebrew culture, *bar* (son of) could be used literally or metaphorically. In the metaphorical sense, to be the son of someone meant being a follower of that person. So when this sorcerer called himself Bar-Jesus, he was probably claiming to be a follower of Jesus of Nazareth. However, his teachings were contrary to what Jesus taught. So Elymas Bar-Jesus was probably the first in a long line of cultists who have hijacked the name of Jesus to disguise their antichristian teaching.

This cultist greatly provoked the spirit of Saul because he interfered with Saul's proclamation of the good news of Jesus Christ. Luke records Saul's response:

Then Saul, who was also called Paul, filled with the Holy Spirit, looked straight at Elymas and said, "You are a child of the devil and an enemy of everything that is right! You are full of all kinds of deceit and trickery. Will you never stop perverting the right ways of the Lord? Now the hand of the Lord is against you. You are going to be blind, and for a time you will be unable to see the light of the sun."

Immediately mist and darkness came over him, and he groped about, seeking someone to lead him by the hand. When the proconsul saw what had happened, he believed, for he was amazed at the teaching about the Lord. (Acts 13:9-12)

Even in his annoyance, Saul was filled with the Holy Spirit. He looked at this man and said, "You are a child of the devil and an enemy of everything that is right! You are full of all kinds of deceit and trickery." You always knew where you stood with the apostle Paul. He never sugarcoated his opinion.

Then he said, "Will you never stop perverting the right ways of the Lord?" Another way to put this is, "Will you not stop making crooked the straight paths of the Lord?" Saul was declaring the straight paths of Jesus, but this man was teaching deviations and detours and blind alleys. He was confusing and misleading the proconsul.

Finally, Saul did something he had never done before. He told Elymas, "Now the hand of the Lord is against you. You are going to be blind, and for a time you will be unable to see the light of the sun." And Elymas was instantly plunged into darkness. What more proof of the power of God did the proconsul need? Sergius Paulus believed and was amazed at the teaching about the Lord.

Barnabas and Saul spent considerable time on the island of Cyprus, and they undoubtedly had a number of fascinating experiences there. Yet Luke records only one incident that took place there—the story of Sergius Paulus and Elymas the sorcerer. Why did Luke select this one incident and not others? Answer: Because this is the point at which Saul became Paul the apostle.

When Paul confronted Elymas, he exercised for the first time his office of apostleship. When Paul, who was "filled with the Holy Spirit," pronounced God's judgment against Elymas, and it was instantly carried out, he demonstrated the first sign of an apostle. This miraculous sign authenticated Paul as one who had been selected by the Lord Jesus as one of His apostles—as one who would lay the foundation of the church and write the New Testament Scriptures.

In pronouncing God's judgment against the sorcerer, Paul echoed the apostle Peter's pronouncement when Ananias and Sapphira threatened the church with their hypocrisy (Acts 5). In both the cases, judgment was immediate. Only true apostles had the power to pronounce such instant judgment.

Notice, too, Luke's use of Paul's name in this passage. In verse 9, Luke writes, "Then Saul, who was also called Paul." This is the first time Saul is referred to as Paul. This signifies an important change in Paul's identity, and particularly his identity as an apostle. Note also that once Saul becomes Paul, we no longer hear about Barnabas and Saul. Instead, we hear about Paul and Barnabas or even Paul and his companions, as we see in the next verse:

From Paphos, Paul and his companions sailed to Perga in Pamphylia, where John left them to return to Jerusalem. (Acts 13:13)

The ministry of the apostle Paul has begun, and it is characterized by the power of Paul's teaching. Sergius Paulus, the proconsul of Cyprus, believed at the moment God imposed His judgment on Elymas the sorcerer. But Luke tells us that it was not the miraculous temporary blinding of the sorcerer that impressed the proconsul. Rather, he was persuaded by the power of Paul's teaching. Luke writes, "When the proconsul saw what had happened, he believed, for he was amazed at the teaching about the Lord." The miracle didn't persuade the proconsul; it validated Paul's teaching.

That's the life-changing power of the good news of Jesus Christ.

CONFIRMATION OF LUKE AS A RELIABLE HISTORIAN

In the mid-nineteenth century, liberal scholars led by Ferdinand Christian Baur (1792-1860) founded the Tübingen school of theology, named after Tübingen University, where Baur was a professor of church history. These scholars attempted to explain the development of early Christianity as a purely human phenomenon, without any involvement by God. They questioned the reliability of the book of Acts, claiming that it was a forgery written in the second century A.D.

The Scottish archaeologist Sir William Mitchell Ramsay (1851-1939) was strongly influenced by this school of thought. While in his late twenties, Ramsay set out to prove that the book of Acts was filled with historical inaccuracies and could not have been written by Luke. As Ramsay conducted archaeological research throughout the region of Paul's missionary journeys, he was gradually forced to reverse his views.

Ramsay was astonished when one of his colleagues, General Louis Palma di Cesnola, announced an amazing discovery. Cesnola was an Italian-born Union Army general during the American Civil War who earned the Medal of Honor for heroism. He was also, like Ramsay, an archaeologist; years later, he was named the first curator of New York's Metropolitan Museum of Art. When Cesnola was appointed U.S. ambassador to Cyprus, he spent much of his free time exploring ancient sites, including places visited by Barnabas and Saul. In 1877, Cesnola uncovered an inscription a short distance north of Paphos bearing the name Sergius Paulus and the title *proconsul*.

Prior to that discovery, liberal scholars had claimed there was no evidence that Sergius Paulus ever existed. The events in Acts 13, they said, never happened. But Cesnola's find was indisputable, and it confirmed the accuracy of Luke's account.

Cesnola's discovery, along with other evidence that Sir William Ramsay uncovered, forced Ramsay to admit that the book of Acts was historically reliable. He later uncovered evidence showing that Sergius Paulus and his family converted to Christianity and became prominent members of the first-century Christian community—further evidence that the account in Acts 13 is true. Ultimately, Ramsay was compelled to conclude that "Luke is a historian of the first rank" and "should be placed along with the very greatest of historians."

There is a good reason why Luke's account has been proven so reliable: The Holy Spirit is the author of the events of Acts and the account of Acts. You cannot explain the early expansion of the church as a purely human phenomenon. The book of Acts is a record of the strategy of the Spirit. As you and I align ourselves with that strategy, we'll see lives transformed, we'll see the church expand, and we'll see new chapters of the book of Acts written in our lives.

23

THE IMPACT OF FORGIVENESS

Acts 13:13-52

Pastor and seminary professor Robert Boyd Munger often told young seminarians, "A prepared messenger is more important than a prepared message." As we continue through Acts 13, we see that the apostle Paul is truly God's prepared messenger to the first-century world. In this chapter, we come to Paul's first recorded sermon. He delivered this message in a synagogue on a Sabbath morning, and it shook a city. As we examine this message in detail, we will see why it had such an impact in the first century and why it is a revolutionary message today.

THE DEFECTION OF JOHN MARK

As we have just seen, Paul, Barnabas, and young John Mark are departing the island of Cyprus, setting sail from the city of Paphos, and crossing to Asia Minor (modern-day Turkey). Luke writes:

> From Paphos, Paul and his companions sailed to Perga in Pamphylia, where John left them to return to Jerusalem. From Perga they went on to Pisidian Antioch. On the Sabbath they entered the synagogue and sat down. After the reading from the Law and the Prophets, the synagogue rulers sent word to them, saying, "Brothers, if you have a message of encouragement for the people, please speak." (Acts 13:13-15)

Why did John Mark leave Paul and Barnabas to return to Jerusalem? The Scriptures do not say. Perhaps there was friction between Mark and Paul early in their relationship. Later, Paul and Mark become close friends and partners in ministry, prompting Paul to tell Timothy, "Get Mark and bring him with you, because he is helpful to me in my ministry" (2 Timothy 4:11; see also Colossians 4:10; Philemon 1:24).

Some scholars suggest that John Mark, having been raised in a wealthy home, was not used to the hardships of missionary work. Perhaps, as their ship approached the rugged coasts of Asia Minor, John Mark became fearful of the dangers ahead, from robbers and from their religious enemies. Whatever his reasons, Mark left Paul and Barnabas at Pamphylia and returned alone to Jerusalem.

Paul and Barnabas went on to the Antioch in the region of Pisidia, in the Roman province of Galatia. (There were several cities called Antioch in those days, and this is not the same city as the Antioch in Syria where Barnabas and Saul had preached and taught earlier.) Paul's letter to the Galatians was written to Christians in the various cities of Galatia, including Iconium, Lystra, Derbe, and Pisidian Antioch.

According to Paul's custom, they went first to the synagogue and preached to the Jews there. Under the tradition of the synagogues, visiting strangers were invited to speak. So Paul gave a sermon, which has been preserved for us in Acts 13.

PART 1 OF PAUL'S MESSAGE: GOD AND THE HISTORY OF ISRAEL

Paul's message divides into three themes or sections. Let's look at each section of this powerful sermon:

> Standing up, Paul motioned with his hand and said: "Men of Israel and you Gentiles who worship God, listen to me! The God of the people of Israel chose our fathers; he made the people prosper during their stay in Egypt, with mighty power he led them out of that country, he endured their conduct for about forty years in the desert, he overthrew seven nations in Canaan and gave their land to his people as their inheritance. All this took about 450 years.
>
> "After this, God gave them judges until the time of Samuel the prophet. Then the people asked for a king, and he gave them Saul son of Kish, of the tribe of Benjamin, who ruled forty years. After removing Saul, he made David their king. He testified concerning him: 'I have found David son of Jesse a man after my own heart; he will do everything I want him to do.'
>
> 'From this man's descendants God has brought to Israel the Savior Jesus, as he promised. Before the coming of Jesus, John preached repentance and baptism to all the people of Israel. As John was completing his work, he said: 'Who do you think I am? I am not that one. No, but he is coming after me, whose sandals I am not worthy to untie.'" (Acts 13:16-25)

Notice that Paul's opening section is similar to the opening section of Stephen's message in Acts 7, just before his death by stoning. Stephen stood before the Sanhedrin, including a young Saul of Tarsus, and recounted the history of Israel in hopes of showing the religious leaders that Jesus was the fulfillment of Israel's longing for its Messiah. Paul never forgot the power of that message, and he now draws on similar themes for his sermon.

Notice, too, that Paul's recounting of history does not focus on human achievements. It focuses on God. Paul's message is clear: God is the center of history. He is the One who moves and shapes events. Paul lists ten actions of God:

1. The God of Israel chose the fathers of Israel.
2. He made the people of Israel prosper during their stay in Egypt.
3. With His power, God led them out of Egypt.
4. He patiently endured their sins and ungrateful conduct for forty years.
5. He overthrew seven nations in Canaan.
6. He gave the land of Canaan to His people as their inheritance.
7. He gave them judges until the time of Samuel the prophet.
8. He gave them Saul to be their first king.
9. He removed Saul and made David their king.
10. Out of the descendants of David, God brought forth the Savior, Jesus.

The history of the nation of Israel is focused on one event. Everything culminates in the coming of Jesus the Messiah. As confirmation of this fact, Paul cites John's testimony to the greatness of Jesus.

Now this was a devastating point. In the provinces, away from Jerusalem, John the Baptist was regarded as a great prophet. Here Paul quotes John's testimony regarding Jesus: "He who is coming after me, whose sandals I am not worthy to untie, is the Lamb of God who takes away the sin of the world." That is the first movement of Paul's sweeping argument.

PART 2 OF PAUL'S MESSAGE: THE TIMELESS FACTS OF THE GOSPEL

In the second section of Paul's sermon, he presents the timeless facts of the gospel: the ministry, death, and resurrection of Jesus. Luke records Paul's words:

> "Brothers, children of Abraham, and you God-fearing Gentiles, it is to us that this message of salvation has been sent. The people of Jerusalem and their rulers did not recognize Jesus, yet in condemning him they fulfilled the words of the prophets that are read every Sabbath. Though they found no proper ground for a death sentence, they asked Pilate to have him executed. When they had carried out all that was written about him, they took him down from the tree and laid him in a tomb. But God raised him from the dead, and for many days he was seen by those who had traveled with him from Galilee to Jerusalem. They are now his witnesses to our people." (Acts 13:26-31)

I once read an article by a prominent liberal theologian who said, "The Christian gospel is almost impossible to define." The apostle Paul would have been surprised to hear that. He never had any trouble defining the gospel. It consisted of the great acts of God in history—the coming of the Lord Jesus, His ministry among human beings, His crucifixion for the sins of humanity, and His resurrection as the Scriptures had promised.

Remember Paul's words to the Christians in Corinth: "Now, brothers, I want to remind you of the gospel I preached to you, which you received and on which you have taken your stand. . . . For what I received I passed on to you as of first importance: that Christ died for our sins according to the Scriptures, that he was buried, that he was raised on the third day according to the Scriptures" (1 Corinthians 15:1, 3-4). That is the good news of the gospel.

Preaching at the synagogue in Pisidian Antioch, Paul says, "The people of Jerusalem and their rulers did not recognize Jesus, yet in condemning him they fulfilled the words of the prophets that are read every Sabbath." Why did the religious leaders who condemned Jesus not recognize Him? They were deeply religious people who knew the Old Testament prophecies concerning the Messiah. The words of the prophets, Paul said, "are read every Sabbath." Why, when the Messiah came, did they not see who He was?

First, the people were misled by faulty expectations. They believed the Messiah would come as a conquering hero, a richly arrayed king. When Jesus arrived on the scene as a poor and humble man, the son of a carpenter from Nazareth, without wealth, power, or prestige, they paid no attention to Him. They did not recognize Him.

Second, the people did not understand the Scriptures. They focused on the passages that depicted the Messiah as a conqueror and ignored the passages that depicted Him in His sufferings, passages such as Psalm 22 and Isaiah 53. The religious leaders could recite the Scriptures from memory, yet they didn't understand what the Scriptures meant. So when the long-awaited Messiah finally arrived, they not only failed to recognize Him but rejected and killed Him. So, Paul says, they fulfilled the prophecies by condemning Jesus and turning him over to Pilate for crucifixion.

PART 3 OF PAUL'S MESSAGE: THE MINISTRY AND RESURRECTION OF CHRIST

In the third section, Paul takes two great truths of the gospel—the ministry of Jesus and His resurrection—and shows how these truths were foretold in the Scriptures:

> "We tell you the good news: What God promised our fathers he has fulfilled for us, their children, by raising up Jesus. As it is written in the second Psalm:
>
> > "'You are my Son;
> > today I have become your Father.'
>
> The fact that God raised him from the dead, never to decay, is stated in these words:

"'I will give you the holy and sure blessings promised to David.'

So it is stated elsewhere:

"'You will not let your Holy One see decay.'" (Acts 13:32-35)

Paul refers to the resurrection when he quotes from Psalm 16:10, "'You will not let your Holy One see decay.'" The psalmist clearly predicted that a man would come who would never see corruption. His body would not decay in the grave. Skeptics claim that the messianic psalms don't refer to Jesus but to experiences in David's life. But Paul answers that argument in his sermon:

"For when David had served God's purpose in his own generation, he fell asleep; he was buried with his fathers and his body decayed. But the one whom God raised from the dead did not see decay." (Acts 13:36-37)

Paul makes it devastatingly clear: You cannot apply Psalm 16:10 to David. That passage says, "You will not let your Holy One see decay," but David died, and his body decayed. That passage can apply to only one person—to Someone who, despite undergoing death, did not undergo corruption. That person, of course, is Jesus. Psalm 16:10 can only be a reference to the resurrection.

Next, Paul goes to the heart of the gospel message:

"Therefore, my brothers, I want you to know that through Jesus the forgiveness of sins is proclaimed to you. Through him everyone who believes is justified from everything you could not be justified from by the law of Moses." (Acts 13:38-39)

To the Hebrew mind, this is an astonishing statement. The people at the synagogue honored the law of Moses and thought that the Ten Commandments were the greatest word God ever gave to humanity. They tried to live up to God's law but felt great inner conflict and guilt when they failed to meet its impossible demands. Now Paul comes to declare that human beings are not accepted by God on the basis of the Law. They can be accepted and forgiven only through faith in Jesus Christ.

If you were raised in a Christian home, you're used to hearing that salvation is by grace through faith in Jesus. But this message came as a shock to the people in that synagogue. They had never heard such a message before. Through Jesus, Paul says, 'everyone who believes is justified." What does it mean to be justified?

Most people think it means to have your sins forgiven. It does mean that, but it means a great deal more. Justification means to have your sins forgiven in such a way that God's honor and integrity are preserved. What if God forgave your sin by saying, "Don't worry about it. Let's forget it ever happened"? What would that say about God's character? It would mean that He doesn't think sin and righteousness are important. It would mean that He's not a God of justice and truth. In effect, he would become an accessory to your sins after the fact.

But God does not wink at sin. He placed our guilt upon His own Son. Jesus paid the price of our sin so that we could go free. God's honor and character were preserved. That is justification. Because of the cross, nobody can point to God and say, "You let guilty people off scot-free!" God obeys His own laws and carries out justice, yet He is still able to pour out His grace upon us. That is what it means to be justified.

Because we have been justified by faith, we don't have to focus on keeping the Law, hoping against hope that we can somehow be good enough to be accepted by God. Instead, we can accept the free gift of justification and live a life of gratitude for His love and forgiveness.

The people in that synagogue had never heard such a message before. Paul evidently saw some disapproving faces as he spoke, because he immediately added:

"Take care that what the prophets have said does not happen to you:

> "'Look, you scoffers,
>   wonder and perish,
> for I am going to do something in your days
>   that you would never believe,
> even if someone told you.'" (Acts 13:40-41)

I don't think Paul spoke these words in anger. I think he spoke them in sadness. He was saying, "When you hear this message of God's grace, you are at a crossroads. You can accept His grace or reject it. There's no third alternative. If you reject His love, you throw your life away. Only God's love can rescue you."

THE POWER OF GUILT AND THE POWER OF FORGIVENESS

One weekday morning, I was working in my study at the church when I heard a woman shouting. I hurried out to the church auditorium and saw a young woman pacing in agitation in front of the cross. I recognized her, because she had come for counseling a week earlier. As she paced back and forth, she cried out, "Yes, there is a God! Yes, there is a God! He'll forgive me! I know He will! I know He will!"

The woman was in an agony of spirit. I hesitated for a moment, wondering how to approach her without startling her. I took a step and cleared my throat—

And she looked at me with frightened eyes. Instantly, she went limp and fell facedown on the floor. I rushed to her side and helped her to one of the pews. While she composed herself, I remembered why she had come for counseling the previous week.

She had told me she was married and a Christian, and she'd been having an affair with an older man. She had rationalized the affair, saying, "How can it be wrong if it makes me happy? As long as my husband never finds out, no one will be hurt."

I said, "If your husband betrayed you, and you never found out, would you agree that you were not harmed?"

She didn't have an answer for that. Even so, I was unable to persuade her to end the adulterous relationship. She had left my counseling room determined to continue the affair. I asked her why she had come to the church.

"The man I had an affair with called me today," she said. "He says it's over. And for the first time, I see how blind I've been. Until today, I didn't realize how I was hurting my husband. I didn't realize I was destroying myself with sin. I just wanted what I wanted, and I didn't care about anything else. Now the affair is over, and the guilt is more than I can stand! I came here to find God and ask Him to forgive me! But what I've done is so terrible, He can never forgive me!"

I went through the Scriptures with her, showing her what God's Word said about repentance and forgiveness, but she refused to accept it. "I can't just be forgiven!" she said. "God will never forgive me until I pay for what I did! But I don't know how to pay for it! I don't know what to do!"

I told her that there is no condemnation for those who are in Christ Jesus and that He would wash the guilt away if she would turn to Him in repentance. She refused to accept what I told her, but she eventually calmed down. She called her husband, and he came over to the church. The three of us sat down, and she confessed her sin to him. He was hurt, but he forgave her and wanted to work on restoring the relationship.

Weeks passed. The woman continued to be depressed and guilt-ridden, so her husband took her to the hospital to be treated for depression. Two days after she checked in, she threw herself from a tenth-floor window of the hospital. She was driven to suicide by an inability to accept forgiveness. That is the destructive power of guilt.

If we cannot relieve the pressure of guilt, it will destroy us. That's why Paul's message had such a powerful impact in that city. He told the people that the only way to be free from guilt is by accepting the work of Another on their behalf. God's love is poured out on that basis, and that alone.

Now see the impact of Paul's message on the people:

> As Paul and Barnabas were leaving the synagogue, the people invited them to speak further about these things on the next Sabbath. When the congregation was dismissed, many of the Jews and devout converts to

Judaism followed Paul and Barnabas, who talked with them and urged them to continue in the grace of God.

On the next Sabbath almost the whole city gathered to hear the word of the Lord. When the Jews saw the crowds, they were filled with jealousy and talked abusively against what Paul was saying.

Then Paul and Barnabas answered them boldly: "We had to speak the word of God to you first. Since you reject it and do not consider yourselves worthy of eternal life, we now turn to the Gentiles. For this is what the Lord has commanded us:

"'I have made you a light for the Gentiles,
   that you may bring salvation to the ends of the earth.'"

When the Gentiles heard this, they were glad and honored the word of the Lord; and all who were appointed for eternal life believed. (Acts 13:42-48)

The gospel affects the heart, awakens the slumbering spirit, and forces human beings to choose sides. You must decide for Jesus or against Him. There is no neutrality, because to ignore Him is to reject Him. Some people, when confronted by the gospel, cry out to Him for forgiveness. Others continue on to destruction. That's what we see here.

Paul preached the gospel message in the synagogue. Some of those who heard him were convinced—and converted. Others were filled with jealousy and hostility. When Paul and his gospel were rejected, he told his Jewish hearers that their Scriptures authorized him to now take this same gospel to the Gentiles. Quoting Isaiah 49:6, Paul said, "I have made you a light for the Gentiles, that you may bring salvation to the ends of the earth."

GOD'S SOVEREIGNTY AND OUR RESPONSIBILITY

Luke relates that when the Gentiles heard this (that is, the Gentiles who were in the synagogue because they had converted to Judaism), they were overjoyed. They glorified the word of the Lord, which Paul had brought to them, "and all who were appointed for eternal life believed."

Now, that is a fascinating statement. It is important that we do not reverse the order of those words. Luke does not say, "and as many as believed were appointed for eternal life." He says that all who were appointed for eternal life believed. The divine appointment came first, then the faith.

Paul began this message by showing that God has been active throughout history, reaching out to human beings. Humanity didn't try to find God; it was God who reached down to find and rescue lost humanity. When men and women believe, they are responding to what God has done in reaching out to them.

Luke records that all who were appointed for eternal life believed. It's a paradox, but it's true: Our salvation involves a mysterious interaction between God's sovereignty and our responsibility, between God's election and our free will.

Finally, Luke tells us what resulted from Paul's preaching at the synagogue:

> The word of the Lord spread through the whole region. But the Jews incited the God-fearing women of high standing and the leading men of the city. They stirred up persecution against Paul and Barnabas, and expelled them from their region. So they shook the dust from their feet in protest against them and went to Iconium. And the disciples were filled with joy and with the Holy Spirit. (Acts 13:49-52)

This passage suggests that Paul and Barnabas remained in that city for an extended time, probably several weeks. During that time, the gospel went out into the surrounding region. The story of Jesus and the deliverance from guilt penetrated individual hearts and an entire society. Many believed. Many others became enraged.

Some of the religious leaders, when they saw they could not defeat Paul and Barnabas in an open debate, went behind the scenes and stirred up the Ladies' Chowder and Marching Society of Pisidian Antioch, or, as Luke called them, "the God-fearing women of high standing." They were the devoutly religious but somewhat snooty society matrons of the community. The religious leaders also stirred up the leading merchants and civic leaders—the first-century equivalent of the Chamber of Commerce. By manipulating these powerful women and men of the city, the jealous religious leaders drove Paul and Barnabas out of the region. In response, Paul and Barnabas shook the dust from their feet as a protest, then proceeded on to Iconium.

The last sentence of Acts 13 is beautiful: The disciples whom Paul and Barnabas had converted and who remained in that city "were filled with joy and with the Holy Spirit." When the Spirit dwells in a human life, the heart floods with joy. When we know we are justified, that our sins are forgiven, and that we who deserve nothing have received all things from God, how else could we respond but with joy?

24

COUNTERATTACK!

Acts 14

Over the years, scores of evangelical organizations have proclaimed the motto, "Evangelize the world in our generation!" This is a perfectly scriptural goal. Jesus, in the Great Commission, told us, "Go into all the world and preach the good news to all creation" (Mark 16:15).

But as we look around the world, we see that all of those organizations have fallen short of that goal. Generation after generation has passed, and the world has not been evangelized. There are still regions where the good news of Jesus Christ has not penetrated. This is not because these organizations have not been committed. It's not because they have sent out too few missionaries or failed to supply adequate resources. They failed because they have not followed the apostolic pattern.

As we have seen, Paul and Barnabas were the pattern setters. They began the final phase of the Great Commission, taking the gospel to the uttermost parts of the earth (Acts 1:8). They have set the pattern for Christian witness in the world, in every age of history. If we follow this pattern, we will manifest the accomplishments of the book of Acts. We will see people come to Christ and rejoice in the freedom of His forgiveness. And yes, we will see rising opposition and persecution from those whose power is threatened by the gospel.

So it's important that we pay close attention to the pattern that Paul and Barnabas have set for us in this section of Acts.

OPPOSITION IN ICONIUM

In Acts 14, Paul and Barnabas minister in three cities—Iconium, Lystra, and Derbe. In two of the cities, they meet violent opposition. Let's examine Luke's account:

> At Iconium Paul and Barnabas went as usual into the Jewish synagogue. There they spoke so effectively that a great number of Jews and Gentiles believed. But the Jews who refused to believe stirred up the Gentiles and poisoned their minds against the brothers. So Paul and Barnabas spent considerable time there, speaking boldly for the Lord, who confirmed the message of his grace by enabling them to do miraculous signs and wonders. The people of the city were divided; some sided with the Jews, others with the apostles. (Acts 14:1-4)

Iconium was a Gentile city with a large colony of Jews who met every Sabbath at the synagogue. Paul and Barnabas went to the synagogue first, as was Paul's custom. When they spoke at the synagogue, their message provoked an immediate response. "They spoke so effectively," Luke said, "that a great number of Jews and Gentiles believed." When God's truth is boldly proclaimed, there's always an immediate effect.

The gospel is not a bland or innocuous message. It affects hearts and minds like a ton of bricks falling from on high. It makes people sit up and take notice. Above all, it divides people into two camps: those who believe and those who reject Jesus. That's what happened at the synagogue in Iconium. When Paul and Barnabas declared the gospel of Jesus Christ, some believed, and some became enraged.

When the gospel is proclaimed without compromise, it arouses opposition. Luke writes, "But the Jews who refused to believe stirred up the Gentiles and poisoned their minds against the brothers." In this synagogue there were Gentiles who wanted to learn the truth about God. The pagan beliefs of their culture offered them no hope, so they turned to the Jews and their monotheistic belief system for hope.

Luke tells us that some of the Jews in that synagogue refused to believe the gospel message. They were unpersuadable. They would not even consider the possibility that Paul's gospel was the truth. Instead, they stirred up people against Paul and Barnabas, spreading lies that poisoned the minds of many.

POISONED MINDS

There were numerous letters and documents circulated in the first few centuries of the church that resembled New Testament documents but were never accepted as Scripture—and with good reason. These documents became known as the New Testament Apocrypha (the word *apocrypha* comes from the Greek *apókryphos,* meaning "of unknown or spurious validity").

One of these apocryphal books was called The Acts of Paul and Thecla. This fanciful account takes place in Iconium, and it tells the story of a romance that supposedly took place between the apostle Paul and a young woman named Thecla. The romance was so scandalous, according to this account, that it shattered the young woman's family and turned the whole city against Paul and Thecla.

This tale is libelous fiction, and scholars believe it was written at least two centuries after Paul lived. But it may have been based on the false rumors and suspicions the religious leaders in Iconium concocted to destroy Paul's reputation and poison the minds of the people against him.

Notice that, in Iconium, Paul and Barnabas do not face the same open opposition they encountered in Pisidian Antioch. Here, they are attacked by a subtle whispering campaign. Lies are spread behind their backs, and it's hard to defend against such lies. Even so, Luke tells us, "Paul and Barnabas spent considerable time there, speaking boldly for the Lord." Though their reputations were smeared, they were not driven out of the city. They were able to continue ministering in spite of the opposition they faced.

The two missionaries were probably in Iconium for several months, possibly as long as six months. Luke tells us that God confirmed the authority of their message with signs and wonders. These miracles were visual parables of the spiritual freedom that is available to all through faith in Jesus Christ.

You and I may not have an apostle's power to work signs and wonders, but nonbelievers should see God at work in our lives. They should say, "There's something amazing about the way he endures mistreatment without seeking revenge," or, "There's something uncanny about the way she demonstrates such joy and peace in spite of everything she's going through!" Our lives should exhibit the supernatural reality of God—a quality that can't be explained in terms of our personality, temperament, or circumstances. When God is at work in our lives, people can detect His presence.

Notice how the gospel divides the city of Iconium. "The people of the city were divided," Luke wrote. "Some sided with the Jews, others with the apostles." That's what the gospel always does. Though the good news may bring peace to individual hearts, it always brings division to society at large.

Jesus said, "Do not suppose that I have come to bring peace to the earth. I did not come to bring peace, but a sword" (Matthew 10:34). He was not referring to a sword of violence. He meant that the good news would be bad news to some, and people would be divided depending on their response to the gospel. The gospel is a sword that divides believers from unbelievers.

ON TO LYSTRA

Paul and Barnabas are referred to for the first time as apostles in Acts 14. In verse 4, Luke writes: "The people of the city were divided; some sided with the Jews, others with the apostles." In verse 14, Luke again uses the term: 'But when the apostles Barnabas and Paul heard of this . . . "

In time, the opposition against the two apostles intensified, as Luke records:

> There was a plot afoot among the Gentiles and Jews, together with their leaders, to mistreat them and stone them. But they found out about it and fled to the Lycaonian cities of Lystra and Derbe and to the surrounding country, where they continued to preach the good news. (Acts 14:5-7)

The opponents of Paul and Barnabas, Jews and Gentiles, plotted to silence them by stoning them to death. So the two missionaries left Iconium and went to the Gentile city of Lystra, where there was no Jewish synagogue. With no synagogue in which to begin their ministry, where should they begin? Luke tells us:

> In Lystra there sat a man crippled in his feet, who was lame from birth and had never walked. He listened to Paul as he was speaking. Paul looked directly at him, saw that he had faith to be healed and called out, "Stand up on your feet!" At that, the man jumped up and began to walk.
>
> When the crowd saw what Paul had done, they shouted in the Lyca-onian language, "The gods have come down to us in human form!" Barn-abas they called Zeus, and Paul they called Hermes because he was the chief speaker. The priest of Zeus, whose temple was just outside the city, brought bulls and wreaths to the city gates because he and the crowd wanted to offer sacrifices to them. (Acts 14:8-13)

Here we see how God opened up the city of Lystra so that Paul and Barn-abas could preach and minister with power. The two missionaries did not need to form a committee and develop a strategy to evangelize the city in a system-atic way. They went to the city and did what God had sent them to do: They preached. Since there was no synagogue there, they went to the marketplace or the town square, and they began sharing the gospel with any who would listen.

And as they proclaimed the gospel, Paul saw a man sitting in the market-place—a man who was lame from birth. We don't know how long Paul and Barnabas had been in Lystra, but they might have been there for days. In fact, they might have had conversations with this man over several days. Perhaps that's how Paul knew that the man had great faith in Paul's gospel. In any case, Paul looked at him and, being led by the Spirit, said, "Stand up on your feet!" Though the lame man had never walked in his life, he had faith enough to obey Paul's words—

And he walked.

It doesn't matter if your disability is physical, emotional, or spiritual. The moment you begin to obey God's Word is the moment your bondage ends and you begin to walk by faith. This miracle is a parable for all of us who are broken in some area of our lives.

The message of this miracle cracked the city wide open. The whole pop-ulace immediately took note of Paul and Barnabas. But even as these men preached with great power, the enemy was at work behind the scenes. Satan caused the superstitious people of Lystra to misinterpret the meaning of the miracle so that they would miss the truth.

The people began to cry out, "The gods have come down to us in human form!" They thought that Barnabas was Zeus, the supreme deity of the Greek pantheon. This was no doubt because of the full beard and dignified bearing of Barnabas. And the people thought that Paul, the chief spokesman of the two, was Hermes, the messenger of the gods. What a subtle attack on Satan's part! Instead of provoking a direct persecution, Satan appealed to the egos of the two apostles. After all, who wouldn't be flattered at being welcomed as gods?

This sort of incident has happened at other times in history. For example, when Captain James Cook of the British Navy landed at Kealakekua Bay in Hawaii, he was welcomed as the god Lono, who descended to earth on a rainbow. Captain Cook and his men were given anything they wanted, and they were quite happy to mistaken for gods.

But on February 14, 1779, Captain Cook did something that angered one of the Hawaiian men. The man grabbed hold of the captain. Angered at being manhandled, Captain Cook knocked the man down. The Hawaiian man retaliated, hitting the captain on the head with a club. Captain Cook staggered, groaning—and when the Hawaiians saw this, they shouted, "He's not a god!" And they fell on him and killed him.

Paul and Barnabas faced a situation similar to that faced by Captain Cook, but they refused to be treated as gods. Paul and Barnabas had too much Christian character to be taken in by Satan's flattery. They knew that popularity is a trap that can ruin a servant of God.

THREE INSIGHTS

Luke tells us how the two apostles responded to being worshiped as gods:

> But when the apostles Barnabas and Paul heard of this, they tore their clothes and rushed out into the crowd, shouting: "Men, why are you doing this? We too are only men, human like you. We are bringing you good news, telling you to turn from these worthless things to the living God, who made heaven and earth and sea and everything in them. In the past, he let all nations go their own way. Yet he has not left himself without testimony: He has shown kindness by giving you rain from heaven and crops in their seasons; he provides you with plenty of food and fills your hearts with joy." Even with these words, they had difficulty keeping the crowd from sacrificing to them. (Acts 14:14-18)

Here, Paul and Barnabas show us the pattern for evangelizing non-religious people: Start with nature. When they went to the Jews in the synagogues, they started with Scripture. But when they went to the Gentiles in Lystra, they started with the truth about God that was visible in the world around them. In this passage, Paul and Barnabas list three insights that should have been plain to these people because of their experience with the world of nature.

First, there is one living God behind all of creation. The multitude of pagan deities they worshiped was nothing more than a system of superstitions. According to the pagan system, there was a god for everything—a god of water, a god of trees, a god of rocks, a god of sex, a god of life, a god of death, and so forth. These gods were capricious and petty. They competed with each other and were often wicked.

Paul says, in effect, "Look at the world around you. Haven't you noticed that nature is a unity that blends and harmonizes together? It functions beautifully because it was designed and created by one God—the living God." Paul declared to them that nature bears witness to the reality of God.

Second, the living God, the God who is One, permits human beings to exercise free will, and that is what makes evil possible in the world. "In the past," the apostles say, God "let all nations go their own way." Here the two missionaries answer the question posed by skeptics: "How can a loving, just, and all-powerful God permit evil, sin, and suffering? Why doesn't He put an end to war and hate and injustice?"

The pagans in Lystra were aware of these arguments, and Paul answers by saying, "God allowed people and nations to go their own way, to exercise their own free will. The only way he could put an end to evil is by taking away our freedom of choice, which is the source of our human dignity. God will not take that from us." That is Paul's argument, and the pagans have no answer for it.

Third, God will not allow evil to go too far. He does not allow calamity and tragedy to engulf humanity and wipe the human race from the face of the earth. Even though humanity sins and rebels against God, He has shown His love by giving rain, fruit, harvest, and joy in various times of life. That's the God whom Paul and Barnabas proclaimed to these pagan Gentiles.

With that, the first onslaught of the enemy was driven back. The city of Lystra was open to the gospel. Paul and Barnabas were able to proclaim God's truth in power.

THE STONING OF PAUL

But Satan doesn't give up. Luke records the next assault, and it is vicious:

> Then some Jews came from Antioch and Iconium and won the crowd over. They stoned Paul and dragged him outside the city, thinking he was dead. But after the disciples had gathered around him, he got up and went back into the city. The next day he and Barnabas left for Derbe. (Acts 14:19-20)

The enemy counterattacks as soon as the power of the gospel is unleashed. This time, Satan dispenses with subtlety and falls back on his most reliable weapon: violence. He incites Paul's enemies in Pisidian Antioch and Iconium to travel to Lystra and turn the crowd against him, and the crowd stones Paul.

Stoning is a grisly and brutal form of execution. Heavy, sharp-edged stones are hurled at the victim, cutting the flesh, breaking the bones, and injuring the internal organs. The victim usually dies due to a combination of blood loss and internal injuries. Paul's enemies stoned him until he seemed lifeless. Then they dragged him outside the city gates and threw him on the rubbish dump.

This may be the incident in which Paul received the marks in his body that he spoke of in his letter to the Galatians: "let no one cause me trouble, for I bear on my body the marks of Jesus' (Galatians 6:17). Lystra was one of the Galatian churches, and he may have wanted to remind the believers there of the stoning he endured there.

You can imagine Barnabas and the faithful converts they had made gathered around Paul, thinking him dead, weeping over him. Perhaps Paul's friends had already begun to plan his funeral and burial, when the apostle sat up and said, "Hold the undertaker! You're not going to bury Paul yet!"

Paul was not raised from the dead. Luke makes it clear that his enemies were mistaken in "thinking he was dead.' Paul was not miraculously resurrected, but he was miraculously spared from death. It is inconceivable that a man could have survived such punishment unless God supernaturally sustained his life.

Paul and the others went back to the city of Lystra. The next day, Paul and Barnabas continued on to the next city, Derbe.

ENCOURAGING BODY LIFE

In the final section of Acts 14, we return to an important theme that threads its way throughout the book of Acts: body life. Luke writes:

> They preached the good news in that city and won a large number of disciples. Then they returned to Lystra, Iconium and Antioch, strengthening the disciples and encouraging them to remain true to the faith. "We must go through many hardships to enter the kingdom of God," they said. Paul and Barnabas appointed elders for them in each church and, with prayer and fasting, committed them to the Lord, in whom they had put their trust. (Acts 14:21-23)

Notice the courage Paul and Barnabas displayed. They had been expelled from Antioch of Pisidia, threatened in Iconium, and stoned in Lystra, yet they went back to those same three cities to encourage the disciples. In spite of threats and peril, Paul and Barnabas continued to strengthen the church. The Christian life is more than merely being converted; it is growing in Christ.

Notice three important things the apostles did to encourage body life in those cities.

First, they taught the disciples. You strengthen disciples by teaching them the Word of God, so Paul and Barnabas expounded the Word to them.

Second, they encouraged the disciples "to remain true to the faith." Paul and Barnabas went back over the Old Testament record and pointed out how men and women of God had lived by faith in ages past and how God had blessed their faithfulness.

Third, they prepared them to endure tribulation. Paul and Barnabas told the disciples, "We must go through many hardships to enter the kingdom of God." In other words, "Don't be surprised when trouble comes. It will make you grow stronger in your character and faith."

Luke goes on to say, "Paul and Barnabas appointed elders for them in each church and, with prayer and fasting, committed them to the Lord, in whom they had put their trust." These two apostles not only taught the disciples but also recognized the spiritual gifts among them and put them into key positions of leadership and ministry. They commissioned them with a time of prayer and fasting.

Because Paul and Barnabas made sure that these believers were well-grounded in the faith, the churches grew and expanded. They sent missionaries out to evangelize the region. We will see the results of their labors later in Acts.

Finally, Paul and Barnabas returned to the church in Antioch from which they had been sent out. Luke writes:

> After going through Pisidia, they came into Pamphylia, and when they had preached the word in Perga, they went down to Attalia.
>
> From Attalia they sailed back to Antioch, where they had been committed to the grace of God for the work they had now completed. On arriving there, they gathered the church together and reported all that God had done through them and how he had opened the door of faith to the Gentiles. And they stayed there a long time with the disciples. (Acts 14:24-28)

So Barnabas and Paul gathered the people together and held a body life celebration! What an exciting time it must have been, as the believers in Antioch heard the stories of the many people who came to Christ on Cyprus and in Asia Minor. Yet it must have also been a sobering experience to see Paul's body now seamed with scars and to hear of the persecution and opposition that the gospel stirred up.

Paul and Barnabas endured great hardship for the sake of the gospel—and we know Jesus Christ as our Lord and Savior because of their faith, obedience, and courage. The Lord now calls us to follow in the footsteps of these two mighty apostles, to move out and meet the challenge of this dark world, and to follow the pattern of evangelism they have set before us. May we, like Paul and Barnabas, rejoice to see the power of God advancing in our day.

25

WHAT IS GOD DOING?

Acts 15:1-21

I once asked a young couple to reach out to another couple who were newcomers to the church. I suggested they invite this couple over and welcome them to our church. The young man and young woman looked at each other, then at me. "Oh, no!" they said. "We don't want to socialize with them! They're not our kind of people!"

I was speechless. I couldn't believe I had heard such a shocking denial of the inclusiveness of the gospel. The Lord Jesus intended for His church to be a melting pot of ages, races, backgrounds, social strata, and personality types. I can't think of a more unchristian statement than, "They're not our kind of people."

All people are the Lord's kind of people. As we come to Acts 15, we will meet some men who try to split the church into "our people" and "the wrong people."

THE EMERGENCE OF FALSE CHRISTIANITY

In Acts 15, we see the emergence of false Christianity. You'll never understand the true nature of the church until you understand that false Christians are almost always present in any Christian gathering. Many millions of churchgoers are not truly a part of the body of Jesus Christ. They may hear the truth preached every Sunday, but it hasn't penetrated their lives. They have accepted a counterfeit Christianity. Luke introduces the problem in these verses:

> Some men came down from Judea to Antioch and were teaching the brothers: "Unless you are circumcised, according to the custom taught by Moses, you cannot be saved." This brought Paul and Barnabas into sharp dispute and debate with them. So Paul and Barnabas were appointed, along with some other believers, to go up to Jerusalem to see the apostles and elders about this question. (Acts 15:1-2)

This is a greatly condensed account of events that occurred over a period of months. Luke says that certain Jewish brethren, who were supposedly Christians, came from Judea to Antioch. They confronted the Gentile believers who had been converted to Christ out of pagan idolatry, and said, in effect, "Unless you Gentiles are circumcised, as we Jews are, you cannot be saved. In order to become a Christian, you must first become a Jew."

This teaching was a direct challenge to the gospel of grace that Paul and Barnabas had proclaimed, and it split the church at Antioch wide open. This has always been Satan's strategy for destroying the church: Divide and conquer.

Christians no longer divide over the issue of circumcision, but Satan's strategy of division is still in force. Today, churches divide over spiritual gifts (particularly tongues), Scripture interpretation, mode of baptism, views on divorce, ordination of women or gays for ministry, issues of race, war and peace, abortion, and the politics of the right or left. Some churches have even split over the color of the carpet or whether or not to put padding on the pews.

Now there's division brewing in Antioch. Because the church is so new and the Christians in the church are relatively untaught, this new teaching regarding circumcision seems plausible. These people from Judea seem sincere. They are deeply committed to the belief that all Christians, including Gentile Christians, need to comply with the law of Moses and be circumcised.

Moreover, the people from Judea seem to have scriptural support for their claims. They went through the Scriptures and cherry-picked verses here and there, yanking them out of context just as cultists do today. To someone who didn't know any better, it would seem that their claims were based solidly in Scripture, and that's why the faith of the Christians in Antioch was shaken.

These people from Judea based their claims on the assumption that all truth had been given in the Old Testament. The Scriptures, however, were not yet completed. God was revealing new truth. In his letter to the Ephesians, Paul wrote that the truth about the Jews and the Gentiles becoming one body in Christ was a mystery, hidden from the people of Old Testament times:

> In reading this, then, you will be able to understand my insight into the mystery of Christ, which was not made known to men in other generations as it has now been revealed by the Spirit to God's holy apostles and prophets. This mystery is that through the gospel the Gentiles are heirs together with Israel, members together of one body, and sharers together in the promise in Christ Jesus. (Ephesians 3:4-6)

Because this truth was not plainly stated in the Old Testament, it was difficult to prove that the acceptance of Gentiles into the church was not a violation of the Scriptures.

THE FIRST ECUMENICAL COUNCIL

Though we are not directly told so in Acts, this is undoubtedly the same incident Paul recounts in Galatians 2. There Paul tells us that the apostle Peter was in Antioch and felt perfectly at ease eating with the Gentile Christians. But then the men from Judea arrived, and they claimed that the Gentiles could not be saved unless they were circumcised according to the law of Moses. Peter was swayed by their claims, so he stopped eating with the Gentiles and went over to the kosher table.

When Barnabas saw Peter practicing segregation against the Gentiles, he fell into the same segregationist mindset, until Paul straightened him out. Then Paul rebuked the apostle Peter for his inconsistency. Now you can see what Luke meant when he said that this issue "brought Paul and Barnabas into sharp dispute and debate" with the men from Judea. This issue threatened to divide Christianity for all time.

So the church in Antioch appointed Paul and Barnabas to go to Jerusalem to meet with the apostles and elders to determine whether or not the Gentile believers had to be circumcised. This doesn't mean that Paul had any doubt in his mind. He wrote in Galatians, "I went in response to a revelation and set before them the gospel that I preach among the Gentiles" (Galatians 2:2). Paul knew he had received a direct revelation from the Lord, and he was prepared to defy all twelve apostles in Jerusalem if they disagreed.

For a while the fate of the gospel hung upon one man's faithfulness. Paul went to Jerusalem not because he wanted advice but because getting a ruling from the apostles was the only way to silence the Judaizers (those who wanted to impose the laws of Judaism on the Gentile believers). Paul was confident that church leaders would repudiate the false doctrine of the Judaizers and rule firmly in favor of grace. So Paul and Barnabas went to Jerusalem. Luke describes what happened there:

> When they came to Jerusalem, they were welcomed by the church and the apostles and elders, to whom they reported everything God had done through them.
>
> Then some of the believers who belonged to the party of the Pharisees stood up and said, "The Gentiles must be circumcised and required to obey the law of Moses."
>
> The apostles and elders met to consider this question. After much discussion, Peter got up and addressed them: "Brothers, you know that some time ago God made a choice among you that the Gentiles might hear from my lips the message of the gospel and believe. God, who knows the heart, showed that he accepted them by giving the Holy Spirit to them, just as he did to us. He made no distinction between us and them, for he purified their hearts by faith. Now then, why do you try to test God by putting on the necks of the disciples a yoke that neither we nor our fathers have been able to bear? No! We believe it is through the grace of our Lord Jesus that we are saved, just as they are."

The whole assembly became silent as they listened to Barnabas and Paul telling about the miraculous signs and wonders God had done among the Gentiles through them. (Acts 15:4-12)

From this account, it seems as if there was one great meeting in Jerusalem. In fact, there were three.

First there was a body life service when Paul and Barnabas arrived. They were fresh from their triumphant missionary journey through the Galatian cities, so they received a joyous welcome. Paul and Barnabas told of the spiritually hungry people who received the Word and the mobs that assaulted them. The Christians in Jerusalem were stirred by these accounts.

The next day there was a private meeting that Paul mentions in Galatians but that Luke does not record. In that meeting, Paul and the other apostles and elders discuss theology. By the end of the meeting, Paul concluded, "Those men added nothing to my message" (Galatians 2:6). In other words, Paul had learned directly from the Lord everything that the Lord had taught the other apostles during His earthly ministry. Paul's gospel was identical to theirs, and they recognized Paul as a genuine apostle. Paul added, "James, Peter and John, those reputed to be pillars, gave me and Barnabas the right hand of fellowship when they recognized the grace given to me" (Galatians 2:9).

On the next day, there was a third meeting in which the church leaders took up the issue of whether the Gentiles had to be circumcised in order to be saved.

THE GREAT DEBATE

Luke records that there was much debate at this meeting. All sides were heard. Peter, who was normally impetuous and quick to speak, kept silent for quite a while. He listened to all the different arguments, then rose to make three points.

First, Peter reminded the people that God had taught him a great lesson and stripped him of his prejudices against the Gentiles. He told them how, in the home of Cornelius, he had learned that God had a great love for the Gentiles as well as the Jews.

Second, he stated openly—and challenged his hearers to deny it—that the effort to obey the Law had been a crushing burden on the Jewish people throughout history. "Now then," he said, "why do you try to test God by putting on the necks of the disciples a yoke that neither we nor our fathers have been able to bear? No!"

Peter's third point was the most compelling of all: "We believe it is through the grace of our Lord Jesus that we are saved, just as they are." In other words, "We Jews have often tried to save ourselves by our own self-righteousness—and we can't do it! The Gentile, who never had the Law, seems to accept God's grace more readily than we do. But we Jews are saved in the same way as the Gentiles: by grace through faith alone."

That statement was so stunning that everyone in the room was silenced— even the Judaizers who were present. They all stopped talking and started thinking. The New International Version translation suggests that the people were silent in order to listen to Paul and Barnabas, who spoke after Peter, but in the original Greek text, it seems more likely that the silence Luke mentions was a thoughtful silence due to the power of Peter's statement.

In that moment of silence, Paul and Barnabas stood and confirmed the words of Peter by telling about the miraculous signs and wonders God had done through them among the Gentiles. These signs and wonders confirmed that Paul and Barnabas were apostles, and it may have been at this point that these two men received the right hand of fellowship from the other apostles.

THE CONCLUSION OF JAMES

Luke records that James, the chairman of the meeting, spoke up and summarized the results of the meeting:

> When they finished, James spoke up: "Brothers, listen to me. Simon [Peter] has described to us how God at first showed his concern by taking from the Gentiles a people for himself. The words of the prophets are in agreement with this, as it is written:
>
> > "'After this I will return
> > and rebuild David's fallen tent.
> > Its ruins I will rebuild,
> >   and I will restore it,
> > that the remnant of men may seek the Lord,
> >   and all the Gentiles who bear my name,
> > says the Lord, who does these things'
> >   that have been known for ages.
>
> "It is my judgment, therefore, that we should not make it difficult for the Gentiles who are turning to God. Instead we should write to them, telling them to abstain from food polluted by idols, from sexual immorality, from the meat of strangled animals and from blood. For Moses has been preached in every city from the earliest times and is read in the synagogues on every Sabbath." (Acts 15:13-21)

This is a crucial statement, made by the flesh-and-blood brother of the Lord Jesus. James was raised in the same Galilean home where Jesus grew up. He had not believed in Jesus during the Lord's earthly lifetime. After the resurrection, the Spirit brought to James's mind all the things Jesus had done that confirmed that He truly was the Son of God. So James became not merely a believer but one of the leaders of the early church.

His summation of the great debate is organized around four main points.

First, James underscored what God had done toward the Gentiles. Citing the earlier words of Peter, James said, "God at first showed his concern by taking from the Gentiles a people for himself." Now, this was a direct contradiction of the claims of the Judaizers, who said, "Without circumcision, the Gentiles cannot be saved." James pointed out that the Gentiles were already saved, and God had not required of them any legalistic rite such as circumcision. The Judaizers could hardly argue this point.

Second, James pointed out that when God appears to do a new thing, it can be accepted as the authentic activity of God only if it agrees with God's written Word. James recited an Old Testament passage, Amos 9:11-12, in which God promises that Jews and "the Gentiles who bear my name" will seek Him side by side in David's restored tent. The salvation of the Gentiles aligns with this Old Testament passage.

We desperately need to understand this principle. There are many strange activities taking place in our times that people claim to be the work of the Holy Spirit, yet these activities are not in line with the Word of God. People naively go along with various supernatural manifestations without searching the Scriptures to see if these manifestations are truly of God. The Spirit of God never contradicts the Word of God. If any manifestation violates Scripture, we can be sure it is not of God, period.

Jack Sparks, one of the founders of the Christian World Liberation Front and the Spiritual Counterfeits Project, once told me of a meeting in Berkeley he attended where supernatural manifestations took place. Guitars and books levitated and floated around the room. Jack knew that this was the result of demonic influence in that place. Yet there were some naive Christians present who said, "Look! God is at work here! It's a miracle!" Such activity does not correspond with the Word of God, so it cannot be the activity of God, no matter how impressive it seems.

Third, James offered practical suggestions designed to lay the controversy to rest. He proposed that the council write a letter to the Gentile Christians, telling them that they should "abstain from food polluted by idols, from sexual immorality, from the meat of strangled animals and from blood." By observing these four simple prohibitions, Gentile Christians would avoid offending the Jews.

The Gentiles were to avoid two immoral activities—idolatry and sexual immorality. And they were to be sensitive to Jewish sensibilities regarding two dietary issues—eating meat from strangled animals and eating blood. So James was saying that the Gentiles should be moral in their conduct and considerate toward their Jewish brothers and sisters. In this way, the Jews and Gentiles, despite their cultural differences, could live in harmony in the body of Christ.

Fourth, James defined the supreme purpose of God. He said that Peter had "described to us how God at first showed his concern by taking from the Gentiles a people for himself." James pointed out the great historical significance of this issue: God was calling from among the Gentiles a people for Himself. In view of the immense importance of this truth, James concluded, it would be wrong to burden the Gentile believers with a requirement to obey the law of Moses.

And the matter was settled. Note, it was not settled by a majority vote. The matter was summarized by Peter and James, and no doubt, as they spoke, heads nodded and Amens were uttered around the room. In this way, the mind of the Holy Spirit was expressed through a sense of unity that was recognized by everyone present.

The conclusion reached by this council continues to affect our lives. James and the other Spirit-filled apostles agreed upon a truth that has guided the church for twenty centuries: God has placed believing Gentiles and believing Jews together to form His church. God has created a unified community where there is "neither Jew nor Greek, slave nor free, male nor female, for you are all one in Christ Jesus" (Galatians 3:28). That is your legacy as a spiritual descendant of the first-century Christians.

26

HOW GOD GUIDES

Acts 15:22–16:10

In the late 1800s, a minister named Milton Wright stood in the pulpit of his church and announced, "You have heard that men are trying to build machines that will enable them to fly like birds. You have also heard that every such attempt has ended in failure. Why? Because men were not meant to fly like birds. These foolish men are trying to do what is contrary to the will of God!"

Bishop Wright couldn't have been more wrong about the will of God. In fact, he was proven wrong in 1903 by his two inventive sons, Wilbur and Orville.

It's not easy to know the will of God. In fact, the most common questions I hear from Christians, especially young Christians, are "What does God want me to do?" and "Where does God want me to go?" The issue of God's will always seems to revolve around what and where.

But I'm convinced that the important thing to God is not "What should I do?" or "Where should I go?" Those questions are important to us, but not to God. The question He cares about is a how question: "How will I do God's will? Will I rely on my own wisdom, strength, and resources—or on His?" That's what God is truly interested in. All other questions are simple compared with that.

I often tell young Christians that it's not difficult to allow God to direct you into what He wants you to do and where He wants you to do it. God will do that. You can hardly avoid knowing His will if you make yourself available to Him. God will open the doors of opportunity. He will direct your path.

PRINCIPLE 1: UNANIMOUS AGREEMENT REVEALS THE MIND OF THE SPIRIT

In Acts 15 and Acts 16, we find seven practical principles for discerning God's will. The first appears in Luke's account of the conclusion of the council at Jerusalem:

> Then the apostles and elders, with the whole church, decided to choose
> some of their own men and send them to Antioch with Paul and Barnabas.
> They chose Judas (called Barsabbas) and Silas, two men who were leaders
> among the brothers. With them they sent the following letter:

The apostles and elders, your brothers,

To the Gentile believers in Antioch, Syria and Cilicia:

Greetings.

We have heard that some went out from us without our authorization and disturbed you, troubling your minds by what they said. So we all agreed to choose some men and send them to you with our dear friends Barnabas and Paul—men who have risked their lives for the name of our Lord Jesus Christ. Therefore we are sending Judas and Silas to confirm by word of mouth what we are writing. It seemed good to the Holy Spirit and to us not to burden you with anything beyond the following requirements: You are to abstain from food sacrificed to idols, from blood, from the meat of strangled animals and from sexual immorality. You will do well to avoid these things.

Farewell. (Acts 15:22-29)

Here we see an important principle regarding God's guidance. The early church settled this question by first hearing everybody's viewpoint. There was a debate, and everyone had a chance to express a viewpoint on the teachings of Scripture.

You'll remember that, at the end of the council, James summed up the consensus of the discussion and underlined two points: First, he took note of the activity of God. He said that God had already answered the question for them by saving the Gentiles without requiring any rituals. Second, James took note of the Word of God. The conclusion of the council agreed with Scripture, as expressed by the prophet Amos. By combining the actions of God with the Word of God, the council came to the unanimous conclusion that expressed the mind of the Spirit.

So this is the first principle of guidance from God, especially in doctrinal matters: Unanimous agreement reveals the mind of the Spirit.

Notice that the council conveyed this decision to the people in Antioch not only by letter but also by appointing men to go and explain it to them. Here God underscores an important lesson: People learn best by having truth presented in a twofold way. Some people learn better through reading, others through hearing—but everyone learns better when both means are used. So these two men, Judas called Barsabbas and Silas, were sent to Antioch to explain the written letter and make certain that its meaning was clear.

PRINCIPLE 2: PERSIST IN LEARNING AND TEACHING THE WORD OF GOD

The second principle is set forth in the next paragraph:

The men were sent off and went down to Antioch, where they gathered the church together and delivered the letter. The people read it and were glad for its encouraging message. Judas and Silas, who themselves were prophets, said much to encourage and strengthen the brothers. After spending some time there, they were sent off by the brothers with the blessing of peace to return to those who had sent them. But Paul and Barnabas remained in Antioch, where they and many others taught and preached the word of the Lord. (Acts 15:30-35)

The Gentile Christians must have been greatly relieved to receiving the letter from the apostles, assuring them that they did not have to submit to the Jewish rituals. Luke tells us that when Judas and Silas arrived with Paul and Barnabas, they "said much to encourage and strengthen the brothers."

After Judas and Silas left, Luke says, "Paul and Barnabas remained in Antioch, where they and many others taught and preached the word of the Lord." In other words, the believers in Antioch, led by Paul and Barnabas, gave themselves to the most fundamental activity of the Christian life: learning and teaching God's Word.

Here we see the second principle in this passage: Persist in learning and teaching the Word of God. Studying God's Word is always in the will of God. Not only did Paul and Barnabas teach and preach but "many others" also. This was a church where the spiritual gifts of teaching and preaching were widely exercised.

I once visited the ruins of Baalbek, located in a valley between Beirut and Damascus. At the foot of the valley, on the Orontes River, was this very city of Antioch. In the first century, Christian communities sprang up all around that valley. As I walked around those ruins, I was amazed to see a temple to Jupiter, the supreme deity of the Romans; a temple to Bacchus, the god of wine; a temple to Venus, the goddess of sex; and a number of temples to other gods. These temples were all part of a huge complex.

Turning to my guide, I asked, "When were these temples built?"

"The temples," he said, "were built by the Romans in the first century A.D. to counteract the rapid spread of Christianity in this area."

I was astounded! The Romans went to great expense to build those temples. They quarried the columns in Egypt and painfully moved the stone blocks on rollers across desert sands or on barges down the Nile. Why? Because they were desperate to stop the spread of Christianity in that region. And who was spreading Christianity? The people we are reading about—the teaching, preaching Christians in Antioch.

PRINCIPLE 3: SHOW RESPONSIBLE CONCERN FOR OTHER PEOPLE

Now let's look at the third principle:

Some time later Paul said to Barnabas, "Let us go back and visit the brothers in all the towns where we preached the word of the Lord and see how they are doing." (Acts 15:36)

These two apostles felt responsible for the people they had led to Christ in Antioch of Pisidia, Iconium, Lystra, and Derbe. The said to each other, "Let's go see how they're doing. Let's make sure they're growing in the Lord." That is a perfectly proper leading of the Holy Spirit.

God doesn't give us detailed instructions for every situation. He expects us to use our own judgment and act responsibly. If you do those things that seem caring and responsible, then the Spirit of God will be with you in it. Don't wait for an engraved invitation from heaven. If you sense an opportunity to show responsible concern for another human being, act on it. That's the third principle, and it is always consistent with God's will.

PRINCIPLE 4: SOMETIMES DIFFERENCES REQUIRE A SEPARATION
The fourth principle arises out of a dispute between Paul and Barnabas:

> Barnabas wanted to take John, also called Mark, with them, but Paul did not think it wise to take him, because he had deserted them in Pamphylia and had not continued with them in the work. They had such a sharp disagreement that they parted company. Barnabas took Mark and sailed for Cyprus, but Paul chose Silas and left, commended by the brothers to the grace of the Lord. He went through Syria and Cilicia, strengthening the churches. (Act 15:37-41)

The two apostles could not agree on whether or not to take young John Mark with them. Barnabas wanted to give his cousin another chance, but Paul, knowing how perilous the journey would be, didn't think Mark was dependable. Luke records this sad note: "They had such a sharp disagreement that they parted company."

Who was right? Paul or Barnabas? I think we miss the point if we try to make either Barnabas or Paul out to be wrong or right. I believe both men were right. How is that possible? The answer seems obvious: Paul was focused on the ministry. Barnabas was focused on the man. Both are valid areas of emphasis.

Paul probably said, "We can't afford to take along someone who may desert us again! Remember what the Lord said: 'No one who puts his hand to the plow and looks back is fit for service in the kingdom of God'" (see Luke 9:62). And Paul would be right to say that. Christian ministry is demanding work, and human souls hang in the balance. Those who undertake the challenge of ministry should persevere to the end. Ministry is not for wimps!

Barnabas probably said, "Yes, the ministry is important—but I also feel a burden for young John Mark. He shows great promise, in spite of his past failure. Paul, you say he was wrong to quit, and I agree, but we'd be wrong to give up on John Mark. He failed us once—but who hasn't failed? Where would anyone be if there were no second chances? If we show that we believe in him, God will use him greatly someday."

The fourth principle: There are times when the differences in viewpoint require a separation. God willed that Barnabas should take Mark and go to Cyprus, which had not been visited since the churches had been founded there. And God willed that Paul take Silas and go into Syria and Cilicia, because the churches there needed his ministry.

However, I don't believe it was God's will that they quarrel. God wanted them to minister in different directions, but He did not want them to be angry with each other. When it's necessary for believers to go their separate ways, they should do so with joy and love for each other.

PRINCIPLE 5: BECOME ALL THINGS TO ALL PEOPLE IN ORDER TO SAVE SOME

For the fifth principle, we ignore the chapter division and proceed to Acts 16:

> He came to Derbe and then to Lystra, where a disciple named Timothy lived, whose mother was a Jewess and a believer, but whose father was a Greek. The brothers at Lystra and Iconium spoke well of him. Paul wanted to take him along on the journey, so he circumcised him because of the Jews who lived in that area, for they all knew that his father was a Greek. As they traveled from town to town, they delivered the decisions reached by the apostles and elders in Jerusalem for the people to obey. So the churches were strengthened in the faith and grew daily in numbers. (Acts 16:1-5)

Paul returns to Lystra, where he was stoned and nearly killed. One of those he led to Christ in that city was a young man named Timothy. Paul had observed various spiritual gifts in this young man—probably gifts of ministry, teaching, preaching, wisdom, and knowledge. Paul took Timothy with him so that he could disciple him, just as Jesus discipled the Twelve.

But there was a problem: Timothy was half Jewish (on his mother's side) and half Greek (on his father's side). The Hebrew people had a practical way of thinking about matters of lineage: They reckoned a person's line of descent through the mother. Thus Timothy was considered a Jew.

Luke then records a surprising incident: "Paul wanted to take him along on the journey, so he circumcised him because of the Jews who lived in that area." Isn't that amazing? Why did Paul circumcise Timothy?

At first glance, Paul seems to be violating his own principles regarding Jewish rituals. In Galatians, Paul tells us that when he went to Jerusalem for the meeting of the council, he took with him a Greek man named Titus (Galatians 2:1-5). The Judaizers who came to Antioch had wanted to circumcise Titus, but Paul refused to allow it. He would not concede that a Gentile had to become a Jew in order to become a Christian.

But if Paul refused to circumcise Titus, why did he circumcise Timothy?

Here we find the key to knowing the mind of God in situations where cultural customs and rituals are involved: Always determine the underlying principle at stake, then act accordingly. If Paul had permitted Titus to be circumcised, it would have meant yielding to a mindset of legalism. But the situation with Timothy was fundamentally different, in spite of superficial similarities.

Because of his Jewish mother, Timothy was viewed as a Jew, not a Gentile. In order not to offend the Jews among whom he must labor, Paul submitted to this Old Testament ritual and circumcised Timothy. Paul stated the principle that governed this action when he wrote to the Corinthians, "I have become all things to all men so that by all possible means I might save some" (1 Corinthians 9:22).

This approach may seem contradictory on the surface, but everything is reconciled once you discover the underlying principle for the decision. If our focus is on saving the lost, then we will always be willing to become all things to all people in order to save some. That is the fifth principle.

PRINCIPLE 6: LISTEN FOR THE CONFIRMING OR DENYING VOICE OF THE SPIRIT

Next, Luke introduces us to the sixth principle:

> Paul and his companions traveled throughout the region of Phrygia and Galatia, having been kept by the Holy Spirit from preaching the word in the province of Asia. When they came to the border of Mysia, they tried to enter Bithynia, but the Spirit of Jesus would not allow them to. So they passed by Mysia and went down to Troas. (Acts 16:6-8)

Paul did not wait for a voice from heaven to tell him where to go next or what he should do. He took the most logical and sensible course. He went wherever it appeared there was an open door for ministry. As it turned out, the Holy Spirit did not want him to go into Bithynia. "They tried to enter Bithynia," Luke said, "but the Spirit of Jesus would not allow them to."

I believe these words indicate that Paul experienced what we call the inner witness of the Spirit. The Spirit of God will often confirm or deny that we are pursuing a correct course. The prophet Isaiah said, "Whether you turn to the right or to the left, your ears will hear a voice behind you, saying, 'This is the way; walk in it'" (Isaiah 30:21). We need to listen for the confirming or denying voice of the Spirit, telling us whether or not we are pursuing the right course. That is the sixth principle.

We often feel the voice of the Spirit as a sense of inner peace, confirming that we've chosen the right course. But sometimes, we feel a troubling sense that we are headed in the wrong direction. That's what Paul experienced when he tried to go into Bithynia. Later, Paul did go to Bithynia, but only when the time was right according to God's timetable.

PRINCIPLE 7: REMAIN OPEN TO UNMISTAKABLE AND SUPERNATURAL LEADING

Next, look at what Paul experiences when he goes to Troas:

> During the night Paul had a vision of a man of Macedonia standing and begging him, "Come over to Macedonia and help us." After Paul had seen the vision, we got ready at once to leave for Macedonia, concluding that God had called us to preach the gospel to them. (Acts 16:9-10)

God in His sovereignty can choose any means of directing us. Sometimes he speaks to us in such an unmistakable way that we can't help knowing that this is a direct communication from God.

There was a similar occurrence when I was called to serve as pastor of Peninsula Bible Church. My name was suggested to the search committee by three different individuals, and none of these three knew that the other two individuals were also writing to the committee. All three letters arrived in the same week. When the search committee received three letters, all suggesting that they seek out a young man named Ray Stedman, they took it as an unmistakable message from the Spirit of God.

Paul had a vision of a man of Macedonia who pleaded, "Come over to Macedonia and help us." This was a vision from God. Though the vision occurred at night, it was not a dream. It was a vivid and meaningful visual experience sent to him by God.

I love Paul's response. Luke writes, "After Paul had seen the vision, we got ready at once to leave for Macedonia, concluding that God had called us to preach the gospel to them." At once! They responded immediately, and they responded in faith. When the prompting of the Spirit came, Paul didn't stop to question. He acted, confident that God would correct him if he was mistaken in any way.

Notice that when Paul received this vision, he was already moving out on a missionary venture. He was taking the gospel into previously unreached territory. When the vision came, Paul knew his exact destination: Macedonia.

And there's another interesting facet to this passage. It's at this point that Luke appears to have joined the missionary company. In verse 8, Luke writes, "So they passed by Mysia and went down to Troas." But in verse 10, he writes, "We got ready at once to leave for Macedonia." Between these verses, "they" became "we." In this way, Luke quietly indicates that he has now joined the expedition.

Luke does not say where he came from or how he got there. We don't know what his connection with Paul might have been. Perhaps he met the apostle

Paul in one of those Greek cities along Paul's journey. In any case, Luke joins Paul at this point and is part of the missionary company as it prepares to move on toward Europe.

The seventh principle for determining God's will is clear: Remain open to an unmistakable and supernatural confirmation of His will for your life. The Spirit of God may give you a vision, or He may send a series of letters that all converge on a single direction or decision. He may make His will clear to you in some other unmistakable and supernatural way. Be open to His leading, and when He shows you His will, be ready to act on it eagerly and immediately.

These are seven of the ways God guides us by His Spirit. As you seek His will for your life, make sure you do everything in total dependence upon His power and His life operating within you. Remember, only God can do God's work. As Paul once wrote, "And whatever you do, whether in word or deed, do it all in the name of the Lord Jesus, giving thanks to God the Father through him" (Colossians 3:17).

27

D-DAY AT PHILIPPI

Acts 16:11-40

The Roman emperor Tiberius Claudius Caesar came to power in A.D. 41, about a dozen years after the crucifixion and resurrection of Jesus. He ruled at the time of Paul's missionary journeys. If you asked Claudius what was the most significant event of his reign, he might have pointed to his restructuring of the Roman Senate, or the expansion of the empire into Asia Minor and Judea, or the conquest of Britannia.

But the events that made headlines in his day are almost forgotten now. Emperor Claudius could not have imagined that the one event that still affects world events twenty centuries later was the decision of a Jew named Paul to cross the Dardanelles, the narrow strait dividing Europe from Asia. It seems like such an obscure event, yet, in the reckoning of hindsight, Paul's quiet invasion of Europe truly changed the course of Western civilization. Perhaps no event except the crucifixion of Christ has so affected the world as Paul's decision to cross that narrow neck of water.

We can compare Paul's momentous decision with D-Day, June 6, 1944, when the Allies landed on the beach at Normandy, France, and changed the course of World War II. When Paul and his companions crossed from Asia to Europe, it was D-Day for the church—the day the good news of Jesus Christ invaded Europe.

THE GOSPEL INVADES PHILIPPI

Paul, Silas, and Timothy have been joined by Luke, the author of Acts. They are in the city of Troas when Paul experiences a vision (Acts 16:9-10). As a result, Luke records:

> From Troas we put out to sea and sailed straight for Samothrace, and the next day on to Neapolis. From there we traveled to Philippi, a Roman colony and the leading city of that district of Macedonia. And we stayed there several days.
>
> On the Sabbath we went outside the city gate to the river, where we expected to find a place of prayer. We sat down and began to speak to the women who had gathered there. (Acts 16:11-13)

Paul and his company arrive in Philippi. About a century earlier, a great battle had been fought outside the walls of the city. In that battle, Brutus and

Cassius, the murderers of Julius Caesar, were defeated by the combined forces of Antony and Octavian, who later became the emperor Augustus. Because of the help the Philippians gave Octavian's armies, he granted them Roman citizenship after he ascended the throne. The people of Philippi were proud of their status as Roman citizens.

When Paul and company entered the city they faced a difficult problem: How do you gain credibility among pagans who don't know you and have no knowledge of the Scriptures? Paul began by proclaiming the revolutionary message about Jesus.

The historical nature of the gospel rivets the attention. It's the story of a man who did remarkable works and preached a never-before-heard message. In a dramatic turn of events, He was taken and crucified on a hill outside the walls of Jerusalem. Then came the most startling event of all: He rose from the grave and appeared over a period of forty days to eyewitnesses. Through the death and resurrection of this man, God provides not only release from guilt but also entrance into the joy of eternal life.

In the past, Paul had always started at the synagogue, preaching to the religious Jews. But Philippi was a pagan Gentile city without a synagogue. According to Jewish law, there must be ten adult male Jews in order to have a synagogue. If not, the Jewish people were to meet by a river for prayer. That's why Luke says, "On the Sabbath we went outside the city gate to the river, where we expected to find a place of prayer."

THE PREPARED HEART OF LYDIA

So Paul, Silas, Timothy, and Luke walked along the riverside to find a Jewish prayer meeting. They found one where there were women present, but no men. There Paul and Silas began to preach the gospel, and the response was immediate:

> One of those listening was a woman named Lydia, a dealer in purple cloth from the city of Thyatira, who was a worshiper of God. The Lord opened her heart to respond to Paul's message. When she and the members of her household were baptized, she invited us to her home. "If you consider me a believer in the Lord," she said, "come and stay at my house." And she persuaded us. (Acts 16:14-15)

After we proclaim the revolutionary message of the gospel, we must leave the rest to God. Paul and his companions preached the Word and expected God to act. They didn't know what He would do, because God is always doing new and unexpected things. Because Philippi was such a spiritually dark pagan city, the Spirit used four different methods to open up the people to the message of Jesus Christ.

First, God used prepared hearts. Often, when we take the gospel into a new place, we will find that there are one or more individuals who are ready to respond to the gospel. They are like ripe fruit on a tree, ready to drop into God's hand at the slightest touch. That's the kind of person Lydia was.

Lydia was a businesswoman who sold goods that were dyed with the costly purple dye that was so highly prized in those days. She made a good living, owned her own home, and was eager to show hospitality to Paul and his companions. Her heart was ready to receive the gospel. She'd been prepared by God.

There have been times when I have spoken to groups of hostile non-Christians, and when I have seen them look at me coldly, with their defenses up, I have always been encouraged to realize that there are unquestionably one or two people in that group whom God has prepared. I have never doubted it, and I have always found it to be true. I always try to talk to those whom God has prepared, while ignoring the hostility of the rest.

That's what Paul encountered here. Lydia was ready to believe. When she heard Paul's gospel, she recognized the good news of Jesus Christ as the fulfillment of all her Jewish hopes. So she opened her heart and received the Lord—the first Christian convert on the continent of Europe.

THE SPECTACULAR DELIVERANCE OF THE SLAVE GIRL

Second, God used a spectacular deliverance to open up the city of Philippi to the gospel. Luke writes:

> Once when we were going to the place of prayer, we were met by a slave girl who had a spirit by which she predicted the future. She earned a great deal of money for her owners by fortune-telling. This girl followed Paul and the rest of us, shouting, "These men are servants of the Most High God, who are telling you the way to be saved." She kept this up for many days. Finally Paul became so troubled that he turned around and said to the spirit, "In the name of Jesus Christ I command you to come out of her!" At that moment the spirit left her. (Acts 16:16-18)

One way God arrests attention is by an act of spectacular deliverance. Sometimes He offers physical deliverance, as when He healed the lame man (Acts 3). At other times, He offers spiritual deliverance, as in the case of this teenage slave girl—what we would call a medium or a witch. She had opened herself to possession by an evil spirit, and the spirit used her as a channel to convey messages from the demonic realm. Spiritually unwary people paid money to the slave girl's owners for demonic information.

It's striking that this girl followed Paul and his companions, shouting, "These men are servants of the Most High God, who are telling you the way to be saved." At first glance, she seems to be doing Paul a favor. In reality, this is a satanic attack on the gospel. Satan knows the power of God's Word, and he knew what Paul could accomplish in Philippi if given a chance. So, to derail the gospel message, he attempted to form an alliance with Paul in order to subvert Paul's gospel.

Satan's two principal approaches are outright attack and seduction. If Satan could form an alliance with Paul, he could seduce Paul into betraying the gospel. This was a fiendishly clever attack, because the girl appeared to be on Paul's side, and the announcement she made was true. But Paul wisely refused to allow Satan to give testimony on his behalf.

Evil spirits tried a similar ploy when Jesus ministered in Israel. When the man who was possessed by many spirits fell on his knees before Jesus, he shouted, "What do you want with me, Jesus, Son of the Most High God?" (Mark 5:7). And though the evil spirits told the truth about who He was, Jesus refused to accept their testimony. Instead, He ordered the demons out of the man. Jesus refused the testimony of demons for two reasons.

First, if anyone was drawn to Jesus by the demons' words, they would be coming to Him on the wrong basis, with the wrong motive. Second, the demons were only using the truth for bait. Eventually, the truth would be mingled with error until people could no longer distinguish truth from lies. That's how cults begin: They mingle truth with error until their followers are led completely astray.

Someone once sent me a copy of Edgar Cayce's *Story of Jesus*. Edgar Cayce (1877-1945) was an American psychic who claimed he could channel answers to questions that were asked of him about health, the future, religion, reincarnation, and astrology. People called him the sleeping prophet because he would go into a sleep-like trance and utter information that allegedly came from the spirit world. His *Story of Jesus* is a mishmash of occultism and Christianity, weaving New Testament truth with absurd revelations about Jesus having been reincarnated many times, including having been a leader named Amilius on the lost continent of Atlantis. Cayce is also the source of the legend that Jesus traveled to India to study Eastern religion. Many people have been misled by this and other concoctions of error mingled with truth.

That is the threat Paul faces. Finally he became so troubled by the evil spirit's sly opposition through this possessed girl that he turns and says to the spirit, "In the name of Jesus Christ I command you to come out of her!" Instantly, the girl was delivered.

SATAN PROVOKES MOB VIOLENCE

Third, God permits satanic activity to open up the city of Philippi to the gospel.

As always, Satan was quick to twist that incident to his own purposes. He used this event to provoke men to oppose the apostle Paul. It may seem superficially that Paul is confronted by merely human opposition, but make no mistake, this is a satanic attack. We must understand that when Satan provokes people to attack Paul and his companions, this attack is permitted by God. This is the third means God uses to open up the city of Philippi. Let's see what happens next:

> When the owners of the slave girl realized that their hope of making money was gone, they seized Paul and Silas and dragged them into the marketplace to face the authorities. They brought them before the magistrates and said, "These men are Jews, and are throwing our city into an uproar by advocating customs unlawful for us Romans to accept or practice."
> The crowd joined in the attack against Paul and Silas, and the magistrates ordered them to be stripped and beaten. After they had been severely flogged, they were thrown into prison, and the jailer was commanded to guard them carefully. Upon receiving such orders, he put them in the inner cell and fastened their feet in the stocks. (Acts 16:19-24)

Paul tells us that "our struggle is not against flesh and blood, but against the rulers, against the authorities, against the powers of this dark world and against the spiritual forces of evil in the heavenly realms" (Ephesians 6:12). Those evil rulers and spiritual powers took a keen interest in everything the apostle Paul did. When we see violent opposition to Paul, we can be sure that this opposition was satanically inspired.

God permitted this satanic attack for a good reason: He knew that this attack would open a door for a church to be planted in this city. Whenever violence opposes Christian witness, it's a sign that evil is deeply entrenched there. Writing to the Christians in Corinth, Paul calls this embedded evil a stronghold. Moreover, he says, "The weapons we fight with are not the weapons of the world. On the contrary, they have divine power to demolish strongholds" (2 Corinthians 10:4).

There was a stronghold of evil in Philippi, and God used this attack on Paul and Silas to demolish its power. The fall of that stronghold would open the surrounding region to the gospel. When the effort to penetrate a region with the gospel meets violent opposition, you can be sure you are attacking a stronghold of evil.

This stronghold was expressed in the pride of the Philippians because of their status as Roman citizens. Notice the clever argument of the slave girl's owners. They hauled Paul and Silas before the magistrates and said, "These men are Jews and are throwing our city into an uproar by advocating customs unlawful for us Romans to accept or practice." Paul and Silas, they claimed, had injured precious Roman pride.

The people responded to this charge with emotion, not logic, and formed a lynch mob. Even the magistrates, who were supposed to settle such matters with reasoned application of the law, were swept up in the emotion of the moment. They ordered that Paul and Silas be stripped and flogged.

After the beating, Paul and Silas were tossed into the dungeon. Their feet were locked in stocks so that they couldn't turn over. They either had to sleep sitting up or lie down with their bleeding backs against the cold, filthy dungeon wall.

GOD'S DRAMATIC INTERVENTION

Fourth, God used dramatic intervention to open up the city of Philippi to the gospel. Luke writes:

> About midnight Paul and Silas were praying and singing hymns to God, and the other prisoners were listening to them. Suddenly there was such a violent earthquake that the foundations of the prison were shaken. At once all the prison doors flew open, and everybody's chains came loose. (Acts 16:25-26)

There's nothing unusual about an earthquake in this region. To this day, temblors are common in northern Macedonia. The earthquake was natural; the timing was supernatural. God released the earthquake at the moment of His choosing, and He set Paul, Silas, and the other prisoners free.

The most dramatic aspect of this story is not the earthquake. It's the fact that Paul and Silas were singing at midnight. It was a sacred concert that literally brought the house down. Imagine these two men, their backs raw and bloody, suffering incredible injustice in that wretched hole. They never asked, "God, how could you let this happen?" No, they praised God. They sang a first-century version of "How Great Thou Art."

I believe Paul and Silas rejoiced because they knew that Satan had panicked. Our enemy usually relies on stealth and subtlety, but when he resorts to violence, it's a sign of desperation—and that meant victory for Paul and Silas. As Paul would later write to the Christians in Philippi, "Now I want you to know, brothers, that what has happened to me has really served to advance the gospel" (Philippians 1:12). Their backs had been cut to ribbons, but the Lord had prevailed through His unstoppable resurrection power.

Paul and Silas rejoiced because they understood that physical and emotional suffering produce Christian maturity. They had benefited by this experience. Again, Paul would later write to the believers in Philippi, "For it has been granted to you on behalf of Christ not only to believe on him, but also to suffer for him" (Philippians 1:29). Suffering is part of God's program for making us mature in Christ. It's part of the Christian curriculum. Without suffering, you will never be what God wants you to be.

Returning to the narrative, we see that the ground shook and the prison was opened. Luke tells us what happened next:

The jailer woke up, and when he saw the prison doors open, he drew his sword and was about to kill himself because he thought the prisoners had escaped. But Paul shouted, "Don't harm yourself! We are all here!"

The jailer called for lights, rushed in and fell trembling before Paul and Silas. He then brought them out and asked, "Sirs, what must I do to be saved?"

They replied, "Believe in the Lord Jesus, and you will be saved—you and your household." Then they spoke the word of the Lord to him and to all the others in his house. At that hour of the night the jailer took them and washed their wounds; then immediately he and all his family were baptized. The jailer brought them into his house and set a meal before them; he was filled with joy because he had come to believe in God—he and his whole family. (Acts 16:27-34)

The jailer knew he would be executed if his prisoners escaped. Rather than allow his superiors to take his life, he drew his sword to commit suicide. He was about to plunge it into his heart when Paul shouted, "Don't harm yourself! We are all here!" The jailer was amazed to see that Paul spoke the truth. Not one prisoner had escaped. Falling to his knees before Paul and Silas, he asked, "Sirs, what must I do to be saved?"

Paul and Silas answer the jailer in terms of eternal things: "Believe in the Lord Jesus, and you will be saved—you and your household." Some commentators have misinterpreted their reply as meaning that the jailer's faith could save his household. Clearly, that's not what Paul and Silas meant. In effect, they are saying, "Believe in the Lord Jesus, and you will be saved, and those in your household who believe will also be saved."

The Philippian jailer believed, and so did the people in his household, and all were saved. Here again we see the spontaneous emergence of body life—a church is born right before our eyes! Paul and Silas had already converted Lydia and perhaps some of the other women in the town, but you don't have a church until you have men and women, and various classes of people. With the conversion of the jailer and his household, including his servants, the Philippian church has been founded.

Note how the jailer now responded to Paul and Silas, his newfound brothers in Christ: He washed their wounds. That's a beautiful picture of Christian love—and of the transformation that takes place through Christian conversion. Hours earlier, this man had thrown Paul and Silas into a dungeon, locked them in stocks, and may have even cursed them as they sang. Now they were guests in his house, and he was providing for their needs and their comfort. This is the way brothers in Christ love one another—and this is body life.

Luke tells us that the jailer "was filled with joy because he had come to believe in God—he and his whole family." He was filled with joy as a new believer, and he could celebrate with Paul and Silas the defeat of Satan in Philippi.

CITIZEN PAUL

So this is D-Day for the gospel. The word of Jesus Christ has invaded Europe, demolished one of Satan's strongholds, and established a beachhead in the city of Philippi in Macedonia. In the final section of this passage, Paul solidifies his victory on behalf of the body of Christ:

> When it was daylight, the magistrates sent their officers to the jailer with the order: "Release those men." The jailer told Paul, "The magistrates have ordered that you and Silas be released. Now you can leave. Go in peace."
>
> But Paul said to the officers: "They beat us publicly without a trial, even though we are Roman citizens, and threw us into prison. And now do they want to get rid of us quietly? No! Let them come themselves and escort us out."
>
> The officers reported this to the magistrates, and when they heard that Paul and Silas were Roman citizens, they were alarmed. They came to appease them and escorted them from the prison, requesting them to leave the city. After Paul and Silas came out of the prison, they went to Lydia's house, where they met with the brothers and encouraged them. Then they left. (Acts 16:35-40)

Paul had the officials in Philippi over a barrel, and he proceeded to extract apologies and concessions from them. The magistrates who previously mistreated him had to apologize to Paul and Silas and beg them to go in peace. Paul replied, in effect, "Okay, we'll go—but in our own time. Before we go, we want to visit with our brothers and sisters in Philippi."

Who were these brothers? I believe some were prisoners who were converted by their encounter with Paul and Silas. Many were probably converted even before the quake, and that's why they willingly remained in the prison with Paul and Silas instead of escaping.

Why did Paul raise the issue of his Roman citizenship? Why didn't he tell the authorities before he was flogged? Everything Paul did, he did for the sake of the gospel and for the Christians in Philippi. Imagine how the believers in Philippi were gladdened to see that the highest officials in the city humbled, forced to meet Paul and Silas on their terms, and forced to apologize for judicial malpractice. Paul's action elevated the church in Philippi to a much higher status than it otherwise would have had. Paul endured a flogging for the sake of the church in Philippi.

Paul's final act before leaving was to gather the brethren together and encourage them to go on with the Lord. When you read the letter to the

Philippians, written from Paul's Roman prison, you see that he was still teaching and encouraging them.

That's the pattern the early Christians followed. The minute believers came together, they began sharing body life together—bearing one another's burdens, praying for one another, rejoicing together, and living out the life of Jesus Christ through their own lives. That is the pattern the church needs to rediscover.

28

RABBLE AND NOBLES

Acts 17:1-15

The seaport city of Thessalonica was founded more than three centuries before Christ and was named after the sister of Alexander the Great. After the kingdom of Macedon fell in 168 B.C., Thessalonica came under Roman rule. By the first century A.D., the city had a sizable Jewish population. After establishing a beachhead for the gospel in the city of Philippi, Paul and his companions moved on to Thessalonica, where he began ministering among his Jewish brethren. Luke writes:

> When they had passed through Amphipolis and Apollonia, they came to Thessalonica, where there was a Jewish synagogue. As his custom was, Paul went into the synagogue, and on three Sabbath days he reasoned with them from the Scriptures, explaining and proving that the Christ had to suffer and rise from the dead. "This Jesus I am proclaiming to you is the Christ," he said. Some of the Jews were persuaded and joined Paul and Silas, as did a large number of God-fearing Greeks and not a few prominent women. (Acts 17:1-4)

Paul and Silas followed the Via Egnatia, or Egnatian Way, a road built by the Romans two centuries earlier. Because it was made from precision-fitted stones, the road still looked new in Paul's day, and parts of it are still in good condition today. The Via Egnatia connected several Roman provinces in what we now know as Greece, Macedonia, Albania, and European Turkey. The cities Luke mentions—Amphipolis, Apollonia, and Thessalonica—were all points along that road.

The apostle Paul, led by the Spirit, passed through some cities while stopping to preach in others. Paul always chose the most strategic centers where the gospel might take root and then branch out into the surrounding area. The most strategic population center in this region was Thessalonica. I have stood on the old Roman wall that formed the northern boundary of the city. From the wall, I saw the Via Egnatia winding down out of the hills, and I pictured Paul and his companions walking down that road into the city.

Let's consider the distances involved. From Philippi to Amphipolis was a distance of thirty-three miles—a long day's journey on foot. From Amphipolis to Apollonia was another thirty miles, another day's journey. Thessalonica is thirty-seven miles beyond Apollonia, which is a full day's journey at a brisk pace. So it took Paul at least three days to go from Philippi to Thessalonica. So Luke concisely reported a journey of a hundred miles with a single sentence.

When Paul and his friends entered Thessalonica, they sought a Jewish synagogue. The Lord had instructed Paul to take the gospel to the Jews first, and that was always his pattern. In the synagogue in Thessalonica, he reasoned with the people from the Scriptures over a span of three Sabbath mornings.

What was Paul doing during the rest of the week? We know from Acts 18:3 that Paul was a tentmaker by profession. He tells us in one of his letters to the Thessalonians, "We were not idle when we were with you, nor did we eat anyone's food without paying for it. On the contrary, we worked night and day, laboring and toiling so that we would not be a burden to any of you" (2 Thessalonians 3:7b-8).

ONE MESSIAH OR TWO?

When Paul taught from the Scriptures on the Sabbath, he dealt head-on with the issue that was the most difficult for the Jewish mind to accept: the death and resurrection of Christ. The Jewish people were looking for the Messiah, and they would have accepted Jesus of Nazareth as the Messiah if He had come in the form they expected: a conquering king who would subdue all enemies, rule over nations, and bring an end to war and oppression. But they could not accept a Messiah who had to suffer and die a criminal's death on a Roman cross. This was a great offense to them.

Some Jewish rabbis proposed the idea that there were two Messiahs prophesied in Scripture. One they called *Mashiach ben David*, or Messiah the son of David. This was the glorious, triumphant king. The other they called *Mashiach ben Yosef*, Messiah the son of Joseph, meaning that this Messiah would be a descendent of Joseph, who was sold into slavery by his brothers. According to this view, Mashiach ben Yosef would be a suffering forerunner preparing the way for the conquering Messiah, Mashiach ben David. They didn't understand that the suffering Messiah and the triumphant Messiah were one and the same—and He had to suffer first, then reign.

Paul taught from the Scriptures that there is only one Messiah. "This Jesus I am proclaiming to you," he said, "is the Christ." He probably taught the people from such passages as Isaiah 53 and Psalm 22, which spoke of the sufferings of the Messiah. Then, when he spoke of the resurrection of Jesus, he probably quoted Psalm 16:9-10: "Therefore my heart is glad and my tongue rejoices; my body also will rest secure, because you will not abandon me to the grave, nor will you let your Holy One see decay."

With passages such as these, Paul reasoned with the Jews in order to prove to them that Jesus was the long-awaited Messiah. And Luke records that three groups of people responded to the gospel: "Some of the Jews were persuaded and joined Paul and Silas, as did a large number of God-fearing Greeks and not a few prominent women."

First, there were the religious Jews. Religious people are the hardest to reach. They already have a set of beliefs and are emotionally attached to them. It can be hard to reason with such people and get them to look at new evidence in a logical way. But Paul, with his gifts for teaching and preaching, managed to reach a few of the religious Jewish people in Thessalonica.

Second, there were the Greeks—unprejudiced Gentiles who, weary of the pagan philosophies, had come to the synagogue to hear the truth about the one true God. Now Paul came with this amazing new message. As these Gentiles heard the word of the gospel, they were tremendously impressed, and they believed.

Third, a group of leading women of the city responded to the gospel. Luke emphasizes the conversion of women in several places in Acts. The gospel had a particular appeal to women, especially to prominent women of the upper classes. Why? It's likely that these women had an understanding of the philosophies of Greek culture and had found these philosophies to be empty and unsatisfying to the soul.

Moreover, the Greek culture was permeated with degrading sexual practices that devastated women and left them full of shame and self-loathing. Many of these women turned toward the enlightened morality of Judaism, only to find themselves burdened with oppressive rules and rituals that again left them empty.

Finally, Paul came, bringing the glad news that, in Jesus Christ, there is neither male nor female, bond nor free, Jew nor Gentile, black nor white, nor any other distinction. All the walls that separate people from each other and from God had been torn down. These women responded joyously to the liberating gospel of Jesus Christ.

So the message of Paul and his companions had a tremendous effect upon the city. God invaded the city of Thessalonica through the prepared hearts of those who were ready and ripe for the good news.

THE RABBLE RISE UP AGAINST PAUL AND SILAS

But Satan was not idle. He struck back immediately. As we shall see, however, God uses even the schemes of the devil to further His own purposes. Luke writes:

> But the Jews were jealous; so they rounded up some bad characters from the marketplace, formed a mob and started a riot in the city. They rushed to Jason's house in search of Paul and Silas in order to bring them out to the crowd. But when they did not find them, they dragged Jason and some other brothers before the city officials, shouting: "These men who

have caused trouble all over the world have now come here, and Jason has welcomed them into his house. They are all defying Caesar's decrees, saying that there is another king, one called Jesus." When they heard this, the crowd and the city officials were thrown into turmoil. Then they made Jason and the others post bond and let them go. (Acts 17:5-9)

Here we see a familiar pattern: The religious leaders were unable to out-reason and out-debate Paul and Silas. Jealous of the missionaries' ability to win converts to Christ, the religious leaders resorted to violence. They went around the marketplace and gathered up the rabble, the bad characters, the loafers and malcontents, and incited them to a fever pitch, turning them against Paul and Silas for no reason whatsoever. That's how easily a crowd can be turned into a lynch mob.

But God is fully in control. Just before the mob arrives, He sends Paul and Silas away, so they are not there when the crowd arrives. The mob has to be satisfied with dragging out Jason, who offered lodging to the missionaries. The mob drags Jason and some other Christians before the city authorities, and they make accusations against Paul and Silas, who are not present. There is just enough truth in their false charges to make them sound credible. Paul and Silas are accused of two crimes.

First, the leaders of the mob accused Paul and Silas of being notorious troublemakers. They said, "These men who have caused trouble all over the world have now come here!" Perhaps these religious leaders had heard about the trouble in Philippi. There was a nugget of truth to what they said. These Christians had indeed turned the world upside down.

But the fact is that the world was already upside down, a wretched jumble of misery and sin. When you turn something upside down that is already upside down, you are turning it right-side up. The world has been upside down since the Fall, so wherever the gospel penetrates, a little corner of the world is set aright. As men and women respond to the gospel, God's original plan for humanity begins to be worked out in their lives, and they experience healed relationships, forgiveness of sin, and freedom from shame. The world desperately needs to be turned upside down by the grace of God.

Second, the leaders of the mob accused Paul and Silas of challenging Caesar's authority by preaching another king—Jesus. This reveals the nature of Paul's message: He has been declaring the lordship and kingship of Jesus. Paul has been preaching the kingdom that Jesus proclaimed—a spiritual kingdom that encompasses all of humanity. Every human being is a subject of that kingdom, like it or not. Those who rebel against His kingship are rebellious subjects, but they are subjects nonetheless.

These religious leaders have interpreted Paul's preaching as a challenge and an insult to the authority of Caesar. It's not clear whether these religious leaders misunderstood Paul or if they deliberately twisted his words to portray him as a political insurrectionist. Most likely, they saw Paul's preaching as a challenge to their authority as religious leaders, so they distorted Paul's message for their own purposes.

The city officials settled the matter by having Jason post bond. This makes it sound as though Paul and Silas were out on bail, awaiting trial, but if that is so, these two Christian leaders jumped bail. As we will see, they left by night. It's unthinkable that Paul and Silas would deliberately cheat justice, so the bond Jason posted was evidently an amount of money paid as a guarantee that Paul and Silas would leave Thessalonica and never return.

Paul may have referred to this promise not to return to Thessalonica when he wrote in his first letter to the Thessalonians: "But, brothers, when we were torn away from you for a short time (in person, not in thought), out of our intense longing we made every effort to see you. For we wanted to come to you—certainly I, Paul, did, again and again—but Satan stopped us" (1 Thessalonians 2:17-18). How did Satan stop them? Perhaps by this official guarantee, made in Paul's absence, that he would never return.

THE NOBLE BEREANS

The next stop for Paul and company is the city of Berea. Luke writes:

> As soon as it was night, the brothers sent Paul and Silas away to Berea. On arriving there, they went to the Jewish synagogue. Now the Bereans were of more noble character than the Thessalonians, for they received the message with great eagerness and examined the Scriptures every day to see if what Paul said was true. Many of the Jews believed, as did also a number of prominent Greek women and many Greek men. (Acts 17:10-12)

I visited Berea along with Dr. Dick Hillis, the noted missionary evangelist. It's a pleasant little city in the foothills of the Olympic Mountains, about sixty miles southwest of Thessalonica. The ancient synagogue of Berea has been excavated, and archaeologists have determined that it is the synagogue mentioned in this passage. Dr. Hillis and I were privileged to stand on the steps of the synagogue where Paul preached in Berea.

We also visited the Greek evangelical church in Berea. We were there on a weekday, so there was no worship service at the time. I went up to the pulpit and found a beautiful Greek Bible there. I opened it to Acts 17 and read, in the original language of Luke, these very words: "Now the Bereans were of more noble character than the Thessalonians, for they received the message with great eagerness and examined the Scriptures every day to see if what Paul said was true" (Acts 17:11).

Luke draws a sharp contrast between the impulsive rabble in Thessalonica and the noble Bereans. Why did Luke call them noble? It's because they took nothing on blind faith but checked everything Paul said against the Scriptures. A noble person has not only an open mind but a cautious and studious heart. Noble people think, reason, and investigate the truth for themselves.

Those who are too lazy to search out the truth are lost in a sea of relativism and confusion. They let others do their thinking for them and are easily manipulated, like the rabble in Thessalonica. If you don't want to end up as a tool of manipulative leaders, you must have the nobility of mind to check out the truth according to Scripture.

It is dangerous to let any leader do your thinking for you. If you do, you'll be misled and won't recognize his errors until it's too late. Many false teachers began their ministries in evangelical churches, teaching biblical truth, but in time they veered off into heresy and took their gullible followers with them. Some false teachers, like Jim Jones of the People's Temple, drag their followers into the grave; in 1978, he compelled more than nine hundred followers to commit suicide by drinking a cyanide-laced drink. If they had nobly investigated the truth for themselves, those people would not have died.

Question every human teacher. Indeed, question everything I write in this book. Compare my teaching with the words with Scripture. The Word of God is the authority, not Ray Stedman or any other human teacher. Be as noble as these Bereans. Search the Scriptures for yourself.

The account concludes with a familiar pattern:

> When the Jews in Thessalonica learned that Paul was preaching the word of God at Berea, they went there too, agitating the crowds and stirring them up. The brothers immediately sent Paul to the coast, but Silas and Timothy stayed at Berea. The men who escorted Paul brought him to Athens and then left with instructions for Silas and Timothy to join him as soon as possible. (Acts 17:13-15)

The religious leaders were not content to drive Paul out of Thessalonica. They pursued him sixty miles away, bringing with them their now-familiar tactic of stirring up crowds with emotional harangues. They attacked Paul and Silas, and once again, Paul was forced to slip out of the city by night. One wonders if Paul was ever able to walk out of a city in broad daylight.

Paul went by sea to Athens, leaving Silas and Timothy in Berea to establish the church. Paul is free to leave because he has left a church behind. God has planted a believing community as a lighthouse in the midst of the darkness of this fallen world. The believers Paul leaves behind will push back the darkness as they exercise their spiritual gifts and proclaim the liberating truth.

When a church moves into a community, the entrenched evil in that community comes under attack, and Jesus said that the gates of hell cannot prevail against the church's attack. There may be a stiff battle for a while, but eventually the forces of light will win and the community will experience deliverance.

Even those who are not yet Christians will be able to think and perceive more clearly. From this day forward, the enemy will find it much more difficult to cloud people's minds in the city of Berea.

The gospel always improves the life of a community. That's why Paul was so concerned that the newly converted Christians he left behind in Berea and Thessalonica would learn to make use of the power of God that was now available to them.

What lay ahead for Paul? Two of the greatest centers of power, learning, culture, and moral depravity in the Roman Empire: Athens and Corinth. In those two cities, the great missionary apostle would face some of his most serious and dangerous challenges.

29

ATHENS VERSUS PAUL

Acts 17:16-34

Five hundred years before Christ, Athens was a powerful Greek city-state—the cradle of Western civilization, home to Plato's Academy and Aristotle's Lyceum. It was the city of Pericles, Demosthenes, Socrates, Sophocles, and Euripides—the thinkers whose ideas shaped the world for centuries.

But that was the glory of ancient Athens. By the time Paul arrived in Athens, it was no longer a powerful city-state, no longer the political hub of an empire. Under the Roman Caesars, Corinth had become the commercial and political center of Greece. Four hundred years had come and gone since the golden age of Greece, and Athens was long past its zenith. Though still a major center of art, philosophy, and learning, Athens had lost its political importance.

It appears that Paul did not originally intend to stay long in Athens. His real objective was Corinth, the political capital, for Paul followed a strategy of establishing churches in areas where their influence would affect the surrounding regions.

ALONE IN ATHENS

Paul had left Berea in the company of certain unnamed Christians. These men escorted Paul to Athens and then returned to their homes in Berea. They returned to Berea with a message from Paul, asking Silas and Timothy to join him in Athens as soon as possible. So Paul waited alone in Athens, and Luke tells us what happened next:

> While Paul was waiting for them in Athens, he was greatly distressed to see that the city was full of idols. So he reasoned in the synagogue with the Jews and the God-fearing Greeks, as well as in the marketplace day by day with those who happened to be there. A group of Epicurean and Stoic philosophers began to dispute with him. (Acts 17:16-18a)

While Paul was waiting at Athens, he went sightseeing, as any tourist would. Athens is the site of the great temples of the Acropolis, which is crowned by the Parthenon. It is also the site of many other beautiful buildings, theaters, marketplaces, and gardens. As the apostle walked around the city, he saw literally hundreds of statues and shrines dedicated to the many Greek gods—false gods worshiped by the Athenians.

Luke tells us that Paul's spirit was troubled when he saw the idolatry of Athens. The Greek word used here, *paroxuno*, is the word from which we get our word *paroxysm*, meaning a fit of violent emotion. Paul felt an intense paroxysm of the spirit as he saw the city given over to idolatry. Paul was not angry with the people who worshiped these idols. The citizens of Athens had never heard of the living God. In fact, the presence of so many idols revealed that the people of Athens had a deep spiritual hunger, even though idolatry represents a tragic distortion of our human capacity for faith in God. Faith in false gods offers only the darkness of superstition.

In response to the delusion he saw all around him in Athens, Paul began to preach the soul-delivering truth of Jesus. There were three groups to whom he spoke in Athens.

First, he went into the synagogue, as was his custom. There he spoke to the religious people, the Jews and devout Gentile converts. Like Paul, they hated the idolatry of the city but could do nothing about it. Paul preached the gospel to them, but with seemingly little effect.

Second, he went to the ordinary citizens of the city in the agora, the marketplace of Athens. He preached to the tradesmen, shopkeepers, and customers who went about their business. He spoke to crowds and individuals. Most were too busy buying and selling to stop and hear Paul's message.

Third, he went to the philosophers, the intellectual elite of the city. Two kinds of philosophers are mentioned: the Epicureans and the Stoics. If you think that there are no Epicureans or Stoics left in the world, you're mistaken. Though they go by other names, the people who live by these philosophies are still with us.

PAUL VERSUS THE ATHEISTS AND PANTHEISTS

The Epicureans were atheists and materialists. They denied the existence of God and the afterlife. They believed that this life is the only existence we will ever know, and so human beings should get the most out of life before they die. To the Epicureans, pleasure is the highest virtue. Their motto is "Eat, drink, and be merry, for tomorrow we die." To this day, the prevailing attitude in society is "live for the moment."

The Stoics, followers of the philosopher Zeno, were pantheists. They believed that everything is God and that God does not exist as a separate being. God is in the rocks and trees and sky and everything around us. Their attitude toward life was one of resignation. They prided themselves on their fatalistic endurance of hardship without complaint or self-pity. There are many among us who face life with stoic resignation.

Luke tells us how these two groups responded when they heard Paul's message:

Some of them asked, "What is this babbler trying to say?" Others remarked, "He seems to be advocating foreign gods." They said this because Paul was preaching the good news about Jesus and the resurrection. Then they took him and brought him to a meeting of the Areopagus, where they said to him, "May we know what this new teaching is that you are presenting? You are bringing some strange ideas to our ears, and we want to know what they mean." (All the Athenians and the foreigners who lived there spent their time doing nothing but talking about and listening to the latest ideas.) (Acts 17:18b-21)

The atheist Epicureans were contemptuous of Paul's message. "What is this babbler trying to say?" they asked as they dismissed him and his gospel.

But the Stoics were interested in what Paul had to say. This is not because they had a genuine desire to know Jesus Christ but because they were intrigued by the fact that Paul seemed to preach two new gods—one named Jesus and the other named Resurrection. The Greeks were accustomed to hearing philosophical concepts personified as gods. In Athens, there were altars to Reason, to Virtue, and to various other concepts, so why not an altar to Resurrection? They were interested because, as Luke said, they "spent their time doing nothing but talking about and listening to the latest ideas," much as many people do today.

Ancient Athens contained the same cross-section of humanity we see: religious recluses who wall themselves off from an idolatrous society; superstitious idolaters living lives of quiet desperation; atheistic materialists who live for today; and self-sufficient fatalists who take pride in their stoic resignation. Paul came to this society with a word of deliverance from God: believe in the resurrected Lord Jesus Christ, and you will be saved. This was a message the people of Athens had never heard before, so they invited Paul to present his message before a meeting of the Areopagus.

PAUL'S INTRODUCTION

If you visit Athens today, you'll be taken up a small, rocky hill west of the Acropolis. Your guides will tell you that this is Mars Hill where Paul addressed the Athenian philosophers. I doubt that this is so. While the word *Areopagus* does mean "Mars Hill," the Areopagus was also the name of a court of judges who had final authority over the city of Athens at that time. Paul was probably brought before this court, which met in one of the porches beside the city marketplace.

In his message before the Areopagus, Paul gave us a splendid example of how the gospel delivers human beings. There are three parts to this message, beginning with his attention-arresting introduction:

Paul then stood up in the meeting of the Areopagus and said: "Men of Athens! I see that in every way you are very religious. For as I walked around and looked carefully at your objects of worship, I even found an altar with this inscription: TO AN UNKNOWN GOD. Now what you worship as something unknown I am going to proclaim to you." (Acts 17:22-23)

Note the graciousness of Paul's words. He did not denounce the Athenians for their idolatry. In fact, he complimented their interest in spiritual things. He said, in effect, "I have walked around your city, and I can see that you are a very religious people." The Greek word used in the text was *deisidaimonesteros*, a compound word that literally means "god-fearers." Paul is not saying that the Athenians fear the one true God (*theos*); he is saying they fear lesser gods or spirits (*daimon*). In any case, the Athenians understood that he was complimenting them for having a consciousness of, and a capacity for, the things of God.

He went on to say, in effect, "While walking around your city, I found one particular altar dedicated to an unknown god." There were several of these altars in Athens. Why had the Athenians erected altars to anonymous gods?

According to Athenian legend, a deadly plague was stopped centuries earlier when the people of Athens turned a flock of sheep loose within the city. Wherever the sheep were found, they were slain and sacrificed as an offering to a god. If a sheep was slain near the altar of a recognized god, the people dedicated the sacrifice to that god. But if a sheep was slain where there was no altar nearby, an altar was quickly erected and the animal was sacrificed to an unknown god.

Paul had learned about this legend, so he told the people at Areopagus, "This unknown God is the One I have come to tell you about. I have come to declare to you the God you have unknowingly and ignorantly worshiped for years." Paul's introduction reveals the emptiness of paganism. If you do not worship the true God, there is no end to your searching. Paul understands the spiritual anguish of human beings crying out for a God they know must exist but cannot find.

My friend Dave Roper once told me of an evangelistic rally he attended at Stanford University. During the rally, a student came up and seized Dave by the shoulders. The young man was wild-eyed and upset. He shook Dave by the shoulders and said, "Can you tell me where I can find Dave Roper?"

The young man was so intense, he was scary! Dave almost wanted to say he'd never heard of Dave Roper. But he answered, "I'm Dave Roper."

At this, the young man relaxed. He said, "Can you tell me how I can find God?"

That was the hunger of this young man's heart. That was the hunger of so many people in Athens. They hungered for the unknown God, the God they could not find.

PAUL'S FIRST POINT: GOD IS THE MAKER AND GIVER OF ALL THINGS

After his introduction, Paul proceeded to make the first of two points. First, he unfolded the truth about the living God that is obscured by idolatry:

> "The God who made the world and everything in it is the Lord of heaven and earth and does not live in temples built by hands. And he is not served by human hands, as if he needed anything, because he himself gives all men life and breath and everything else." (Acts 17:24-25)

Here Paul unveils a profound and startling truth to the Athenians. There are not many gods. There is one God, and He is the Maker of all things. God was not created by man; He is the One who made man and everything that exists throughout the universe. He is the Source and Originator of all things.

God is the giver and has no needs. "He is not served by human hands, as if he needed anything," Paul says, "because he himself gives all men life and breath and everything else." Pagan idolatry teaches that the gods demand gifts from human beings. Paul says, "That's wrong! The true and living God does not need gifts from you. He Himself is the giver of life and breath and all good gifts."

People fall into the same error today. They think that idolatry is practiced only by primitive people, yet they themselves are ensnared in idolatry. They sacrifice their time, effort, energy, and devotion to the demanding gods they have made. An idol is anything that occupies the primary place of importance in your life. Some people have made wealth and material possessions their god. Others have made a god of fame, and they will sacrifice anything to attain it. Some people make idols of alcohol or drugs or gambling or some other addiction. That's why the most successful addiction recovery programs are those that replace the idol of addiction with a relationship with God.

False gods promise to provide the things we want most in life: meaning, purpose, joy, satisfaction, and security. But false gods are liars. The things we want most in life can come only from a relationship with the one true eternal God. Only He can give us the desires of our hearts.

Paul told the Athenians that God does not live in temples made by human hands. As he said this, I'm sure he pointed up toward the Parthenon, for it was revered as the home of Athena, the goddess for whom Athens was named. God does not live in buildings. He needs no roof over his head. He created the universe and everything in it.

PAUL'S SECOND POINT: GOD DRAWS ALL OF HUMANITY TO HIMSELF

Paul now makes the second of his two points: God draws people to Himself. To the Athenians, the gods dwelt high on Mount Olympus, remote from humanity. People had to go through perilous journeys to find the gods and placate them. But the true and living God has reached out to humanity. He is not remote, He does not hide. He is near:

"From one man he made every nation of men, that they should inhabit the whole earth; and he determined the times set for them and the exact places where they should live. God did this so that men would seek him and perhaps reach out for him and find him, though he is not far from each one of us." (Acts 17:26-27)

The one true God is the Lord of history. He made man as one race, originating from one source. Despite differences of pigment, stature, and feature that exist around the world, there is only one race of human beings, and all descend from one source. God has determined where and how long they shall live. He allows one nation to rise, another to fall. God does not do so arbitrarily or capriciously but strategically: He arranges events so that human beings might find Him. That is why He allows history to take place.

All of human history is focused on one single goal: God wants to motivate human beings to seek Him. The Scriptures affirm this truth again and again: "Anyone who comes to him must believe that he exists and that he rewards those who earnestly seek him" (Hebrews 11:6b). And in the Old Testament we read, "'You will seek me and find me when you seek me with all your heart. I will be found by you,' declares the Lord," (Jeremiah 29:13-14a).

I've met scores of people who were in the grip of an idolatrous delusion—seeking fame or success, addicted to drugs or alcohol, compulsively pursuing pleasure and sexual gratification—until some calamity crashed into their lives. Suddenly, they saw their need of God. They realized that God had been calling to them, and they had stubbornly resisted Him—so, at last, they have surrendered to Him. If God is calling you, don't make Him use extreme measures to get your attention. Draw near to God, and He will draw near to you.

WE ARE GOD'S OFFSPRING

Paul concludes with a discourse on our relationship with our Creator:

God did this so that men would seek him and perhaps reach out for him and find him, though he is not far from each one of us. 'For in him we live and move and have our being.' As some of your own poets have said, 'We are his offspring.'

"Therefore since we are God's offspring, we should not think that the divine being is like gold or silver or stone—an image made by man's design and skill. In the past God overlooked such ignorance, but now he commands all people everywhere to repent. For he has set a day when he will judge the world with justice by the man he has appointed. He has given proof of this to all men by raising him from the dead." (Acts 17:27-31)

Paul concludes with a statement of human dignity, rooted in the recognition that we are God's offspring. It is not biblical to tell people that human beings are vile, worthless worms. True, we are powerless to save ourselves, and the highest righteousness we can achieve in our own strength is like filthy rags. But the Bible does not tell us we are worthless worms.

In the Scriptures we learn that we are made in the image of God, and we have a capacity to respond to God. We are made for God. We have a love for building and creating and achieving goals because we were made in the image of a God who is a builder, a creator, and a master planner. Human inventiveness and creativity are echoes of the creative genius of God. We seek fellowship with one another because God seeks fellowship with us, and we are made in His image. God's likeness, stamped upon us at creation, is the source of our greatest dignity.

Paul points out that since we were made in God's image with a capacity to know Him, it's insulting to God and degrading to ourselves to worship an idol. "Therefore since we are God's offspring," Paul says, "we should not think that the divine being is like gold or silver or stone—an image made by man's design and skill." Paul is deeply troubled by the tragedy of prostituting our noble capacity for God through idolatry.

"In the past God overlooked such ignorance," Paul says, "but now he commands all people everywhere to repent." When Paul speaks of the past, he is not talking about Old Testament times. He is speaking of the past of each individual who is hearing him speak. He's saying, in effect, "Prior to this moment, you were ignorant, and God took your ignorance of Him into account. But now you have heard the truth, and God commands you to repent of your idolatry and turn to Him."

Once that person learns the truth about Jesus, he or she becomes responsible to respond to that truth through repentance. Paul says that God "commands all people everywhere to repent," to change their minds, to turn around and walk in a new direction. Paul then states three great facts that underscore the importance of repentance.

First, there is a day of judgment coming. "For he has set a day," Paul says, "when he will judge the world." The day of judgment has been fixed and circled in red on God's calendar. You and I don't know when that day will come, but the Father knows the exact date when every life will be evaluated.

Second, there is an unchallengeable Judge. 'He will judge the world with justice," Paul says, "by the man he has appointed." That man is Jesus. The One who will evaluate every human life will not be some remote deity upon Mount Olympus but a man who has lived among us, who knows what human life is like. He has been tempted and tested in every way as we are, yet without sin. He will pass judgment on that day.

Third, God has made these facts known through a historic event, an irrefutable truth: God raised Jesus from the dead. That is the foundational reality upon which Christianity rests. If you can disprove the resurrection of Jesus, you can destroy Christianity in one blow. As long as that fact remains, Christianity is unshaken.

THE ATHENIANS' REACTION

In the closing verses of this passage, Luke relates the reaction of the Athenians:

> When they heard about the resurrection of the dead, some of them sneered, but others said, "We want to hear you again on this subject." At that, Paul left the Council. A few men became followers of Paul and believed. Among them was Dionysius, a member of the Areopagus, also a woman named Damaris, and a number of others. (Acts 17:32-34)

Some Athenians mocked Paul's words. That's still the reaction of many people today. When they hear of Jesus and His resurrection, they ridicule the subject.

Others put off making a decision. Paul had just called them to repentance, but they said, in effect, "You are an interesting fellow, and you have many fascinating ideas. We'd like to hear more from you—tomorrow. No, we don't wish to repent right now, thanks. We don't want to get swept up in the emotions of the moment. We wish to view this entire subject with intellectual detachment. Come back tomorrow, and give us more evidence that we may study." This was an intellectual delaying tactic.

But there were still others who responded immediately to Paul's message. They heard, they believed, and they repented. The ones who repented were the earnest, honest seekers after truth. They wanted answers to life's questions, and the moment they heard the good news of Jesus Christ, they knew they had found it. The story of the crucified and resurrected Lord broke through their darkness, and their hungry hearts responded.

"A few men became followers of Paul and believed," Luke concludes. "Among them was Dionysius, a member of the Areopagus, also a woman named Damaris, and a number of others." Dionysius the Areopagite was one of the judges—an intellectual Greek, a ruler of the city—and now he was also a Christian.

With him was a woman named Damaris. I'm glad that Luke included the name of a woman. This is one of many instances in the New Testament that show us how the gospel of Jesus Christ elevated the status of women in that culture.

These few people formed the nucleus of the church in Athens. Why, then, do we never hear anything else in the New Testament about the Athenian church? I suspect that the letters to the Corinthians were also shared with the church in Athens, because the cities were not far apart. We don't know what ultimately happened to the church in Athens. We only know that here, amid the darkness of pagan idolatry, the light of Jesus Christ shone—and the body of Christ took form in that city.

Next, we will see Paul move on to Corinth, one of the most strategically important cities in the first-century world.

30

THE CROSS IN CORINTH

Acts 18:1-22

Athens and Corinth were twin centers of evil in the first-century world. Athens was the intellectual capital of the Roman Empire. Corinth was the center of immorality and sensuality of the Roman Empire. These two cities symbolized the forces that still seek to enslave the hearts of people: intellectual pride and sensual lust.

Paul now leaves Athens and moves fifty miles west, to the city of Corinth. At the time Paul visited there, Corinth was the capital of the Roman province of Greece, which they called Achaia. It was a center of commerce and trade, located on a narrow neck of land between the Adriatic and Aegean Seas. Corinth was a beautiful city in a magnificent natural setting. Some of the Corinthian temples of Paul's day are still standing.

Corinth was a center for worship of Aphrodite, the Greek goddess of love and beauty (the Romans called her Venus). The great temple of Aphrodite stood on the Acrocorinth, the rocky hill overlooking the city. Every evening, a thousand prostitute-priestesses of the temple would come down into the streets to ply their sensual trade. Thus Corinth was known as the hub of sensual indulgence for the Roman world. Corinthians were usually portrayed in Greek drama as morally depraved drunkards.

So the apostle Paul came to Corinth, a city much like the celebrated sin capitals of today's world—San Francisco, Las Vegas, Rio de Janeiro, Amsterdam, Bangkok. It was infested with certain strongholds of evil that the apostle describes in his second letter to the Corinthians—places where evil was entrenched and difficult to dislodge: "The weapons we fight with are not the weapons of the world. On the contrary, they have divine power to demolish strongholds" (2 Corinthians 10:4).

We saw such a stronghold of evil in Philippi (Acts 16), where Paul and Silas were unjustly beaten and imprisoned by city officials. Whenever the gospel encounters violent opposition, you usually find a stronghold of evil. In Corinth, the pagan belief system created a stronghold that was intensely resistant to the gospel. There was rampant sexual perversion, racial strife, and political tyranny. We live in Corinthian conditions today, and the same kind of satanic stronghold that Paul encountered there is found in cities and towns across our country and around our world.

PAUL, THE TENTMAKER-EVANGELIST

The apostle arrived as a stranger, knowing no one, yet confident that God would open the door to ministry. Luke tells us how he went about it:

> After this, Paul left Athens and went to Corinth. There he met a Jew named Aquila, a native of Pontus, who had recently come from Italy with his wife Priscilla, because Claudius had ordered all the Jews to leave Rome. Paul went to see them, and because he was a tentmaker as they were, he stayed and worked with them. Every Sabbath he reasoned in the synagogue, trying to persuade Jews and Greeks. (Acts 18:1-4)

Again, Paul follows the familiar pattern by beginning his ministry in the synagogue. He made his living by working as a tentmaker, and while he was working at his trade, probably in the Corinthian marketplace, Paul encountered a fellow Jew who was also a tentmaker. This man was Aquila. Along with his wife, Priscilla, he had just been forced out of Rome by an anti-Jewish decree of Claudius.

Since Paul plied the same trade as Aquila and his wife, the three of them worked together, and it wasn't long before Paul led Aquila and Priscilla to Christ. They became faithful ministry partners of the apostle Paul and are frequently mentioned in the pages of Scripture.

Paul has set an example for us all. As believers, we should take advantage of every situation where we can build relationships with people so that we can share the good news of Jesus Christ. The workplace is a natural environment for building friendships. At the same time, we should remember not to use company time for evangelism. We owe full diligence to our employers when we are on the clock. But we can invite our co-workers over for weekend barbecues, be available to them in times of crisis, and set a good example of Christlikeness at all times.

THE ARRIVAL OF SILAS AND TIMOTHY

When Silas and Timothy arrived from Macedonia and rejoined Paul, the apostle took a different approach toward ministry in Corinth. Luke writes:

> When Silas and Timothy came from Macedonia, Paul devoted himself exclusively to preaching, testifying to the Jews that Jesus was the Christ. But when the Jews opposed Paul and became abusive, he shook out his clothes in protest and said to them, "Your blood be on your own heads! I am clear of my responsibility. From now on I will go to the Gentiles."
>
> Then Paul left the synagogue and went next door to the house of Titius Justus, a worshiper of God. Crispus, the synagogue ruler, and his entire household believed in the Lord; and many of the Corinthians who heard him believed and were baptized. (Acts 18:5-8)

Paul's efforts in Corinth were initially successful, but it was not long before the preaching of the crucified Christ aroused bitter opposition in the synagogue. As long as Paul dwelt upon the predictions of a glorious, conquering Messiah, the people listened attentively. But when Paul spoke of the suffering and crucified Messiah, the people openly opposed him.

So Paul shook his garments before them—a Middle Eastern gesture that means, "I no long have any relationship with you!" He told them, in effect, "I've tried to spare you from spiritual death, and you refuse to hear me! I tried to warn you, but you've sealed your own fate. Since you reject this message, I will go to the Gentiles of this city."

Luke includes a fascinating detail: When Paul went to the Gentiles, he didn't go far. He went next door, to the house of Titius Justus. Not only did this Gentile live next to the synagogue, but in the Greek text it's clear that his house and the synagogue shared a common wall. This is significant because we next see that Crispus, the ruler of the synagogue, was won to Christ. Both he and his household believed. So even after Paul went to the Gentiles, he continued to have influence at the synagogue.

Among the other citizens of Corinth there was a tremendous response. Many who heard Paul believed and were baptized. Paul did not often conduct baptisms himself because he didn't want people to brag about being baptized by the apostle Paul. He later wrote to the Christians in Corinth:

> I am thankful that I did not baptize any of you except Crispus and Gaius, so no one can say that you were baptized into my name. (Yes, I also baptized the household of Stephanas; beyond that, I don't remember if I baptized anyone else.) (1 Corinthians 1:14-16)

Silas and Timothy undoubtedly helped by conducting many of the baptisms.

ASSAILING THE STRONGHOLDS OF CORINTH

The next section reveals Paul's emotional state while he was in Corinth:

> One night the Lord spoke to Paul in a vision: "Do not be afraid; keep on speaking, do not be silent. For I am with you, and no one is going to attack and harm you, because I have many people in this city." So Paul stayed for a year and a half, teaching them the word of God. (Acts 18:9-11)

In the original Greek text, the Lord literally says to Paul, "Stop being afraid, but keep right on speaking." This reveals that Paul was indeed afraid, and that's understandable. A pattern was developing—a pattern that always seemed to end in violent opposition. Paul would start by preaching to the Jews in the synagogue. When they rejected his message, he would turn to the Gentiles and see many conversions. This aroused jealousy and hostility among the Jewish religious leaders, and soon he was either arrested or beaten or ousted from the city.

We tend to think of Paul as practically fearless, but Paul experienced fear just as we do. In a letter to the Corinthians, he wrote, "I came to you in weakness and fear, and with much trembling" (1 Corinthians 2:3). Paul greatly feared what he would have to suffer in Corinth. Why? Because the strongholds of evil in that city were violently opposed to him.

When Paul entered Corinth, the entrenched powers of darkness were shaken and disrupted by the spiritual awakening he brought. That, after all, is the only legitimate mark of a successful church. Many churches today measure success by what happens within the congregation—greater membership, attendance, involvement, or giving. It's wonderful when good things happen within a congregation, but that's not the mark of success. A church is successful only when it affects the world around it.

The Lord Jesus said, "You are the salt of the earth. . . . You are the light of the world" (Matthew 5:13-14). The church was never intended to be a safe, cloistered retreat from the brokenness of society. It was intended to be salt, a preservative for a corrupt and decaying world. It was intended to be light, a source of brilliant illumination, pushing back the darkness of sin and spiritual ignorance.

God has painted a bull's-eye on the world. If the church does not hit that bull's-eye, the church has failed. If I enter a city and I see church buildings on every corner while that city is locked into cycle after cycle of violence, hatred, immorality, shattered families, and so forth, I know there's something wrong with the church in that city.

All the evils of our day were present in Corinth in Paul's day. True, there was no Internet pornography in that day, but every form of lust and perverted desire could be indulged in ancient Corinth. And as Paul brought this radical, revolutionary message of the gospel to the heart of the city, he threatened the strongholds of evil that kept men and women in bondage to sensuality, addiction, and corruption.

As the apostle Paul began to see lives transformed by the gospel in that city, he knew it was only a matter of time before the evil spiritual forces fought back. Paul feared Satan's retaliation—and with good reason. He had been stoned, beaten, imprisoned, and more. He had looked death in the eye on several occasions, and like any human being in Paul's circumstances, he had experienced fear.

That's why the Lord appeared to Paul in a vision. That's why the Lord spoke to him so graciously and reassuringly, telling him in effect, "Paul, don't let your fears defeat you! Stop being afraid! Be bold! Speak out! Keep right on preaching because I have people in this city who will protect you."

I'm reminded of how, in football, the quarterback is protected in much the same way. The linemen form a protective pocket around the quarterback, and the quarterback drops back into the pocket. There he is protected long enough to throw a pass or hand the ball to the running back. That's what the Lord says to Paul: "Yes, the enemy is after you, but I have built a pocket around you. Just concentrate on moving the ball and gaining ground, because you are surrounded by protectors."

These are words of powerful encouragement: "I have many people in this city." God had sovereignly chosen people among the Corinthians who would be His people. For the moment, they were still pagans, but the Lord knew they were there. He knew He could send Paul into that city, even though it was an enemy stronghold, and His people who would rise up and serve as Paul's allies and protectors.

Paul was greatly strengthened and encouraged by the vision. For a year and a half, he continued in Corinth without being persecuted. He was able to preach the truth and establish a large, vibrant church in Corinth.

While Paul was in Corinth, he wrote his first and second letters to the Thessalonians, the believers he had converted in Acts 17. These two letters are the earliest-written of all of Paul's New Testament letters. The apostle undoubtedly wrote to other churches during that time, but those letters have not been preserved. Some of Paul's lost letters are mentioned in the New Testament. The Thessalonian letters, however, were preserved because they contain the full-orbed teaching of the New Covenant that is crucial to an understanding of New Testament doctrine.

TRUTH ON THE SCAFFOLD, WRONG ON THE THRONE

Of course, opposition is practically inevitable, but when the attack against Paul finally comes, God's restraining hand is in control of events:

> While Gallio was proconsul of Achaia, the Jews made a united attack on Paul and brought him into court. "This man," they charged, "is persuading the people to worship God in ways contrary to the law."
>
> Just as Paul was about to speak, Gallio said to the Jews, "If you Jews were making a complaint about some misdemeanor or serious crime, it would be reasonable for me to listen to you. But since it involves questions about words and names and your own law—settle the matter yourselves. I will not be a judge of such things." So he had them ejected from the court. Then they all turned on Sosthenes the synagogue ruler and beat him in front of the court. But Gallio showed no concern whatever. (Acts 18:12-17)

The Jewish religious leaders brought Paul into the courtroom of Gallio, the Roman proconsul of Achaia. This courtroom has been excavated, and you can visit the site. In Greek, the place is called the *bema*, "the scale," meaning the judgment seat. I have walked around in this courtroom and visualized the apostle Paul standing before the proconsul Gallio, who was the prosecutor and judge in that courtroom.

The life and career of Junius Annaeus Gallio is well documented in secular history. He was the older brother of the philosopher Seneca, who was at that time serving as tutor to the young Nero, who would one day succeed Claudius as emperor. Seneca dedicated his treatises *De Ira* and *De Vita Beata* to Gallio. Both Seneca and the poet Statius spoke of Gallio as a man of personal charm, calm disposition, and impartial justice. Because Gallio's tenure as proconsul of Achaia can be dated at A.D. 51 to 53, we know that the events of Acts 18 took place somewhere in that three-year span of time.

The Jewish religious leaders accused Paul of violating Roman law by promoting a new religion. "This man," they said, "is persuading the people to worship God in ways contrary to the law." The law they referred to was Roman law, not Jewish law. They probably supported their accusations by citing some of Paul's claims about Jesus—His teachings, His crucifixion, His resurrection—and they undoubtedly twisted Paul's words.

But Gallio was an astute man. Through his example, we see how God often uses governmental authorities to preserve the peace and permit the gospel to go forth. Luke points out that Paul didn't even get to speak in his own defense. "Just as Paul was about to speak," Luke says, the judge threw the case out of court. In effect, Gallio said, "Look, if this man had violated Roman law, I would judge him. But it's obvious that this dispute is about fine distinctions between Jewish religious factions. Case dismissed!"

This was an important precedent-setting decision. Gallio had ruled, in effect, that Christianity was, in the eyes of the Romans, a sect of Judaism. And Judaism was an officially recognized religion within the empire. This meant that Paul was free to preach the gospel throughout the Roman Empire and was not in violation of Roman law.

Now notice what happens to Sosthenes, the ruler of the synagogue. The previous ruler of the synagogue, Crispus, had evidently resigned his position when he became a Christian (Acts 18:8). Sosthenes, the successor of Crispus, had tried to have Paul punished under Roman law, but he had bungled the matter so badly that the Jewish religious leaders became enraged. They seized Sosthenes and beat him in the courtroom, right in front of Gallio, the Roman judge. Gallio was unmoved even by this display of disorder in the court.

It appears that this beating did Sosthenes a lot of good. In Paul's first letter to the Corinthians we read, "Paul, called to be an apostle of Christ Jesus by the will of God, and our brother Sosthenes" (1 Corinthians 1:1). By the time Paul wrote his first letter to the Christians in Corinth, Sosthenes had become Paul's companion and secretary.

I would never recommend physical violence as means of evangelism, but it seemed to work in this case. Sosthenes' eyes were opened when his fellow religious leaders turned against him. Deciding that their opposition to Christianity might not be a just cause after all, Sosthenes gave heed to the gospel, received Jesus as Lord, and became a co-laborer with Paul.

Acts 18 is a beautiful picture of how God stands watch over His people and achieves His purpose through their lives. This is the same principle James Russell Lowell described in his poem "The Present Crisis":

> Truth forever on the scaffold, Wrong forever on the throne,—
> Yet that scaffold sways the future, and, behind the dim unknown,
> Standeth God within the shadow, keeping watch above his own.

THE CONCLUSION OF PAUL'S SECOND MISSIONARY JOURNEY

Luke traces the end of the second missionary journey with just a few words:

> Paul stayed on in Corinth for some time. Then he left the brothers and sailed for Syria, accompanied by Priscilla and Aquila. Before he sailed, he had his hair cut off at Cenchrea because of a vow he had taken. They arrived at Ephesus, where Paul left Priscilla and Aquila. He himself went into the synagogue and reasoned with the Jews. When they asked him to spend more time with them, he declined. But as he left, he promised, "I will come back if it is God's will." Then he set sail from Ephesus. When he landed at Caesarea, he went up and greeted the church and then went down to Antioch. (Acts 18:18-22)

Paul stayed a long time in Corinth after Gallio dismissed his case—perhaps as long as two years. The Christian faith was now legally accepted, so Paul had an open door for ministry, and he took advantage of it. Finally, he took Priscilla and Aquila with him and sailed from Cenchreae, one of the ports of Corinth.

Luke makes an interesting observation: "Before he sailed, he had his hair cut off at Cenchrea because of a vow he had taken." Luke refers here to a religious vow. According to the Law, this was a way of expressing thanks to God, undoubtedly for the success of his ministry in Corinth.

Paul and his companions went first to Ephesus in the Roman province of Asia. Earlier, in Acts 16:6-8, Paul was forbidden by the Spirit to preach the word of the Lord in the region of Asia Minor that included Ephesus. But on this occasion, at the close of his second missionary journey, Paul was allowed to come into that city.

As usual, Paul began at the synagogue. The people there received his message and asked him to stay longer. Paul, however, was eager to return to Jerusalem, so he left Aquila and Priscilla to minister there while he continued on to Caesarea on the coast of Palestine. From there, Luke says, Paul "went up [to Jerusalem] and greeted the church." In other words, he spent some time in

Jerusalem and reported on all that God had done during his second missionary journey.

Finally, Paul returned to Antioch. He had begun his second missionary journey at Antioch some two to three years earlier, and now he has reached the conclusion of that journey in the same city.

THE PATTERN OF PAUL

Through this account of the second missionary journey of Paul, God is showing us that if we follow His pattern for evangelism, He will creatively orchestrate the circumstances of each situation to achieve His goals. What is His pattern for evangelism? It's the pattern of Acts: The early Christians always began by preaching of the Word. Then, as people came to Christ, the church was formed. In the church, believers began to experience body life—loving one another, praying for one another, and putting their spiritual gifts to work. As the body of Christ began to function, the innovative Holy Spirit led believers into creative evangelistic approaches for each specific situation. Thus the Word went out with power and affected the surrounding community.

This is still God's pattern for advancing His church into the world. The lesson of Acts 18 is that God is prepared to work through us to bring down strongholds of evil, to shake up entire communities, and to set men and women free. This will take place as the body of believers operates as God intended it to.

The work of ministering and witnessing for God was never intended to be the exclusive domain of a few professional Christians. God calls all believers to be His witnesses. God has commissioned all believers to recognize and exercise their spiritual gifts. When all of us, not just a few of us, begin to function as the body of Christ, it won't be long before the world around us is affected and changed.

31

HALFWAY CHRISTIANS

Acts 18:23–19:7

As we follow along with Paul on his missionary journeys, we catch profound glimpses of his personality and character. We see him in all of his human contradiction—his courage and his fears, his outspoken boldness and his soft-spoken humility, his hardheaded practicality and his sensitive spirituality, his proclamation of truth and his ministry of grace. Again and again, as Paul goes from situation to situation, we see a servant of God who has been refined by trials and defined by faith.

At this point in Acts, Paul has returned from his second missionary journey. He has gone to the church in Jerusalem, where he reported all that God had done during his travels in Asia Minor and Europe. Then he went back up to Antioch of Syria, where he enjoyed a brief but well-deserved rest. Luke tells us what happened next:

> After spending some time in Antioch, Paul set out from there and traveled from place to place throughout the region of Galatia and Phrygia, strengthening all the disciples. (Acts 18:23)

Paul set off on his third missionary journey alone. On this trip, he covered familiar ground, ministering among friends whom he had personally led to Christ. Whereas his first two journeys were focused on planting churches in new territories, the primary purpose of this journey was to strengthen the churches already established. So Paul devoted this journey to the training of the disciples. He went among the churches in Galatia and Phrygia, teaching them the Word of God. Paul knew that they could not grow stronger as Christians without a continually increasing understanding of the Word, so teaching was Paul's means of "strengthening all the disciples."

APOLLOS AND THE MESSAGE OF JOHN THE BAPTIST

In the next section, Luke introduces us to a key figure in the early church:

> Meanwhile a Jew named Apollos, a native of Alexandria, came to Ephesus. He was a learned man, with a thorough knowledge of the Scriptures. He had been instructed in the way of the Lord, and he spoke with great fervor and taught about Jesus accurately, though he knew only the baptism of John. (Acts 18:24-25)

Apollos was not a Christian at this point. He was a Jewish orator trained in the Hebrew schools at Alexandria in Egypt. He was well versed in the Scriptures, but his understanding was limited by the fact that he had learned only "the baptism of John," meaning the message preached by John the Baptist. This meant that Apollos possessed a great deal of truth because John, the forerunner of Jesus, had pointed the way to Jesus. But John died before the crucifixion and resurrection of Christ, so the truth Apollos had received was incomplete. John's message consisted of three great truths. First, John told the people that the forgiveness of sins was possible on the basis of repentance, and there was no longer any need to bring a sacrifice or offering. This was a startling message to the Jews. They had been told that the only way to receive forgiveness of sin was through an animal sacrifice. Because the blood of the slain animal symbolized the shed blood of Jesus, God accepted, temporarily at least, the blood of the animal on behalf of the people and forgave their sins. But John came with the startling word that God wanted repentance, not sacrifice.

Second, John told the people to express their repentance through water baptism, a symbolic act of cleansing. John announced that as people repented and changed the direction of their lives, turning away from sin and toward God, He forgave their sins. The symbol of forgiveness was the washing of baptism. John insisted that their repentance had to be real and that their lives had to produce the fruit of true repentance.

Third, John announced that One was coming after him who would complete the work John had begun. Repentance is just a beginning. It doesn't give us eternal life. It doesn't provide power for effective living. John announced that the coming One would bring true salvation and power for living: ""I baptize you with water. But one more powerful than I will come, the thongs of whose sandals I am not worthy to untie. He will baptize you with the Holy Spirit and with fire" (Luke 3:16).

So Apollos knew these three truths, but he knew nothing of the cross, or of the resurrection, or of the coming of the Holy Spirit on the day of Pentecost. His message was incomplete.

APOLLOS AND THE INSTRUCTION OF PRISCILLA AND AQUILA

Luke records what happened next:

> He began to speak boldly in the synagogue. When Priscilla and Aquila heard him, they invited him to their home and explained to him the way of God more adequately.
>
> When Apollos wanted to go to Achaia, the brothers encouraged him and wrote to the disciples there to welcome him. On arriving, he was a great help to those who by grace had believed. For he vigorously refuted the Jews in public debate, proving from the Scriptures that Jesus was the Christ. (Acts 18:26-28)

Here we see the first instance of an excellent Christian tradition: inviting the preacher home to dinner!

Though Aquila and Priscilla were Christians, they continued to meet on the Sabbath with the Jews in the synagogue. They probably held meetings in their home as well, probably on Sunday, the day of resurrection. But on this particular Sabbath, they were in the synagogue and heard Apollos preach. They saw that his knowledge went only as far as the teaching of John the Baptist, so they graciously invited him home to dinner with them and helped him understand the gospel more completely.

Though Aquila and Priscilla are relatively new in the faith, having been led to Christ by Paul in Corinth just a few years earlier, they show an amazing depth of spiritual maturity. They don't criticize Apollos for preaching an incomplete gospel. They don't accuse him of heresy. Instead, they invite him to their home and fill in the gaps of his knowledge. They undoubtedly explained both the Old Testament prophecies of Christ and the events that fulfilled those prophecies, the crucifixion and resurrection.

To his everlasting credit, Apollos humbly sat under the teaching of these two members of his congregation and listened to their instruction. Apollos must have rejoiced to learn that John's proclamation had been fulfilled and that the One John had baptized now provided the way of salvation for all people. It may have taken time for him to grasp the implications of the cross, the resurrection, and the coming of the Holy Spirit, but it was all good news, and he received it joyfully.

Apollos immediately decided to go to Corinth in Achaia, probably because there was a congregation of believers there who had been instructed by the apostle Paul. Aquila and Priscilla were led to Christ by Paul in Corinth, so Apollos wanted to go where he could learn more about this good news. The brethren in Ephesus sent letters of recommendation with him so that the brethren in Corinth would receive him.

Because of his deep knowledge of the Old Testament Scriptures, Apollos was a great help to the Corinthian believers. He strengthened the faith of the Christians and answered the arguments of opponents. Armed with the knowledge he had received from Aquila and Priscilla, he strengthened the believers who were planted in Corinth by Paul. That's why Paul says in 1 Corinthians 3:6 that he planted and Apollos watered.

HALFWAY CHRISTIANS

In the next section, Paul again takes center stage:

> While Apollos was at Corinth, Paul took the road through the interior and arrived at Ephesus. There he found some disciples and asked them, "Did you receive the Holy Spirit when you believed?"

They answered, "No, we have not even heard that there is a Holy Spirit."

So Paul asked, "Then what baptism did you receive?"

"John's baptism," they replied. (Acts 19:1-3)

In Acts 18:23, we saw Paul traveling throughout Galatia and Phrygia, strengthening the believers there. Now we see Paul arriving in Ephesus, just as he had promised at the close of his second journey (Acts 18:19-21). As was his custom, Paul undoubtedly went to the synagogue in Ephesus. There he encountered some disciples. We are not told whose disciples they were, but if we link this account with the previous account concerning Apollos, it seems that they must have been disciples of Apollos. They were men and women whom Apollos had told about Jesus, according to the teachings of John, but these teachings were incomplete.

Paul heard these disciples speaking about Jesus, and at first he thought they were Christians. But the longer he observed them, the more he realized that something was missing. I'm sure there was puzzlement in Paul's voice when he finally asked them, "Did you receive the Holy Spirit when you believed?"

The Greek text makes it clear that Paul's understanding is that the Spirit would be given at the instant of genuine conversion, and that is why Paul was puzzled. These disciples knew about Jesus and appeared to be followers of Jesus, but something was missing. Perhaps Paul saw that there was no joy in their lives or that they were not exercising the gifts of the Spirit.

So Paul asked them, "Did you receive the Spirit when you believed?" The disciples answered, "No, we have not even heard that there is a Holy Spirit." So Paul asked, "Then what baptism did you receive?" They replied, "John's baptism."

At that moment, Paul understood what the problem was: These people were halfway Christians. They had come as far as repentance and the forgiveness of sins, but they knew nothing about the work of the Holy Spirit.

THE BIBLICAL GIFT OF TONGUES

Paul began to instruct these halfway Christians, as Luke explains:

Paul said, "John's baptism was a baptism of repentance. He told the people to believe in the one coming after him, that is, in Jesus." On hearing this, they were baptized into the name of the Lord Jesus. When Paul placed his hands on them, the Holy Spirit came on them, and they spoke in tongues and prophesied. There were about twelve men in all. (Acts 19:4-7)

Here Luke summarizes in two sentences what was certainly hours of teaching by the apostle Paul about the life, death, and resurrection of Jesus and about the coming of the Holy Spirit. After he had instructed them in this way, they were then rebaptized in the name of Jesus. This is significant, for it clearly shows that the baptism they had received, based on an incomplete knowledge of Jesus, was not Christian baptism.

When these people were rebaptized by Paul, he laid his hands upon them. He was not imparting any supernatural power on them. Rather, he was signifying his identification with them. Paul made a symbolic statement that he and they were part of one body—the body of Christ. The moment he performed this act of identification, the Spirit came into their lives. They believed on Jesus, and the Spirit came immediately.

The mark of the coming of the Spirit was the exercise of spiritual gifts. Many people who read this passage note only that these believers spoke in tongues. But there are two gifts mentioned here. These believers immediately began exercising their spiritual gifts, the first of which was speaking in tongues. This is listed as one of the gifts of the Spirit in 1 Corinthians 12. It's natural that this gift would be given, for, as Paul tells us in 1 Corinthians 14, the gift of tongues is a witness to those who do not believe.

These twelve disciples were Jews. They had sat under the teaching of Apollos and were regarded as a sect of Jews. Then they became Christians, but their friends were still religious Jews. Now these disciples were filled with the Holy Spirit, and they used the gift of tongues to praise God in languages they had never learned—and they did so publicly as a sign to unbelievers that God was powerfully at work in their lives. (For a more complete discussion of the gift of tongues, see chapter 3, "Speaking of Tongues.")

Along with the gift of tongues was the gift of prophesying. This is the ability to open and expound the Scriptures in power and truth. The Greek word for "prophesied" is *propheteuo*, which is derived from two other Greek words: *pro phaino*. The word *pro* means "before," and *phaino* means "to cause to shine." A prophet is a person who stands before the Word of God and causes it to shine. The gift of prophecy illuminates people's lives with the power and truth of the Scriptures. Peter uses the term this way: "And we have the word of the prophets made more certain, and you will do well to pay attention to it, as to a light shining in a dark place" (2 Peter 1:19).

These twelve new Christians of Ephesus began to prophecy as the Spirit illumined their minds. They declared the truth of Scripture with power. This was a sign to the apostle that they had moved into the full experience of the Christian life. Paul specifically tells us, "Tongues, then, are a sign, not for believers but for unbelievers; prophecy, however, is for believers, not for unbelievers" (1 Corinthians 14:22). Here, believers and unbelievers were present, so the Spirit caused both gifts to be manifested.

There are many people today who believe in Jesus but do not manifest much evidence of the Spirit in their lives. Often, when I go to speak at different churches, I'm tempted to ask, "Did you receive the Holy Spirit when you believed?" There's no sign of the Spirit. They are not exercising their gifts. They are simply taking up pew space.

The Holy Spirit is given when we believe in the Lord Jesus. But the work of the Spirit in our lives doesn't end there. We are to keep on believing in the Lord Jesus and to keep manifesting the power and vitality of the Spirit in our lives. As Paul wrote, "So then, just as you received Christ Jesus as Lord, continue to live in him" (Colossians 2:6).

If we lack the evidence of the Spirit in our lives—if we do not demonstrate His grace and power in our lives—it's probably because we do not truly believe in Him. We believed in Him once, and we still say, "Oh, I believe in Jesus," but do we trust Him to lead us in our daily lives? Do we ask Him to do great things through us? Do we ask Him to lead us to someone who needs to hear His gospel? Do we have a sense of anticipation about the ministry He is going to do through us?

Or, when we say, "I believe in Jesus," are we merely looking back ten, twenty, or fifty years to a profession of faith we have long since neglected? Do you truly believe in Jesus? If you would say, "Yes," then my next question would be, "Is the evidence of the Spirit's power manifested in your life?" If you can't honestly answer "Yes," then you have ceased believing in Jesus.

Jesus makes Himself available to us continually, moment by moment, to fulfill every demand life makes upon us, if we believe in Him. The question Paul asked those halfway Christians in Ephesus so long ago is still the question you and I must answer: "Did you receive the Holy Spirit when you believed?"

32

OUT, WITCHCRAFT!

Acts 19:8-20

When Paul came to Ephesus, he found the city gripped by pagan religion, sensuality, and satanic darkness. The great temple of the goddess Artemis was located there. It was one of the seven wonders of the ancient world, and people traveled from all over the Roman Empire to see it. However, the rituals performed there in worship of Artemis are too loathsome to describe.

In Acts 19, Luke gives us a fascinating account of how the gospel can affect an entire region through a small band of Christians. God never wins His battles by majority vote. He always uses a small, outnumbered force, employing approaches completely unlike the methods of the world, and He achieves results that are humanly impossible.

Ephesus was a center of witchcraft, demon worship, astrology, and superstition. With so many pagan priests, magicians, witches, warlocks, and quacks of every description, the city was not unlike so many cities in the United States today.

The occult was once considered a thing of the distant past in America. That changed in the late 1960s with the rise of the New Age counterculture. Today, occult practices are everywhere. We attend PTA meetings and wait in supermarket checkout lines with people who live in unimaginable spiritual darkness and engage in degrading practices. Large parts of our culture are in bondage to demonic forces beyond our comprehension. So Paul's experience in first-century Ephesus is highly relevant to the spiritual challenges we face.

IN THE HALL OF TYRANNUS

Paul came to Ephesus and assaulted the strongholds of evil in that city. It was from Ephesus that Paul wrote to the church at Corinth: "The weapons we fight with are not the weapons of the world. On the contrary, they have divine power to demolish strongholds. We demolish arguments and every pretension that sets itself up against the knowledge of God, and we take captive every thought to make it obedient to Christ" (2 Corinthians 10:4-5).

And it was to Ephesus that Paul wrote from Rome: "For our struggle is not against flesh and blood, but against the rulers, against the authorities, against the powers of this dark world and against the spiritual forces of evil in the heavenly realms" (Ephesians 6:12). Those words underscore Paul's view of this city. He saw Ephesus as a stronghold of darkness that could be overcome only by the weapons of spiritual warfare.

Strongholds of evil are just as real and dangerous today as they were twenty centuries ago. In this account, we see what can happen when a church lays hold of the weapons of spiritual warfare and begins to operate as God intended.

Paul began his ministry in Ephesus where he always began—at the synagogue:

> Paul entered the synagogue and spoke boldly there for three months, arguing persuasively about the kingdom of God. But some of them became obstinate; they refused to believe and publicly maligned the Way. So Paul left them. He took the disciples with him and had discussions daily in the lecture hall of Tyrannus. This went on for two years, so that all the Jews and Greeks who lived in the province of Asia heard the word of the Lord.
>
> God did extraordinary miracles through Paul, so that even handkerchiefs and aprons that had touched him were taken to the sick, and their illnesses were cured and the evil spirits left them. (Acts 19:8-12)

Paul began by speaking of the kingdom of God—the rightful rule of God over human hearts and His desire to bless us and bring us into a place of fellowship with Him. The kingdom of God, Paul said, arrived with the coming of Jesus Christ. This kingdom was opposed to the rule of Satan. Wherever the gospel went, it liberated human beings from the tyranny of satanic control.

At first, the people welcomed Paul's message. You'll recall that the Jewish colony in Ephesus had previously welcomed Paul and invited him to return and speak. So, as promised, he returned. For three months, every Sabbath day, Paul reasoned with them out of the Scriptures concerning the kingdom of God. But when the people realized that submission to the lordship of Jesus meant turning away from the emptiness of religious legalism, opposition arose.

People who take pride in their outward religiosity and respectability don't like to hear that they have to come to Christ on the same humble basis as every other sinner: "Nothing in my hands I bring / Simply to Thy cross I cling." Religious respectability is the toughest nut to crack in the satanic kingdom.

So the proud religious people of the synagogue rose up against Paul and started a smear campaign against the Way, the Christian church. Paul withdrew from the synagogue and moved into rented quarters, the hall of Tyrannus, a lecture room where the Greek teachers taught philosophy.

Some manuscripts include an interesting detail that the New International Version omits: Paul had the use of the hall from eleven o'clock in the morning until four in the afternoon. During this time, the people of Ephesus took what Spanish cultures call a *siesta*, an afternoon map. The Ephesians closed up their shops, went home, had a leisurely meal, worked in the garden, slept, and so forth. The shops reopened at around four, and business went on until nine or ten at night. This was a normal work day in Ephesus.

Paul was a businessman. He made tents during the morning hours to support himself. At eleven o'clock, when the businesses closed down, he went to the hall of Tyrannus, where he taught for five hours every day for two years. Five hours a day, six days a week, fifty-two weeks a year for two years adds up to 3,120 hours of teaching. Imagine the impact of all of that teaching! No wonder Luke says that "all the Jews and Greeks who lived in the province of Asia heard the word of the Lord."

The Roman province of Asia was larger than the state of California, and there were many cities in the province. Paul did not teach all of those people in the province of Asia. Rather, Christians heard him in the lecture hall of Tyrannus, and they took the great truths he taught and told them to people throughout the region. Many people came to Christ, and many churches were formed. In two years, the entire province had been reached with the gospel of Jesus Christ.

EXTRAORDINARY MIRACLES

During this time, the church at Colosse was begun by Epaphras and Philemon, who carried the gospel to the cities in the Lycus valley. Other believers, perhaps Trophimus and Tychicus, young men from this province, took the gospel to other cities of the region. They may have founded the churches to which John later wrote his letters in the book of Revelation—Smyrna, Sardis, Thyatira, Pergamum, Philadelphia, and Laodicea. Some of these churches were probably begun by Christians whose names have been lost to history but who had sat under Paul's teaching in the hall of Tyrannus.

Luke tells us that the word Paul spoke was confirmed by signs:

> God did extraordinary miracles through Paul, so that even handkerchiefs and aprons that had touched him were taken to the sick, and their illnesses were cured and the evil spirits left them. (Acts 19:11-12)

Note that word *extraordinary*. These miracles were unusual. They were of a different kind than before. These miracles were performed when pieces of cloth touched Paul and were carried away to the sick, so that healings took place at a distance from Paul. Now, there was no inherent power or virtue in these cloths, and we can be misled if we do not understand Luke's meaning.

Some words in the original Greek text are difficult to translate into English. The New International Version says that "even handkerchiefs and aprons that had touched him" were used to heal the sick. These were not handkerchiefs or aprons in the usual sense. The Greek word in the text was *soudarion*, literally meaning "sweat cloth." These were the bands of cloth Paul used to wipe the sweat from his eyes while toiling as a tentmaker.

And the aprons in the original Greek were *simikinthion*, meaning "half-girding." They were leather shop aprons worn by workmen, not dainty little kitchen aprons. These cloths and aprons were associated with labor, and they symbolized the toil Paul went through in order to make the gospel available to the people.

A number of so-called faith healers have appropriated this practice for their own ends. They anoint little linen cloths and mail them out to people with a promise of miraculous healing, but they are really offering unbiblical superstition. That's not what Luke describes in this scene.

The cloths used here are symbols that God employs to underscore the fact that Paul is allowing himself to be used as a conduit for the power of God. It's like the staff of Aaron, the brother of Moses, in Exodus 7. There God told Aaron to throw his staff down on the ground, and when he did, the staff became a serpent. Later, in Numbers 17, God caused Aaron's staff to bud and blossom and bear ripe almonds as a sign that God had chosen Aaron and his tribe to serve as priests in Israel. There was nothing magical about the rod. It was a symbol of God's affirmation of Aaron's ministry.

The sweatbands and work aprons of Paul were symbols of the honest, dignified labor of the apostle. They pictured his humble heart and servant's obedience. That's what God wants to teach us through these pictures of healing cloths. These were more than miracles; they were, Luke tells us, extraordinary miracles. Through these extraordinary miracles, God confirmed that Paul was a diligent and humble laborer who was willing to stoop to a lowly trade so that the power of God would be released.

THE SEVEN SONS OF SCEVA

Paul's work in Ephesus threatened the stronghold of evil there. We know this by the way the powers of darkness attempted to form an alliance with Paul. As we have seen before, this is Satan's favorite trick. He tries to join the team so that he can subvert it from within. Luke writes:

> Some Jews who went around driving out evil spirits tried to invoke the name of the Lord Jesus over those who were demon-possessed. They would say, "In the name of Jesus, whom Paul preaches, I command you to come out." Seven sons of Sceva, a Jewish chief priest, were doing this. [One day] the evil spirit answered them, "Jesus I know, and I know about Paul, but who are you?" Then the man who had the evil spirit jumped on them and overpowered them all. He gave them such a beating that they ran out of the house naked and bleeding.
>
> When this became known to the Jews and Greeks living in Ephesus, they were all seized with fear, and the name of the Lord Jesus was held in high honor. (Acts 19:13-17)

The seven young men were the sons of a Jewish high priest, and they recognized an opportunity to use this new religion, Christianity, to advance their own cause. Employing these two names, Jesus and Paul, as though they were a magic formula, these men tried to cast out evil spirits.

We have people like the sons of Sceva today. They are called mediums, fortune tellers, psychics, yogis, gurus, channelers, clairvoyants, remote viewers, palm readers, witches, and on and on. They know how to impress the ignorant with their occult jargon. Some are con artists. Others meddle with real spiritual forces that they don't begin to understand. Like the sons of Sceva, they think they are in control of spirits, but they soon find that the spirits control them.

What happened to these seven sons is both serious and funny. They adjured the evil spirit by the names of Jesus and the Christian preacher, Paul. The evil spirit was angered that these men tried to invoke the name of Jesus against it when they clearly had no authority to use His name. The demon replied, "Jesus I know, and I know about Paul, but who are you?"

It's significant that the Greek text uses two different words for "know." The demon says, in effect, "Jesus I know very well, in a deep and innate way." The demon, of course, had once been an angel in the courts of God before having fallen with Satan. So this demon undoubtedly had an experience with the Son of God that went back thousands of years. The evil spirit knew Jesus very well.

Next the demon says, "And I know about Paul—I'm acquainted with him. I don't have the same deep knowledge of Paul that I have of Jesus, but I'm aware of who he is." The demon might have been involved in some of the attacks against Paul in the past. Paul, a humble servant of the Most High God who lived in reliance upon the Spirit, had no doubt proven to be a formidable opponent for this evil spirit.

Then the demon said, "But who are you?" The seven sons of Sceva had no answer to that question, so the evil spirit, using the body of the possessed man, pounced on all seven sons at once. The demon beat them, slashed at them, and terrified them. You can imagine those seven men tumbling out the doors and windows with their clothes ripped, their flesh bloodied, and their eyes wide with horror.

Perhaps because of the grotesque and almost slapstick nature of the incident, the story was told all over Ephesus. Jews and Greeks heard about it. The result was that the name of Jesus was magnified among all the people, because His name intimidated the rulers of the invisible realm of the spirits.

This was the first sign of weakness in the stronghold of darkness in Ephesus. As Jesus said, "If Satan drives out Satan, he is divided against himself. How then can his kingdom stand?" (Matthew 12:26). Here we see the kingdom of Satan divided. These seven would-be exorcists, followers of a satanic philosophy, thought they could control the evil spirit. Instead, it sent them fleeing.

The stronghold of evil in Ephesus could not withstand the weapons of Christian warfare—righteousness, faith, and love.

HIDDEN POWER

Luke tells us what took place next:

> Many of those who believed now came and openly confessed their evil deeds. A number who had practiced sorcery brought their scrolls together and burned them publicly. When they calculated the value of the scrolls, the total came to fifty thousand drachmas. In this way the word of the Lord spread widely and grew in power. (Acts 19:18-20)

Notice that the cleansing of witchcraft from this city began with the Christians. Luke says, "Many of those who believed now came and openly confessed their evil deeds." The Christians began to clean up their own lives, confessed their hidden practices, and repented of them. These were new Christians, and in their spiritual immaturity they probably didn't realize at first that they were doing anything wrong.

But as they sat under the teaching of the apostle Paul and learned about the kingdom of God, they began to see that occultism, astrology, and other superstitious practices held them in bondage. They confessed their sin and repented.

This precipitated another mass repentance. The pagans in the city took a second look at their own practices. Many had practiced the magic arts and owned books containing spells and incantations. Luke says, "A number who had practiced sorcery brought their scrolls together and burned them publicly." In this way, they were set free from their deadly delusion.

The church is the light of the world. When the church cleanses itself of sin, light breaks forth upon the surrounding culture. People begin to experience freedom from sinful practices. That's what happened in Ephesus. The believers and the pagans surrendered their occult literature, and this proved to be an expensive repentance. The value of the books came to fifty thousand pieces of silver—a tremendous sum. This meant that many people in Ephesus were forsaking their old livelihood in order to expunge the demonic evil from their lives.

This account shows how witchcraft gets its claws into people. Human beings are not easily invaded by demonic forces. Though supernatural forces are operating all around us, God made man to be a king and has built into us certain safeguards that keep us free from demonic control. Demons can't simply force their way into a human life and take possession, though they would like to. They must first find a way to coax us into yielding our will to their influence. Only when we voluntarily give way can they take possession and dominate our lives.

I once taught a home Bible class in the Bay Area of California. After one session, a young lady took me aside and said, "I've been having some strange experiences. A year and a half ago, when I was a school teacher in Alaska, another girl and I roomed together. During those long winter evenings, when there was nothing to do, we whiled away the time with a Ouija board. We got various messages and thought it was just a game.

"But I became aware of some strange thoughts when I'd go to bed at night. I'd think of certain obscene words. At first I could put them out of my mind and go to sleep, but they gradually became more insistent. Finally, I couldn't sleep until I obeyed the inner voices and started to write down the filthy words.

"I told my roommate about this, and she said she was having the same experience. Even now, after I've moved back to California, I find that I can't get to sleep until I write out, sometimes for hours at a time, all the filthy things these voices insist I say. Is God making me do this?"

"Absolutely not!" I said. "You are being influenced by the powers of darkness." I turned to Deuteronomy and showed her what the Word of God says: "Let no one be found among you who sacrifices his son or daughter in the fire, who practices divination or sorcery, interprets omens, engages in witchcraft, or casts spells, or who is a medium or spiritist or who consults the dead" (Deuteronomy 18:10-11).

She was tremendously helped by the realization that these practices are an abomination to the Lord. I showed her how to receive Jesus as her Lord and Savior. I told her to pray and ask God for help whenever she felt this kind of influence.

Several weeks later, I saw her in a restaurant, and she said, "I can't thank you enough for what you told me. It's been wonderful to be free of those awful voices. I've been doing what you suggested, and I'm finding that the Lord keeps the voices away."

All occult practices are satanic tricks to entice us into opening our minds and yielding our wills to demonic influence. Books and Web sites about occult practices promise that you can discover hidden power known only to a few. It's true that you can find hidden power in the occult, but you don't control that power. It controls you.

HIDDEN POWER

Paul and his companions assaulted the stronghold of evil and cracked it wide open. As a result, Luke said, "the word of the Lord spread widely and grew in power." Ephesus was shaken to its corrupt core. God intended for His church to go on the offensive against the strongholds of evil.

There are demonic strongholds all around us—fortresses of witchcraft, addiction, sexual immorality, pornography, child abuse, gambling, crime, racism, atheism, intellectual pride, and on and on and on. The people trapped in these strongholds need to be freed from their bondage to sin and delusion. Our mission as believers is to launch a relentless assault of love and light against those demonic fortresses.

God is not willing that any should perish. He longs to deliver people from these strongholds, and He has given the church all the power it needs to accomplish the task. But first we must awaken from our slumber and come alive. We must truly, authentically become the body of Christ. May God open our minds and hearts to understand the weapons we have at our disposal and the power that is ours through reliance upon Him.

33

DANGEROUS CHRISTIANITY

Acts 19:21–20:1

What is a Christian?

I believe the most apt description is this: "A Christian is a person who is completely fearless, continually cheerful—and constantly in trouble." That surely describes the apostle Paul.

Christianity is a dangerous faith. If you do not think so, you have not begun to live it. We are followers of the One who said, "Do not suppose that I have come to bring peace to the earth. I did not come to bring peace, but a sword" (Matthew 10:34).

Paul came to Ephesus and found an enemy stronghold defended by demonic powers. The people were held in bondage to spiritual darkness. Using the mightiest weapons ever known—the spiritual weaponry of truth, love, and faith—Paul attacked the stronghold. Within two years, the enemy's grip on Ephesus was broken.

After the great Ephesian bonfire, when the people burned their books of black magic in the public square, it appeared that Paul's work was done. The Marines had landed, and the situation was well in hand. So Paul began to think of moving on.

THREE MATTERS ON PAUL'S MIND

There were three matters occupying Paul's mind. Luke tells us:

> After all this had happened, Paul decided to go to Jerusalem, passing through Macedonia and Achaia. "After I have been there," he said, "I must visit Rome also." He sent two of his helpers, Timothy and Erastus, to Macedonia, while he stayed in the province of Asia a little longer. (Acts 19:21-22)

What were the three issues that pressed on Paul's mind?

First, he was concerned about the new Christians who had come to Christ in Macedonia and Greece (Achaia). Paul had planted churches in Thessalonica, Berea, Philippi, Athens, and Corinth, and he wanted to pass through Macedonia and Achaia again. He longed to impart more truth to the believers there.

Paul knew it was not enough to start strong in the Christian life. Christians need to keep growing stronger and deeper in the faith. If you don't learn how to live it every day in the power of the Holy Spirit, you will never be effective as a Christian. So Paul longed to teach them the truths that would keep them growing in the faith.

Second, Paul had an intense desire to penetrate the Roman Empire with the good news. He wanted to plant the gospel in the city of Rome. "I must visit Rome also," he said. As Dr. G. Campbell Morgan observed, "That's not the 'must' of the tourist; that's the 'must' of the missionary."

Third, Luke hints that Paul has a great concern to help the famine-stricken saints in Jerusalem. This is not stated explicitly in the text, but we know that a great famine had descended upon Judea by this time. The Christians in Jerusalem were suffering, and Paul longed to help them. So he sent Timothy and Erastus into Macedonia while he stayed behind and prepared to go to Jerusalem.

A BAD LIE VERSUS A GREAT TRUTH

Why did Paul stay behind before going to Jerusalem? Luke does not tell us here, but we learn the answer from one of Paul's letters: Paul wanted to tell the churches in the region about the need in Jerusalem and to collect an offering for the suffering Christians there. He wrote the believers in Corinth:

> Now about the collection for God's people: Do what I told the Galatian churches to do. On the first day of every week, each one of you should set aside a sum of money in keeping with his income, saving it up, so that when I come no collections will have to be made. Then, when I arrive, I will give letters of introduction to the men you approve and send them with your gift to Jerusalem. If it seems advisable for me to go also, they will accompany me.
>
> After I go through Macedonia, I will come to you—for I will be going through Macedonia. Perhaps I will stay with you awhile, or even spend the winter, so that you can help me on my journey, wherever I go. I do not want to see you now and make only a passing visit; I hope to spend some time with you, if the Lord permits. But I will stay on at Ephesus until Pentecost, because a great door for effective work has opened to me, and there are many who oppose me. (1 Corinthians 16:1-9)

As Paul wrote in this letter, he planned to stay in Ephesus until Pentecost, but he soon changed his mind. Luke tells us in Acts 19 what caused his plans to change:

> About that time there arose a great disturbance about the Way. A silversmith named Demetrius, who made silver shrines of Artemis, brought in no little business for the craftsmen. He called them together, along with the

workmen in related trades, and said: "Men, you know we receive a good income from this business. And you see and hear how this fellow Paul has convinced and led astray large numbers of people here in Ephesus and in practically the whole province of Asia. He says that man-made gods are no gods at all. There is danger not only that our trade will lose its good name, but also that the temple of the great goddess Artemis will be discredited, and the goddess herself, who is worshiped throughout the province of Asia and the world, will be robbed of her divine majesty." (Acts 19:23-27)

The silversmiths at Ephesus were organized into a trade union. They made silver idols of the goddess Artemis, and Paul and his gospel were bad for business. There were so many pagans converting to Christ that nobody wanted to buy their idols anymore. The head of the union was a man named Demetrius. It's interesting to note that archaeologists have found an inscription bearing the name Demetrius in the ruins of Ephesus.

Demetrius called a union meeting and told his fellow smiths that Paul was ruining their livelihood and threatening the religion of the goddess Artemis. Paul had to be silenced, Demetrius said, or else "the temple of the great goddess Artemis will be discredited, and the goddess herself . . . will be robbed of her divine majesty."

The Temple of Artemis at Ephesus was one of the seven wonders of the world. Commissioned by King Croesus of Lydia, the temple had been built over a span of 120 years. Artemis was represented by a statue of a many-breasted woman, a grotesque representation of motherhood. In effect, Demetrius was saying that Paul was attacking the symbol of motherhood—what we would call Mom and apple pie. With these emotional arguments, Demetrius whipped the crowd to a fever pitch.

Why did Demetrius accuse Paul of threatening Artemis? Paul had never spoken a word against the religion of Ephesus. He never denounced the temple. He never attacked the pagan superstition of the Greeks. Later, we will hear the city clerk admit that Paul and his fellow Christians have not blasphemed the goddess or desecrated the temple.

This is a significant insight into the evangelistic style of Paul. He never faulted or criticized paganism. He simply proclaimed the Christian faith with such power that it was instantly more appealing than the old pagan ways. Christianity displaced paganism not by attacking it but by offering a better way. Christians declared the good news of Jesus Christ, and the people saw that their pagan religion was meaningless by comparison.

Demetrius thought he could rally his fellow silversmiths to beat back the Christian faith. He didn't understand that a bad lie can never defend against a great truth.

MOB MENTALITY

Demetrius has done his best to stir up the mob. Luke records the mob's response:

> When they heard this, they were furious and began shouting: "Great is Artemis of the Ephesians!" Soon the whole city was in an uproar. The people seized Gaius and Aristarchus, Paul's traveling companions from Macedonia, and rushed as one man into the theater. Paul wanted to appear before the crowd, but the disciples would not let him. Even some of the officials of the province, friends of Paul, sent him a message begging him not to venture into the theater.
>
> The assembly was in confusion: Some were shouting one thing, some another. Most of the people did not even know why they were there. (Acts 19:28-32)

In our culture, protesters march and riot, and news reporters interview them and ask, "Why are you here? What message are you trying to send?" And the people often have no answer. They've come to join the crowd and experience the excitement. They haven't a clue what the hubbub is about. Luke writes, "Most of the people did not even know why they were there."

How big was this commotion? Archaeologists have excavated the theater in Ephesus where these events took place. It's the only sizable part of the city that may still be seen. It is a huge theater with capacity to seat twenty thousand people. So this was a large and dangerous crowd.

Paul wanted to go before the crowd and speak, but his friends knew that the mood of the crowd was ugly, and they held him back. Even Paul's friends, the Asiarchs, the Roman rulers of the province of Asia, sent word to him not to go before the crowd. (This is a revealing insight. Paul made friends among the rulers of the province. Though Luke doesn't say that the Asiarchs were Christians, they were clearly impressed by Paul's earnest profession of the gospel, and they worried about his safety.)

Luke shows that it would have been impossible for Paul to quiet the mob:

> The Jews pushed Alexander to the front, and some of the crowd shouted instructions to him. He motioned for silence in order to make a defense before the people. But when they realized he was a Jew, they all shouted in unison for about two hours: "Great is Artemis of the Ephesians!" (Acts 19:33-34)

When mob mentality takes over, reason evaporates. The mob has no argument other than to chant one mindless slogan over and over again for two solid hours: "Great is Artemis of the Ephesians! Great is Artemis of the Ephesians!" This slogan stirred their pride and churned their emotions.

The Jews who were present worried that the mob might turn against the Jewish population of Ephesus. It was probably no secret in Ephesus that the monotheistic Jews detested idol worship because it was an abomination to the one true God. Jewish opposition of idolatry had never been effective enough to hurt the profits of the pagan idol-smiths, but Paul and his gospel had put a serious dent in their livelihood. The Jews worried that the backlash against Paul might turn into a backlash against all Jewish people in Ephesus. So they pushed the Jewish metalworker Alexander forward and made him speak to the pagan crowd.

Who was Alexander? He was very likely the same Alexander to whom Paul referred in his letter to Timothy, written after Timothy had become the bishop of the church at Ephesus: "Alexander the coppersmith did me much harm; the Lord will repay him according to his deeds' (2 Timothy 4:14 NASB). Though Alexander was a Jew, he bore a Greek name, so he was apparently a Grecian (Hellenized) Jew who made his living as a metalworker. He may have even worked in the idol-making industry, which would have given him some standing with the pagan silversmiths. Perhaps that's why the Jews chose him to speak to the mob.

The crowd, however, refused to hear Alexander. They drowned him out with chants of "Great is Artemis of the Ephesians!" The mob's emotions had become dangerously volatile. The slightest provocation could have sent thousands of frenzied people raging through the streets, killing and destroying. At that crucial moment, someone stepped forward to take charge of the potentially explosive situation.

AN ANSWER FOR UPROAR

Luke tells us what happened next:

> The city clerk quieted the crowd and said: "Men of Ephesus, doesn't all the world know that the city of Ephesus is the guardian of the temple of the great Artemis and of her image, which fell from heaven? Therefore, since these facts are undeniable, you ought to be quiet and not do anything rash. You have brought these men here, though they have neither robbed temples nor blasphemed our goddess. If, then, Demetrius and his fellow craftsmen have a grievance against anybody, the courts are open and there are proconsuls. They can press charges. If there is anything further you want to bring up, it must be settled in a legal assembly. As it is, we are in danger of being charged with rioting because of today's events. In that case we would not be able to account for this commotion, since there is no reason for it." After he had said this, he dismissed the assembly. (Acts 19:35-41)

Mob violence was narrowly averted by the city clerk, a man whose office in that culture corresponded to that of mayor. The city clerk's name is not given, but he's an admirable politician and an effective orator. He intervenes at the right psychological moment. The crowd, having exhausted itself with two hours of chanting, is ready to listen. So the city clerk rises and makes three eminently reasonable points.

First, he says, in effect, "Yes, I agree with your slogan. The goddess Artemis is great, so she doesn't need us to defend her. We can count on Artemis to defend herself, so why should we get upset? Nobody can overthrow our goddess, so let's calm down."

Second, he makes a point about Paul. He says, in effect, "Paul and his companions have not blasphemed the goddess. They have not robbed the temple. They have not committed any sacrilege whatsoever. So why not let the court handle this matter. And if the court doesn't satisfy you, we can always go to the legislature. The legal channels of protest are open to us, so let's calmly avail ourselves of them."

Third, he warns the crowd not to annoy the powers that be, the rulers in Rome, who were well known for clamping down harshly on civil disorder. "If there's a riot," he said, in effect, "and we can't explain what it was all about, we'll have the Romans on our necks—and we'll lose our freedom."

The city clerk was looking out for himself, to be sure. If there was trouble in Ephesus, and the Romans had to intervene, his head would be the first to roll. But everyone in the crowd knew that when the Romans intervened, there was plenty of punishment to go around. The Ephesians didn't want to risk the wrath of the empire.

So God used this pagan city clerk to calm the murderous passions of the mob and protect His servants. As Paul wrote to the Christians in Rome, "The authorities that exist have been established by God" (Romans 13:1). In spite of its cruelty, corruption, and excesses, the Roman Empire maintained order—and God used the pagan city clerk of Ephesus and the threat of intervention by the pagan Roman Empire as a means of protecting Paul.

AFTER THE UPROAR

Ignore the chapter division between Acts 19 and Acts 20 (though the Scripture text is inspired by God, the chapter and verse divisions are not, and they often interrupt the flow of the text). In the first verse of Acts 20, we find the conclusion of this story:

> When the uproar had ended, Paul sent for the disciples and, after encouraging them, said good-by and set out for Macedonia. (Acts 20:1)

Paul called the Christians together and gave them a message of encouragement. Luke doesn't record Paul's message, but I believe Paul tells us about this incident in 2 Corinthians: "We do not want you to be uninformed, brothers, about the hardships we suffered in the province of Asia. We were under great pressure, far beyond our ability to endure, so that we despaired even of life. Indeed, in our hearts we felt the sentence of death. But this happened that we might not rely on ourselves but on God, who raises the dead. He has delivered us from such a deadly peril, and he will deliver us. On him we have set our hope that he will continue to deliver us" (2 Corinthians 1:8-10).

During this uproar, when twenty thousand people were chanting and surging with rage, Paul undoubtedly "despaired even of life" and "felt the sentence of death." He could see no way out of the situation.

But after the uproar ended and the dust settled, Paul could see God's hand in everything that happened. The Lord had allowed this uproar to happen "that we might not rely on ourselves but on God, who raises the dead."

That's the heart of the Christian message. Our sufficiency is not in ourselves but in God. Even when all hope is gone and it seems that nothing lies before us but death, God is able to achieve His purposes—because He is the One who raises the dead.

I believe that Paul's message of encouragement to the believers was along these lines. He probably said to them, "God allowed this event to happen in order to teach us all a lesson in faith. I admit it—the mob was so ugly that I truly thought we were done for. But I learned that when our circumstances tumble out of our control, God wants us to rely on Him alone. If He is able to raise the dead, then what is too hard for Him? Our God works in us to do exceedingly, abundantly above all that we could ask or think, according to His power at work in us."

That's the message I believe Paul implanted in the hearts of those Ephesian believers before he departed for Macedonia. And that's the lesson Paul wants you and me to learn from this situation as well. It's the perspective we need whenever we face pressure, danger, and despair. The trials we face are allowed by God so that we might learn to rely not on ourselves but on the Mighty One who raises the dead.

34

LAST WORDS

Acts 20:2-38

John Wesley preached his final sermon on February 17, 1791, in the borough of Lambeth. His text was Isaiah 55:6: "Seek the Lord while he may be found; call on him while he is near." The next day, he fell ill and went to bed. On March 2, he turned to his friends and family who were gathered around his deathbed. "The best of all is, God is with us," he said. "Farewell, farewell." Those were the last words of John Wesley.

We have come to the last section of the third division of Acts. I call this third section (Acts 13–20) the Pattern Setters because it is here that we find the pattern for all Christian witness in any culture, in any era of history. Here, in Acts 20, the story of Paul the pattern setter takes a somber turn. Like Wesley on his deathbed, Paul senses that his life and ministry are coming to a close. He begins to say farewell to those who have meant so much to him during his missionary journeys.

PAUL'S TRAVELING SEMINARY

We last saw Paul as he departed from Ephesus following the riot of the silversmiths' union. The good news of Jesus Christ had changed the cultural landscape of the city and destroyed the market for silver idols of the goddess Artemis. Luke now picks up the account as Paul travels from Ephesus through Macedonia and into Greece:

> He traveled through that area, speaking many words of encouragement to the people, and finally arrived in Greece, where he stayed three months. (Acts 20:2-3a)

Paul moved through cities where he had founded churches, including Philippi, Thessalonica, and Berea. He probably spoke to the believers in Athens. He finally came to Corinth, where he stayed for three months. Paul's ministry, from the time he left Ephesus until he left Corinth, probably lasted a year or more, yet Luke records that entire period of Paul's life in a single sentence.

There are many incidents in the life of Paul that I would like to know more about. He had many experiences that were not recorded. For example, he visited the region we now call Albania and Yugoslavia but was then called Illyricum. Paul briefly refers to his travels there (Romans 15:19), but we don't know any details of that experience. Someday in eternity, I would like to hear Paul tell of his travels there.

Paul's goal for this journey was to encourage the believers. He wanted to establish churches that would stand for generations. He also collected contributions from the Gentile churches for the relief of the famine-stricken church in Jerusalem. Several men were appointed by each church to go with Paul to take the gifts to Jerusalem.

Luke tells us who some of those men were:

> Because the Jews made a plot against him just as he was about to sail for Syria, he decided to go back through Macedonia. He was accompanied by Sopater son of Pyrrhus from Berea, Aristarchus and Secundus from Thessalonica, Gaius from Derbe, Timothy also, and Tychicus and Trophimus from the province of Asia. These men went on ahead and waited for us at Troas. But we sailed from Philippi after the Feast of Unleavened Bread, and five days later joined the others at Troas, where we stayed seven days. (Acts 20:3-6)

Paul had planned to sail directly from Corinth to the Syrian coast, so that he could walk to Jerusalem in time for the Passover feast. But he heard rumors of a plot against his life, probably involving murder at sea. So Paul took a different path. He went through Macedonia, through Thessalonica and Philippi, and was joined by Luke (in verse 5, Luke's use of pronouns changes from "them" to "us"). Paul sailed on to Troas with Luke and the other young men.

Some of Paul's companions were slaves or former slaves. Secundus, which means "the second," was a slave name. Slaves didn't bother to name their children but numbered them instead—the first, the second, the third, and so forth. It may be that Tertius, who wrote the letter to the Romans as Paul's secretary, was the brother of Secundus, because Tertius means "the third."

Paul insisted that these men go with him to Jerusalem so that he could not be accused of mishandling the funds. He also discipled and mentored these men as they traveled. In effect, Paul operated a traveling seminary, teaching these young men the ins and outs of Christian ministry as they journeyed over land and sea.

DON'T FALL ASLEEP IN CHURCH

Next, Luke gives us an intimate glimpse into a startling incident in Troas:

> On the first day of the week we came together to break bread. Paul spoke to the people and, because he intended to leave the next day, kept on talking until midnight. There were many lamps in the upstairs room where we were meeting. Seated in a window was a young man named Eutychus, who was sinking into a deep sleep as Paul talked on and on.

When he was sound asleep, he fell to the ground from the third story and was picked up dead. Paul went down, threw himself on the young man and put his arms around him. "Don't be alarmed," he said. "He's alive!" (Acts 20:7-10)

This is the first mention in the New Testament of believers worshiping on Sunday, the first day of the week. The Christian church moved worship from Saturday, the Hebrew Sabbath, to Sunday, the day our Lord's resurrection. The church in Troas had evidently met for a communion service ("we had come together to break bread"), and Paul was called upon to teach from the Scriptures. Because Paul was leaving the next day and had so much to tell the people, he continued speaking until midnight.

Someone has said that preaching is the art of speaking in other people's sleep. That was certainly the case here. Seated in a window, a young man named Eutychus fought a losing battle to stay awake. Luke observes, "There were many lamps in the upstairs room where we were meeting." Lamps burn oxygen while giving off carbon monoxide. The lateness of the hour, combined with the effect of the lamps, caused the young man to doze—and fall from the third floor window. When the people reached him, he was dead.

Some skeptics question whether Eutychus died. But the issue is settled by a physician's testimony: Luke, the writer of Acts, was an eyewitness. Throughout the book of Acts, Luke has been a careful and accurate chronicler of the facts. Luke does not say that Eutychus appeared to be dead. Luke says the young man "fell to the ground from the third story and was picked up dead." He was clearly certain of his facts.

Paul rushed down to where the young man lay, fell on him, and embraced him. Then, to everyone's amazement, Paul announced that the young man was alive! So God used Paul to perform an amazing miracle of raising this young man from the dead. This miracle was another confirmation of Paul's apostleship.

Luke provides another touching detail at the close of this story:

Then he went upstairs again and broke bread and ate. After talking until daylight, he left. The people took the young man home alive and were greatly comforted. (Acts 20:11-12)

The communion service was interrupted by the young man's fall. Once he was restored, the believers went back upstairs and finished celebrating the Lord's Supper. They spent a wonderful time enjoying body life and praising God for the miracle they had just witnessed. They enjoyed such a wonderful time together that Paul couldn't tear himself away. He stayed with them until dawn.

PAUL'S PLANS—AND A CHANGE OF PLANS

Luke continues:

> We went on ahead to the ship and sailed for Assos, where we were going to take Paul aboard. He had made this arrangement because he was going there on foot. (Acts 20:13)

Luke does not tell us why Paul chose this route. He sent his companions by ship around a point that jutted into the sea, a voyage of about forty miles. Meanwhile, he cut across the neck of the peninsula, a hike of about twenty-five miles. He walked alone, perhaps because he wanted to think and pray, much as the Lord Jesus would sometimes draw aside for private times with the Father. Luke continues:

> When he met us at Assos, we took him aboard and went on to Mitylene. The next day we set sail from there and arrived off Kios. The day after that we crossed over to Samos, and on the following day arrived at Miletus. Paul had decided to sail past Ephesus to avoid spending time in the province of Asia, for he was in a hurry to reach Jerusalem, if possible, by the day of Pentecost.
>
> From Miletus, Paul sent to Ephesus for the elders of the church. (Acts 20:14-17)

Paul was trying to keep a schedule. He had originally planned to reach Jerusalem in time for the Passover. When he was unable to do so, he tried to arrive in time for the day of Pentecost. He not only wanted to celebrate the anniversary of the coming of the Holy Spirit, but he wanted to celebrate the Hebrew feast of Pentecost as well. He maintained a deep love for the Jewish people and traditions. He longed to reach his people with the good news that their Messiah had come.

To save time, Paul sent word to Ephesus and asked the elders to join him at the port city of Miletus, about fifteen miles from Ephesus. They came, and Paul met them with a great message about their ministry. That message occupies the rest of Acts 20.

Notice that Paul believes in planning ahead, yet he is always ready to change his plans when God gives him new opportunities. We are easily frustrated when things don't go as we planned, but Paul never objects when God issues new instructions.

PAUL'S DEFENSE OF HIS MINISTRY

We come now to Paul's great charge to the Ephesian elders. Here, the apostle lets us see into his heart and soul—perhaps the most intimate personal glimpse in Scripture.

In those ancient cities, people could not meet together in one large church building. There were probably several thousand Christians in Ephesus, but they could not gather in one large place, so they met in homes. In a letter to Corinth, Paul speaks of the church in Ephesus that met at the house of Aquila and Priscilla, and there were many other house churches in that city. The teachers of these house churches were the elders, and Paul had summoned these elders to meet him at Miletus.

Paul begins with a defense of his ministry:

> When they arrived, he said to them: "You know how I lived the whole time I was with you, from the first day I came into the province of Asia. I served the Lord with great humility and with tears, although I was severely tested by the plots of the Jews." (Acts 20:18-19)

Some people think that Paul is arrogantly congratulating himself, talking about how he served God faithfully in spite of his suffering and the opposition he endured. But if you understand how severely Paul was being attacked at this time, you'll see why he speaks this way. It appears that Paul's enemies were accusing him of being prideful and insincere, so Paul says, "I served the Lord with humility and with tears. This ministry has meant everything to me." Paul continues:

> "You know that I have not hesitated to preach anything that would be helpful to you but have taught you publicly and from house to house. I have declared to both Jews and Greeks that they must turn to God in repentance and have faith in our Lord Jesus." (Acts 20:20-21)

Paul always set forth the whole counsel of God. He taught publicly in the Jewish synagogues and the pagan marketplaces. He taught privately, in small groups, from house to house. His message always came down to two key concepts: Repentance toward God and faith in Jesus Christ. That is the Christian message condensed into two words: repentance and faith.

Repentance means that you change your mind about your life. You stop thinking, acting, and living the way you have been. Faith means that you place your trust in the Lord and allow Him to live His life through you.

The Christian life was meant to be an exciting, compelling adventure. An adventure always entails risk—and risk-taking requires faith. You must have faith that when you risk for God, He will stand with you. In order to begin the adventure of the Christian life, you must repent and have faith. That's the essence of Paul's gospel.

Next, Paul describes another characteristic of his ministry among them:

> "And now, compelled by the Spirit, I am going to Jerusalem, not knowing what will happen to me there. I only know that in every city the

Holy Spirit warns me that prison and hardships are facing me. However, I consider my life worth nothing to me, if only I may finish the race and complete the task the Lord Jesus has given me—the task of testifying to the gospel of God's grace.

"Now I know that none of you among whom I have gone about preaching the kingdom will ever see me again. Therefore, I declare to you today that I am innocent of the blood of all men. For I have not hesitated to proclaim to you the whole will of God." (Acts 20:22-27)

Paul says that his ministry for God is going to cost him everything. He knows that with every footstep he goes deeper into danger, hardship, and affliction. The Holy Spirit has been preparing him for the road ahead, and he says, "I consider my life worth nothing to me, if only I may finish the race and complete the task the Lord Jesus has given me—the task of testifying to the gospel of God's grace." Nothing matters to Paul except finishing the race and completing his mission.

Vladimir Lenin, the first head of the Soviet Union, used to say that communists are "dead men on furlough." As revolutionaries, they should view themselves as already dead, so that they would be ready to die at any moment. That's how Paul saw himself. That's how all committed Christians should see themselves: dead men and dead women on furlough. We should want nothing but to see God exalted.

Paul tells these elders that he has successfully completed his ministry among them. "I declare to you today that I am innocent of the blood of all men. For I have not hesitated to proclaim to you the whole will of God." In other words, "I have given you the truth, and I've held nothing back. You know all you need to know in order to serve Christ. Now the rest is up to you."

PAUL'S CHARGE TO THE EPHESIAN ELDERS

Next, Paul speaks about the responsibilities of these elders to the flock (the believers) at Ephesus. There are three considerations the apostle lays before them to govern their ministry. Paul's first charge: Feed the flock.

"Keep watch over yourselves and all the flock of which the Holy Spirit has made you overseers. Be shepherds of the church of God, which he bought with his own blood." (Acts 20:28)

The primary responsibility of a pastor is to teach the Scriptures. That's what Paul means when he says, "Feed the flock." If a pastor does not teach the Scriptures, he is starving the people he is supposed to feed.

Moreover, these elders were to begin with themselves. "Keep watch over yourselves," Paul says. In other words, these elders were to feed on God's Word and live in obedience to His truth, so that they would be able to care for His flock.

Paul goes on to say, "Be shepherds of the church of God, which he bought with his own blood." Here, Paul underscores the seriousness of their ministry. Nothing is more precious to God than His church, which Jesus purchased with His blood.

Paul's second charge to the Ephesian elders: Watch for perils. He says:

"I know that after I leave, savage wolves will come in among you and will not spare the flock. Even from your own number men will arise and distort the truth in order to draw away disciples after them." (Acts 20:29-30)

Paul warns of two deadly dangers ahead. First, evil people will come in among them like wolves disguised as sheep. They will be unregenerate men and women who talk and act like Christians, who may even think of themselves as Christians, but they will undermine the church from within. They will be religious but will deny the power of true faith. Paul's warning has come true again and again throughout Christian history.

Second, men will arise from among the elders themselves who will teach distorted doctrines. These false teachers will deceive people and divide the church, forming cliques of followers around themselves. This warning has also proven true again and again.

Paul's third charge to the Ephesian elders: Do everything in the same spirit that Paul exemplified. He tells them:

"So be on your guard! Remember that for three years I never stopped warning each of you night and day with tears.

"Now I commit you to God and to the word of his grace, which can build you up and give you an inheritance among all those who are sanctified. I have not coveted anyone's silver or gold or clothing. You yourselves know that these hands of mine have supplied my own needs and the needs of my companions. In everything I did, I showed you that by this kind of hard work we must help the weak, remembering the words the Lord Jesus himself said: 'It is more blessed to give than to receive.'" (Acts 20:31-35)

Paul urges the elders to follow his example in three ways.

First, they should admonish the flock with tears. They should speak the truth in love, as he wrote in Ephesians 4:15. A true shepherd will admonish the flock, but lovingly, not harshly.

Second, they should use the Word. He says, "Now I commit you to God and to the word of his grace, which can build you up and give you an inheritance among all those who are sanctified." God's Word builds us up and reveals our inheritance as children of the King, but we must teach it.

Third, they should be selfless. Paul uses himself as an example: "I have not coveted anyone's silver or gold or clothing. You yourselves know that these hands of mine have supplied my own needs." In other words, "I didn't go into the ministry to get rich. In fact, I've worked at a fulltime job in order to supply my own needs. So follow my example and labor selflessly."

The final paragraph describes a heartbreaking service of farewell:

> When he had said this, he knelt down with all of them and prayed. They all wept as they embraced him and kissed him. What grieved them most was his statement that they would never see his face again. Then they accompanied him to the ship. (Acts 20:36-38)

I'm glad Paul was wrong. The people of Ephesus did see Paul's face one last time. In 1 Timothy we learn that Paul paid another visit to Ephesus after this one. But he didn't know that at the time, so this was a bittersweet parting. Before Paul stepped aboard the ship, they wept, embraced, and prayed for each other. As Paul boarded the ship before sailing out of their sight, his last words to them were not unlike those of John Wesley before he slipped into eternity: "The best of all is, God is with us. Farewell, farewell."

PART IV

THE PRISONER OF THE LORD

Acts 21–28

35

PAUL'S MISTAKE

Acts 21:1-26

Paul, a prisoner of Christ Jesus . . .” These are the opening words of Paul's epistle to Philemon. He calls himself a prisoner of the Lord or a prisoner of Jesus Christ in two other letters, Ephesians and 2 Timothy, but Philemon is the only letter that begins with those words.

When Paul calls himself a prisoner of the Lord Jesus, we catch a glimpse of the apostle's heart. As we are about to see, Paul will soon become a prisoner of the Roman Empire. Paul will languish for two years in the prison at Caesarea, then spend roughly three more years as a detainee in Rome.

But Paul wants to make it clear that he is not a victim of the Roman Empire. Rather, he is a victorious and willing prisoner of the Lord Jesus. The chains of his physical confinement mean little to him. His only goal is to go where the Lord sends him and do what the Lord tells him, so that God will be exalted by Paul's life, or his death, or even his imprisonment. That's the attitude each of us should have as fellow prisoners of the Lord with Paul.

A WARNING FROM THE SPIRIT

I'm convinced it wasn't necessary for Paul to be a prisoner. The Lord Jesus, when He first called Paul on the Damascus road, said that Paul would suffer greatly for Him, but the Lord did not specifically say that Paul would be a prisoner. The Lord's prediction was amply fulfilled by such hardships as being beaten, stoned, flogged, and so forth. Paul had been thrown in jail a few times, but usually only for a day or two.

The Lord Jesus told Paul he would stand before kings and give his testimony, and it was, in fact, his status as a prisoner that finally brought him before kings. But I don't believe Paul had to go before kings in chains.

I know that Paul wrote some of his finest letters from prison, but was it prison that made those letters so powerful? After all, the greatest of all his letters, Romans, was not written in prison. The prison letters, such as Colossians, Ephesians, and Philemon, are evidence of God's ability to salvage His good from our mistakes.

One of the most instructive sections of Acts is the one now before us— Luke's somber account of Paul's mistake. It opens with the story of Paul's last journey to Jerusalem. The apostle Paul and his friends have left the Ephesian elders on the beach at Miletus and are now aboard the ship. Luke writes:

After we had torn ourselves away from them, we put out to sea and sailed straight to Cos. The next day we went to Rhodes and from there to Patara. We found a ship crossing over to Phoenicia, went on board and set sail. After sighting Cyprus and passing to the south of it, we sailed on to Syria. We landed at Tyre, where our ship was to unload its cargo. Finding the disciples there, we stayed with them seven days. Through the Spirit they urged Paul not to go on to Jerusalem. But when our time was up, we left and continued on our way. All the disciples and their wives and children accompanied us out of the city, and there on the beach we knelt to pray. After saying good-by to each other, we went aboard the ship, and they returned home. (Acts 21:1-6)

Luke gives us an itinerary of the ship's progress down the coast of Asia Minor and across a reach of the Mediterranean toward the coasts of Syria and Palestine. Luke, who was aboard, probably kept a log of the journey. When the ship stopped in ancient Tyre, north of Palestine, they looked up certain disciples who urged Paul, "through the Spirit," Luke notes, not to go up to Jerusalem.

Many Christians have struggled with this passage. It's hard to believe that Paul would disobey the Holy Spirit. Yet, taken at face value, that's exactly what Luke says. The Spirit spoke to Paul through these disciples, and Paul ignored the Spirit's urging.

We would prefer to soften the implications of this statement and say it was only a warning of trouble ahead. But the apostle hardly needed any warning. He knew that trouble lay ahead. He had told the Ephesian elders, "I only know that in every city the Holy Spirit warns me that prison and hardships are facing me" (Acts 20:23).

Some say that Paul was right and that he was following the Spirit's inner leading. It was the disciples who were wrong, and they should not have tried to stop him. The problem is that, in order to take this position, you have to ignore those three crucial words: "through the Spirit." Their urging of Paul didn't come from their fleshly will, but rather it came "through the Spirit." Luke is clear on this point.

We must face the full implications of those words. Luke was Paul's friend and would not have willingly written anything to put Paul in a bad light. But Luke, being led by the Holy Spirit in writing this inspired book, had to set down the truth. So he wrote that the disciples urged Paul "through the Spirit" not to go to Jerusalem. The original Greek text is strong here—much stronger than our English text. They didn't merely urge Paul but practically ordered him, "Stop going up to Jerusalem!"

Luke records: "But when our time was up, we left and continued on our way." That was Paul's mistake. The Spirit urged Paul to change course, but Paul continued on his way. Why did Paul make this decision?

PAUL'S MOTIVE—AND HIS MISTAKE

If we are to learn from Paul's action, we have to see where it began. Luke previously gave us this insight into Paul's thinking while he was still in Ephesus: "After all this had happened, Paul decided to go to Jerusalem, passing through Macedonia and Achaia. 'After I have been there,' he said, 'I must visit Rome also'" (Acts 19:21). Paul intensely desired to go, first, to Jerusalem and, second, to Rome. Jerusalem was the heart of the Jewish nation; Rome was the heart of the Gentile empire. Why did Paul urgently wish to go to Jerusalem? He explains in his letter to the Romans:

> I speak the truth in Christ—I am not lying, my conscience confirms it in the Holy Spirit—I have great sorrow and unceasing anguish in my heart. For I could wish that I myself were cursed and cut off from Christ for the sake of my brothers, those of my own race, the people of Israel. Theirs is the adoption as sons; theirs the divine glory, the covenants, the receiving of the law, the temple worship and the promises. Theirs are the patriarchs, and from them is traced the human ancestry of Christ, who is God over all, forever praised! Amen. (Romans 9:1-5)

It's difficult for Gentiles to understand the emotions of the apostle Paul. He was not only a Christian among Christians but a Jew among Jews, and he deeply loved his people. He loved their heritage of the patriarchs and the promises, the rituals and ceremony, the traditions and the Law. Paul knew that on Pentecost there would be a great gathering of Jews from all over the world, and he urgently wanted to be there.

We also know that Paul had the gift of prophecy. In Romans 11 he prophetically tells us that the welfare of the world hangs on what happens to Israel. The world will never solve its problems until the prophecies concerning Israel have been fulfilled. A day will come when Israel turns to Jesus the Messiah, and then the entire world will undergo a dramatic transformation. Until that day comes, the world must suffer crisis after crisis, sorrow upon sorrow. We will never solve the political, economic, ecological, moral, and social problems of our day until Israel is in a right relationship to Jesus Christ.

Paul, watching the signs of the times, felt that the day of the Lord's return was drawing near. He probably felt that the time had come that God had decreed for Israel to be evangelized, so he made up his mind to go to Jerusalem and to work toward the fulfillment of those prophecies by preaching to his people.

Living two thousand years after these events, we easily forget that first-century Christians didn't anticipate such a long period of time—at least twenty centuries—before the Lord's return. As Jesus said, the times and seasons were not for us to know. God has always expected His church, in every age, to be ready and waiting for the Lord's return. Paul believed that the Lord's return was imminent, and he wanted to reach his people before it was too late. So he made plans to be in Jerusalem on the day when the Jews would be gathered together so that he could proclaim the gospel to them.

Paul's motive was pure. He was driven by a love for his Jewish countrymen and a holy passion for God's truth. But Luke makes it clear that God had other plans for Paul. The Lord did not want the apostle to be in Jerusalem at that time. Though Paul had a love for his Jewish brethren, though he had led many Jews to faith in Christ, the Lord had given Paul a ministry to the Gentiles. Paul always started with the Jews at the synagogue in every city, yet his ministry was primarily to the Gentiles.

Paul's mistake lay in insisting on doing what his heart longed to do. Yes, he was zealous for the glory of Jesus Christ, but he let his compassionate heart for the Jews blind him to God's express will. The Spirit repeatedly tried to deter him from going to Jerusalem, but Paul would not be deterred.

The apostle Paul was on guard against the snares of sin. He knew the deadly power of sexual immorality and lust, the appeal of pride and prestige, the seduction of materialism and greed. Satan undoubtedly tried to tempt Paul to sin, without success. So Satan found a more subtle enticement. Instead of tempting Paul to sin, Satan tempted Paul to do right—but at the wrong time. In the end, Paul tried to fulfill God's program, but on his own timetable. That's what trapped him.

THE PROPHECY OF AGABUS

Next, Luke records that Paul had a second motive for going to Jerusalem:

> We continued our voyage from Tyre and landed at Ptolemais, where we greeted the brothers and stayed with them for a day. Leaving the next day, we reached Caesarea and stayed at the house of Philip the evangelist, one of the Seven. He had four unmarried daughters who prophesied.
>
> After we had been there a number of days, a prophet named Agabus came down from Judea. Coming over to us, he took Paul's belt, tied his own hands and feet with it and said, "The Holy Spirit says, 'In this way the Jews of Jerusalem will bind the owner of this belt and will hand him over to the Gentiles.'"
>
> When we heard this, we and the people there pleaded with Paul not to go up to Jerusalem. Then Paul answered, "Why are you weeping and breaking my heart? I am ready not only to be bound, but also to die in Jerusalem for the name of the Lord Jesus." When he would not be dissuaded, we gave up and said, "The Lord's will be done."
>
> After this, we got ready and went up to Jerusalem. Some of the disciples from Caesarea accompanied us and brought us to the home of Mnason, where we were to stay. He was a man from Cyprus and one of the early disciples. (Acts 21:7-16)

At Caesarea, they came into the home of Philip the evangelist, the man who led the Ethiopian eunuch to Christ. There they encountered Agabus, a well-known prophet of the Lord (we met him previously in Acts 11, when he predicted famine in Jerusalem). In dramatically visual demonstration, Agabus took Paul's sash from around his waist and bound his own feet and hands. Then he said, "The Holy Spirit says, 'In this way the Jews of Jerusalem will bind the owner of this belt and will hand him over to the Gentiles.'"

This was a last effort by the Spirit to awaken and warn Paul. After Agabus prophesied, everyone, including Luke, tried to dissuade Paul. Luke writes, "When we heard this, we and the people there pleaded with Paul not to go up to Jerusalem." Paul's associates recognized the voice of the Spirit, yet Paul himself was strangely deaf.

Paul had succumbed to what is often called a martyr complex. Convinced he was going to die, he was determined to go resolutely to his fate. There is a boldness, bravery, and earnestness in his words, but also a fatalistic resignation: "Why are you weeping and breaking my heart? I am ready not only to be bound, but also to die in Jerusalem for the name of the Lord Jesus."

We can't fault his courage, but the fact remains that he didn't have to go. Indeed, the Spirit told him not to go. This is what happens when human beings are misled by noble but misguided inner urgings to accomplish a task that God has not assigned.

Perhaps Paul saw himself as following in the footsteps of his Lord. The Gospel accounts tell us that Jesus was steadfastly determined to go to Jerusalem, even against the pleadings of His disciples. Paul may have seen himself in a similar role. The difference is that Jesus had the Spirit's witness within that it was the will of the Father for Him to suffer and die in Jerusalem. Paul had the Spirit's repeated pleadings to turn back.

When Paul refused to be persuaded, his friends said, "The Lord's will be done." That's what you say when you don't know what else to say. In other words, "Lord, it's up to you. We tried, but we can't stop him. He's strong-willed and deluded. Only you can dissuade him now. Your will be done."

FREE TO LIVE AS A GENTILE OR A JEW
Next, we see the welcome that Paul and his companions received in Jerusalem:

When we arrived at Jerusalem, the brothers received us warmly. The next day Paul and the rest of us went to see James, and all the elders were present. Paul greeted them and reported in detail what God had done among the Gentiles through his ministry.

When they heard this, they praised God. Then they said to Paul: "You see, brother, how many thousands of Jews have believed, and all of them are zealous for the law. They have been informed that you teach all the Jews who live among the Gentiles to turn away from Moses, telling them not to circumcise their children or live according to our customs." (Acts 21:17-21)

James and the other elders greet Paul and then tell him of a misunderstanding that has arisen. It's been rumored that Paul is telling Jewish Christians that they should ignore the law of Moses and reject the old Jewish rites and traditions, such as circumcision. This is a false charge. Paul never taught the Jews to abandon the Law. He only taught that the Gentiles should not be subject to these Jewish provisions.

All along, Paul has taught the Jews from their own Scriptures that the beautiful symbols of Judaism are pictures that point to Jesus Christ. The ritual sacrifices represent the sacrifice of Jesus upon the cross. Jesus did not come to do away with the Old Testament rituals but to fulfill them. Throughout the book of Acts we see Jewish Christians going to the temple and offering sacrifices. The sacrifices ended when the temple was destroyed in A.D. 70 (in fulfillment of Jesus' prophecy in Luke 21:20-24).

Luke goes on, continuing the words of James and the Jerusalem elders to Paul:

"What shall we do? They will certainly hear that you have come, so do what we tell you. There are four men with us who have made a vow. Take these men, join in their purification rites and pay their expenses, so that they can have their heads shaved. Then everybody will know there is no truth in these reports about you, but that you yourself are living in obedience to the law. As for the Gentile believers, we have written to them our decision that they should abstain from food sacrificed to idols, from blood, from the meat of strangled animals and from sexual immorality."

The next day Paul took the men and purified himself along with them. Then he went to the temple to give notice of the date when the days of purification would end and the offering would be made for each of them. (Acts 21:22-26)

Paul was following his own announced practice. He said that when he was with the Jews, he became as a Jew; when he was with the Gentiles, he became as a Gentile; when he was with the weak, he limited himself and became as weak as they. He did this to reach people at their own level. He was free in Christ to live as a Gentile among the Gentiles or a Jew among the Jews. So Paul adopted this Jewish purification rite in order to clear up the misunderstanding that had arisen about him.

LEARNING TO HEAR THE VOICE OF THE SPIRIT

There's a crucial lesson for you and me as we examine Paul's mistake: There are no guarantees that we won't miss the mind of God. We can have great spiritual maturity and a deep understanding of Scripture and still we can be blind to God's clear guidance in our lives. That's why we often see men and women who have been greatly used by God suddenly trapped by a sin that ruins their spiritual legacy.

The flesh is our enemy. It seeks to catch us off guard. The flesh can awaken a desire in us that seems noble and good but that violates the leading of the Spirit of God. The Spirit persistently warned Paul, and Paul persistently ignored the warning. We desperately need to hear and obey the Spirit's voice.

God did not abandon Paul. The Lord used him in a great and powerful way during the last years of his life. Yes, Paul had to go through great suffering, but the Spirit was with him through it all.

We can be grateful that Scripture honestly records the failures of even a great man like Paul. The lesson of Paul's mistake is that we must listen to the voice of God—then heed it. As we learn to rely on the arm of the Spirit instead of the arm of the flesh, we will discover what it means to truly know and do God's will for our lives.

36

TROUBLE IN JERUSALEM

Acts 21:27–22:29

Sometimes, your efforts to solve a problem only make it worse. That's the situation Paul encountered at Jerusalem.

Upon his arrival, Paul learned that there was widespread misunderstanding about his teaching. Many Jewish Christians in Jerusalem kept the rituals and sacrifices at the temple. They heard rumors that Paul taught Jewish Christians to reject the law of Moses and the temple rituals, but Paul had never said such a thing. He had only insisted that the Gentiles not be subject to the law of Moses in order to become Christians.

To allay the suspicions of the Jewish Christians in Jerusalem, Paul decided to go to the temple, along with four young Jewish companions. They would follow the Jewish rituals and shave their heads according to Nazarite tradition, and all would see Paul's deep respect for the law of Moses and the traditions of Judaism.

That was Paul's plan. Unfortunately, his plan only made matters worse.

TROUBLE ERUPTS

Paul and his four companions had nearly completed the prescribed rites when trouble broke out. Luke records what happened:

> When the seven days were nearly over, some Jews from the province of Asia saw Paul at the temple. They stirred up the whole crowd and seized him, shouting, "Men of Israel, help us! This is the man who teaches all men everywhere against our people and our law and this place. And besides, he has brought Greeks into the temple area and defiled this holy place." (They had previously seen Trophimus the Ephesian in the city with Paul and assumed that Paul had brought him into the temple area.) (Acts 21:27-29)

Who instigated this trouble? Not the Jews in Jerusalem. The troublemakers came all the way from the Roman province of Asia. The capital of that province was Ephesus. So these may have been the same Jews who had opposed Paul at the synagogue in Ephesus (Acts 19:8-9). Here they are again, hot on his trail, stirring up trouble.

Perhaps Alexander, the coppersmith from Ephesus, was one of those involved. Years later, during his imprisonment in Rome, Paul would write to Timothy in Ephesus, "Alexander the coppersmith did me much harm; the

Lord will repay him according to his deeds" (2 Timothy 4:14 NASB). It may be that it was here, during the trouble in Jerusalem, that Alexander caused Paul the great harm he spoke of to Timothy.

God had repeatedly tried to deflect Paul from Jerusalem because He knew that these troublemakers were there. The Spirit knew it would be fruitless to attempt to evangelize Israel at this time. The stubborn hearts of the people were not ready.

Paul had experienced amazing success in the Gentile regions of the Roman Empire, and God would have allowed that success to continue. After the decision of the Roman judge at Corinth (Acts 18:12-17), Paul had access to every Roman city to preach the gospel. Instead, he went to Jerusalem, where his presence provoked a riot.

Notice the false charge against Paul. His enemies accused him of defiling the temple by bringing Gentiles there. Had anyone seen Paul take a Gentile into temple area? Of course not. But they had seen Paul walking in the city with a Greek Christian, Trophimus the Ephesian—so they assumed he must have taken Trophimus into the temple. That's how flimsy their evidence was.

"AWAY WITH HIM!"

Luke records what happened next:

> The whole city was aroused, and the people came running from all directions. Seizing Paul, they dragged him from the temple, and immediately the gates were shut. While they were trying to kill him, news reached the commander of the Roman troops that the whole city of Jerusalem was in an uproar. He at once took some officers and soldiers and ran down to the crowd. When the rioters saw the commander and his soldiers, they stopped beating Paul.
>
> The commander came up and arrested him and ordered him to be bound with two chains. Then he asked who he was and what he had done. Some in the crowd shouted one thing and some another, and since the commander could not get at the truth because of the uproar, he ordered that Paul be taken into the barracks. When Paul reached the steps, the violence of the mob was so great he had to be carried by the soldiers. The crowd that followed kept shouting, "Away with him!" (Acts 21:30-36)

There is probably no more vivid and dramatic account in the New Testament than Luke's eyewitness record here. I once stood in Jerusalem on the site of the Roman fortress of Antonia, and I imagined the tumultuous scene—the crowds gathered for the great day of the feast, the people running toward the temple from every directions, the faces twisted with rage, the shouts of accusation, the flailing fists, the arrival of the Roman soldiers, the cries of "Away with him! Away with him!"

Luke tells us that the crowd seized the apostle Paul, beat him with fists, kicked him with their feet, and tried to stamp the life out of him. The people began to beat him to death. Only the arrival of the Roman guards saved him. The Romans charged into the mob and carried Paul to safety on their shoulders. The crowd, seeing that Paul was getting away, became all the more enraged and began battling the Roman soldiers.

A MOB BECOMES AN AUDIENCE

No sooner does Paul escape when he demonstrates the amazing extent of his faith by making an unusual request:

> As the soldiers were about to take Paul into the barracks, he asked the commander, "May I say something to you?"
>
> "Do you speak Greek?" he replied. "Aren't you the Egyptian who started a revolt and led four thousand terrorists out into the desert some time ago?"
>
> Paul answered, "I am a Jew, from Tarsus in Cilicia, a citizen of no ordinary city. Please let me speak to the people."
>
> Having received the commander's permission, Paul stood on the steps and motioned to the crowd. When they were all silent, he said to them in Aramaic: (Acts 21:37-40)

The mob had just tried to kill Paul, yet he seized that moment as an opportunity for witness. He said to the Roman commander, "Please let me speak to the people."

The commander was startled when Paul addressed him in Greek. This Roman thought he knew who Paul was—an Egyptian terrorist leader. But when the commander heard Paul speak in the cultured accents of Greece, he knew that Paul was no terrorist. In fact, there was something about Paul that impressed the Roman commander. So he permitted Paul to speak to the crowd.

PAUL'S DEFENSE

In Acts 22, Luke relates Paul's defense:

> "Brothers and fathers, listen now to my defense." When they heard him speak to them in Aramaic, they became very quiet.
>
> Then Paul said: "I am a Jew, born in Tarsus of Cilicia, but brought up in this city. Under Gamaliel I was thoroughly trained in the law of our fathers and was just as zealous for God as any of you are today. I persecuted the followers of this Way to their death, arresting both men and women and throwing them into prison, as also the high priest and all the Council can testify. I even obtained letters from them to their brothers in

Damascus, and went there to bring these people as prisoners to Jerusalem to be punished." (Acts 22:1-5)

When Paul indicated with his hand that he wanted to speak, a hush fell over the crowd. An unruly mob became an attentive audience.

Paul spoke to the crowd in Aramaic. Everything he said in this introductory paragraph was designed to win over a hostile crowd. He reminded the people that he himself was a Jew. He spoke to them in their own language—Aramaic, a dialect of Hebrew. He told them he was born in the university city of Tarsus, where he studied under Gamaliel, one of the five greatest Jewish scholars of all time. Paul clearly wanted to impress these people with his formidable credentials.

Then Paul reminded them that he was once zealous in persecuting Christians. The Sanhedrin could bear witness that he was genuinely committed to wiping out the Christian cause. Next, he told the crowd the simple story of his conversion:

"About noon as I came near Damascus, suddenly a bright light from heaven flashed around me. I fell to the ground and heard a voice say to me, 'Saul! Saul! Why do you persecute me?'

"'Who are you, Lord?' I asked.

"'I am Jesus of Nazareth, whom you are persecuting,' he replied. My companions saw the light, but they did not understand the voice of him who was speaking to me.

"'What shall I do, Lord?' I asked.

"'Get up,' the Lord said, 'and go into Damascus. There you will be told all that you have been assigned to do.' My companions led me by the hand into Damascus, because the brilliance of the light had blinded me." (Acts 22:6-11)

Paul practiced the most powerful form of witness: simple testimony from his experience. Whenever you tell your own story—the story of what Jesus has done for you and how He has changed your life—you are on solid ground. You are the world's best authority on your own life, so you can speak with unassailable conviction.

Paul recounted his conversion story—the story of his deep hostility to Christianity and his encounter with the risen Lord on the road to Damascus. What an effect this story must have had upon the crowd! What a rare privilege it must have been to hear the apostle Paul's conversion story from his own lips. Paul continues:

"A man named Ananias came to see me. He was a devout observer of the law and highly respected by all the Jews living there. He stood beside me and said, 'Brother Saul, receive your sight!' And at that very moment I was able to see him.

"Then he said: 'The God of our fathers has chosen you to know his will and to see the Righteous One and to hear words from his mouth. You will be his witness to all men of what you have seen and heard. And now what are you waiting for? Get up, be baptized and wash your sins away, calling on his name.'" (Acts 22:12-16)

The details of Paul's conversion, which took place some thirty years earlier, are etched in his memory. This was the moment God commissioned Paul to be an apostle. There were three parts to this commission.

First, Paul was chosen to know the will of God. Ananias said, "The God of our fathers has chosen you to know his will." This is important because Paul was chosen to be a pattern setter—a model of what Christians are to be. An apostle is not a super-saint but a role model, living at our level, showing us how the Christian life is to be lived.

In order to be a pattern setter for us, Paul had to know the will of God. This does not mean knowing where God wanted him to go and what God wanted him to do. Paul had to learn that the will of God for all Christians is to have an intimate relationship with His Son. Our relationship with Him is the source of our power to live for Him.

Second, Paul was to see the Lord Jesus. Ananias said, "The God of our fathers has chosen you . . . to see the Righteous One." Paul looks back and says, in effect, "This is what made me an apostle: I have seen Jesus Christ many times. He has appeared to me, and talked to me. He taught me directly the truths that the other apostles learned when they were with him as disciples."

Third and finally, Paul was to hear the Lord's own voice. Ananias said, "The God of our fathers has chosen you . . . to hear words from his mouth." Paul had received his message directly from Jesus, and when he went preaching and teaching, he declared the message that he had heard from the Lord's mouth. Like the Twelve, Paul had been personally instructed in the truth by the Lord Jesus Himself—and being personally instructed by the Lord was an identifying sign of a true apostle.

PAUL'S ENCOUNTER WITH JESUS IN JERUSALEM

Next, Paul describes his amazing encounter with Jesus in Jerusalem:

"When I returned to Jerusalem and was praying at the temple, I fell into a trance and saw the Lord speaking. 'Quick!' he said to me. 'Leave Jerusalem immediately, because they will not accept your testimony about me.'

"'Lord,' I replied, 'these men know that I went from one synagogue to another to imprison and beat those who believe in you. And when the blood of your martyr Stephen was shed, I stood there giving my approval and guarding the clothes of those who were killing him.'

"Then the Lord said to me, 'Go; I will send you far away to the Gentiles.'" (Acts 22:17-21)

It seems odd that Paul would include this episode in his defense. Though it explains why he ultimately went to the Gentiles, he now seems to testify against himself. He is recounting an episode that occurred in Jerusalem three years after his conversion. He came back to Jerusalem with the intention of being the apostle to Israel. Convinced that he was equipped to reach Israel with the gospel, he underwent a series of humbling experiences, including being let down over the city wall of Damascus in a basket.

Paul even recounts how the Lord said to him, "Go; I will send you far away to the Gentiles." Up to that point, his audience has listened attentively. But the moment he mentions that Jesus had sent him to the Gentiles, the crowd erupts in fury:

The crowd listened to Paul until he said this. Then they raised their voices and shouted, "Rid the earth of him! He's not fit to live!" (Acts 22:23)

Paul had offended their racial and religious pride. The idea that God would consider bringing the Gentiles and Jews into the same realm of blessing was unthinkable. They rightly understood that, as Jews, they were God's chosen people, but they had misinterpreted what it meant to be chosen by God. They believed that they were superior to the Gentiles, and that their chosen status meant that all other people were rejected by God. So when Paul said that God had sent him to the Gentiles, their pride was offended.

Many evangelical Christians are guilty of the same spiritual pride. We believe that God has chosen us, that we in the church are God's elect. So we resist going out to the poor, the illegal aliens, the homeless, the addicts, the prisoners, the AIDS sufferers, the least, the last, and the lost. God always judges such self-righteous pride, because His grace is available to all—

And the ground is level at the foot of the cross.

CITIZEN PAUL

Luke goes on to record:

As they were shouting and throwing off their cloaks and flinging dust into the air, the commander ordered Paul to be taken into the barracks. He directed that he be flogged and questioned in order to find out why the people were shouting at him like this. (Acts 22:23-24)

The Roman commander has not understood a word of Paul's message, which was delivered in Aramaic. When the crowd erupted in rage, the commander didn't know what to make of it, so he ordered Paul scourged to find out what he said that angered the mob.

Luke tells us what happened next:

> As they stretched him out to flog him, Paul said to the centurion standing there, "Is it legal for you to flog a Roman citizen who hasn't even been found guilty?"
>
> When the centurion heard this, he went to the commander and reported it. "What are you going to do?" he asked. "This man is a Roman citizen."
>
> The commander went to Paul and asked, "Tell me, are you a Roman citizen?"
>
> "Yes, I am," he answered.
>
> Then the commander said, "I had to pay a big price for my citizenship."
>
> "But I was born a citizen," Paul replied.
>
> Those who were about to question him withdrew immediately. The commander himself was alarmed when he realized that he had put Paul, a Roman citizen, in chains. (Acts 22:25-29)

Roman law forbade any citizen of Rome to be bound without due process of law. Furthermore, no citizen was to be beaten under any circumstances, even if convicted. The penalty was death. So the Roman commander knew he was in trouble. He had come within moments of administering a bloody scourging to a Roman citizen.

As in Ephesus, God used the government to protect his apostle. Previously, Paul was saved by the intervention of the city clerk of Ephesus. This time, it was the Roman Empire itself that protected Paul. The powers that be are ordained by God, and He uses them to accomplish His purpose in the world.

In this incident from Paul's life, we see a profound life principle: God will sometimes let us stumble into disasters of our own making—and we must reap the consequences of our actions. But even so, God never abandons us. He finds a way to work out our tangled circumstances and restore us to usefulness again.

Though Paul will remain a prisoner of Caesar—and a prisoner of the Lord Jesus—he will carry on his ministry of preaching, teaching, and blessing lives. And, as we shall see, Paul will realize his cherished dream of taking the gospel of Jesus Christ to the heart of the Roman Empire.

God never abandons His people.

37

LOVE THAT NEVER LETS GO

Acts 22:30-23:35

Paul is a prisoner of the Romans. He is in the custody of a bewildered Roman commander who can't figure out what to make of this amazing man. The commander permitted Paul to speak to the crowd in the Aramaic language—and everything seemed to go smoothly until Paul said something that caused the crowd to erupt in rage.

Luke continues his account:

> The next day, since the commander wanted to find out exactly why Paul was being accused by the Jews, he released him and ordered the chief priests and all the Sanhedrin to assemble. Then he brought Paul and had him stand before them. (Acts 22:30)

Here, the commander calls all the high priests and elders of the Sanhedrin to the Roman fortress of Antonia, overlooking the temple courts. He brings Paul before them, and the mighty apostle seizes this crisis as an opportunity to address the leaders of the Jewish people he so deeply loves.

PAUL'S INSULT

Acts 23 opens with Paul's address to the Jewish leaders:

> Paul looked straight at the Sanhedrin and said, "My brothers, I have ful-filled my duty to God in all good conscience to this day." At this the high priest Ananias ordered those standing near Paul to strike him on the mouth. Then Paul said to him, "God will strike you, you whitewashed wall! You sit there to judge me according to the law, yet you yourself vio-late the law by commanding that I be struck!"
>
> Those who were standing near Paul said, "You dare to insult God's high priest?"
>
> Paul replied, "Brothers, I did not realize that he was the high priest; for it is written: 'Do not speak evil about the ruler of your people.'" (Acts 23:1-5)

Paul seems almost uncaring of the consequences of his words—like a man burning his bridges behind him. He does not begin with his usual courtesy. The customary address to the Sanhedrin was a standardized form that began, "Rulers of Israel, and elders of the people . . ." Paul places himself on the same level with these rulers, undoubtedly because he was once a member of the Sanhedrin, and he addresses them simply as, "my brothers."

This breach of protocol offended the Jewish leaders. Yes, Paul had once sat on the council, but that was thirty years ago. Since then, a fierce enmity had arisen between Paul and the Sanhedrin. For Paul to come now and brashly address them as "brothers" and equals offended their religious pride.

Paul also said that he had lived in all good conscience before God, implying that there was no possible ground of accusation against him. Though this was a true statement, the high priest interpreted it as an insult, as if Paul were saying, "This meeting is a pointless waste of time, because I did nothing wrong." So the high priest commanded that Paul be slapped across the mouth—a degrading insult. The law commanded that no Israelite should ever be struck in the face, and the high priest was wrong to order it.

Paul's anger flashed. He responded, "God will strike you, you whitewashed wall! You sit there to judge me according to the law, yet you yourself violate the law by commanding that I be struck!" This was a typically Judaic way of calling someone a hypocrite. The only whitewashed walls in Israel were the walls of tombs. Jesus used this same figure of speech: "Woe to you, teachers of the law and Pharisees, you hypocrites! You are like whitewashed tombs, which look beautiful on the outside but on the inside are full of dead men's bones and everything unclean" (Matthew 23:27).

Paul probably recognized Ananias. The man was well known for his gluttony, corruption, and collaboration with the Roman oppressors. Paul was offended that this notorious hypocrite would command him to be struck in violation of the law. But Paul did not know that Ananias had recently been appointed high priest. The council was summoned hastily, so Ananias probably didn't have time to don the robe of his office.

The moment someone informed Paul that he had insulted the high priest, Paul was instantly repentant for insulting the ruler of the tribunal. But the damage was done. If Paul ever had a chance for a fair trial, that chance was gone forever.

RULED BY THE FLESH

By going to Jerusalem in disobedience to the Spirit, Paul placed himself in a position of being mastered by the flesh. Paul tells us in Romans 6:16 that if we yield to the flesh, we become the servant of the flesh. When the flesh rules one area of our lives, then even when we want to obey the Spirit in other areas, we cannot. The flesh always carries us farther than we want to go. As Paul warns, we must not "give the devil a foothold" in our lives (Ephesians 4:27), for once we do, everything we attempt for God comes out according to the flesh, not according to the Spirit.

That's what happens to Paul. He tries to walk in the Spirit but cannot. The flesh is in command. There are certain unmistakable marks of the flesh in this account.

First, Paul is not in control of his emotions. When struck, he lashes out in anger, insulting the high priest. Then he has to retract his words.

Second, Paul shows a prideful disdain for others. Though he is normally courteous, he sets that aside while addressing the Sanhedrin. Thinking himself the equal of these men, he treats them with a touch of disdain. They sense it, and they resent it.

Third, Paul relies on his wits to get himself out of this dilemma. Instead of relying on God's wisdom, he falls back on human cleverness, as Luke records:

> Then Paul, knowing that some of them were Sadducees and the others Pharisees, called out in the Sanhedrin, "My brothers, I am a Pharisee, the son of a Pharisee. I stand on trial because of my hope in the resurrection of the dead." When he said this, a dispute broke out between the Pharisees and the Sadducees, and the assembly was divided. (The Sadducees say that there is no resurrection, and that there are neither angels nor spirits, but the Pharisees acknowledge them all.)
>
> There was a great uproar, and some of the teachers of the law who were Pharisees stood up and argued vigorously. "We find nothing wrong with this man," they said. "What if a spirit or an angel has spoken to him?" The dispute became so violent that the commander was afraid Paul would be torn to pieces by them. He ordered the troops to go down and take him away from them by force and bring him into the barracks. (Acts 23:6-10)

At first glance, it appears that Paul has pulled off a brilliant diversion. He's managed to divide the Pharisees from the Sadducees. I doubt that Paul had this stratagem planned out. He simply realized that his cause appeared lost, so he identified himself with the Pharisees in order to win some support.

The Sadducees were the liberals on this council. They denied the supernatural and had no belief in the existence of spirits, angels, or the resurrection. The Pharisees were the ultraconservatives, the legalists who adhered strictly to the Law. When Paul identified himself with the Pharisees (he was, in fact, a Pharisee before his conversion), he touched a nerve of old disputes between the Pharisees and Sadducees.

Instantly, the Pharisees were ready to defend Paul on the grounds that his conversion might be the result of a visitation by a spirit or an angel. They wouldn't acknowledge that it was the Lord Jesus whom Paul had seen, but they were willing agree that something supernatural had occurred in Paul's life.

Though Paul succeeded in polarizing the council, he effectively dashed his hopes of giving his testimony before the leaders of the nation. Now he's become nothing more than a pawn in a shouting match between warring Jewish factions.

THE SCARS OF SIN

Meanwhile, the Roman commander observed this scene with growing puzzlement: What is it about this man Paul that always results in a ruckus?

The commander ordered his troops to take Paul away and put him in the barracks under protective custody. So Paul was led to the barracks, dejected and defeated. He had his chance to address the Sanhedrin and point them to their Messiah, but his hopes had been dashed.

Yet God had a lesson to teach the apostle Paul: The hour of discouragement is always God's time to act. He often waits for us to reach our lowest point—and then, when our self-sufficiency has run its course, leaving us broken and bankrupt, He rebuilds us in His image. Remember the opening words of our Lord in the Sermon on the Mount: "Blessed are the poor in spirit, for theirs is the kingdom of heaven" (Matthew 5:3). Blessed are we when we have come to the end of ourselves and don't know what to do! That's when God can work. Luke tells us what happened next:

> The following night the Lord stood near Paul and said, "Take courage! As you have testified about me in Jerusalem, so you must also testify in Rome." (Acts 23:11)

Literally, the Lord Jesus told Paul, "Be of good cheer!" or even "Cheer up!" This reveals the state of Paul's heart. He is defeated and discouraged, but he's not abandoned. The Lord has come to restore him to ministry. He tells Paul, "As you have testified about me in Jerusalem, so you must also testify in Rome." The desire of Paul's heart will yet be fulfilled, and he will bear witness for Christ in the capital of the Gentile world.

In the Lord's words, we can detect a hint of the limitation that Paul has imposed on himself by disobeying the Spirit. The Lord Jesus puts it this way: "As you have testified about me in Jerusalem, so you must also testify in Rome." The emphasis here is on the manner by which Paul's witness will go forth: "As you have testified about me in Jerusalem . . ." How did Paul testify in Jerusalem? As a prisoner in chains, stripped of his freedom. Had Paul obeyed, he would have been free to travel around the Roman world, preaching the gospel.

The Lord visited Paul in prison and restored him to spiritual health. Though Paul's restoration didn't erase the consequences of his wrong choices— consequences I call the scars of sin—it's a wonderful thing to be restored by God. Paul still faced two years of imprisonment in Caesarea, followed by at least three more years of confinement in Rome. But from this point forward, everything Paul did would have that wonderful infusion of the Spirit's power—power to make amazing things happen.

Paul's experience is instructive for us all. Christians sometimes feel that they can sin, then confess it to the Lord, and it will be as if it never happened. But that's not the way life works. While it's true that God will forgive our sins and will not hold our sins against us, there is always a price to pay for sin. When we violate God's will and ignore the pleading of His Spirit, we incur the natural and inescapable consequences of sin.

God will forgive our sexual sin, but we may have to live with broken relationships, painful memories, pregnancy, or sexually transmitted disease. God will forgive our sin of greed and dishonesty, but we may have to live with the broken trust, lost career, or public shame that results. God's forgiveness is free, but sin always exacts a price. That's what Paul experiences here. These are the scars of sin.

THE PLOT AGAINST PAUL

As Luke continues the account, we see how God graciously works out His purpose in the life of the restored apostle Paul:

> The next morning the Jews formed a conspiracy and bound themselves with an oath not to eat or drink until they had killed Paul. More than forty men were involved in this plot. They went to the chief priests and elders and said, "We have taken a solemn oath not to eat anything until we have killed Paul. Now then, you and the Sanhedrin petition the commander to bring him before you on the pretext of wanting more accurate information about his case. We are ready to kill him before he gets here." (Acts 23:12-15)

Paul's religious opponents plot to get Paul away from the protection of the Roman guardhouse and into the streets of Jerusalem, where they can pounce on him. Forty would-be assassins make a desperate vow to neither eat nor drink until they have killed the apostle. The plot has every chance of succeeding, but the conspirators have not reckoned with God's protective hand:

> But when the son of Paul's sister heard of this plot, he went into the barracks and told Paul.
>
> Then Paul called one of the centurions and said, "Take this young man to the commander; he has something to tell him." So he took him to the commander.
>
> The centurion said, "Paul, the prisoner, sent for me and asked me to bring this young man to you because he has something to tell you."

The commander took the young man by the hand, drew him aside and asked, "What is it you want to tell me?"

He said: "The Jews have agreed to ask you to bring Paul before the Sanhedrin tomorrow on the pretext of wanting more accurate information about him. Don't give in to them, because more than forty of them are waiting in ambush for him. They have taken an oath not to eat or drink until they have killed him. They are ready now, waiting for your consent to their request."

The commander dismissed the young man and cautioned him, "Don't tell anyone that you have reported this to me." (Acts 23:16-22)

Paul can do nothing to protect himself, but Paul doesn't need to be concerned. The Lord is watching over him. Paul is God's man in God's place, carrying out God's plan.

To those who don't believe in divine intervention, this story would seem to involve a great deal of coincidence. The plot just happens to be overheard by Paul's nephew—and the nephew goes to the commander and reveals the plot. Of course, where God is concerned, there is no such thing as coincidence. He is sovereign over all events.

Luke tells us what the commander did next:

Then he called two of his centurions and ordered them, "Get ready a detachment of two hundred soldiers, seventy horsemen and two hundred spearmen to go to Caesarea at nine tonight. Provide mounts for Paul so that he may be taken safely to Governor Felix." (Acts 23:23-24)

Imagine this scene: The Roman commander ordered a detachment of 200 soldiers, 70 horsemen, and 200 hundred spearmen—470 armed men to protect one Christian. Paul was guarded by a small army because God wanted Paul to know that he had nothing to fear from his enemies.

The Roman commander sent a letter to Governor Felix, and that letter was another key to God's protection of Paul. Luke writes:

He wrote a letter as follows:

Claudius Lysias,

To His Excellency, Governor Felix:

Greetings.

This man was seized by the Jews and they were about to kill him, but I came with my troops and rescued him, for I had learned that he is a Roman citizen. I wanted to know why they were accusing him, so I brought him to their Sanhedrin. I found that the accusation had to do with questions about their law, but there was no charge against him that deserved death or imprisonment. When I was informed of a plot to be carried out against the man, I sent him to you at once. I also ordered his accusers to present to you their case against him. (Acts 23:25-30)

The commander obviously wrote this letter to make himself look good in the eyes of the governor. He handled the truth rather loosely, implying that he had rescued Paul because he learned that Paul was a Roman citizen. Of course, we know that the commander learned that Paul was a Roman citizen mere moments before he was to have Paul flogged. Though the commander wrote a self-serving letter, it was practically a letter of acquittal for Paul. The commander went on record as saying Paul had done nothing worthy of death or imprisonment. This letter laid the groundwork for a favorable disposition of the case. Once more, God used unbelievers to accomplish His purpose.

PAUL GOES TO CAESAREA

Next, Luke takes us to Caesarea with Paul to face the Roman governor:

So the soldiers, carrying out their orders, took Paul with them during the night and brought him as far as Antipatris. The next day they let the cavalry go on with him, while they returned to the barracks. When the cavalry arrived in Caesarea, they delivered the letter to the governor and handed Paul over to him. The governor read the letter and asked what province he was from. Learning that he was from Cilicia, he said, "I will hear your case when your accusers get here." Then he ordered that Paul be kept under guard in Herod's palace. (Acts 23:31-35)

From Jerusalem to the Fortress of Antipatris in Caesarea was a distance of sixty miles. Paul and the soldiers covered the first forty miles by a rapid forced march. The next morning, the horsemen brought Paul the remaining twenty miles to the palace of the Roman governor in Caesarea. When the governor read the letter from the Roman commander in Jerusalem, he was favorably disposed toward Paul. He only asked one question about Paul: "What province does he come from?"

There were two kinds of provinces in the Roman Empire—those controlled by the Roman Senate and those controlled by the emperor (imperial provinces). The governor learned that Paul was from Cilicia, which, like Judea, was an imperial province. Because Paul was a citizen of an imperial province, the governor had to account to the emperor himself for Paul's treatment. So we can already see how God was arranging circumstances to pave the way for Paul to go to Rome—

Where he would meet the emperor Nero face to face.

38

THE DISCIPLINE OF DELAY

Acts 24

Marcus Antonius Felix, the Roman governor of the province of Judea, was a fascinating character. Much is known of him, thanks to the secular historians Tacitus and Suetonius. He was a successor to Pontius Pilate (there were several intervening governors who held the post between Pilate and Felix). By the time the apostle Paul came before him, Felix had been governor of the province of Judea for five years.

Felix and his brother Pallas were born slaves, but Pallas gained favor with the Roman emperor and won his freedom. Through the influence of Pallas, Felix was also freed and was later appointed governor—the first slave-born man to ever govern a Roman province. Tacitus alluded to the slave-born status of Felix in this highly critical assessment from his *Histories*: "Antonius Felix indulged in every kind of cruelty and immorality, wielding a king's authority with all the instincts of a slave."[1]

This slave-born governor was married at different times to three different princesses. His first wife was Drusilla of Mauretania, a second cousin of the emperor Claudius and a granddaughter of Antony and Cleopatra. Felix divorced her and married another Drusilla—the Judean princess Drusilla, daughter of King Herod Agrippa I, the king who executed the apostle James (Acts 12). This Jewish Drusilla had been the wife of the king of Emesa, a city in Syria, but Felix seduced her and married her. She was his wife during these events in Acts 24. Felix later married a third princess, though little else is known about her, not even her name.

Felix was famed for his corruption and his willingness to exchange political favors for bribes. His term as governor of Judea was marked by an increase in crime, civil unrest, and political feuding. A notoriously brutal man, he once put down an uprising of Jewish Zealots by hiring an organized crime syndicate called the Sicarii (dagger men) to hunt down and execute the Zealots. Historians also believe Felix hired the Sicarii to murder the Jewish high priest Jonathan.

This was the man who would judge the fate of the apostle Paul.

---

1. Tacitus, *The Histories,* vol. 2, trans. W. Hamilton Fyfe (Oxford: Clarendon, 1912), 213.

PAUL'S ACCUSERS

In the opening verse of Acts 24, Luke introduces us to Paul's accusers:

> Five days later the high priest Ananias went down to Caesarea with some
> of the elders and a lawyer named Tertullus, and they brought their charges
> against Paul before the governor. (Acts 24:1)

Ananias, the high priest, wanted revenge against Paul for the insult of calling him a "whitewashed wall." Along with Ananias was a delegation of elders
who probably included Pharisees and Sadducees. And there was one officious
little Roman lawyer named Tertullus. We know Tertullus was short of stature
because his name is the diminutive of Tertius. Tertullus means "little Tertius."

We know that Luke was also present, since only an eyewitness could capture the atmosphere of the scene as Luke does. Luke records the accusations
against Paul:

> When Paul was called in, Tertullus presented his case before Felix: "We
> have enjoyed a long period of peace under you, and your foresight has
> brought about reforms in this nation. Everywhere and in every way, most
> excellent Felix, we acknowledge this with profound gratitude. But in
> order not to weary you further, I would request that you be kind enough
> to hear us briefly." (Acts 24:2-4)

Luke carefully records the pompous, flowery speech of Tertullus. Through
his words alone, we can see what kind of man this lawyer was: a flatterer, a
yes-man, a fawning little toady—and a liar. "Most excellent Felix," he said,
"we have enjoyed a long period of peace under you, and your foresight has
brought about reforms in this nation." Both Tertullus and Felix know this was
a lie. Felix was corrupt, and had corrupted the entire nation. The province was
continually rocked by murder, riot, and scandal, all of which could be laid at
the door of Felix.

Perhaps the governor showed growing impatience with the false flattery
of Tertullus. In any case, the lawyer decided to hurry things along a bit: "But
in order not to weary you further," he said, "I would request that you be kind
enough to hear us briefly." And then he got to the point:

> "We have found this man to be a troublemaker, stirring up riots among
> the Jews all over the world. He is a ringleader of the Nazarene sect and
> even tried to desecrate the temple; so we seized him. By examining him
> yourself you will be able to learn the truth about all these charges we are
> bringing against him."
>
> The Jews joined in the accusation, asserting that these things were
> true. (Acts 24:5-9)

Luke has undoubtedly condensed a long and windy speech to a brief outline. There were three principal charges leveled against Paul, slanted in such a way as to prejudice the Roman governor against the apostle.

The first charge: Paul was a revolutionary, a man who stirred up riots and revolt against the empire. There were few things the Romans hated more than civil disorder. They had a far-flung empire to administer, and they handled political troublemakers with an iron fist.

The second charge: Paul was a religious extremist, a "ringleader of the Nazarene sect." Felix had certainly heard of this religious group known variously as the Way or Christians or the Nazarenes (after Jesus of Nazareth). He also knew that there were many self-proclaimed messiahs running around, gathering followers, and promising to throw out the Roman occupation forces. Tertullus implied that Paul was one of them.

The third charge: Paul had defiled the Jewish temple by bringing in Gentiles. Though the Romans didn't care about the Jewish religion, they cared a great deal about maintaining order in the Jewish province. Any hint that the sacred temple had been profaned could enflame the rage of the Jewish people.

PAUL'S DEFENSE

Next, Luke records Paul's masterful defense:

> When the governor motioned for him to speak, Paul replied: "I know that for a number of years you have been a judge over this nation; so I gladly make my defense." (Acts 24:10)

Paul, being an honest man, could not make fawning, flattering statements about Felix. He opened by making as complimentary statement as he could muster: "I know that for a number of years you have been a judge over this nation; so I gladly make my defense." No flattery, just fact. Then Paul answers the charges, one by one.

First, he answered the charge that he was a revolutionary:

> "You can easily verify that no more than twelve days ago I went up to Jerusalem to worship. My accusers did not find me arguing with anyone at the temple, or stirring up a crowd in the synagogues or anywhere else in the city. And they cannot prove to you the charges they are now making against me." (Acts 24:11-13)

In other words, "I wasn't in the city long enough to incite a riot. My accusers have never seen me disputing at the temple or causing trouble anywhere in town. They can't prove a word of these accusations." Paul demolished his enemies' first accusation.

Next he answered the charge of being a religious extremist:

"However, I admit that I worship the God of our fathers as a follower of the Way, which they call a sect. I believe everything that agrees with the Law and that is written in the Prophets, and I have the same hope in God as these men, that there will be a resurrection of both the righteous and the wicked. So I strive always to keep my conscience clear before God and man." (Acts 24:14-16)

Paul boldly pleaded guilty to being a follower of the Way, which is consistent with his faith in God and his reverence for the Hebrew Scriptures. He said, in effect, "This so-called sect stresses the same hope that is taught in the Scriptures—the hope of the resurrection of the dead, both the just and unjust. My fellow Jews in this room believe in this hope just as I do. So my conscience is clear, and I plead guilty to the charge of being devoted to faith in God—but is that a crime? What Roman law have I broken by living a life of righteousness and faith?"

Having demolished the second accusation, Paul turned to the third charge:

"After an absence of several years, I came to Jerusalem to bring my people gifts for the poor and to present offerings. I was ceremonially clean when they found me in the temple courts doing this. There was no crowd with me, nor was I involved in any disturbance. But there are some Jews from the province of Asia, who ought to be here before you and bring charges if they have anything against me. Or these who are here should state what crime they found in me when I stood before the Sanhedrin—unless it was this one thing I shouted as I stood in their presence: 'It is concerning the resurrection of the dead that I am on trial before you today.'" (Acts 24:17-21)

Paul's argument was simple: "Not only was I *not* defiling the temple," he said, in effect, "I was doing good, bringing gifts and offerings for the poor that had been collected in Macedonia. I had followed the ritual of ceremonial cleansing. I went to the temple and worshiped like any Jew should. I brought no Gentiles with me, and I was minding my own business, causing no disturbance whatsoever. My accusers aren't even here to testify. If they have evidence against me, why aren't they here?"

Having dismantled the unfounded charges against him, Paul would be exonerated by any fair-minded judge. But as we shall see, an unaccountable delay—one of God's mysterious delays—will keep him in custody.

THE PATHWAY OF PRISON

Instead of deciding Paul's fate, Felix delays, as Luke records:

Then Felix, who was well acquainted with the Way, adjourned the proceedings. "When Lysias the commander comes," he said, "I will decide your case." He ordered the centurion to keep Paul under guard but to give him some freedom and permit his friends to take care of his needs. (Acts 24:22-23)

We met Lysias earlier, though this is the first time his name is given. Lysias is the commander of the Roman garrison in Jerusalem. Why does Felix want Lysias to come? He has already received a letter from Lysias that exonerates Paul. Clearly, Felix is delaying a decision in order to hear more from this fascinating man, the apostle Paul. Felix is curious because, as Luke tells us, he is already well acquainted with the Way. He knows something about Christianity, and he wants to hear more. So though Paul is clearly innocent, Felix keeps him in custody.

Governor Felix is being used as an instrument of God's will. This delay is the work of a loving, heavenly Father. Remember that Paul, by ignoring the warnings of the Holy Spirit, chose a pathway that led to his imprisonment. Though he was forgiven and restored, he still had to endure the consequences of his earlier choice. He had chosen a pathway that led through prison, and he couldn't simply return to the pathway of freedom.

Even though Paul remains in custody, God is able to use him in a mighty way:

Several days later Felix came with his wife Drusilla, who was a Jewess. He sent for Paul and listened to him as he spoke about faith in Christ Jesus. As Paul discoursed on righteousness, self-control and the judgment to come, Felix was afraid and said, "That's enough for now! You may leave. When I find it convenient, I will send for you." At the same time he was hoping that Paul would offer him a bribe, so he sent for him frequently and talked with him. (Acts 24:24-26)

Paul has some liberty, including permission to receive visitors. But he remains in the custody of the Romans and is unable to go anywhere he pleases. From time to time, Felix sends for Paul so they can talk. The governor's motives are mixed. He seems genuinely interested in Paul's message, yet he also hopes Paul will offer him a bribe.

THE GOVERNOR TREMBLES

The gospel message has a profound effect on Felix. Luke tells us that as he listened, he was afraid. In the Greek text, the meaning is stronger: Felix literally trembled with terror. He felt the impact of the apostle's clear, logical presentation of God's truth. Paul boldly spoke to this morally bankrupt official about the kind of life God expected of human beings.

What is wrong with the world today? People don't love one another. They fight and hate each other. They intimidate and exploit each other. Their hearts are filled with greed, lust, bitterness, envy, theft, and revenge. Unrighteous human behavior is at the root of pollution, poverty, crime, oppression, and war.

Ask anyone on the street, "What's wrong with the world today?" They'll tell you that *other* people behave badly in some way. They seldom point a finger of blame at themselves. Paul, with his keen understanding of human life, lays out before the governor the truth about righteousness.

Then Paul goes on to talk about self-control. Here's a word that appears only one time in Paul's letters, when he lists the fruit of the Spirit in Galatians 5. If the Holy Spirit is in us, He will produce the life of Christ in us. Then our lives will be characterized by "love, joy, peace, patience, kindness, goodness, faithfulness, gentleness and self-control" (Galatians 5:22-23).

Finally, Paul warned Felix of the judgment to come. No wonder Felix trembled! There is a time ahead of us when we shall each be evaluated, without exception. All the hidden secrets of the heart will be on display before God. How would you feel if you knew that all your thoughts for the past hour had been recorded and were about to be played back? Would you be proud of those thoughts—or ashamed? You may think, "I'm glad such a thing could never happen." But such a thing *will* happen. We will be held accountable for our actions, our words, and our thoughts.

In light of God's demand for righteousness, what provision have you made for the day of judgment? What have you done with Jesus? Is He your Lord and Savior, your Friend and Advocate with the Father? Or will you stand alone, with all your sins and guilt on display when the day of judgment comes?

When Felix heard about the judgment, he trembled. He remembered the things he had done—deeds he thought no one would ever know about. The people he had harmed. The immoral acts. The bribes. The corruption. The murders he had ordered.

Trembling with fear, Felix said, "That's enough for now! You may leave. When I find it convenient, I will send for you." He knew he couldn't withstand the day of God's judgment, but he wasn't ready to turn control of his life over to God. So he put off the problem of God's judgment to another day. That's why Felix delayed Paul's release.

Felix knew that Paul spoke the truth. He even brought his wife, Drusilla, to hear what Paul had to say. This indicates that Felix genuinely wanted something from God, but he was conflicted, because he also wanted something from Paul: money.

Jesus said that we cannot serve two masters. We can't serve God and money. We *must* choose between God and the world. We dare not procrastinate. Putting off the choice is a choice in itself—and a tragic one. This moment is too important to waste. We must seek God today, while He can still be found. Tomorrow may be too late.

Imagine, Felix had one of the rarest opportunities ever afforded a human being: the opportunity to spend hours with the apostle Paul, listening to the deep and marvelous truths that were revealed to him by the Lord Jesus. But Felix didn't appreciate the opportunity he had. He let it pass by.

Luke records that Felix called Paul to him many times. They talked again and again. But after that first meeting, Felix never again trembled with fear. That was the closest he ever came to giving his life to the Lord. Eventually, the opportunity passed. That's the danger people face when they procrastinate. Eventually, the opportunity evaporates. Put off a decision—and soon the moment is gone.

THE DISCIPLINE OF DELAY

Luke tells us what happened to Felix—and to Paul:

> When two years had passed, Felix was succeeded by Porcius Festus, but because Felix wanted to grant a favor to the Jews, he left Paul in prison. (Acts 24:27)

Secular historians tell us what happened to Felix. There was a riot in Caesarea between the Jews and Greeks who lived there. When the Jews appeared to be winning, Felix sent Roman troops to help the Greeks. The Roman soldiers attacked the Jews, killing several thousand. The soldiers looted and burned the homes of the Jewish leaders.

The Jews complained to Nero—and Nero summoned Felix to Rome to answer for his mishandling of the situation. Before he left, Felix tried to regain his lost favor among the Jews by keeping Paul in prison. Then Felix went to Rome and passed into history.

Meanwhile, Paul, who was clearly innocent, remained in jail. He wanted nothing more than to be free to preach the gospel and strengthen the churches. But he could do none of those things. He was forced to accept the discipline of delay.

We've all had the experience of praying for relief, only to have our hopes dashed. Months or years pass, and we are still right where we were. And we wonder, "Why is God delaying? Why doesn't He act?" So it is with the apostle Paul.

God's delays are always times of learning. He uses those times in our lives to teach us lessons we could never learn in any other way. While Paul remained in prison, he wrote some of his greatest letters: Ephesians, Philippians, Colossians, and Philemon. Paul once wrote of the lessons he learned in prison:

I know what it is to be in need, and I know what it is to have plenty. I have learned the secret of being content in any and every situation, whether well fed or hungry, whether living in plenty or in want. I can do everything through him who gives me strength. (Philippians 4:12-13)

That is what you learn in a time of waiting. Are you in a prison right now—locked into circumstances you feel helpless to change? You may have been put there by your own sins. Or you might have been put there by the loss of your career or a troubled marriage or a bankruptcy or an illness. You can't understand why God delays.

It may be that God is allowing you to learn the discipline of delay. He is leaving you in a place where you can learn the secret Paul learned while a prisoner in Caesarea: "I can do everything through Jesus, who gives me strength."

39

BEFORE GOVERNORS AND KINGS

Acts 25–26

Prophecy is being fulfilled.

After Paul's conversion on the Damascus road, the Lord Jesus appeared to a godly man named Ananias and said, "This man [Paul] is my chosen instrument to carry my name before the Gentiles and their kings and before the people of Israel" (Acts 9:15). In these closing chapters of Acts, that prophecy is being fulfilled. Paul has appeared before the Gentile governor Felix. Now, in Acts 25 and Acts 26, he will appear before governor Festus and the Jewish ruler, King Agrippa. Soon, he will go to Rome to face the emperor Nero. Luke writes:

> Three days after arriving in the province, Festus went up from Caesarea to Jerusalem, where the chief priests and Jewish leaders appeared before him and presented the charges against Paul. They urgently requested Festus, as a favor to them, to have Paul transferred to Jerusalem, for they were preparing an ambush to kill him along the way. Festus answered, "Paul is being held at Caesarea, and I myself am going there soon. Let some of your leaders come with me and press charges against the man there, if he has done anything wrong." (Acts 25:1-5)

It has been two years since Paul stood trial before Governor Felix. Now another man, Porcius Festus, has been appointed by the emperor to govern the Roman province of Judea. We do not know much about Festus from secular history, though most historians describe him as a just man. Even so, we see clearly that there are limits to the integrity of Festus. Though not as corrupt as his predecessor, Festus behaves as a typical politician.

As soon as Festus takes office, the Jewish religious leaders take him aside and immediately try to bend him to their will. They propose that he send Paul to Jerusalem for trial. This is part of a plot to assassinate Paul along the way. In Acts 23, we saw these same religious leaders plot to kill Paul during his transfer from Jerusalem to Caesarea. In fact, forty would-be assassins bound themselves with an oath not to eat or drink until they had killed Paul. One wonders how they survived for years without food or water!

AN APPEAL TO CAESAR

The Roman governor Festus insists questioning Paul himself. Luke writes:

After spending eight or ten days with them, he went down to Caesarea, and the next day he convened the court and ordered that Paul be brought before him. When Paul appeared, the Jews who had come down from Jerusalem stood around him, bringing many serious charges against him, which they could not prove.

Then Paul made his defense: "I have done nothing wrong against the law of the Jews or against the temple or against Caesar."

Festus, wishing to do the Jews a favor, said to Paul, "Are you willing to go up to Jerusalem and stand trial before me there on these charges?"

Paul answered: "I am now standing before Caesar's court, where I ought to be tried. I have not done any wrong to the Jews, as you yourself know very well. If, however, I am guilty of doing anything deserving death, I do not refuse to die. But if the charges brought against me by these Jews are not true, no one has the right to hand me over to them. I appeal to Caesar!"

After Festus had conferred with his council, he declared: "You have appealed to Caesar. To Caesar you will go!" (Acts 25:6-12)

Paul has been in prison for two years, hoping to be released. There is no legal reason to hold him. The Roman judge, Felix, has already acknowledged that he could find no wrongdoing in Paul. Now, in his second trial, the arguments against Paul are the same as before—and just as unfounded.

Finally, Festus shows that he is a true politician. Luke records that "Festus, wishing to do the Jews a favor, said to Paul . . ." And he tried to maneuver Paul into going to Jerusalem to stand trial. In other words, Paul was a political pawn, and Festus wanted to use him to gain favor with the people.

Paul might have been tempted to take Festus up on his offer. After several years of waiting, he could go to Jerusalem, be tried once and for all—and perhaps he would be set free. What should Paul do? Should he seize a possible opportunity for freedom by going to Jerusalem or remain in the custody of the Gentiles? Yet Paul also must have known that he could never get a fair trial from the religious leaders in Jerusalem. Recalling the Lord's promise that he would go to Rome, Paul probably considered his options, then announced, "I appeal to Caesar."

At that point, Festus had no choice in the matter. Roman law gave Paul the right to have his case heard before the emperor. Festus conferred with his advisors, then turned to Paul and said, "You have appealed to Caesar. To Caesar you will go!"

THE LAST OF THE HERODS

At this point, we have an interesting development. A Jewish king enters the scene:

A few days later King Agrippa and Bernice arrived at Caesarea to pay their respects to Festus. Since they were spending many days there, Festus discussed Paul's case with the king. He said: "There is a man here whom Felix left as a prisoner. When I went to Jerusalem, the chief priests and elders of the Jews brought charges against him and asked that he be condemned.

"I told them that it is not the Roman custom to hand over any man before he has faced his accusers and has had an opportunity to defend himself against their charges. When they came here with me, I did not delay the case, but convened the court the next day and ordered the man to be brought in. When his accusers got up to speak, they did not charge him with any of the crimes I had expected." (Acts 25:13-18)

Festus is clearly troubled by the case of the apostle Paul. When King Agrippa arrives, Festus seeks his advice. He tells the king that he had expected certain political charges to be leveled against Paul, but the accusations were of an entirely different nature:

"Instead, they had some points of dispute with him about their own religion and about a dead man named Jesus who Paul claimed was alive. I was at a loss how to investigate such matters; so I asked if he would be willing to go to Jerusalem and stand trial there on these charges. When Paul made his appeal to be held over for the Emperor's decision, I ordered him held until I could send him to Caesar."

Then Agrippa said to Festus, "I would like to hear this man myself." He replied, "Tomorrow you will hear him." (Acts 25:19-22)

So the foundation has been laid for Paul to come before King Agrippa. This will not be another trial. King Agrippa and Bernice have come to pay their respects to the new Roman governor, and Festus arranges to bring Paul before them as the evening's entertainment. Knowing King Agrippa's religious background, Festus thinks the king will be amused and intrigued by the charges against Paul.

Who was King Agrippa? Marcus Julius Agrippa, also called Herod Agrippa II, was the last of the Herods. He was the brother of Bernice and Drusilla, who was, you recall, the second wife of the Roman governor Antonius Felix. The Herods were not Jews in the strictest sense. They were Edomites, descendents of Esau, the twin brother of Jacob, who adhered to the Jewish religion.

The first of the line was Herod the Great, who killed the babies in Bethlehem when our Lord was born. His son, Herod Antipas, was the king who had John the Baptist beheaded in prison. The son of Herod Antipas, Herod Agrippa I, put the apostle James to death by the sword. And now we come to his son, Agrippa II, who was appointed by the Romans as tetrarch (a subordinate ruler) of Galilee. He had authority to appoint the high priest in Jerusalem and administer the temple. He was loyal to Rome, not to the Jews.

King Agrippa's wife was Bernice. As I previously noted, Agrippa was the brother of Bernice and Drusilla. You may wonder, "Were Agrippa and Bernice husband and wife—or brother and sister?" Answer: They were both. Though brother and sister, they lived together incestuously as man and wife, a violation of Jewish law.

Paul is now called to appear before this morally depraved couple. He knows that this is his last chance to reach Israel for Christ, and he hopes against hope that the king will repent so that the nation might follow. Luke writes:

> The next day Agrippa and Bernice came with great pomp and entered the audience room with the high ranking officers and the leading men of the city. At the command of Festus, Paul was brought in. Festus said: "King Agrippa, and all who are present with us, you see this man! The whole Jewish community has petitioned me about him in Jerusalem and here in Caesarea, shouting that he ought not to live any longer. I found he had done nothing deserving of death, but because he made his appeal to the Emperor I decided to send him to Rome. But I have nothing definite to write to His Majesty about him. Therefore I have brought him before all of you, and especially before you, King Agrippa, so that as a result of this investigation I may have something to write. For I think it is unreasonable to send on a prisoner without specifying the charges against him." (Acts 25:23-27)

Governor Festus is baffled by Paul. He is required to send Paul to the emperor to answer charges, but what is Paul charged with? Festus knows that the political charges against Paul have been disproved, but he can hardly send a prisoner to the emperor without a charge. That would only make Festus appear inept. So Festus asks King Agrippa to help him formulate a charge against Paul that will withstand imperial scrutiny.

PAUL AND THE KING
Paul, chained to a Roman guard, is brought before King Agrippa. As we turn to Acts 26, Paul presents his defense:

> Then Agrippa said to Paul, "You have permission to speak for yourself."
> So Paul motioned with his hand and began his defense: "King Agrippa, I consider myself fortunate to stand before you today as I make my defense against all the accusations of the Jews, and especially so because you are well acquainted with all the Jewish customs and controversies. Therefore, I beg you to listen to me patiently.

"The Jews all know the way I have lived ever since I was a child, from the beginning of my life in my own country, and also in Jerusalem. They have known me for a long time and can testify, if they are willing, that according to the strictest sect of our religion, I lived as a Pharisee. And now it is because of my hope in what God has promised our fathers that I am on trial today. This is the promise our twelve tribes are hoping to see fulfilled as they earnestly serve God day and night. O king, it is because of this hope that the Jews are accusing me. Why should any of you consider it incredible that God raises the dead?

"I too was convinced that I ought to do all that was possible to oppose the name of Jesus of Nazareth. And that is just what I did in Jerusalem. On the authority of the chief priests I put many of the saints in prison, and when they were put to death, I cast my vote against them. Many a time I went from one synagogue to another to have them punished, and I tried to force them to blaspheme. In my obsession against them, I even went to foreign cities to persecute them." (Acts 26:1-11)

The substance of Paul's argument before King Agrippa is that he stands condemned for being a good Jew. He is trying to appeal to the Jewish sympathies of the Edomite king, in hopes of penetrating the man's spiritual darkness. Paul's argument is brilliantly constructed.

First, he points out that even his Jewish accusers can testify to his credentials as a Pharisee, raised according to the traditions of the strictest sect of the Jews.

Second, he states that, with respect to the resurrection of the dead, he does not preach anything that he didn't believe as a Pharisee. Speaking to the entire court, he asks, "Why should any of you consider it incredible that God raises the dead?" Certainly a Jew should not think it incredible, because God had already promised the resurrection of the dead. Paul is earnestly trying to appeal to the Jewish faith of the king.

Third, he demonstrates his intense commitment to his Jewish beliefs by the way he persecuted the church. His intent is to prove to Agrippa that he has impeccable credentials as a Jew.

PAUL'S TESTIMONY

Next, Paul offers the most compelling form of Christian witness. He gives his personal testimony.

"On one of these journeys I was going to Damascus with the authority and commission of the chief priests. About noon, O king, as I was on the road, I saw a light from heaven, brighter than the sun, blazing around me and my companions. We all fell to the ground, and I heard a voice saying to me in Aramaic, 'Saul, Saul, why do you persecute me? It is hard for you to kick against the goads.'

"Then I asked, 'Who are you, Lord?'

"'I am Jesus, whom you are persecuting,' the Lord replied. 'Now get up and stand on your feet. I have appeared to you to appoint you as a servant and as a witness of what you have seen of me and what I will show you. I will rescue you from your own people and from the Gentiles. I am sending you to them to open their eyes and turn them from darkness to light, and from the power of Satan to God, so that they may receive forgiveness of sins and a place among those who are sanctified by faith in me.'" (Acts 26:12-18)

Here is the heart of Paul's message—his transforming experience with Jesus Christ. Reciting the words of Jesus, as Paul heard them on the Damascus road, Paul gives us the Lord's diagnosis of the human condition: Human beings live in darkness. They are enslaved by Satan and lost in their sins.

In two thousand years, nothing has changed. People are lost in darkness, unable to see the truth, groping their way through life. Behind the curtain of darkness that enfolds the human race, there is a great enemy, Satan, a malevolent intelligence that twists and distorts human thinking, making people doubt the truth and believe a lie.

We hear these lies all the time. "Live for the moment." "I am the master of my fate." "Whoever dies with the most toys wins." Satan wants us to believe that we can find peace and satisfaction apart from God. He wants us to waste our lives chasing after wealth, possessions, status, pleasure, sex, power, and other idols. But the gospel turns our darkness into light and turns people away from the power of Satan to the power of God. They are no longer slaves to the lying propaganda of Satan; they can finally receive the truth of God. And it all comes by faith in Jesus Christ.

People today often ask, "Why do Christians insist that Jesus is the only way to God? Jesus may be *one* way, but He's surely not the *only* way. What about Buddhism, or Hinduism, or Islam, or some of the other great religions? The adherents of those religions are sincere and religious. Why do Christians insist that Jesus is the only way?" The answer: That's what Jesus Himself said. You can't call yourself a Christian and deny what Christ said—and He said, "I am the way and the truth and the life. No one comes to the Father except through me" (John 14:6).

When Jesus came forth from the tomb, He solved the mystery of death. No one else has ever solved this problem. Only Jesus has conquered death, and that is why only Jesus is worthy to be followed.

"I AM NOT INSANE"

Paul goes on to say that he provoked the wrath of his enemies by declaring the truth of the gospel. That's why they have persecuted him. Then he underscores once more the essential facts of the gospel—the death and the resurrection of Jesus Christ:

> "So then, King Agrippa, I was not disobedient to the vision from heaven. First to those in Damascus, then to those in Jerusalem and in all Judea, and to the Gentiles also, I preached that they should repent and turn to God and prove their repentance by their deeds. That is why the Jews seized me in the temple courts and tried to kill me. But I have had God's help to this very day, and so I stand here and testify to small and great alike. I am saying nothing beyond what the prophets and Moses said would happen—that the Christ would suffer and, as the first to rise from the dead, would proclaim light to his own people and to the Gentiles." (Acts 26:19-23)

Festus suddenly interrupts Paul's discourse:

> At this point Festus interrupted Paul's defense. "You are out of your mind, Paul!" he shouted. "Your great learning is driving you insane."
>
> "I am not insane, most excellent Festus," Paul replied. "What I am saying is true and reasonable. The king is familiar with these things, and I can speak freely to him. I am convinced that none of this has escaped his notice, because it was not done in a corner. King Agrippa, do you believe the prophets? I know you do."
>
> Then Agrippa said to Paul, "Do you think that in such a short time you can persuade me to be a Christian?"
>
> Paul replied, "Short time or long—I pray God that not only you but all who are listening to me today may become what I am, except for these chains."
>
> The king rose, and with him the governor and Bernice and those sitting with them. They left the room, and while talking with one another, they said, "This man is not doing anything that deserves death or imprisonment."
>
> Agrippa said to Festus, "This man could have been set free if he had not appealed to Caesar." (Acts 26:24-32)

Paul seldom got to finish a sermon. He was constantly being interrupted. On this occasion, he was interrupted by the skeptical questioning of a Roman rationalist. Festus believed only in what he could see with his own eyes. When Paul spoke of the resurrection, it was more than he could stand.

Festus said, in effect, "Paul, you're crazy! You're talking about raising the dead! Everyone knows that when you're dead, you're dead!"

Paul replied, in effect, "Everything I say is the truth. God has shattered the power of death and has made life available to humanity—life as He intended it to be lived."

THE ENSLAVED KING

Then Paul turned to Agrippa. He clearly wanted to reach this man. It was his last chance to reach the Jewish people, and the essence of Paul's message to the king was this: "I'm sure you're aware of the teaching about the resurrection, because these truths have not been taught in secret. The Lord Jesus preached and taught, lived and died, right in front of everyone in Israel. I know the king believes the Old Testament prophets—and the prophets foretold the coming of the Messiah. Clearly, Jesus was the Messiah that the prophets wrote about. He fulfilled the Old Testament prophecies."

The king undoubtedly squirmed uncomfortably under Paul's preaching. There was a serious obstacle in the king's life, preventing him from accepting Jesus as his Lord and Savior: The king was enslaved by his lusts. He lived in sin with his own sister. He didn't want to give up the pleasures of sin, so he shrugged off everything Paul said to him.

King Agrippa's reply to Paul has often been mistranslated. For example, the King James Version mistakenly translates the king's reply as, "Almost thou persuadest me to be a Christian." That's not what Agrippa said. He did not say that Paul came close to convincing him. The New International Version is much closer to the sense of the original Greek text: "Do you think that in such a short time you can persuade me to be a Christian?" Those words drip with sarcasm.

With a heavy heart, Paul replied, in effect, "King Agrippa, whether it takes a lot of time or a little, I urgently want to win you to Christ, along with your wife and everyone in this room. I wish you could all be as I am, except for these chains. Even though you are a king, a man of power and wealth, I do not envy you; in fact, I wish that you were truly as blessed as I am, and that you could have the peace and joy of knowing the Lord Jesus."

It was a challenging message, spoken by a prisoner in chains to a king upon his throne. But Agrippa is a Herod, an Edomite, a descendent of Esau. He is true to his heritage. Speaking through the prophet Malachi, God said, "I have loved Jacob, but Esau I have hated. . . . Edom may say, 'Though we have been crushed, we will rebuild the ruins.' But this is what the Lord Almighty says: 'They may build, but I will demolish. They will be called the Wicked Land, a people always under the wrath of the Lord'" (Malachi 1:2-4).

Why does God say that He loves Jacob but hates Esau? Is He arbitrary and unfair? Does He simply choose Jacob over Esau without reason? No. Throughout Scripture, Esau is a symbol for a rebellious, arrogant, stubborn spirit that refuses God's grace and demands its own way. Agrippa, a true son of Edom, chooses his fate in the same way. He demonstrates his own rebellious, arrogant, stubborn spirit in true Edomite style. He turns his back on God's love, spurns Paul's message of everlasting life—

And then the last of the Herods fades from history.

Having heard all he wishes to hear, the king rose from his throne. His wife and Governor Festus also stood, along with the other dignitaries. They departed, chatting and laughing, leaving Paul behind. As they talked together, they remarked about the fact that Paul had clearly done nothing that deserved punishment. In fact, notes Festus, Paul could have been set free if he hadn't insisted on making his appeal to Caesar.

Paul remained in Roman custody, yet his words continue to echo down through the centuries. They are words of love for lost humanity: "I pray God that not only you but all who are listening to me today may become what I am, except for these chains."

40

SHIPWRECKED!

Acts 27

I'm a landlubber, not a sailor. But I've talked to experienced sailors about the account of Paul's sea voyage to Rome. They tell me that Luke's description of sailing techniques and storm survival tactics are remarkably detailed. They are essentially the same skills that sailboat enthusiasts learn today. Luke was a doctor, not a sailor, but he was such a careful historian that his account contains more insight into ancient sailing practices than all other ancient manuscripts combined.

Acts 27 divides into four major movements: Part 1, Setting sail for Rome (Acts 27:1-8); part 2, A dangerous tempest (Acts 27:9-20); part 3, A word of encouragement (Acts 27:21-27); and part 4, Disaster and deliverance (Acts 27:28-44). Let's take a closer look at this true-life adventure tale.

PART 1: SETTING SAIL FOR ROME

The first section of this account reads like a page from a ship's log. It gives us the list of important passengers on the voyage and explains some of the problems they faced as they sailed from Caesarea. Paul is on his way to Rome to appear before the emperor. He goes as a prisoner, usually chained to a Roman guard. Luke tells us:

> When it was decided that we would sail for Italy, Paul and some other prisoners were handed over to a centurion named Julius, who belonged to the Imperial Regiment. We boarded a ship from Adramyttium about to sail for ports along the coast of the province of Asia, and we put out to sea. Aristarchus, a Macedonian from Thessalonica, was with us. (Acts 27:1-3)

Luke lists the personalities of this drama. Paul is the hero, of course. He is in the custody of Julius, a Roman centurion who treats Paul with respect and kindness. As a member of the Imperial Regiment, Julius commands an elite unit of soldiers.

The phrase "we boarded a ship" shows that Luke is with them as Paul's friend and personal physician. Luke's presence may suggest that Paul suffered from a physical illness or impairment and needed a doctor's care. Also aboard is Aristarchus, a young man Paul met in Thessalonica on his second missionary journey. His devotion to Paul was so great that he may have volunteered to be Paul's servant on the voyage.

They set sail from Caesarea, move up the coast of Palestine, and make their way toward Asia Minor (modern Turkey). Luke continues:

> The next day we landed at Sidon; and Julius, in kindness to Paul, allowed him to go to his friends so they might provide for his needs. From there we put out to sea again and passed to the lee of Cyprus because the winds were against us. When we had sailed across the open sea off the coast of Cilicia and Pamphylia, we landed at Myra in Lycia. There the centurion found an Alexandrian ship sailing for Italy and put us on board. We made slow headway for many days and had difficulty arriving off Cnidus. When the wind did not allow us to hold our course, we sailed to the lee of Crete, opposite Salmone. We moved along the coast with difficulty and came to a place called Fair Havens, near the town of Lasea. (Acts 27:4-8)

Landing at Sidon, a port city still thriving in modern Lebanon, the sailing party disembarked. Julius permitted Paul to meet with friends who ministered to his needs.

They set sail from Sidon and immediately encountered contrary winds. At that time of year, the winds usually blew from the northeast, which would have helped them on their way to Rome. But they were met by a strong northwest wind and were forced to take refuge behind the isle of Cypress and hug the Asian coast, tacking against the wind.

They arrived at the Lycian port of Myra, where they hired a much larger vessel, undoubtedly a grain ship carrying wheat from Alexandria in Egypt, the granary of the Roman Empire. It was a huge ship with (we later learn) space for 276 crewmen and passengers. The centurion evidently leased the vessel because he was in charge of it for the rest of the voyage. Again they encountered contrary winds and made slow progress, tacking back and forth on a zigzag course. Several days of sailing gained them only a couple hundred miles. They had to sail under the lee of the isle of Crete to make any headway.

The adverse winds make us wonder: Why would the apostle Paul experience such difficulties from natural forces when he was going where God wanted him to go? God, who controls the wind and the waves, could surely have given Paul an easier journey.

This is a question we all face in our lives. From time to time we wonder why, when we are being obedient to God's will, we experience great adversity and trial. If God wants us to accomplish tasks that bring glory to Him, then why doesn't he smooth out our circumstances and make the job easier? We will glimpse an answer to this question before we reach the end of Acts 27.

PART 2: A DANGEROUS TEMPEST

Luke continues his eyewitness narrative of the journey:

Much time had been lost, and sailing had already become dangerous because by now it was after the Fast. So Paul warned them, "Men, I can see that our voyage is going to be disastrous and bring great loss to ship and cargo, and to our own lives also." But the centurion, instead of listening to what Paul said, followed the advice of the pilot and of the owner of the ship. Since the harbor was unsuitable to winter in, the majority decided that we should sail on, hoping to reach Phoenix and winter there. This was a harbor in Crete, facing both southwest and northwest. (Acts 27:9-12)

Though a prisoner, Paul is given considerable freedom. When he offers advice, he is listened to with courtesy and respect, even though his advice is not always followed. When Paul predicts disaster, he is not prophesying. He's simply speaking out of common sense. He warns that their lives will be lost, but this warning does not prove prophetic.

Paul knows it's too late in the year to try to make it to Rome. The great fast of the Day of Atonement has already passed, which means it is now early October. Navigating the Mediterranean is dangerous in the late fall and early winter. Storms arise without warning and last for days. Knowing this, Paul urges the centurion to winter in the little port of Fair Havens, near the town of Lasea.

The captain and owner of the ship, along with most of the crew, differ with Paul, and Luke records the reason why: "The harbor was unsuitable to winter in." In other words, these men think that the dinky little town of Fair Haven is boring! Sailors crave excitement, so they prevail upon the centurion, who has the last word, to head for Phoenix, a seaport fifty miles up the coast of Crete. So they set out for Phoenix—and sail right into the teeth of a storm:

When a gentle south wind began to blow, they thought they had obtained what they wanted; so they weighed anchor and sailed along the shore of Crete. Before very long, a wind of hurricane force, called the "northeaster," swept down from the island. The ship was caught by the storm and could not head into the wind; so we gave way to it and were driven along. As we passed to the lee of a small island called Cauda, we were hardly able to make the lifeboat secure. When the men had hoisted it aboard, they passed ropes under the ship itself to hold it together. Fearing that they would run aground on the sandbars of Syrtis, they lowered the sea anchor and let the ship be driven along. We took such a violent battering from the storm that the next day they began to throw the cargo overboard. On the third day, they threw the ship's tackle overboard with their own hands. When neither sun nor stars appeared for many days and

the storm continued raging, we finally gave up all hope of being saved.
(Acts 27:13-20)

As soon as the sailors had one day of good weather, they cast all caution to the wind and set sail. This is typical human nature. You and I are often fooled by seemingly favorable circumstances. There's something we want to do so badly that we'll take any favorable circumstance as a good omen, even if we know, deep down, it's wrong. We ignore the facts and plunge ahead—and we live to regret it. That's what these sailors did.

Soon after setting sail, they encountered a tremendous tempest, a north-easter blowing away from the land. The hurricane-force wind was so strong that they couldn't sail against it and get back to land, even though they were close to shore. They had to let the ship be driven before the wind.

They had a hard time securing the lifeboat. In those days, the lifeboat wasn't carried onboard but was towed behind the ship. If a storm arose, the boat would be hauled up into the ship, but this storm came up so suddenly and with so much force that they were unable to secure it until they ran under the lee of a small island.

They even found it necessary to run ropes under the ship and tie up the hull in order to hold it together. The weight of the grain, shifting in the storm, threatened to tear the ship apart. As the tempest raged, the sailors feared that they would be driven onto the great sand bank, the Syrtis, along the coast of North Africa, one of the great hazards of sailing the Mediterranean. If the ship struck the Syrtis, they would be marooned miles from shore.

As the storm increased in fury, they threw much of the cargo overboard, along with the mainsail and tackle. Luke adds, "When neither sun nor stars appeared for many days and the storm continued raging, we finally gave up all hope of being saved." Having no compass or other navigational aids in those days, the sailors had nothing to guide them but the stars. When the stars disappeared, they were truly lost.

Note these significant words: "We finally gave up all hope of being saved." When Luke says "we," he always includes Paul. So Paul, too, gave up hope—but not hope of survival. The Lord had promised that Paul would go to Rome, and he relied on that promise. But Paul probably became convinced that the ship would be wrecked and lives would be lost—perhaps the lives of his friends, Luke and Aristarchus.

So Paul reached the point of despair.

PART 3: A WORD OF ENCOURAGEMENT

Next, Luke tells us of a word of hope from a supernatural source:

After the men had gone a long time without food, Paul stood up before them and said: "Men, you should have taken my advice not to sail from

Crete; then you would have spared yourselves this damage and loss. But now I urge you to keep up your courage, because not one of you will be lost; only the ship will be destroyed. Last night an angel of the God whose I am and whom I serve stood beside me and said, 'Do not be afraid, Paul. You must stand trial before Caesar; and God has graciously given you the lives of all who sail with you.' So keep up your courage, men, for I have faith in God that it will happen just as he told me. Nevertheless, we must run aground on some island." (Acts 27:21-26)

Paul is concerned about these men. They have been so distressed and fearful that they have not eaten in days. So Paul stood before them—the Greek text says that he literally "stood forth"; he stood out among them, not only physically but in his commanding attitude. In that moment, he became the de facto leader of the voyage.

His opening words sound like an I-told-you-so, for he says, "Men, you should have taken my advice not to sail from Crete." But he's not rubbing it in. He's simply reminding them that he was right from the beginning, which means they should heed him now. He's establishing his credentials as a man of foresight and wisdom.

Despite all evidence to the contrary, Paul then announces, "Not one of you will be lost; only the ship will be destroyed." He knows this because an angel came to him the night before and reaffirmed the Lord's word that Paul would stand before Caesar and he should not be afraid. This indicates that fear had crept into Paul's heart.

The angel also told him, "God has graciously given you the lives of all who sail with you." Paul has been praying for the lives of the men traveling with him. God has heard his prayer and granted him their lives. This shows us the tremendous power of prayer. God wants to do mighty things in our lives—if we but ask him. As James 5:16 tells us, the prayers of righteous people literally release great power.

So Paul and his companions will be spared, but there is still a frightening ordeal ahead. After encouraging them, Paul tells them that they must maintain their courage because, as the Lord has revealed to him, "we must run aground on some island."

PART 4: DISASTER AND DELIVERANCE

The remainder of Acts 27 tells of the disaster and the deliverance that followed:

On the fourteenth night we were still being driven across the Adriatic Sea, when about midnight the sailors sensed they were approaching land. They took soundings and found that the water was a hundred and twenty feet deep. A short time later they took soundings again and found it was ninety feet deep. Fearing that we would be dashed against the rocks, they dropped four anchors from the stern and prayed for daylight. In an attempt to escape from the ship, the sailors let the lifeboat down into the sea, pretending they were going to lower some anchors from the bow. Then Paul said to the centurion and the soldiers, "Unless these men stay with the ship, you cannot be saved." So the soldiers cut the ropes that held the lifeboat and let it fall away. (Acts 27:27-32)

The wind and waves threaten to tear the ship apart, and the sailors hear breakers in the distance. They are approaching the shore—but what shore? It's pitch-black, and the sailors can see nothing. Will the ship be dashed against the rocks? They drop sea anchors from the stern to slow the ship. Their fear grows.

A few sailors hatch a plot to steal the lifeboat and save their own skins. Paul learns of the plot (Luke doesn't tell us how), and the apostle goes to Julius and says, "Unless these men stay with the ship, you cannot be saved." It's going to take every experienced sailor to beach the ship safely. The centurion wastes no time. He orders the soldiers to set the lifeboat adrift. Now everyone aboard is literally in the same boat.

Even though God promised Paul that every life would be spared, Paul told the centurion, "Unless these men stay in the ship, you will not be saved." God's promises involve human activity. He works out his promises through human choices and actions, and His announced purpose does not cancel human free will. The fact that God announces his promise does not mean we may fold our hands and say, "Well, it'll all work out one way or another." We must act in partnership with God's will in order to receive His promise.

Next, Luke shows us the deadly peril they faced as the ship was flung toward the unseen shore:

> Just before dawn Paul urged them all to eat. "For the last fourteen days," he said, "you have been in constant suspense and have gone without food—you haven't eaten anything. Now I urge you to take some food. You need it to survive. Not one of you will lose a single hair from his head." After he said this, he took some bread and gave thanks to God in front of them all. Then he broke it and began to eat. They were all encouraged and ate some food themselves. Altogether there were 276 of us on board. When they had eaten as much as they wanted, they lightened the ship by throwing the grain into the sea. (Acts 27:33-38)

Fourteen days without food! Having lost their appetites due to fear and despair, the crewmen face an incredible test of endurance while in a weakened condition. Once again, Paul stands forth to remind his companions of God's promise. He strengthens their courage, saying, "Now I urge you to take some food. You need it to survive. Not one of you will lose a single hair from his head." Then, setting an example, he takes bread, gives thanks, breaks it, and eats it. Just the sight of Paul taking nourishment strengthens the resolve of the other men.

Paul is a man of faith—and a man of faith is a man of action. Amid discouraging circumstances, Paul acts on a different basis than those without faith—and the result is that all are encouraged. One man with hope in his heart can alter the fate of 275 other people and help prepare them for the challenge ahead.

THE THREAT OF NATURE—AND MAN

Luke describes what takes place with the coming of the dawn:

> When daylight came, they did not recognize the land, but they saw a bay with a sandy beach, where they decided to run the ship aground if they could. Cutting loose the anchors, they left them in the sea and at the same time untied the ropes that held the rudders. Then they hoisted the foresail to the wind and made for the beach. But the ship struck a sandbar and ran aground. The bow stuck fast and would not move, and the stern was broken to pieces by the pounding of the surf.
>
> The soldiers planned to kill the prisoners to prevent any of them from swimming away and escaping. But the centurion wanted to spare Paul's life and kept them from carrying out their plan. He ordered those who could swim to jump overboard first and get to land. The rest were to get there on planks or on pieces of the ship. In this way everyone reached land in safety. (Acts 27:39-44)

The sun comes up, and the crew sees a bay ahead (it is known today as St. Paul's Bay on the island of Malta). They decide to beach the ship, so they lighten the ship by throwing everything overboard that can be spared. Then they hoist the foresail to the wind and make for the beach. Unfortunately, the ship runs aground some distance from the shore and begins to break up in the surf. They are forced to abandon ship.

The soldiers decide that, to prevent any escapes, they must kill all the prisoners. Roman law required any soldier who allowed a prisoner to escape to receive that prisoner's sentence—and there were no valid excuses for an escape, not even a shipwreck. The centurion, Julius, is unwilling to see Paul killed, so he countermands the execution order and accepts full responsibility for the outcome. Paul's life is spared, along with the lives of an unknown number of prisoners.

The sailors, soldiers, passengers, and prisoners struggle ashore and, as God has promised, not a single life is lost. The crew and passengers have survived the threat of nature, and the prisoners have survived the threat of man. The chapter concludes with an almost audible sigh of relief: "In this way everyone reached land in safety."

WHY WE SUFFER SHIPWRECKS IN LIFE

One question remains: Why do we encounter shipwrecks while doing God's will? Why does He permit adversity in our lives? The Scriptures provide several answers.

First, adversity is often the result of opposition from Satan. In Paul's letter to the Romans, he said he had tried many times to go to Rome and was prevented. In his letter to the Ephesians, he wrote, "For our struggle is not against flesh and blood, but against the rulers, against the authorities, against the powers of this dark world and against the spiritual forces of evil in the heavenly realms" (Ephesians 6:12).

It's likely that Paul was prevented from going to Rome at least in part by Satan. I believe Satan fought Paul every step of the way. He sent the contrary winds, the storm, and other hindrances—anything to keep Paul out of the strategic center of the Roman Empire. That was Satan's citadel, and he feared that the mighty apostle would come in the power of the risen Lord and demolish his stronghold there.

Second, God often allows adversity in our lives to teach us to trust Him. God is greater and stronger than Satan, and He could put a stop to Satan's opposition in an instant. But God didn't do so in this situation, and He often does not do so in your life and mine. Why? Because God can use the opposition of Satan to teach us lessons that we couldn't learn in any other way.

In addition to Paul, there were 275 people on the ship—at least two believers (Luke and Aristarchus), plus a number of sailors, soldiers, and prisoners. They all watched Paul's response to the most extreme peril imaginable, and they saw a man of faith, a man of action, a servant of Jesus Christ. God spoke to them through this man, and none came through that experience unchanged.

Paul himself learn lessons about God's presence and protection, even all appeared to be lost. At every critical moment, the Lord Jesus was alongside Paul, guiding, encouraging, and protecting. As Paul moved closer and closer to his appointment with Nero, one of the cruelest tyrants in history, he knew the Lord was ever with him.

Third, God sometimes allows adversity for reasons we will never understand in this life. We find this principle in the Book of Job. This godly man Job goes through incredible suffering, and God never tells Job the reason for his suffering—but there *is* a reason. At the beginning of the book we see a dialogue between God and Satan that reveals that there is an unseen victory that takes place in the heavenly realms when God's people maintain their faith while enduring affliction.

We may never know about the people we helped win during our earthly lifetime, but it is a real and momentous event that makes possible great progress for His kingdom. When we endure shipwrecks and disasters with faith in God, we strike a blow against Satan—

And we bring honor and glory to our Lord.

41

THE END OF THE BEGINNING

Acts 28

In 1952, Billy Graham conducted his first Greater London Crusade, a twelve-week event in which thousands committed their lives to Jesus as Lord and Savior. All of England was affected, yet some liberal church leaders disapproved of his message. They said that no thinking Christian believes in such myths as the virgin birth, the resurrection, or the atonement, in which Jesus took our sins upon Himself. One liberal English churchman said, "Billy Graham has set the church back two hundred years!"

Hearing that comment, Billy Graham replied, "If I've only set the church back two hundred years, then I've failed. I intend to set the church back two thousand years!"

As we come to the last chapter of God's unfinished book, I want to set the church back to those early days when Paul and his fellow apostles were spreading the good news and planting churches throughout the Roman world. I want to set the church back to that time when the Holy Spirit came upon the church with power and God's people were filled with an extravagant love for Him and one another.

Acts 28 is the last chapter of the book of Acts, but it is only the last page of the first chapter of church history. The same church that was born in Acts 2 is still alive and dynamically involved in human affairs in the twenty-first century. The book of Acts is God's unfinished book—and you and I are still writing new pages for the world to read.

THE VIPER AND THE APOSTLE

Acts 27 ended with a cliffhanger. The apostle Paul and his companions were on their way to Rome when they were shipwrecked on the island of Malta. They lost their ship, provisions, and cargo, but they escaped with their lives, just as Paul had promised. As Luke picks up the story, we find Paul, Julius the centurion, and the rest of the ship's company on the beach at Malta:

> Once safely on shore, we found out that the island was called Malta. The islanders showed us unusual kindness. They built a fire and welcomed us all because it was raining and cold. Paul gathered a pile of brushwood and, as he put it on the fire, a viper, driven out by the heat, fastened itself on his hand. When the islanders saw the snake hanging from his hand,

they said to each other, "This man must be a murderer; for though he escaped from the sea, Justice has not allowed him to live." But Paul shook the snake off into the fire and suffered no ill effects. The people expected him to swell up or suddenly fall dead, but after waiting a long time and seeing nothing unusual happen to him, they changed their minds and said he was a god. (Acts 28:1-6)

Paul and his companions will spend three months on Malta waiting for the winter to pass so that navigation may resume. Their time on the island will be characterized by numerous healings, beginning with the amazing healing of the apostle Paul from the bite of a poisonous snake.

Luke notes that these events took place among primitive people. The word translated "islanders" in the New International Version is the Greek word *barbaros*, from which we get our English words *barbarian* and *barbarous*. The Greeks considered anybody who spoke a non-Greek tongue to be *barbarous*, because they seemed to speak in nonsense syllables. The Greeks thought the speech of non-Greeks sounded like "bar-bar-bar," So they called them *barbaros*, or barbarians—people who did not speak the civilized Greek tongue.

It's significant that the miracle of the healed snakebite occurred in a place where there was no previous exposure to the gospel. The introduction of the gospel to a previously unevangelized culture is often accompanied by signs and wonders. This is necessary in order to demonstrate the reality of the supernatural kingdom that God rules. Those who first carry the gospel into darkened parts of the world often manifest signs that confirm their authority to speak God's word.

Luke notes that the Maltese people treated Paul and his company with unusual kindness and courtesy. A literal translation of the Greek says they showed "kindness more than ordinary." The Holy Spirit was preparing the hearts of these people to receive the gospel. C. S. Lewis coined a term for such people: "pre-Christians." They have been prepared to be receptive to the gospel by the emptiness of their pagan faith.

One reason many people are unreceptive to the gospel is that they think they already know about Christianity. They have heard about the church, they've seen televangelists, and they think they know what Christianity is all about. They have just enough information (and misinformation) to be jaded and unreachable. They would be more receptive to the message of Jesus Christ if they were "pre-Christian barbarians," hearing the message of Jesus Christ for the very first time.

Paul's witness to the people on Malta began with the remarkable incident of the viper. Note that Paul was engaged in the humble labor of gathering sticks for the fire. He picked up a bundle in which a snake, torpid with the cold, hid among the sticks. When Paul laid the bundle on the fire, the snake was roused by the heat. It struck at Paul and dangled by its fangs from Paul's hand. This showed that the snake's venom must have entered Paul's body. The islanders knew that Paul would suffer and die.

The Maltese islanders had a primitive theological explanation for the viper's attack: Paul must be an evil man. People commonly believe that bad things happen only to bad people. Paul, a prisoner of the Romans, was bitten by a snake, so he must have been a murderer. He had escaped from the sea, they reasoned, but the invisible hand of Justice had sent a snake to finish him off. But when Paul did not sicken and die, the superstitious islanders swung to the opposite pole in their thinking: Paul wasn't a murderer—he was a god.

What should we make of this incident? Paul's miraculous survival is one of the signs of an apostle Paul refers to in 2 Corinthians 12:12—"The things that mark an apostle—signs, wonders and miracles—were done among you with great perseverance." This incident also fulfills the Lord's words in Mark's gospel: "they will pick up snakes with their hands; . . . they will place their hands on sick people, and they will get well" (Mark 16:18). In the last chapter of Acts, we see these two signs manifested by Paul. He picked up serpents without suffering harm, and, as we shall soon see, he laid hands on the sick so that they recovered.

People often misread the Lord's statement in Mark, taking it to mean that signs and wonders ought to accompany any believer. But if you examine the Lord's words in context, it's clear that He is addressing the Eleven (the Twelve, minus the traitor Judas) and rebuking their lack of faith in the resurrection. He tells them that signs and wonders will accompany those of His hearers (the Eleven) who believe in His resurrection. In other words, these signs and wonders will accompany the apostles as confirmation that they believe in the risen Lord and have authority to speak in His name.

Mark reports that, after Jesus ascended into heaven, "the disciples went out and preached everywhere, and the Lord worked with them and confirmed his word by the signs that accompanied it" (Mark 16:19-20). Note that last statement: "The Lord confirmed his word by the signs that accompanied it."

We now see Paul demonstrating the same signs Jesus spoke of. By miraculously surviving the viper attack, Paul demonstrates his authority to speak the word of Christ to these people. This is the first sign of his authority as an apostle.

MANY HEALINGS

Next, Luke relates the second sign of Paul's authority—the healing of the father of Publius:

> There was an estate nearby that belonged to Publius, the chief official of the island. He welcomed us to his home and for three days entertained us

hospitably. His father was sick in bed, suffering from fever and dysentery. Paul went in to see him and, after prayer, placed his hands on him and healed him. (Acts 28:7-8)

Jesus said, "They will place their hands on sick people, and they will get well." Here, Paul has demonstrated this sign as well. It is a clear-cut case of instantaneous healing through prayer and the laying on of hands, reported by Luke the physician.

Publius was the chief official of the island. This reflects an official title given him as head of the Roman government on Malta. He owned land near the site of the shipwreck, and Julius the centurion probably arranged a visit with him. Publius probably heard from Julius or others about Paul, so he invited Paul and his friends to come. As Publius welcomed Paul and his companions, he demonstrated the preparation of his heart by the Spirit. Wherever you find kindness, the grace of God is always behind it.

While Paul visits at the estate of Publius, he learns that the official's father is ill. The man suffers flu-like symptoms—fever and dysentery—so Paul goes to the man, prays, and lays hands on him as an act of identifying with him. The man is instantly healed. This healing confirms Paul as an accredited servant of the Lord Jesus.

Luke goes on to record:

When this had happened, the rest of the sick on the island came and were cured. They honored us in many ways and when we were ready to sail, they furnished us with the supplies we needed. (Acts 28:9-10)

It's important to note that when Luke says that Publius's father was healed, the Greek word means that the man was instantaneously made well. But when referring to the healing of the other islanders, Luke uses a Greek word that refers to a gradual cure. The other islanders were not healed instantaneously as the father of Publius was.

Luke may have been involved in some of these cures in his capacity as a physician. If so, then the healing of the islanders would demonstrate the combined power of the medical arts and the healing grace of God working harmoniously together. Luke notes that the people "honored us in many ways" and "furnished us with the supplies we needed." The people literally gave honorariums—gifts of supplies and money—to express their gratitude.

LEAVING MALTA

At last they are ready to go on to Rome, as Luke records:

After three months we put out to sea in a ship that had wintered in the island. It was an Alexandrian ship with the figurehead of the twin gods Castor and Pollux. We put in at Syracuse and stayed there three days.

From there we set sail and arrived at Rhegium. The next day the south wind came up, and on the following day we reached Puteoli. There we found some brothers who invited us to spend a week with them. (Acts 28:11-14a)

The writer gives us a careful account that even includes a description of the ship. It bore a carved figurehead of Castor and Pollux, the twin sons of Jupiter. The ship was dedicated to these Roman gods. Paul and his companions sailed eighty miles north to the island of Sicily, where they put in at the port of Syracuse. They stayed three days, then crossed the Straits of Messina to Rhegium, at the tip of the toe of the Italian boot. Then a wind from the south sped them up the coast.

They landed at the seaport of Puteoli, now called Pozzuoli, located near Naples. Ships from all over the empire stopped there, especially the grain ships from Alexandria. The largest naval fleet in the ancient world was anchored at Puteoli. There Paul disembarked and was met by a group of Christians. This shows that Christianity had spread amazingly far by this time, about A.D. 60. Paul had never been to Italy before, nor (as far as anyone knows) had any of the other apostles. Yet there were already Christian churches throughout Italy.

After spending a week with the Christians in Puteoli, Paul and his companions set out by foot along the Appian Way toward Rome, 150 miles to the northwest. Though still in the custody of Julius the centurion, Paul enjoyed considerable freedom.

ROME AT LAST!
Luke continues the story of the journey to Rome:

And so we came to Rome. The brothers there had heard that we were coming, and they traveled as far as the Forum of Appius and the Three Taverns to meet us. At the sight of these men Paul thanked God and was encouraged. When we got to Rome, Paul was allowed to live by himself, with a soldier to guard him. (Acts 28:14b-16)

As Paul and company approached Rome, the believers heard of his arrival and came great distances to meet him. Some came from as far away as the Forum of Appius, forty-three miles southeast of Rome, and the Three Taverns, thirty-three miles away. If you go to Italy today, you can retrace Paul's steps along the Appian Way and visit those places.

"At the sight of these men," Luke says, "Paul thanked God and was encouraged." Imagine Paul's anxiety as each step took him closer to Rome. True, this had been his goal for years—but Paul knew that he would have to appear before Nero, one of the cruelest tyrants ever to rule an empire. So the unexpected greetings of these Italian Christians were a great comfort and encouragement to Paul.

Upon his arrival in Rome, Paul again saw God's hand at work, allowing him to be treated courteously and leniently by the Roman authorities. Though he remained under guard, the Romans permitted him to stay in his own rented house.

Paul's habit, whenever he entered a new city, was to take the gospel to the Jews first, then to the Gentiles. Luke relates the last account in Scripture where Paul maintained that priority:

> Three days later he called together the leaders of the Jews. When they had assembled, Paul said to them: "My brothers, although I have done nothing against our people or against the customs of our ancestors, I was arrested in Jerusalem and handed over to the Romans. They examined me and wanted to release me, because I was not guilty of any crime deserving death. But when the Jews objected, I was compelled to appeal to Caesar—not that I had any charge to bring against my own people." (Rom 28:17-19)

Paul invited the local Jewish leaders to come and see him. He could not go to them, because he was under house arrest. It's rather amazing that the Jews in Rome responded to Paul's request. If they had heard of Paul, then they probably knew enough about him to distrust him. Yet they came, and they listened.

Paul explained his predicament, noting that he had done nothing against his nation and his people. Yet his own people had accused him of crimes and handed him over to the Romans. The Romans wanted to release him, but the Jews continued to oppose him. Even so, Paul held no bitterness against his Jewish brothers. In spite of all the persecution he had endured, Paul freely absolved them of guilt. Then he underscored the reason for the opposition that has so often been directed against him:

> "For this reason I have asked to see you and talk with you. It is because of the hope of Israel that I am bound with this chain." (Acts 28:20)

What is "the hope of Israel"? It is the promised coming of the Messiah. To this day, the messianic question has never been settled in the Jewish community. If you want to trigger an argument, you merely have to raise the issue of the Messiah, and you will provoke a reaction. It is still an issue in our day as it was in Paul's.

PAUL'S BIBLE STUDY

Next, Luke records the response of his Jewish audience:

They replied, "We have not received any letters from Judea concerning you, and none of the brothers who have come from there has reported or said anything bad about you. But we want to hear what your views are, for we know that people everywhere are talking against this sect." (Acts 28:21-22)

The Jews in Rome had received no word about the apostle Paul, but they had heard bad things about the Christian church: "We know that people everywhere are talking against this sect." Still, they were curious and wanted to hear more about this new community of followers of the crucified Galilean, Jesus of Nazareth:

They arranged to meet Paul on a certain day, and came in even larger numbers to the place where he was staying. From morning till evening he explained and declared to them the kingdom of God and tried to convince them about Jesus from the Law of Moses and from the Prophets. (Acts 28:23)

What a Bible study that must have been! The Jews came in great numbers to hear Paul lecture and to debate him. The mighty apostle took them systematically through the Scriptures, drawing upon his training as a scholar of the Scriptures, interpreting the wonderful Old Testament passages he knew by heart. He showed them that Jesus of Nazareth was pictured throughout the Old Testament in the books of Moses, the Psalms, and the Prophets. What a tremendous, compelling mountain of proof he set before the people—but look at the discouraging result:

Some were convinced by what he said, but others would not believe. They disagreed among themselves and began to leave after Paul had made this final statement: "The Holy Spirit spoke the truth to your forefathers when he said through Isaiah the prophet:

"'Go to this people and say,
"You will be ever hearing but never understanding;
    you will be ever seeing but never perceiving."
For this people's heart has become calloused;
    they hardly hear with their ears,
    and they have closed their eyes.
Otherwise they might see with their eyes,
    hear with their ears,
    understand with their hearts
and turn, and I would heal them.'" (Acts 28:24-27)

Here we see the perversity of human nature. Paul quoted from Isaiah 6:9-10, a passage that predicts that people would deliberately close their minds because they do not want to hear God's truth. The people fulfilled this passage by walking away.

It's instructive to note that Paul used this passage exactly as Jesus had used it in his last encounter with the Jewish leaders who opposed Him. In John 12, we read:

> Even after Jesus had done all these miraculous signs in their presence, they still would not believe in him. This was to fulfill the word of Isaiah the prophet:
>
> > "Lord, who has believed our message
> > and to whom has the arm of the Lord been revealed?'
>
> For this reason they could not believe, because, as Isaiah says elsewhere:
>
> > "He has blinded their eyes
> > and deadened their hearts,
> > so they can neither see with their eyes,
> > nor understand with their hearts,
> > nor turn—and I would heal them."
>
> Isaiah said this because he saw Jesus' glory and spoke about him. (John 12:37-41)

Notice that last line: John says that Isaiah saw Jesus and beheld his glory and spoke of Him. Isaiah had a glimpse of the coming Messiah—and the Messiah's name was Jesus. For centuries, the Jewish people waited for their Messiah to come, yet, when He came, many didn't recognize Him. As a result, Paul made this heavy-hearted announcement to his Jewish audience as they turned their backs on him:

> "Therefore I want you to know that God's salvation has been sent to the Gentiles, and they will listen!" (Acts 28:28)

One of the great mysteries of the Scriptures is Jewish unbelief. Jesus seems so clearly depicted in the Old Testament as to be unmistakable, yet most Jewish people would say, "This man was not the Messiah the Scriptures foretold."

THE END OF THE BEGINNING

Yet, as we look around at Christendom today, we have to ask, "Are we in the church any different?" We have enshrined Jesus in stained glass and hung his portrait on our walls. We have reinvented him in our own image. Political liberals see Him as a leftist radical taking on the Establishment. Political conservatives see Him as a champion of their values and causes. Philosophers see Him as a great teacher. Mystics see Him as a man who preached enlightenment and peace.

We have reshaped Jesus to make Him look like us. We have twisted His words into an endorsement for our agenda. We call Him Lord while treating Him as our servant. Just as Paul's Jewish hearers did not recognize Him from their own Scriptures, we do not recognize Him from our own New Testament. We have ignored all of the words and actions of Jesus that make us uncomfortable or condemn our way of living. We focus only on our favorite texts, where Jesus behaves as we think He ought to.

The Scriptures show us that Jesus reached out to the poor, the lepers, the outcasts, and the prostitutes. But for some reason, we don't recognize this Jesus. We are deaf to His call to reach out to the poor, the aliens, the AIDS sufferers, the prisoners, the homeless, the addicts, the ones who are broken by sin and shame. We don't want any of the dirt of this world to rub off on us. We don't want any of those people coming into our nice suburban church, sitting in our pews, shaking our hands, making us uncomfortable.

Haven't we missed the Messiah just as completely as those Jews in Rome who turned their backs on Paul? Haven't we utterly failed to understand why Jesus came—and for whom? Haven't we forgotten that He came to save the least, the last, and the lost?

When the Spirit of God moved in our midst, we planted our heels and refused to follow. We have stubbornly insisted on clinging to the dead past instead of taking the new and unexplored pathway where Jesus leads. With this sobering realization in mind, we come to the last two verses of the book of Acts, where Luke tells us:

> For two whole years Paul stayed there in his own rented house and welcomed all who came to see him. Boldly and without hindrance he preached the kingdom of God and taught about the Lord Jesus Christ. (Acts 28:30-31)

I call this statement the end of the beginning. With these words, Luke's account draws to a close, but the story goes on. The book of Acts is just the beginning of the record of the body of Christ at work in the world. It's just the first chapter. The rest of the record is being written as history continues to unfold. Fresh chapters are being written in your life and mine. It's a tremendous privilege to play a part of this divine record.

Luke says that Paul preached and taught "boldly and without hindrance." This phrase describes the freedom of the gospel. Even when God's people are hindered, God's Word is never hindered.

Paul was a man confined. He could not go freely about the city. He was chained day and night to a Roman guard. Yet he could welcome friends into his house, and he could teach and preach there. Paul never chafed under this restraint. His letters from Rome are filled with rejoicing and hope. Philippians,

Ephesians, Colossians, and Philemon are letters that have changed the world. Paul had time to write those letters because he could no longer travel abroad.

Even so, Paul still had to appear before the emperor. History records that while Paul was in Rome, a great persecution of Christians broke out under the emperor Nero. The Roman historian Tacitus describes Nero's mania for torturing and executing Christians. Another historian, Suetonius, lavishes praise on Nero for persecuting the despised Christian sect. The early Christian writer Tertullian wrote that Nero was "the first persecutor" of Christians.

So, as Paul awaited his hearing before Nero, he knew that this man was a Christian's worst nightmare—a cruel sadist invested with the full power of the Roman state. On a whim, he would have Christians crucified or fed to the lions or covered with pitch and burned as torches in his garden. Though Paul had reason to be anxious about his fate, the Word was not hindered. God's people may be persecuted, imprisoned, and killed, but God's Word cannot be bound.

THE FATE OF THE APOSTLE PAUL

The Scriptures do not tell us how the apostle Paul died. Tradition and hints in the Scriptures suggest that, at the end of a two-year period of house arrest in Rome, Paul appeared before Nero, his case was dismissed, and the apostle was released. From Rome, Paul probably went to the island of Crete, in the company of Titus and other companions. He left Titus in charge of the church on Crete, as the letter to Titus tells us.

Paul probably visited the church in Ephesus once again, even though he had said to the Ephesians when he left, "None of you . . . will ever see me again" (Acts 20:25). During that later visit to Ephesus, he left Timothy as the bishop of the Ephesian church.

He had always wanted to go to Spain, as he told the Christians in Rome (Romans 15:24, 28). Some scholars believe Paul may have taken the gospel as far as the British Isles.

Paul was eventually arrested again by the Romans, though it is unclear what crime he was charged with. This time, instead of being allowed to live in a rented house, he was thrown into a dark and fetid dungeon known as Mamertine Prison, which you can still visit in Rome. Originally a stone-walled cistern for storing spring water, Mamertine was converted to a prison more than three centuries before Christ. There the most notorious prisoners of the empire spent their last days before being executed. According to tradition, the apostle Peter was also imprisoned in Mamertine before he was crucified upside-down in Rome.

Paul wrote his second letter to Timothy from Mamertine. You can sense Paul's depressing surroundings in his courageous but lonely words: "For I am already being poured out like a drink offering, and the time has come for my departure. I have fought the good fight, I have finished the race, I have kept the faith" (2 Timothy 4:6-7). He mentions some former friends who have deserted him, then adds, "Only Luke is with me. Get Mark and bring him with you, because he is helpful to me in my ministry. . . . Do your best to get here before winter" (2 Timothy 4:11, 21a).

These are the words of a man who remains faithful to the Lord, even though he is in chains and facing death and though friends have betrayed and abandoned him. His circumstances are bleak, but he is not without hope. He is lonely but not alone. He faces the end of his life knowing that a crown of righteousness awaits him and that he will soon hear his Lord say, "Well done, Paul, my good and faithful servant. Well done."

Tradition tells us that on a day in early spring, Paul was taken from his cell, led outside the walls of Rome, and made to kneel. A Roman soldier stepped forward, drew his sword, and poised it over Paul's neck. The blade flashed in the sunlight—

And the mighty apostle passed from time into eternity.

The account that Luke began to write remains incomplete. God's unfinished book continues as you and I add our chapters to this amazing adventure tale of faith.

Paul and his fellow apostles have set the pattern for us to follow. If we will be obedient to the pattern set forth in Acts, God will supply all the power we need. The life of the body of Christ goes on in the twenty-first century as it did in the first century. The same Spirit who empowered the mighty apostle dwells in us today.

With each new day and each new believer who joins the body of Christ, the book of Acts edges closer to completion. Every morning, let us rise and ask the Lord, "What new page of your unfinished book would you have me write today?"

NOTE TO THE READER

The publisher invites you to share your response to the message of this book by writing Discovery House Publishers, Box 3566, Grand Rapids, MI 49501, USA. For information about other Discovery House books, music, or videos, contact us at the same address or call 1-800-653-8333. Find us on the Internet at http://www.dhp.org/ or send e-mail to books@dhp.org.